The San Rocco Villa
at Francolise

The San Rocco Villa
at Francolise

by

M. AYLWIN COTTON AND GUY P. R. MÉTRAUX

with an introduction by
ALASTAIR SMALL

THE BRITISH SCHOOL AT ROME
AND
THE INSTITUTE OF FINE ARTS
NEW YORK UNIVERSITY
1985

A Supplementary Publication of
The British School at Rome
ISSN 0307–2762
ISBN 0 904152 08 1

Printed in England by Stephen Austin and Sons Ltd, Hertford

To the memory of
JOHN WARD-PERKINS
and
MARTIN FREDERIKSEN

Contents

List of Plates

List of Figures

xvi

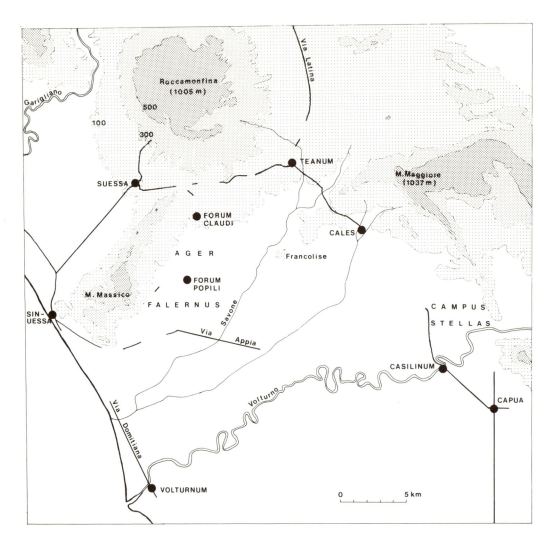

The area around Francolise

Introduction: The Area around Francolise in the Roman Period

From its position on the eastern summit of the hill of Francolise, the villa of San Rocco looks southwards over the North Campanian plain, and westwards to the range of Monte Massico. To the east is the hill of Montanaro which, with the hill of Francolise itself, marks an extension of the limestone formation of Monte Maggiore. A little to the north of Francolise, but out of sight of the villa, lies the course of the river Savone which flows between the hill of Montanaro and the slope of Monte Massico. 14 km. to the northwest of Francolise rises the summit of the extinct volcano Roccamonfina. The geology of the area is relatively simple. The hills of Monte Massico, Francolise and Montanaro consist of Jurassic and Cretaceous limestone, whereas the volcano of Roccamonfina is an intrusion of the Quaternary age. The lava flow from the volcano spread over the northern fringe of the plain as far as Francolise, partly burying the earlier formations but leaving the higher limestone tops exposed. To the south of Francolise the lava gives place to tuffs, ignimbrites and other volcanically derived materials which are distributed over much of the North Campanian plain. In the downstream area of the Volturno these volcanic deposits have been buried by a combination of marine and fluvial sediments of Pleistocene and Recent age.

In terms of land use, the area around Francolise can be divided into four distinct zones: the low lying marshes near the mouths of the Savo (modern Savone) and Volturnus (modern Volturno) rivers; the gradually sloping plain running down towards the marshes from the slopes of Monte Massico; the limestone ridge of Montanaro and Francolise; and the southern slopes of Monte Massico.

The marshes of the lower Savone and Volturno rivers already existed before the Romans began to develop Campania. The route chosen for the Via Appia skirted the worst of these marshes, and the low lying ground probably remained roadless and uncultivated for most of the Roman period.[1] In A.D. 95 Domitian had the Via Domitiana built along the coast with dykes to contain the Volturno river,[2] but by this time the sea level had probably begun to rise[3] causing increased siltation and consequent marsh formation in the lower reaches of the rivers.[4] It seems probable that the rate of erosion in the hills also increased, aggravating the problem of siltation.[5] Whatever the factors involved, the process of marsh formation was gradual, and it was not until the sixth century that the deterioration of the land led to the general abandonment of much of the plain.

Above the marshes, the plain which slopes gradually down from the foot of Monte Massico provided much valuable agricultural land enriched by volcanic debris which was

[1] Cf. Frederiksen, 1959, 83.

[2] Statius, *Silvae* iv carm. 3.

[3] Schmiedt, 1972, esp. 214. Along much of the Tyrrhenian coast the sea level has risen (or the coast sunk) by about 1 m. since the time of Domitian.

[4] For a standard account of the processes involved, see Schumm, 1977, 100 ff. A relative rise in sea level causes aggradation in the lower level of the stream as the stream attempts to regrade its profile to the changed elevational circumstances.

[5] For increased erosion in the hills and a discussion of its causes see Delano Smith, 1979, 317-25. Increased siltation was a widespread phenomenon in the Mediterranean lands in the first millennium A.D. and later. There is little agreement among geomorphologists about the factors involved, but it is generally held that it began in the Roman imperial period and continued throughout the Middle Ages. There was, however, a good deal of regional variation in the time factor. (Delano Smith, 1979; Vita-Finzi, 1969, 101-2).

intensively cultivated by the Romans. The natural vegetation, which still survives in the broad ravines cut by the tributaries of the Savone river, is oak forest, and it seems probable that the whole area was wooded before the Roman intervention. After the Roman land settlement, the area was at first used mostly for arable, but later there was much fruit growing.[6] This part of Campania is still largely given over to orchards.

The hills of Montanaro and Francolise are the two most prominent points of a limestone ridge which runs from Monte Maggiore into the plain, and which ends at Francolise. The lower southern slopes of these hills are mostly used for olive growing, and this was probably also the case in the Roman period, as the olive presses found at both the San Rocco and Posto villas indicate.

The southern slopes of Monte Massico, and the hills above Cales, were the wine growing country *par excellence* in Roman times, being the area where the *vinum Falernum* and *vinum Calenum*[7] were produced. Traces of terracing can still be seen all along the slopes of Monte Massico, and although these have not been dated it seems probable that many go back to the Roman period. Certainly the slopes must have been terraced by the Romans for vine cultivation to have been possible here. These terraces have now mostly been abandoned and vine growing is practised only on a small scale down in the plain.

The Volturno river to the south, the sea to the west, the range of Monte Massico and Roccamonfina to the north, and the ridge of Monte Maggiore to the east, all combined to create a separate entity of the plain around Francolise. But although this forms a single geographical and economic unit it was divided in the Roman period into a number of separate municipal territories.[8] The heart of the plain was the Ager Falernus which was administered, after the municipalisation of Italy, from Forum Popili. The western edge of the plain belonged to Sinuessa, the north-eastern to Teanum and the eastern to Cales. To the south-east was the Campus Stellas, which had a complicated administrative history, but which began and ended as part of the territory of Capua[9] which lay on the other side of the Volturno.

The natural obstacles surrounding the plain left only a few possibilities of easy access, each of which was controlled by a city. The only easy approach from the west is by way of the narrow gap left between the mountains and the sea at Sinuessa where the Romans founded a maritime colony in 296 or 295 B.C. This was the route taken by the Via Appia between Minturnae and Capua: after skirting the ridge of Monte Massico it turned northeast, then south-east to cross the plain above the worst of the marshes.[10] It passed about 7 km. to the south of Francolise. An alternative route, which may have been the original line

[6]Cf. Livy xxii 15. 2: *ea regio praesentis erat copiae non perpetuae, arbusta vineaeque et consita omnia magis amoenis quam necessariis fructibus.* Livy is writing of the Ager Falernus in the time of Hannibal, but the description is probably drawn from his own time. Pliny *Hist. nat.* xv 53 refers to a drink made from the juice of Falernian pears.

[7]Cf. esp. Servius *apud* Verg. *Geor.* ii 143: *vinum a montibus Falernis qui Massici dicuntur.* The term Falernian is used in Plin. *Hist. nat.* xiv 62 specifically of wine from the lowest vineyards. Faustian and Caucinian were produced in vineyards higher up the slopes. But the ancient sources (including Pliny elsewhere: cf.iii 50-60) are not usually so specific. For wine from Monte Massico above Sinuessa: Martial viii lll. The references to Calenian wine give little indication of where it was produced: for the sources see Nissen, 1902, II 694-6. There was also a *vinum Statanum* from an area adjoining the Ager Falernus (Plin. *Hist. nat.* xiv 64-5; xxiii. 33).

[8]See esp. Beloch, 1926, 535-7.

[9]The Campus Stellas was the only part of the Campanian plain left to Capua after the Romans had annexed the Ager Falernus (Livy ix 44. 5). It became Roman *ager publicus* after the surrender of Capua in 211 B.C. (Livy xxvi 16), and it was probably on the Campus Stellas that Sulla's colony of Urbana and Caesar's and Antony's colony of Casilinum were founded. These were later amalgamated with Capua (see n. 67 below).

[10]For the line taken by the Via Appia, see Johannowsky (1975), Vallat (1980) and esp. Pagano (1978). It is now established with reasonable certainty that it followed the course shown on the map Fig. 1, passing Torre Ballerino and the Masseria Aceti.

taken by the Via Appia before the foundation of Sinuessa[11] ran from Minturnae to Capua by way of Suessa Aurunca where the Romans planted a Latin colony in 313 B.C. It crossed Monte Massico by the low pass (just over 200 m.) at Cascano and joined the Via Latina at Teanum. This pass also forms a natural route, taken by the modern SS 7, to Capua by way of Francolise: the discovery of a stretch of Roman road on this line near Ventaroli[12] shows that this route was also used in Roman times. To the north-east the broad gap between Roccamonfina and Monte Maggiore allows easy access to Latium along the line of the Via Latina,[13] and to Molise by way of the Upper Volturno valley. This gap was controlled by Teanum and Cales, both of which lay on the line of the road. To the east, the valley of the Volturno-Calore permits access to Beneventum, Samnium and ultimately Apulia. The entrance to the valley was controlled by Casilinum and Capua.

Communication to the south was limited by the Volturno, the largest river in Campania, which was sufficiently deep and wide to form a serious natural obstacle. The best point in the plain for crossing the river was at Casilinum, where the Roman army invading Campania built a temporary bridge in 342 B.C.[14] There was no permanent bridge until the Romans built the Via Appia.[15] Once the route of the Appia had been established through the Ager Falernus, it was joined by the Latina at Casilinum so that the two roads could use the same bridge. The construction of the bridge must have greatly improved communications between the plain around Francolise and Capua. Much later, in A.D. 95, Domitian built the Via Domitiana along the western edge of the plain, bridging the river near its mouth at Volturnum, so as to provide a much easier route from the north-west part of the plain to the important Roman settlements at Cumae, Baiae and Puteoli.

The cities which controlled these roads, Sinuessa, Suessa Aurunca, Teanum, Cales and to a lesser extent Casilinum and Volturnum, must also have been the local market centres which supplied the villas with equipment and services and absorbed much of their produce. Only a little further away was Capua, which, as the largest city of inland Campania, must also have been an important market centre. Rome and other more distant markets could be reached through the port at Sinuessa. In addition there were several smaller settlements in the plain which served more local needs, like Forum Popili and Forum Claudi in the Ager Falernus; and there were no doubt various *vici* and *pagi,* though we find only occasional mention of them as in the Pagus Sarclanus[16] and the Vicus Caedicii near Sinuessa.[17] The Vicus Caedicii is known to have been inhabited by coloni, and it is probable that many of the larger estates had similar settlements of dependent tenants.

---

[11]Cf. Wiseman, 1970, 130-1. Wiseman suggests that the low line of the Via Appia by way of Sinuessa and the Pons Campanus was not built until 162 B.C. (arguing that the Cn. Domitius cos. recorded on a milestone near Sinuessa (*CIL* X 6870) was the original builder of this stretch of the road, and that he is probably to be identified with the suffect consul of 162). I should prefer an earlier date since this part of the plain was already developed before the Hannibalic War: cf. Livy xxii 13-14.

[12]Information from Mr. Paul Arthur. For other roads in the vicinity of Suessa Aurunca, see Valletrisco (1977).

[13]The Via Latina follows the natural inland route from Rome to Capua by way of the Liri valley. The road, which was of great antiquity, was perhaps first paved in the last half of the fourth century B.C., for it linked Rome with the colonies of Fregellae and Interamna (founded in 328 B.C.) as well as with Cales. The scanty literary and epigraphic evidence is collected by Radke (1973).

[14]Dion. Hal. xv 4. 2. According to Dionysius the river was not less than 4 plethra (approx. 123m.) wide.

[15]A bridge of some kind was presumably built at the river crossing when the Via Appia was made, but the six-arched *ponte romano* which survived, much rebuilt by Frederick II, until the second World War can hardly have been built before the second century B.C.

[16]For an inscription recording the Pagus Sarclanus, Pellegrino (1978).

[17]A Vicus Caedicii is located by Pliny *Hist. nat.* xiv 62 six mp. from Sinuessa. The Vicus was named after a landlord called Caedicius (cf. Festus 45M), a common name in this part of Italy (Wiseman, 1971, 218, no. 76). The vicus was probably acquired by L. Papius Pollio who had coloni there (*CIL* X 4727). For vici as appendages of private estates, see Cicero *ad. Att.* i 4.3 and Shackleton-Bailey's commentary ad. loc.

As can be seen, the villas at Francolise were well situated for communications. They lay close to a branch of the Via Appia which connected them with Suessa Aurunca to the north west, and with Casilinum and Capua to the south east. To the north a road led directly to Teanum,[18] and to the east another must have led to Cales.[19] The Via Appia, 7 km. to the south, gave access to the sea at Sinuessa. There was therefore a variety of markets available for the agricultural and industrial produce of the villa.

For municipal purposes, the villas at Francolise fell within the territory of Cales. This can be deduced from two passages of Pliny's *Natural History* which refer to the spring of mineral water which still rises immediately below the hill of Francolise on its north-west side. In one of these Pliny refers to a spring of mineral water situated 4 miles from Teanum. Since this corresponds to the distance of Francolise from Teanum there can be little doubt that he is referring to the spring at Francolise. In the second he refers to a spring in the territory of Cales. In both passages the spring water is said to be called 'acidula', so that it seems probable that the two refer to the same spring.[20] That being the case, the villas at Francolise must also have fallen within the territory of Cales.

The Roman occupation of the North Campanian plain began in 340 B.C. when they defeated a combined force of Latins and Campanians, and punished both peoples by confiscating valuable parts of their territories. The Ager Falernus, which had belonged to the Campanians, was then divided among the Roman plebs up to the line of the Volturno river. The individual allotments were three and a quarter iugera (approx. 0·82 ha.) in size: rather larger than normal since the terms offered to the Roman settlers presumably had to be unusually advantageous to compensate them for the distance of the area from Rome.[21] A surviving boundary stone commemorates the commission of four which carried out the centuriation and distribution of the conquered land.[22] The work of the commission must have proceeded rather slowly, for it was not until 318 that a new tribe, the Tribus Falerna, was created for the new settlers.[23] This long interval between the occupation of the Ager Falernus and the creation of the tribe probably indicates the amount of work that had to be done, not only in surveying and dividing the land, but also in clearing the forest cover. Two administrative centres, Forum Popili and Forum Claudi,[24] were founded in the Ager Falernus probably in connection with the original settlement. Like other such fora they will have served both as market centres and as places where visiting Roman magistrates could administer justice.[25]

---

[18]This may be inferred from Pliny *Hist. nat.* xxxi 9 which locates a spring at Francolise 4 mp. from Teanum. See n. 20 below.

[19]There was a Via Falerna, maintained by the municipality of Cales, which evidently linked Cales with the Ager Falernus: *CIL* X 3910.

[20]Pliny *Hist. nat.* xxxi 9; ii 230. The spring is also mentioned by Valerius Maximus (i 8. ext. 18) and Vitruvius (viii 3. 17) who locates it at Teanum. The two springs are identified by Nissen (1902, II 695 n. 2).

[21]Livy viii ll. 13-14: *terna (sc. iugera) in Falerno quadrantibus etiam pro longinquitate adiectis.*

[22]*CIL* X 4719

[23]Livy ix 20. 6.

[24]Forum Popili: see Mommsen's remarks in *CIL* X.1 pp. 460-3. The Popilius who gave his name to the Forum cannot be identified with certainty: perhaps M. Popilius Laenas, cos. 316 B.C. in the second Samnite War: Nissen, 1902, II 692.

Forum Claudi: Ruoff- Väänänen, 1978, 31-2 and n. 181. The name is first recorded in the eleventh century, but the site is much earlier. The church, which was the seat of a bishopric in the Middle Ages, has a nave arcade of re-used late antique materials; there are the remains of a cistern in *opus mixtum* a few metres to the north of the church, and numerous traces of settlement on a low hill opposite the church, including fragments of African red slip and Late Roman C pottery. I did not myself see anything of Republican date, but Mr. Paul Arthur tells me that he has found a little black glaze pottery here. The main reason for dating Forum Claudi to the middle Republic is its name, for the fora in Campania seem to have been established before the end of the third century (Ruoff-Väänänen, 1978, 29).

[25]Fora as market centres: Brunt, 1971, 570; as centres for the administration of justice: Ruoff-Väänänen, 1978, 4-9.

INTRODUCTION

In 340 B.C. when the Romans annexed the Ager Falernus, the security of the area must have seemed very uncertain. In 335 B.C., however, they seized Cales from the Aurunci and in the following year refounded it as a Latin colony for 2,500 settlers.[26] This was a master stroke of Roman statecraft, for Cales was a strongpoint from which the Romans could control access to the Ager Falernus (and indeed the whole of Campania) from both Latium and Samnium. The fortifications of the existing Auruncan settlement were preserved[27] but the city was redesigned on a coherent plan,[28] and part of its territory was centuriated.[29] The Roman hold on the Ager Falernus was still further strengthened in 313 or 312 when they suppressed a rebellion of the Aurunci and confiscated all their remaining territory.[30] Suessa Aurunca, which dominates the low pass leading south over the shoulder of Roccamonfina to the Ager Falernus, was founded as a Latin colony on some of the confiscated land. These colonies could provide local protection, but they could not withstand an organised army as subsequent events showed, for in 305 the Samnites made raids into the plain north of the Volturnus,[31] before they were defeated by an army commanded by the Roman consuls.

In 296 or 295[32] a small maritime colony was founded at Sinuessa where traffic from the Ager Falernus reaches the coast. Like other maritime colonies it consisted of Roman citizens who remained under central Roman control, and it was intended to act as a guard-post against attack by sea. But the foundation of the colony must also have made it possible to adopt the low route for the Via Appia following the coast through Minturnae and Sinuessa to beyond the end of the range of Monte Massico, and then passing through the Ager Falernus to join the Via Latina at Casilinum. The route was clearly chosen to facilitate the development of the Ager Falernus, by linking the settlement there with the important market at Capua, and with the coast at Sinuessa.

In securing the Ager Falernus it is probable that at first the Romans were principally interested in developing the plain land for grain production with a view to the Roman market. Certainly by the time of the Second Punic War the whole of the north Campanian plain was producing a surplus of grain, so that the conflict between the Romans and Carthaginians for the possession of Capua was intensified by the importance of controlling this supply.[33] Two episodes in the war throw some light on the conditions in the Ager Falernus at the time. In 217 B.C. Hannibal carried out the famous stratagem[34] by which he escaped from a trap set for him by Fabius Maximus somewhere in the vicinity of Cales by attaching torches to the horns of 2,000 oxen and driving them by night up a slope near Fabius' camp, so creating confusion in the Roman army and allowing the Carthaginians to escape. According to Polybius the 2,000 beasts were selected for their strength from the working oxen which the Carthaginians had collected as spoils from the Ager Falernus.

---

[26]Livy viii 16; Vell. i 14. 3. The Fasti Triumphales record a triumph of M. Valerius Corvus *de Caleneis idibus Mart.* of 335 B.C.

[27]Johannowsky, 1961, 259.

[28]For the city plan of Cales, see Johannowsky, (1961, 259) and the *Atlante aerofotografico delle sedi umane in Italia, Parte Seconda: le sedi antiche scomparse* (Florence: Istituto Geografico Militare, 1970), 104-5 and pl. 106.

[29]Vallat, 1980, 425-7: réseau no. 4.

[30]Hence Livy ix 25: *deletaque Ausonum gens.* For *Ausones* as the term for the Aurunci normally used by Greek sources, see *RE* 4 *s.v.*

[31]Diod. xx 90.3: the Samnites raid τὴν φαλερνιτιν; Livy ix 44: they raid the Campus Stellas.

[32]Vell. i 14. 6 (295); Livy x 21. 7-10 (296).

[33]For cereal production in Campania: Heurgon, 1942, 14-15. Livy records the importation of grain from Campania as early as 476 B.C. (ii 52). For the importance of Campania as a granary in the Second Punic War: Brunt, 1971, 272-3.

[34]Polybius iii 92.

This large number of working oxen must imply that a very large part of the Ager had been brought under the plough, presumably for grain production. Moreover, since farmers with estates of less than 20 iugera can hardly have used a plough to till the land[35] it would seem that the pattern of small-holdings set up by the original land distribution had already given place to one of larger estates before the Hannibalic war.[36] Such estates were probably already being administered from villas like the earliest of those on the slopes of Monte Massico which stood on terraces of polygonal masonry[37] some of which may go back to the third century B.C.

The cities on the edge of the Ager Falernus also underwent a rapid development after the Roman conquest. The Latin colony of Cales became an important centre of pottery manufacture, producing both the moulded black-slipped Calene ware which was frequently exported to Etruria in the second half of the third century[38] and simpler black slipped pottery which was also produced with an eye to the Roman and Etruscan market.[39] But the effects of Roman conquest are perhaps best seen at Teanum. This city remained in the hands of the Sidicini, but it too underwent a rapid development which reflects the strength of Roman influence. At the end of the fourth century it was consolidated as a city,[40] with circuit walls of square cut blocks of stone ornamented with projecting columns;[41] and the first of the great terraces which was to transform its sanctuary at Loreto into one of the most impressive engineering works of Hellenistic Italy was begun.[42] Like many other Campanian cities, it produced its own black-glazed pottery.[43] Sinuessa, which was not an autonomous city, seems to have been slower in developing.

The devastation wrought by Hannibal in this area has left some record in the archaeological[44] as well as the literary[45] sources, but this was probably soon made good. An inscription[46] shows that Cales was reinforced by a fresh settlement of colonists early in the second century B.C. In 194 a maritime colony of three hundred Roman citizens was established at Volturnum on the mouth of the Volturnus river,[47] which had proved itself an important supply base for the Romans during the war over Capua.[48] Like Liternum, which was founded at the same time a little further south, it was intended to protect the Campanian plain from piratical raids.[49] The destroyed sanctuary at Sinuessa was rebuilt.[50] With the

[35]White, 1970, 336. Even with 20 iugera a farmer could only have used plough oxen if he could pasture them on communal grazing.

[36]There is good literary and archaeological evidence to show that large estates were already being created in Italy before the Hannibalic War. The best example is the estate (*ager*) of Fabius Maximus which was spared by Hannibal. Fabius sold it in 217 B.C. and with the proceeds paid the ransom of 247 Roman prisoners (Livy xxii 23). For archaeological evidence for a villa of the third century B.C., see Tocco, *Atti 13 Convegno Magna Grecia*, 461-8.

[37]Johannowsky, 1976, 277. For illustrations of such terraces: Vallat, 1981, 13.

[38]Pagenstecher, 1909; Morel, 1976, 270-1.

[39]Morel, 1976, 270-1.

[40]Johannowsky, 1963, 133.

[41]Blake, 1947, 106; Johannowsky, 1963, 132. Blake, following Della Corte, argues that the projecting columns supported a soldiers' passageway corbelled out from the wall.

[42]Johannowsky, 1963, 133.

[43]Morel, 1976, 271.

[44]According to Johannowsky, 1977, 772 a temple at Mondragone, presumably the sanctuary at Panetelle, was destroyed about this time, and subsequently rebuilt.

[45]Hannibal's raid on the Ager Falernus in 217 is vividly described in Livy xxii 13-14; Polybius iii 92. He ravaged the territory of Teanum and (probably) Cales again in 211 (Livy xxvi 9). Cales and Suessa Aurunca failed to supply troops to the Roman army in 209, pleading inability (Livy xxvii 9) and were subsequently punished (Livy xxix 15). Sinuessa as a maritime colony pleaded exemption from military sevice in 207 (Livy xxvii 38).

[46]*CIL* VI 1283; *Inscr. It.* XIII. 3 no. 70(a).

[47]Livy xxxii 29. 3, xxxiv 45. 1.

[48]Livy xxv 20, 22.

[49]Val. Max. ii 10, 2, for a piratical raid on the villa of Scipio Africanus at Liternum.

[50]See n. 41.

end of the war the economy of the cities soon recovered. Cales continued to produce moulded pottery,[51] and supplied agricultural equipment for villas in Campania.[52] Its prosperity in the second century is revealed by its buildings. Already by the time of C. Gracchus the city possessed public baths[53] and by the end of the century it had a large theatre.[54] In buildings it was rivalled by Teanum, where the terraced sanctuary was further developed with massive concrete substructures in the middle of the century. Teanum too had public baths, which were the scene of the atrocity committed by a Roman consul on a local magistrate which roused the wrath of C. Gracchus.[55] But the most important building at Teanum erected before the end of the second century was its theatre—the first known example of a theatre with an auditorium built up on substructures.[56] The third city of the Ager Falernus, Sinuessa, was slower to develop, because being a Roman colony it lacked its own government, and public buildings had to be authorised by the censors at Rome, where expending money on the colonies was not popular. Even so a reforming censor in 174 defied both his colleague and the senate and placed a contract for what appears to have been a suburb of cottages protected by a defensive wall at Sinuessa.[57]

The increasing prosperity of the cities in the second century B.C. reflects the increasing wealth of the local aristocrats, who probably derived most of the funds which they spent on their cities' fabric from the revenues of their agricultural estates. The Roman conquests of the period brought an abundant supply of slaves to Italy, so that the typical agricultural estate of the second century, vividly depicted for us in Cato's *De re rustica*, came to be based on the exploitation of cheap slave labour. Such estates were run from villas where the animals were stalled, the agricultural equipment was stored, and the slaves and the bailiff who acted for the landlord were housed. The landlord himself might visit the villa only occasionally to supervise the management of his estate. The agricultural and domestic parts of the villa had not yet been separated, for these villas were intended to be functional rather than luxurious. By the time of the Gracchan reforms slavery must have been widely used in agriculture in the north of Campania, for 4,000 slaves were executed at Sinuessa after the slave revolt of 133, far more, apparently, than anywhere else in Italy.[58] Although some of these had no doubt come from further afield, it seems probable that they concentrated near Sinuessa because the number of slaves employed in this part of Italy was unusually large.

Archaeologically the larger villas of the period in the north of Campania are little known, but the building of the earliest phase at San Rocco gives us a vivid impression of the character of a villa of moderate pretensions datable to the beginning of the first century. It afforded a reasonable degree of comfort and had some artistic embellishment, but was still of modest size, suitable for a family with a few slaves. We may compare the villa at Posto[59] in its earliest phase, which was perhaps marginally earlier than that of San Rocco. This was a rather simpler structure consisting of a house with six rooms and an attached farmyard. It could have been run by a single family or by a bailiff with a few slaves.

[51]Morel, 1976, 281: the so-called Megarian bowls.
[52]Cato *De re rustica*. 135. 1.
[53]Gellius *N.A.* iii 3.
[54]Johannowsky, 1976, 272.
[55]Gellius *N.A.* iii 3.
[56]Johannowsky, 1976, 271-2.
[57]Livy xli 27. 12; Servius on Verg. *Aen.* i 421.
[58]Orosius v 9. 4. 450 slaves were crucified at Minturnae.
[59]Cotton, 1979, 16-17.

The Gracchan land reforms of 133 and 123/2 B.C. affected the Ager Campanus,[60] but there is no reliable evidence for Gracchan settlement in the plain north of the Volturno. Admittedly the *Liber Coloniarum* records a Gracchan land division at Cales,[61] but this must be rejected as unhistorical since Cales as a Latin colony would not have been touched by the Gracchan reform.[62] In the first century B.C., however, the area around Francolise saw numerous changes brought about by the civil wars, veteran settlements and agrarian reforms of the period. Suessa Aurunca over the pass to the north of Francolise was the scene of a critical episode in the civil war between the factions of Marius and Sulla,[63] and it is probable that Cales was also involved in the conflict since the suburb of the city appears to have been devastated around this time.[64] The whole area was probably Marian in sympathy[65] and may have incurred reprisals after Sulla's victory. Sulla created a new colony, Urbana, on land immediately to the north of the Volturno, adjoining the territory of Cales.[66] The land was centuriated, but the colony, which was presumably a settlement of vererans, seems never to have prospered.[67] The area around Francolise continued to be affected by proposals for land reform. If Cicero can be believed, Cales, Teanum and the Campus Stellas were among the areas threatened by Rullus' land bill in 63 B.C.[68] That bill came to nothing, but in 59 B.C. Julius Caesar settled some of Pompey's veterans in the Campus Stellas on the north side of the Volturno, as well as at Capua to the south,[69] and later, as dictator, he founded a colony for veterans at Casilinum,[70] and probably at Volturnum.[71]

In spite of the various land assignations of the Late Republic, the Roman aristocracy continued to build large estates in the area around Francolise. Cicero's speeches and correspondence throw some light on these. Pompey had an estate somewhere in the Ager Falernus,[72] as did L. Quinctius, the radical tribune of 74 B.C.[73] Cicero's friend Lepta had a luxury villa near Sinuessa,[74] and Cicero himself bought a more modest property in the

---

[60]Gracchan land distributions in the Ager Campanus are attested by *CIL* X 3807, 3808.

[61] *Gromatici Veteres*, ed. Lachmann, 1848, 232 lines 13-16: *Calis, municipium muro ductum. iter populo non debetur. ager eius limitibus Graccanis antea fuerat adsignatus, postea iussu Caesaris Augusti limitibus nominis sui est renormatus.*

[62]The *lex agraria* carried by Tiberius and renewed by Gaius Gracchus applied only to *ager publicus populi Romani*(for the relevant sources, see Greenidge and Clay, 1960, 4-5, 34). A Gracchan colony at Suessa Aurunca (*Lib. col.* 237) should also be rejected.

[63]Appian *BC* i 85.

[64]Johannowsky, 1961, 266, n. 13; 1970-1971, 470. Note that it was between Teanum and Cales that Scipio made his deal with Sulla in 82 (Cic. *Phil* xii 27).

[65]Marius took refuge in the marshes near Minturnae in 88 B.C.: Liv. *Ep.* lxxvii.

[66]Pliny *Hist. nat.* xiv 62. For the location of Urbana, which can only be identified approximately, see Cuomo, 1974, Vallat 1980, 436. It lay between the territory of Cales and the Volturno about 9 km. south of Francolise.

[67]Neither Urbana nor the adjacent Casilinum (a Caesarian and Antonian colony — see below) appears in Pliny's list of Italian municipalities in Campania and Latium (*Hist. nat.* iii 63-5) which is mostly derived from an Augustan source (Pliny *Hist. nat.* iii 46; Thomsen, 1947, 17-46). In *Hist. nat.* xiv 62 Pliny describes Urbana as a Sullan colony which had recently been merged with Capua (*nuper Capuae contributam*). Assuming that Urbana and Casilinum lost their autonomy at the same time, we may conclude either that they were both allocated to Capua by Augustus (in which case Pliny has taken the word *nuper* from his source: cf. Brunt, 1971, 307), or that the merger was genuinely recent at the time Pliny was writing (in which case Pliny has here updated his source). Since we know that Capua was reinforced by a new veteran settlement in 57 A.D. (Tac. *Ann.* xiii 31. 2), it seems better to suppose that the municipal re-organisation was carried out then. Cf. n. 103 for another case in which Pliny updates his Augustan material.

[68]Cicero, *de leg. ag.* i. 20; ii. 85-86; 96.

[69]Suet. *Div. Iul.* 20. 3.

[70]Nic. Dam. 136f.

[71] *Gromatici Veteres*, ed. Lachmann, 1848, 239 lines 4-7: *Volturnum, muro ductum. colonia iussu imp. Caesaris est deducta. iter populo debetur ped. XX. ager eius a nominibus villarum et possessorum est adsignatus.*

[72]Cic. *Phil* xiii ll.

[73]Cic. *Cluent.* 175.

[74]Cic. *ad fam.* vi 19.

vicinity which provided a convenient stopping-off point on the Via Appia on his journeys between his villas at Cumae and Formiae.[75] Some of the largest estates were probably in arable land[76] and specialised in the production of cereals, but what chiefly attracted the Roman aristrocracy to the plain must have been its fame as a wine producing area. The production of Falernian wine for export can be traced back at least to the first half of the second century B.C.,[77] but it was probably only in the middle of the first century that the *vinum Falernum* became famous.[78] The best of this wine, according to Pliny, came from the *Faustianus ager* which was located half way up the slopes.[79] Fronto connected the name of the vineyard with Faustus Sulla,[80] and it is not unlikely that the famous *cru* was his creation. Sinuessa provided the entrepôt where wine from the plain was bottled in amphorae, and shipped to Rome or overseas, and a large amphora industry developed there to provide the containers.[81]

During the period which followed the dictatorship of Sulla there was a tendency for the villas of the Roman aristocracy to become increasingly magnificent as new standards of luxury were set,[82] and we may surmise that the villas which the great magnates owned in and around the Ager Falernus shared in this development. Recent archaeological surveys seem to confirm that there was an upsurge of villa building in the area in the early first century B.C., and that some of these villas were of impressive size.[83] None of these, however, has been excavated.

The prosperity of the North of Campania in the first half of the first century B.C. is reflected in the continued development of the cities which provided most of the services and markets for the surrounding villas. New or rebuilt fortification walls at Cales[84] and Forum Popili[85] reflect the unsettled conditions of the Sullan period, but other works show clear signs of prosperity. Cales, which had acquired an aqueduct before 82 B.C.,[86] built its magnificent Central Baths at about this time. Its theatre was enlarged, and its principal sanctuary was developed with terraced substructures.[87] At Teanum too, new public baths were built within the 'Sullan' period, and new substructures were built in the Loreto sanctuary.[88]

This upsurge of building seems to have come to an end before the middle of the first century B.C., and it is easy to suppose that the unsettled conditions of the third quarter of the century were not conducive to new building in the municipalities. In the countryside numerous properties changed hands or were divided up as a result of the confiscations and land distributions carried out first by Caesar, then by the triumvirs, and finally by Octavian alone. The scale of the confiscations is impossible to estimate, though Caesar certainly expropriated the properties of many of his enemies, and the confiscations of the triumvirs

---

[75]Cic. *ad fam.* vi 19. 1; *ad Att.* xii 20; xiv 8.

[76]Cf. Horace *Epod.* iv: *Arat Falerni mille fundi iugera.* The passage probably antedates Octavian/Augustus' settlement of veterans in the Ager Falernus in which estates such as these must have been split up.

[77]Mr. Paul Arthur tells me that he has located several kilns near Sinuessa which produced Graeco-italic amphorae. This suggests that the production of wine for shipment goes back at least to the beginning of the second century.

[78]The first literary mention of Falernian is in Catullus 27. 1.

[79]Pliny (*Hist. nat.* xiv 62). There is an alternative reading Faustinianus.

[80]Fronto *De Fer. Als.* 3.2.

[81]Panella (1980), Peacock (1977).

[82]See esp. Varro *RR* i 13. 7.

[83]Vallat, 1981, 13.

[84]Johannowsky, 1961, 259; 1976, 275.

[85]Illustrated in Vallat, 1981, 18.

[86]*CIL* X 4669 refers to the cleansing of an aqueduct in 82 B.C.

[87]Johannowsky, 1961, 260-3; Gros, 1978, 74.

[88]Johannowsky, 1976, 285; 1963, 140.

were notorious. We know, almost by chance, the names of two citizens of Cales, C. Subernius and M. Planius Heres, who had taken the Pompeian side in the war in Spain, and whose properties appear to have been in danger of confiscation. Cicero wrote a highly disingenuous letter to Dolabella in late 46 or early 45, asking leave for them to return.[89]

Much land in the plain around Francolise was redistributed to veterans in this quarter-century. Caesar's colonies at Casilinum and Volturnum have already been mentioned. The colony at Casilinum was refounded by Mark Antony with another *deductio* of veterans in 44.[90] In 41, before the outbreak of the Perusine war, Octavian was based at Teanum[91] where he was evidently occupied with settling the veterans of the battle of Philippi. The *Liber Coloniarum* records an Augustan colony here,[92] probably wrongly, though there may well have been a smaller settlement of veterans, as there probably were at Cales and Forum Popili where the *Liber* also records Augustan *limites*.[93]

The land redistributed to veterans did not always come from confiscated properties,[94] though both Caesar and the triumvirs auctioned confiscated estates to raise money, partly to finance such settlements. So much land was sold in these auctions that the price of properties fell and speculators were able to make purchases at bargain prices.[95] What happened to the villas at Francolise at this time? Vallat believes that they fell within the cadastre of the Augustan land distribution at Cales,[96] but this seems improbable, since although we cannot estimate the size of the estates farmed from them, it is clear that the owner of the San Rocco villa had a very large olive plantation and lived in a considerable degree of comfort, while the owner of the Posto villa must also have had extensive olive groves. These men were not ordinary veterans. Nevertheless the fact that both villas were substantially rebuilt around this time suggests that they may have been acquired by partisans of Octavian who could afford to invest in their properties without fear of their being expropriated for veteran settlements.

When the civil wars had come to an end, and the veteran settlements had been completed, the municipalities in the vicinity of Francolise seem to have entered a new period of prosperity. The peaceful conditions established by Augustus favoured the municipal aristocracy, with the result that various inscriptions of the early Empire record the names of local dignitaries who became patrons of one or other of the municipalities and provided funds for the repair of its fabric or the endowment of special feasts. Cales is particularly rich in such inscriptions. The greatest of the local families was the Vinicii[97] who rose to high

---

[89]Cic. *ad fam.* ix 13. The restoration of their properties is not specifically mentioned; but we are given to understand that Lepta had lent them substantial sums which he stood to lose if they were not reinstated.

[90]Cic. *Phil* ii 102. The colony was subsequently merged with Capua: see n. 67.

[91]Appian *BC* V. 20.

[92]*Gromatici Veteres* ed. Lachmann, 1848, 238, lines 6-9: *Teanum Siricinum, colonia deducta a Caesare Augusto. iter populo debetur ped. LXXXV. ager eius militibus metycis nominibus IIIICL limitibus Augusteis est adsignatus.* See n. 103 below.

[93]*Gromatici Veteres*, 233, line 18 (Forum Populi); 232, line 13 (Calis): see n.61.

[94]See the discussion in Brunt, 1971, 319-31.

[95]Cf. Cic. *ad fam.* ix 10. 3 for the speculative purchases of P. Sulla in 45; Appian *BC* iv 31 for the low prices fetched by the sales of properties of those proscribed in 43.

[96]Vallat, 1980, 424-7 and n. 93; cadastre D on his plan annexe 2. According to Vallat, the cadastre supersedes a previous cadastre (no. C on Vallat's plan), which according to Vallat is likely to be contemporary with the foundation of the Latin colony at Cales in 334. It is not clear from the published evidence that cadastre D does in fact extend over Francolise, but even if this is the case, it does not necessarily follow that Francolise was centuriated in the Augustan period, since the cadastre D might date to any time after the foundation of the original colony, e.g. to the reinforcement of the colony in the early second century B.C. (above, n. 46). Alternatively, as Nicholas Purcell has suggested in a written comment on the manuscript of this chapter, it is possible that the villas at Francolise, being on an uneven piece of terrain and very near the edge of the ager Calenus, may have fallen into a *subsecivum* and so escaped being confiscated.

[97]*RE* IX A 1 110 ff. nos. 5-11; Wiseman, 1971, 274-5, nos. 494-5.

importance under Augustus and Tiberius. M. Vinicius, the patron of Velleius, who had been born in Cales and had risen to hold the consulship twice under Tiberius, rebuilt the roads of the city at his own expense.[98] The Vitrasii, who were also to become a consular family, gave generous benefactions to the city rather later in the first century A.D.[99] At Teanum, the Vipstani who appear in the municipal *fasti* for A.D. 46[100] were probably local landowners as well as eminent members of the Roman senate. Municipal building at Teanum is recorded in another inscription[101] on which the name of the benefactor has been lost. Both Teanum and Cales reached their maximum development in the early Empire. According to Strabo,[102] who wrote in the time of Augustus, Teanum was the largest city on the Via Latina, and the most noteworthy city in the interior of Campania after Capua, though Cales was also considerable. Teanum's importance was marked by the grant of colonial status made to it by Claudius.[103] But the city in this area which developed most in the early Empire was probably Sinuessa, where the mineral springs at Aquae Sinuessanae became popular with the imperial family and other important figures of the time. The baths and associated temple of Aphrodite seem to have attracted the patronage of Drusus and Antonia,[104] and later of their son, the emperor Claudius.[105] Tigellinus came to the baths after his fall, and committed suicide there.[106] The baths and palaestra were rebuilt some time around the middle of the first century A.D.[107] Sinuessa also had its local patrons, no doubt local landowners, who left records of their benefactions on inscriptions, such as the senators C. Clodius Adiutor and Clodius Capito who jointly bequeathed funds for building a temple and paving the forum,[108] or Sex. Caecilius Birronianus who contributed to the construction of the city's amphitheatre.[109] The patronage exercised by such men is exemplified by the inscription from Forum Popili which records a funeral feast which L. Papius Pollio gave to his coloni at Sinuessa and the *vicus Caedicii* in memory of his father.[110] Such men evidently owned large properties in the north of Campania.

Another factor which helped to increase the prosperity of the area in the early empire was the more efficient maintenance of the road system. The Via Appia had already been improved in the late Republic, at least where it crossed the Pontine marshes,[111] and further improvements probably followed under Augustus. Dio records in 27 B.C. that he at first called on senators to pay for repairs to most of the roads, and that when that failed he met

---

[98]Tacitus, *Ann.* vi 15. 1; *AE* 1929, no. 166.

[99]*CIL* X 4643, cf. 4635, 4639, 4873.

[100]Degrassi, 1938, 142-3.

[101]*CIL* X 4792.

[102]Strabo v 3. 9; v 4.10.

[103]Pliny (*Hist.nat.* iii 63) treats Teanum as a colony in his list of Campanian cities, and since his list of colonies is, by his own account, taken from a list drawn up by Augustus (*Hist. nat.* iii 46) it is normally supposed that Teanum was an Augustan colony. This seems to be confirmed by the *Liber Coloniarum* which lists Teanum Sidicinum as a colony founded by Augustus (see n. 92). But as Mommsen argued (*CIL* X. p.471), two *tituli* (*CIL* X 4781 and 4799) show with virtual certainty that it had the appellation Colonia Claudia Firma Teanum, and must therefore be a foundation of Claudius. And this appears to be confirmed by a fragment of the municipal *fasti* which suggests that the city was reorganised as a colony in A.D. 46 (Degrassi, 1938, 140 ff.). It should be noted that Pliny's list of colonies is not drawn exclusively from Augustus (Thomsen, 1947, 41), and that the *Liber Coloniarum* is notoriously unreliable.

[104]*CIGr* 5956

[105]Tac. *Ann.* xii 66.

[106]Tac. *Hist.* i 72.

[107]Johannowsky, 1974, 354.

[108]*CIL* X 3851 and 3852; *AE* 1926, no. 143; *PIR*² 1156 and 1158.

[109]*CIL* X 4737. For the amphitheatre: Pagano and Ferrone, 1977, 20 ff. Some *opus reticulatum* was still visible in the 1920s.

[110]*CIL* X 4727.

[111]The Pontine stretch of the Via Appia had been improved some time before Horace's journey to Brundisium (Heurgon, 1976, 18), perhaps in connection with Caesar's scheme of draining the Pontine marshes.

the expenses either from his own or from public funds.[112] In 20 B.C. he accepted the *cura viarum* and set up a board of *curatores,* of praetorian status, to supervise road building.[113] From then on the upkeep of the principal roads remained the responsibility of the emperor, and the standard of maintenance improved. A major restoration of the Via Appia was carried out under Nerva, attested on our stretch of the road by three milestones located between Sinuessa and Capua.[114] A still more significant development was the opening of the Via Domitiana in A.D.95.[115] This road probably followed an earlier route for part of its way, but by bridging the Volturno near its mouth and paving the road, Domitian greatly improved the communications on the west fringe of the plain. The new road cut 16 miles off the journey to Puteoli in comparison with the Via Appia and so must have drawn much of the traffic destined for the Bay of Naples away from the vicinity of Francolise. These improvements in the road system must have made it easier for villa owners to get their produce to market, and it is probably symptomatic of this that the pattern of amphora production in the early Empire changes, so that whereas the Dressel 1 amphorae, which had been the typical containers for wine in the late Republic, had been produced on the coast near Sinuessa, the Dressel 2s and 4s of the early Empire were frequently produced on villas inland.[116] Evidently it was no longer necessary to transport the wine in wine sacks from the villas where it was produced to the ports where it was decanted into amphorae. The villa owners at Francolise are unlikely to have exported wine, but the improvement in the road system must have facilitated their trade in olive oil, bricks, and no doubt other commodities.

As for the villas of the early Empire, little can yet be said about the country seats of the richest aristocrats who endowed their municipalities so well, though some of these have been located in the area we are looking at.[117] The villas at San Rocco and Posto, however, show that men of more modest wealth also flourished in the first century A.D. L. Billienus, the putative owner of the San Rocco villa in the middle of the century, who used his villa not only for processing oil, but also for making bricks, was probably typical of many villa owners of moderate means.[118] He is a useful reminder that there was no inevitable tendency for small or medium sized estates to be absorbed by larger ones.

After the end of the first century A.D. the north of Campania, like much of the rest of Italy, [119] begins to slip into economic decline. This was perhaps least pronounced in the cities. Cales, indeed, was granted colonial status some time before 289;[120] and some municipal building is attested both at Cales, where a new temple was erected early in the second century A.D.,[121] and at Teanum, where the theatre was substantially rebuilt also in the second century.[122] Moreover, some important individuals still served as patrons of their municipalities and recorded their benefactions in inscriptions, like Vitrasia Faustina at

---

[112]Dio liii 22. 1-2; Suet. *Aug.* 30

[113]Dio liv 8. 4.

[114]*CIL* X 6871, 6873, 6877.

[115]Dio lxvii 14; Statius *Silvae* carm. iv 3; Nissen, 1902, II 712.

[116]Information from Mr. Paul Arthur; publication pending.

[117]Notably at San Limato, close to Sinuessa: Pagano and Ferrone, 1977, 73. For villas of this period in general terms: Vallat, 1981, 18.

[118]Cf. the villa at San Giovanni in Lucania where there is evidence for tile making in the first century A.D.: Small, 1980, 91.

[119]Sirago (1958)

[120]Mommsen *CIL* X.1 p. 471. The date of the grant is uncertain. It could be considerably earlier.

[121]Johannowsky, 1961, 263. Johannowsky dates the building in the first half of the first century A.D., but the thinness of the bricks (average 6 · 5 cm) suggests a date early in the second century: cf. the dimensions of bricks in Ostia: Meiggs, 1973, 542-3.

[122]De Franciscis. *Atti 5 Conv. Magna Grecia* 1965, 191; Johannowsky, ibid. 152.

Cales[123] or Appia Veturia Sabinilla at Forum Popili.[124] In general, however, there is a decrease in the evidence. In the countryside the decline was probably more marked. The reputation of the Falernian wine still stood high and the product continued to be exported,[125] but the small number of amphorae which can be identified as containing it suggests that the quantity produced was no longer what it had been. And although there was probably still some new villa building in the first half of the second century[126] the evidence from Francolise, where the Posto villa was abandoned *ca.* A.D. 160 and the San Rocco villa fifty years later, suggests that this area shared in the general decline of the villa economy which can be detected in much of the Roman empire in the late second century and which lasts throughout the chaotic conditions of the third.[127]

The restoration of stable conditions under Constantine brought about a partial revival of villa building[128] which can be seen in a small way in the re-occupation of the villa at Posto. A few inscriptions from the area around Francolise also indicate a revival of the local aristocracy who owned these villas.[129] By now the Roman economy was largely in kind, so that the maintenance of a good road system was essential for transporting commodities whether for market or for payment of taxes. The later Roman emperors therefore lavished attention on the roads. Our stretch of the Via Appia, which had been restored after flooding by Caracalla,[130] was repaired again under the tetrarchs, Maxentius, Constantine, and Valentinian and Valens.[131] It was still in excellent condition in the time of Procopius.[132]

By the sixth century, however, the economy of the plain was changing. The limited evidence available shows that the creation of marshland was no longer being checked. Volturnum, which was a bishopric at the beginning of the century, had lost its episcopal status by 559,[133] probably because the settlement had declined. Being at the mouth of the Volturno, it must have been specially vulnerable to the changed conditions. But the extent of the change is best demonstrated by the fate of the Via Appia. Whereas the Antonine Itinerary and the Peutinger Table show that the road still followed its traditional route from Minturnae to Sinuessa to Capua, Guido and the Anonymous of Ravenna show it as running from Minturnae by way of Suessa Aurunca to Capua.[134] We must infer that by the seventh century A.D. (the probable date of the Anonymous of Ravenna), the Via Appia where it crossed the Ager Falernus had been swallowed up in marshland, so that traffic for

---

[123]*CIL* X 4635, datable before A.D. 176. For the reading Vitrasia T.f. Faustina, see Mommsen ad loc. Annia T.f. Faustina is also possible.

[124]*CIL* X 4720; *PIR*² no. 956: Appia Veturia Airula Coeciva Sabinilla, a *clarissima femina.* The names Airula and Coeciva are probably corrupt.

[125]Tchernia (1980)

[126]E.g. a villa at the foot of Monte Pizzuto near Sinuessa: Pagano and Ferrone, 1977, 34. The masonry in *opus reticulatum* and *opus latericium* suggests a Trajanic or Hadrianic date.

[127]Percival, 1976, 44. For some other Italian villas which are abandoned in the last half of the second century or beginning of the third, cf. the villa at Settefinestre abandoned in the late second century: Carandini and Tatton-Brown, 1980, 16; the villa at San Giovanni abandoned around the end of the second century: Small, 1980, 92; the villa on the Via Gabina, Site 11, abandoned early in the third century: Widrig, 1980, 129.

[128]In various parts of the empire: Percival, 1976, 45-50. For another Italian villa re-occupied in the fourth century after a period of abandonment, cf. the villa at San Giovanni: Small, 1980, 92.

[129]E.g. L. Mamilianus Crispus (*AE* 1940 p. 48; *PLRE* I p. 232) who was a patron of both Suessa Aurunca and Sinuessa in the early or middle fourth century; Minucius Aeterius, patron of Forum Popili who died in A.D. 367 (*CIL* X 4724; *PLRE* I p. 25); Flavius Lupus at Teanum, a *vir clarissimus* (*AE* 1968, no. 113; *PLRE* I p. 521, after A.D. 402).

[130]*CIL* X 6876: *viam inundatione aquae interruptam restituit.*

[131]The tetrarchs: *CIL* X 6870. Maxentius: ibid. 6869. Constantine: ibid. 6874, 6878. Valentinian and Valens: ibid. 6875.

[132]Procopius, *Bella* v 14:6–11.

[133]*Pelagii I Papae epistulae quae supersunt* (556-61) ed. Dom Pius Gasso, 1956, 67-8.

[134]The evidence is tabulated in Lugli, 1952, 278-9.

Capua now had to leave the coast before Sinuessa to pass over the slope of Roccamonfina and reach Capua by way of Francolise.

These changes brought drastic economic consequences. Much agricultural land must have been abandoned or given over to grazing, either because it was no longer cultivable, or because the harbours through which the produce passed had been abandoned. The famous Falernian vineyards disappeared from the scene.[135] At Francolise the last phase of the Posto villa came to an end early in the sixth century, and the area then seems to have been deserted until the twelfth.[136] There was probably some movement of population into settlements where there was agricultural land available on higher ground, as at Forum Claudi,[137] but in general there must have been a drastic decline in the population of this part of Italy in the sixth century. The *amoenissima pars Italiae*[138] degenerated into the waste land which it remained until the nineteenth century.[139]

ALASTAIR SMALL

[135]By the middle of the sixth century the term 'Falernian' ceases to be used of wine from the Ager Falernus, and comes to be applied to any good wine: Brouette (1948).

[136]Cotton, 1979, 61-2.

[137]The settlement at Forum Claudi appears to have expanded in the later Roman empire and early Middle Ages: see n. 24 above.

[138]Livy xxii 14.

[139]The reclamation of the marshland began in 1539. Much progress was made in the early seventeenth century, but the work was not completed until after 1860: TCI *Guida d'Italia, Campania*, 1963, 119-20.

ACKNOWLEDGEMENTS

The excavation of the San Rocco Villa, with that of Posto (Cotton, 1979), was a joint project of The British School at Rome and The Institute of Fine Arts of New York University, working in collaboration with the Soprintendenza alle Antichità di Campania. The whole project was financed by the Batchelor Fund of The Institute of Fine Arts.

The Directors were Professor Peter von Blanckenhagen and the late Dr. John Ward-Perkins, and Dr. M. Aylwin Cotton was Field Director. John Ward-Perkins had always intended writing the introduction to this report and it is sad that he did not either succeed in doing so or live to see it printed. The authors are fortunate in having this lacuna filled so ably by Professor Alastair Small. All three authors now wish to thank all those who have contributed to the whole undertaking, at all stages, over so long a period.

The then Superintendent for Campania, Professor A. de Franciscis, and his assistant Professor W. Johannowsky, arranged for permission to excavate, visited the site and gave expert advice, arranged professional supervision of the restorations, and helped in every way possible. Agreement to work on the villa platform was given by the Comune of Francolise, to whom it belongs; help over many points was given by the Sindaco, and we were allowed to use the Elementary School for working quarters.

Five seasons of work, in 1962-66, over some 40 weeks, were undertaken. For the first two years, the Senior Supervisor was Walter Widrig (now Assistant Professor in the Department of Fine Arts, Rice University, Houston, Texas). Guy P. R. Métraux (now Associate Professor in the Department of Visual Arts, York University, Toronto) joined the team in 1963, succeeded as Senior Supervisor in 1964-66, and as joint author of this publication deserves special mention. With them, the site supervisors for the American team were Marie Keith (now Assistant Librarian at The Frick Museum), Mary Bator, Vivienne Hibbs and Richard Stapleford (now Assistant Professor, Hunter College, New York). The British supervisory team consisted of Mark Hassall (now Lecturer, The Institute of Archaeology, London University), Kenneth Painter (now Deputy Keeper, Department of Greek and Roman Antiquities, British Museum), Timothy Tatton-Brown (now Director of the Archaeological Unit, Canterbury) and Reginald Brooks (now retired, and Honorary Treasurer of The Royal Archaeological Institute and The Prehistoric Society).

The surveying and planning were the work of Vanessa Wills (Mrs. Peter Winchester) and Hugh Richmond. The final plans were traced and lettered by Sarah Lee (Mrs. Demetrios Michaelides). For the reconstruction drawings of the villa we are fortunate in having had the expertise and artistry of Sheila Gibson. The photography was, for the greater part, the work of the late John Ward-Perkins, the late Ernest Nash, Portia Wallace-Zeuner and Geoffrey Sansbury. As at Posto, Pasquale Morelli was the foreman of a large team of workmen, and his wife and her sisters helped in the pottery shed.

Alastair Small wishes to thank Paul Arthur for much helpful advice on the topography of North Campania, Ian Campbell for guidance on geological matters, and Claude Roberto for assistance in drawing the map which appears on Fig. 1; also the grants committee of the Faculty of Arts of the University of Alberta for a travel grant which made it possible for him to visit North Campania while writing the chapter on the area around Francolise in the Roman period.

Molly Cotton would like to thank also Frank Brown (ex-Director of The American Academy in Rome) and Friedrich Rakob (of The German Archaeological Institute, Rome) whose visits supplemented those of her Directors, all of whom gave advice and helpful interpretations, much needed by a protohistorian tackling two classical sites for the first time.

An apology is offered for the long delay in the publication of this report. As a result, it has, however, benefited from the increasing number of studies by Italian colleagues and others on the subject, so that analogies and pottery dating could be improved.

Grateful thanks are offered to all the specialists who have given so generously of their time and expertise. Their names are given in association with their reports.

The artists who drew the pottery and finds, over so long a period, were numerous, but the bulk of the work is by Patricia Mallett, Catherine Ward-Perkins (Mrs. Mark Hassall), Rosalind Thompson, Anne Brunnell, Susan Walston and Alexandra MacKenzie (Mrs. Henry Hurst). The tile kiln was drawn by Geoffrey Sansbury and the *oletum* by Hugh Richmond. Miss Caroline Stone gave much of her time in preparing the figures for publication. The whole book was seen through the press by Penelope Bulloch.

Finally, at the close of the excavations, it was decided that the site be conserved and be kept open. To achieve this, all remaining mosaic floors were lifted, consolidated, relaid and sanded. The tile kiln was consolidated and given a glass front. Protective roofs, on metal struts, were built over the relaid mosaics, the *figlina* and the *oletum*. The site was fenced, with an entrance gate at the top of the steps from the approach road. These restoration expenses, which much exceeded the cost of the excavation, were paid by The Batchelor Foundation Fund. The finds have been deposited with the Soprintendenza at Naples.

M. AYLWIN COTTON

Chapter I. The Site of the San Rocco Villa and its Environment*

(Pls. I–II and Figs. 1–2)

(Carta d'Italia, map sheet 172 IX 59 Carinola, 211599)

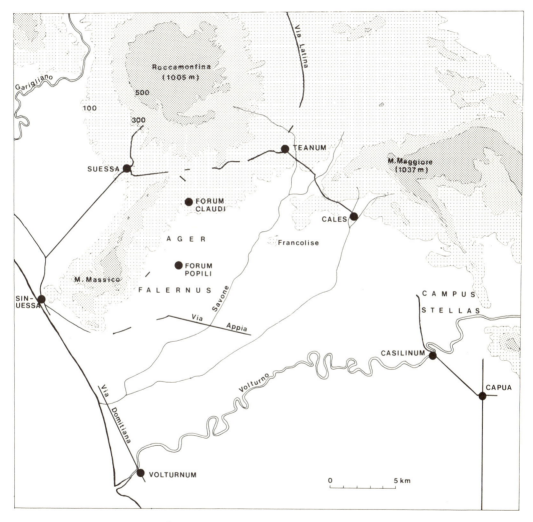

Fig. 1. Map of the area showing the Via Appia

*The authors are deeply indebted to the late Martin Frederiksen, of Worcester College, Oxford, both for reading this chapter and for the many helpful comments and the contributions he made to it.

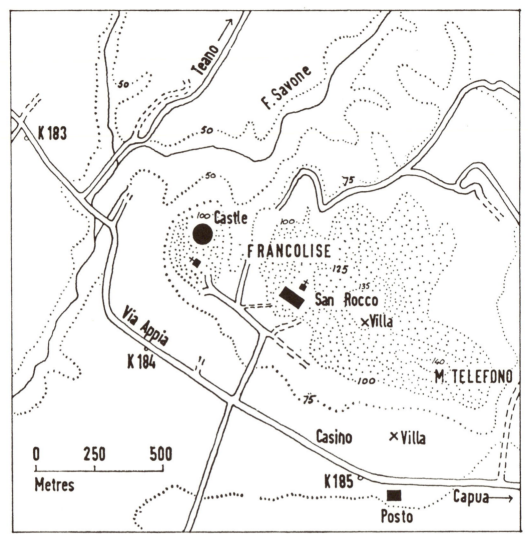

Fig. 2. Map showing the site of the villa

The site of the Roman villa of San Rocco (m.52), dominating the village of Francolise on
the northwest and distant from it by about 0 · 4 km. (Fig. 2), stands on the westernmost
spur of Monte Telefono (m.144), in the foothills of the Monte Maggiore *massif* which
begins above Cales (modern Calvi Risorta), 6 km. to the northeast. The site is so named
after the patron saint of a small chapel to San Rocco which is just north of the Roman
remains.

   The low hills on which the villa stands and the other hills surrounding Francolise are
spurs of white limestone in mantles and aprons of volcanic tufa of more recent geological
origin, which come from the volcanic region of Monte Roccamonfina, 8 km. to the west
above Suessa Aurunca (modern Suessa). The dark clayey earth associated with the limestone, called *argilla* or *argillosus* by Columella (iii 11.9) and Pliny (*Hist. nat.* xxvii 80) contrasts with the soils of a *pozzolana* character described as *tofacea* or *tofus,* such as those
surrounding the site of the Posto villa in the plain. Directly to the northeast of the villa site
on the San Rocco hill, a mantle of blue-grey volcanic tufa, very dense and fine but also

light, has been quarried down to the limestone base for building purposes, actually destroying the northeastern corner of the Period II terraces and cisterns. Geologically, the villa at San Rocco and that at Posto stand in proximity to a variety of soils and rock formations; limestone and *argilla,* tufa and tufaceous soils and, at the San Rocco villa itself, evidence of tile-making points to a nearby clay bed and perhaps one of sand (for tempering the tile fabric). The geological variety of soils corresponds to the topographical variety of situations and insolations of the area. These varieties of aspect gave diversity to agricultural activities — at San Rocco there is evidence of wheat-threshing, olive cultivation, tile-making and animal husbandry — and a pleasant multiplicity of views and moods. To the west, overlooking the hill of Francolise itself, a quiet prospect with a fan of hills and valleys rises to the Mons Massicus (modern Monte Massico), and to the south there is a dramatic far view to the Tyrrhenian Sea across the Ager Falernus, with the line of the Volturnus (modern Volturno) on the left and with the Ager Campanus and the headland of Cumae beyond.[1]

The geological variety of the site is similar to the diversity of hydrological aspects which the immediate area offers. Springs, some of plain, cool water, others affected by subsoil volcanic action and rising warm, mineralized or carbonated, or all three, are numerous and were so in antiquity. Vitruvius (viii 3.17) mentions two of them, and Pliny (*Hist.nat.*ii 230) mentions what appears to be the Acqua Catena or Acqua Cantarone. This spring, situated not far from the San Rocco villa, at the foot of its hill on which Francolise stands, is still in existence and has been frequented by visitors seeking its medicinal powers since the eighteenth century. The spring, locally called Il Bagno, has a constant temperature of 22° and consists of a good tasting water containing bicarbonates and carbonic anhydrides (making it effervescent). According to Pliny (loc.cit.), it had an effect similar to wine.

Apart from the springs, the local watershed affecting residential situations is as follows: rainwater and springs, not finding an absorbent surface in the *argilla* of the limestone hills, quickly run off into the tufaceous soil of the plain and valleys, providing well-watered areas in places, making swamps in others. Some of these characteristics were noted in antiquity, but it is not known whether the local river or stream, the Safo (modern Savone), was as intermittent in its flow as it is now.[2] The quick dispersion of water from the limestone hills was the cause of some concern to the inhabitants of the villa: cisterns, very carefully built and very extensive, are present in both major building phases (Periods I and II). A well was

---

[1.] For the Ager Falernus in general, no systematic single publication gathering together all the known sources exists. Interest has for the most part been focused on Capua and the Ager Campanus to the south, towards and around the Bay of Naples. The Roman geography of the area is discussed by Hülsen, 1909, col. 1971 ff. and most authoritatively, with ancient sources, by Beloch, 1890, 293–374, in the context of Capua and the Ager Campanus. See also Nissen, 1902, 685–96, and Maiuri, 1938, *passim.*

The geographical limits and general characteristics of the Ager alernus in Roman times are discussed by Cuomo, 1974, 29–30 and by Johannowsky, 1975, 3–6. The foundation of the Roman colony at Urbana discussed by Cuomo, 1974, was followed in Gracchan times (?) by the establishment of two *fora,* Forum Popilli and Forum Claudi, perhaps coordinated with the building of villas near Sinuessa; see Johannowsky, 1976, *passim* and 277.

For roads, see Corradi, 1949. For Capua, the most useful references are Heurgon, 1942, 5, 23, 258–9, and Frederiksen, 1959, 94 ff.

However, none of these dwell at any length on the area in the triangle of Teanum Sidicinum, Cales and Suessa Aurunca, an area of which the villas at Francolise form a part; for special problems of the area, see Salmon, 1967, 218–24 and *passim,* and Johannowsky, 1965, 420–3 (Appendix in Alföldi, 1965). The villas at San Rocco and Posto provide the major part of the rural history with which to supplement the rather meagre Roman development of these towns (see n. 5 p.5).

[2.] Beloch, 1890, 290. On the river, see Johannowsky, 1975, 13–14 and the spirited and unconvincing account in Maciariello, 1964, *passim.* The probably exaggerated story of the poisonous springs near Teanum Sidicinum reported by Vitruvius (viii 3, 17) is still, however, a common belief about other springs amongst the local inhabitants. It is to be noted that a spa and bottling plant built in the 1920's around a mineral water spring at Francolise seems to have failed when the gaseous or mineral content of the water changed.

also found. In Period II, the cisterns were fed by a water-channel whose line could not be traced: the channel may have originated at a spring or in some other natural collection point and would have transported water for storage at the villa. The quick run-off of water towards the plain caused occasional stagnation; it may be that the siting of the villa half-way up the hill was decided upon in view of these swamps.

On the siting of the villa half-way up the hill, and on its orientation facing the south-western quadrant and other particulars, Cato and Columella have something to say: indeed, they clarify some of the questions concerning the villa siting. It is literally at the foot of a mountain system as desired by Cato (*De re rustica* i 3) but at that point on the hill prescribed by Columella (i 4.10). In all other respects — the proximity to a town (Cales or Teanum), to a major river (the Volturnus, perhaps partially navigable), to the sea and to good roads (the Via Appia and the Via Latina) — the San Rocco villa would have been a first-rate property in Cato's estimation (i 2-7), and in Columella's as well (i 3.3). More-over, perhaps even more important was the proximity of other villas, not only the Posto villa, but villas of contemporary date and probably of both residential and agricultural character.[3] These nearby villas are on the brow of Monte Telefono, to the north and north east of the San Rocco villa. Substantial remains of cisterns and the débris of extensive mosaic floors can be observed at three points on the hill, and in one case the cisterns were much larger and the villa remains more extensive (but more ruined) than at San Rocco (cf. Chapter II). The masonry of the other villas, of *opus caementicium* or *opus incertum*, is analogous to that of the San Rocco villa and indicates that a residential and agricultural development took place in the environs at approximately the same dates in the first century B.C.

The San Rocco villa and its neighbours on the hillside should be contrasted with the rel-ative simplicity of periods I and IA of the Posto villa. At San Rocco, and very probably at the other villas on the hill, the viability and profitability of agriculture justified, even sup-ported, luxurious houses used either all the year round or sporadically for summer resi-dence. There was no lack of appreciation of the pleasures of country living in the first cen-tury B.C.[4] A pastoral setting, books, views, work on the land interrupted by rustic *diver-tissements*, all came to be an ideal, and we may imagine that Horace's *beatus ille . . .* (*Epodes* 2) might have referred to the proprietor of the San Rocco villa.

The transformation of the landscape with *villae rusticae* to which were attached fine houses or *domus* can almost be symbolised by the mention of the area in Vergil's *Aeneid.* The Romanization of the Ager Falernus, a process given legal force by the Roman acquisition of it in 340 B.C., had, by Vergil's time, led to another need, typically Roman:

[3] For the Posto villa, the main publication is Cotton, 1979; see also the preliminary reports: Blanckenhagen, Cotton and Ward-Perkins, 1965, and Cotton, Blanckenhagen and Ward-Perkins, 1965[2]; and the intervention by Cotton, 1970-71, in Frederiksen, 1970-71, 360 ff. See also Ward-Perkins, 1970[2] 338. Brief mentions occur in White, 1970, 419; McKay, 1975, 104-5; Boëthius and Ward-Perkins, 1970, 319 and Percival, 1976, 56 and fig. 11.

[4] For a review of the elements — cultural and architectural — and of the vast bibliography on this topic see D'Arms, 1970, 11-17 and 116-20. See also Mansuelli, 1958, *passim* and especially André, 1966, 455-527. The model of all such studies is still Della Valle, 1938, 205-67, especially 223-33: see also Mustilli, 1956, 77-97.

the need for Latin origins.[5] Vergil, in listing the Italian forces friendly to King Latinus and to Turnus, mentions the men from Mons Massicus, from Suessa Aurunca, Cales, Teanum Sidicinum and the Volturnus (vii 726-30). The inclusion of the inhabitants of this region — the Francolise region — is an indication of long standing Roman presence in an area which the Romans also knew was not their own.[6] The attempt by Vergil to identify Italic peoples as old adversaries is a tribute more to Roman antiquarianism rather than to any lingering native memory, Ausonian, Sidician or any other.

The region in its Roman aspects, namely the southern part of the Ager Falernus around Cales and Teanum Sidicinum (modern Teano), is of great interest and presents many problems, not all of which can be broached here. The Ager Falernus itself, after its acquisition by Rome in 340 B.C. and the foundation of a Latin colony at Cales, was famous for its wine by the first century B.C. As early as Cato's day, the area was well-known for the high quality of its farm equipment, notably press-pieces (xxii 2), and the region was well supplied with markets and market-days (*nundinae*). The San Rocco and Posto villas would thus have been part of a region in which agricultural and commercial markets were combined with the manufate of agricultural equipment, denoting a dynamic economic interdependence between villas and towns. These clues to the agricultural life of the Francolise region have as yet to be put together with the traces of Roman centuriation in the Ager Falernus, recently traced by Johannowsky, 1975. For the area around the villa at San Rocco itself, however, specific instances of Roman centuriation are not known, and such knowledge is essential because it would indicate the scope and character of farming in the area. Because the land's agricultural produce is still valuable and the area has undergone continuous and continuously changing cultivation, traces of Roman centuriation have disappeared. There are a few other historical indications. Livy (viii 11.14) mentions that, in or shortly after 338 B.C., the Ager Falernus (and probably also the Ager Stellas to the south) was divided among the *plebs* into farms of three *iugera.* This division would probably not have survived: numerous wars intervened, and natural economic processes favouring concentration and agglomeration of property would have affected the Ager Falernus as they did the Ager Campanus and other parts of Italy as well. For the Ager Campanus on the other side of the Volturnus, Gentile, 1955, has shown the definitive effect of Roman centuriation on fields, roads and place-names in the region in the second century B.C., but he did not come to a conclusion about how the development of concentrated farm holdings came about.[7] Certainly the region was the object of much concern

[5.] The principal source for the history of the Ager Falernus is Livy; but see Hülsen, 1909, and Heurgon, 1942, 202. Most recently this area has been studied by Johannowsky, 1975, and 1976. As is the case with the physical description of the area in Roman times (see n. 1 p.3), the history of the Ager Falernus was less important, for Latin and modern writers, than the complexities of the history and administration of the Ager Campanus. On the physical limits of the *ager*, see Beloch, 1890, 360-74, corrected by Levi, 1921-22, 604 ff. and confirmed by Cuomo, 1974, 29-30 and Johannowsky, 1975, 3-6. The foundation of Casilinum (modern Capua), and the confiscation from Capua of the Ager Falernus by the end of the fourth century B.C., led to the obscurity of the area relative to the Ager Campanus, where exciting events — social, military and administrative — document Rome's external and internal development in Late Republican times. For our purposes, the silence of Latin sources on developments in Falernian agricultural administration in the second and first centuries B.C. is a serious handicap in reconstructing the historical context of the San Rocco and Posto villas. One cannot, unfortunately, extrapolate from the events (very well documented by Livy and Cicero among others) in the same period in the Ager Campanus what was going on north of the Volturnus. In any case, the periodic distributions and redistributions of land following the annexation of the Ager Campanus were often a burning social issue; see Tibiletti, 1950, 183 ff.

[6.] Alföldi, 1965, 250-65, 391-419 and appendix by Johannowsky, 1965, 420-23.

[7.] For Campanian markets and market-days, see MacMullen, 1970, 333-41, especially 339-41. For the centuriation of the Ager Falernus, the only study is that of Johannowsky, 1975, 3-35, especially 22-4 and fig. 5 for the Francolise-Carinola region. For the Ager Campanus, see Gentile, 1955, and Castagnoli, 1955, 3 ff.

[8.] See Gentile, 1955 and Scullard, 1959, 26-40, for instances. The subject is also touched on by Skydsgaard, 1969, 31-5, and in Sirago, 1958, *passim* and in the relevant articles in *Dialoghi di archeologia*, iv-v, 1970-71.

in agrarian legislation in Late Republican times, and there seem to have been attempts to 'balance' large holdings with the distribution of small ones.[8]

We do not, however, know what these adjustments meant practically and what consequences they had on agriculture. Positive evidence comes from the villas themselves: at the beginning of the first century B.C. the Posto villa was built in the plain as a small holding with no pretensions to much residential comfort and with a single enclosure for residential and agricultural activities (period I). The San Rocco villa was built on the hill, a simple structure but with rooms of some distinction, both architectural and decorative (Period I). The Posto villa remained *rustica* in character until its latest phases, while the San Rocco villa was always divided into a residential *domus* and a *villa rustica*. Both villas underwent changes, the Posto villa minor ones (period IA), the San Rocco villa more extensive ones (Period IA). At Posto, expansion of the agricultural and residential quarters (period II) took place in pre-Augustan times of *c*. 30 B.C.; at San Rocco, a sudden and much more extensive rebuilding took place at about the same time — a huge *domus* and a very large *villa rustica* came into existence, about 60–70 years after the initial building. After that, for at least 130 years, no physical expansion took place at either villa. Rather, change is represented by diversification around the middle to the end of the first century A.D. Oil processing took place at both villas, tile-making, husbandry, wheat-threshing at San Rocco, and these required structures to be added to the existing ones. The pattern, if we may call it that, is in both cases the same: an unfolding, internal development spanning about 300 years of agricultural activity. Sudden expansion around 30 B.C., following initial construction around 100–90 B.C., was followed by a period lasting until the second half of the first century A.D. when new machinery (presses, kilns) or types of rooms (bath-buildings) were added. After that, until the abandonment of the villas in the late second or early third century A.D., no structural change is registered, nor was there any violent destruction or evidence of gradual reduction of scope and late adaptation to smaller or different uses (the squatter occupations at Posto and San Rocco are not related to the continuing life of the villas, but rather to a reoccupation when the buildings were in a ruinous state).

The relation of the countryside to the local towns — and thus of the villas to their markets — is not clear in detail. For the first century B.C., we do not know enough about the changing relationships between, for example, Capua and the resorts or commercial ports on the Bay of Naples, or between small centres such as Capua and Puteoli. Economic relationships between countryside and towns, towns and cities, cities and ports, ports and regions are difficult to describe in antiquity. Cales, 6 km. to the east, and Teanum, 7 km. to the north, were flourishing towns at all times during the Francolise villas' existence, and both received notable embellishments around the time of the Sullan campaign, just after the San Rocco villa was built.[9] Both Cales and Teanum also received embellishments and new dignities from Augustus, 20 or 25 years after the San Rocco villa was enlarged in Period II.

There are other factors whose effects are impossible at present to assess: the proximity of the Via Appia and the Via Latina or Casilina to the northeast, and also the proximity of other villas.[10] And finally, in the interpretation of the Francolise villas, it is not known to what extent historical events (for example, the after-effects of the Hannibalic invasion or

[9] For Cales, see Hülsen, 1899, col. 1351 ff., but mainly the excavator, Johannowsky, 1961, 258-67, with an account of the excavations. For Teanum, see the useful summary in De Franciscis, 1966, 638-40, but especially Johannowsky, 1963, 131-65, with an account of the excavations. See also Castagnoli, 1955, for the centuriation and a general review by Johannowsky, 1970-71, 460-71, and the valuable discussion, 491-3. For the villas in the area of Teanum Sidicinum, see Della Corte, 1929, 173-5.

[10] On the roads, however, see the Introduction to this volume.

of the Social War) and vagaries of fashion affected the villa's development. On the topic of fashion, we are well informed about the use of resort and maritime villas on the Bay of Naples, but about country living we have little information, except for the rather special attitudes of Vergil, Horace, Pliny the Younger and others.[11]

The San Rocco villa could have been used as a *diversorium* for occasional use on the road between Rome and Puteoli, as a permanent dwelling, as a summer home, as a farm with a house for an absentee landlord (as in Cato's conception), or as some combination of these. In short, the archaeological evidence does not supply definitive answers to all of the questions which it raises.

Villa sites such as that of San Rocco are intrinsically useful in helping to define the historical relationship between Roman country living and the landscape setting. The particulars of construction and development described and analysed below are presented with a view to contributing to one small part of the history of Roman Campania.

---

[11] For a general review of the topic in relation to pastoral themes in poetry, see Rose, 1936, 239-94 and Fraenkel, 1957, *passim,* also André, 1966.

Chapter II. The Villa Sites in the Vicinity of San Rocco

During excavations at San Rocco and Posto, several 'sherding' surveys were made on the hill, revealing the presence of at least three other villas and a small rural structure (see Cotton in Frederiksen, 1970-71, 360 ff.). The basis for identifying these sites as Roman, and as being of analogous date to the structures at San Rocco, lay in the visual similarity of the mortars used, the presence of *opus caementicium* and *opus incertum* walls (very fragmentary), the occurrence of Roman potsherds and the strew of white limestone *tesserae* from mosaic floors.

A small rural structure of unknown use was observed on the north-western slope of the San Rocco hill. About 600 m. from the side of the San Rocco villa, toward the NNW, a largish area (*c.* 100 × 150 m.) of Roman construction débris can be observed on a platform which seems to be man-made. To the NNE, a similar kind of débris and sherd-filled area about the same size could be seen.

To the direct north of the villa, however, near the top of the San Rocco hill, at a spot which affords spectacular views on all sides, the remains of a much larger villa than that of San Rocco could be observed. Short pieces of walls of *opus incertum*, very well built but almost entirely ruinous, were seen, covering an area nearly 250 × 200 m. and built on several man-made terraces. The spread of sherds and tesserae was even more extensive than the area of the architectural ruins. Most important was the cistern system with the platform it supported. As at San Rocco, two contiguous groups of three cisterns were present. Of these, the western group of three cisterns could be visited, with difficulty, in 1966, the eastern group having been almost entirely destroyed or filled. The cisterns visited were fully twice the size of those at San Rocco, and they were built of *opus caementicium* with occasional patches of *opus incertum* facing which seems to tie them closely to the construction dates (at least of Period II) at San Rocco. The central barrel-vaulted cistern was 2.92 m. wide and was paralleled on the north and south by similarly vaulted cisterns 2.70 m. wide. The middle cistern was 5.60 m. high from floor to the springing of the vault; presumably the flanking cisterns were equally high. Small arched doors (0.60 m. wide and 1.20 m. high), at floor level, connected the three parallel cisterns.

The cisterns were at least 30 m. long, and another set of three at least as long ran to their east. It is clear that the villa for which these huge cisterns supplied the water (at least 3,800,000 litres) was of a much larger size than that for which the San Rocco cistern capacity was constructed (*c.* 1,100,000 litres). What is equally clear is that the San Rocco villa was not the only, and certainly not the largest, villa on the hill on which it stands; it was definitely smaller than some villas, certainly it was larger than that of Posto, but in any case it was only one of many.

The implications of these contiguous villa properties on the San Rocco hill are many and various. In the first place, what is striking about their proximity (five substantial villas including San Rocco and Posto in a radius of not more than 600 m.) is that they lie close to each other *in a decidedly rural setting.* One would expect such close proximity in the bay of Naples region, for example, or along a road very near Rome, in an almost suburban setting like the Via Gabina (see Carrington, 1931, and Widrig, 1980), but whilst the San Rocco hill is near large towns (see Chapter I), it is decidedly not as close as Pompeii and Rome were to the examples cited. In the second place, the villas at San Rocco appear to be closer together than similarly proximate villas in south Etruria, whose distribution is better known; see the recently published surveys or reports in Potter, 1980, *passim,* Carandini and Settis, 1979, 35-41, and also Quilici and Quilici Gigli, 1978, *passim.* For earlier remarks on villas in close proximity (but not as close as here), see Brown, 1970-71 in Frederiksen, 1970-71, 362. These two facts — very close proximity and proximity of villas in a rural setting — about the San Rocco hill and its villas in the first century B.C. emphasize the economic and social interdependence of the *familiae,* and certainly points up the fact that residential property in the countryside existed here in a grouping which places villas so close together that the agricultural lands of the estates must have been elsewhere on the hills and in the *ager* below (the whole hill is less than 50 hectares in area or about 200 iugera, much too small to be divided into viable farms by any standard, even ancient ones). At the same time, the villas are sufficiently far apart to have a sense of privacy; from any one of them, the visual distance would be great enough to give a sense of almost rural isolation. The road (see p. 00) which was built in Period II apparently ran from the *ager* up to and through the San Rocco villa and up the hill toward the other villas; the implication is that all the owners on the hill contributed to this convenience-in-common, and a right-of-way agreement existed in some form. Granting this degree of co-operation, can other situations be hypothesized? Some efficient sharing of personnel and equipment might be expected, and strong social and familial or even blood relationships may have been built up. Perhaps the greatest point of contact (and potential conflict!) among the villa owners would have been in the area of land-use. It is clear that, with five villas in close proximity, little land would have been left over for what, at the San Rocco villa, was an important activity in Period IIA (and possibly earlier), namely the cultivation of olive trees and the manufacture of oil. The San Rocco hill was thus mainly a residential area in a rural setting, with agricultural lands of which the major part must have been separate from the villas themselves. There was definitely no 'manorial' organisation, in the sense of a self-sufficient, centralising, virtually independent villa sitting on its own lands as implied by Cato, Varro and Columella: rather, the owners were interdependent in that they had to agree on the purchase, accessibility, and use of the lands in their region. The further implication is, of course, that the large size of the villas, and the distinct impression that at least some of the structures of the *villa rustica* in Period II were slaves' or tenants' quarters (see p. 53f), indicates that the San Rocco area was one in which residences and *villa rusticae* were combined with lands exploited in a large-scale, fully rationalised way commercially, yet not at all in the manner of *latifundia.* The picture is one of co-operation in determining the site of residences and the use of non-contiguous lands. Though far smaller in extent, the creation of a co-operative residential and agricultural area around Francolise can be compared to other known areas, for example: the Ager Veientanus (Kahane *et al.,* 1968), the Ager Capenas (Jones, 1962, 116-207 and Jones, 1963, 100-58), and the area around Pompeii (Carrington, 1931, 110 ff., Day, 1932, 167 ff. and Crova, 1942, *passim.*). Other sources of information on villa areas are to be found in Lacchini, 1972-73, 193-226 (in the Veneto), and in the volumes of the *Forma Italiae* where there are many instances of villas near roads or tracks connecting them. An example of a hill with villas of similar size and situation is published by Lugli, 1921, 263-73, at Albano Laziale. It must be noted, moreover, that none of the information from San Rocco or from these other sites gives a clear picture of the means and extent of land-ownership; on this problem, see Potter, 1980, 74.

If the means and extent of land-ownership and the management of the estates is not clear, it is however clear that the nature of the villas changes, and not all of them change in the same way. Period I at Posto, a little earlier than Period I at San Rocco (see p. 254) is nonetheless just about the same in the number of rooms and enclosed courtyard space and provisions for water, but the San Rocco villa is a little more nicely finished in its decoration than the earliest villa at Posto. And whilst Posto continued throughout its history to be smaller and decidedly simpler than the subsequent periods at San Rocco (periods IA, II and IIA), it did, in its way, keep up with its larger neighbour. On the other hand, the expansion of San Rocco in Period II, of which the most notable elements were provisions for storing large amounts of water, an elegant plan and a sumptuous decorative environment, was on a scale inconsistent with the Posto villa and inconsistent with its own past as a simple structure, but consistent with the large size, mosaic floors and cistern-construction of the other villas on the hill. In Period IIA the construction of tile-kilns and an *oletum* (see pp. 66–76) confirms the picture of well-organised agricultural business and building-trade in the fourth stage of the villa's structural life, but in the second, complex stage of its economic life.

Although we cannot know, precisely, what the pattern of development was in the other villas on the San Rocco hill, two conclusions present themselves: that in Periods I and IA at both San Rocco and Posto, the small size of the villas indicates a small property with a consequentially modest social status for the owners. The villas developed in a parallel but independent way. Then, with the construction of the Period II villa at San Rocco and comparably large ones nearby it on the hill, the situation changed: Posto remained small, whilst the villas on the hill had more land, though not neccessarily contiguous with the villas themselves, more space and a higher social status for the owners. Thus, parallel and independent development on a small scale at the beginning of the first century B.C. gives way, in the last years of the Republic (Period II), to cooperation amongst large landlords, leading eventually to durable investment in the form of farm equipment (the kilns and *oletum*) and luxuries (the *balineum*) later on (Period IIA). At this point the site of Posto, whilst remaining small, emulates the establishments on the hill as best it can (see Cotton, 1979, *passim*), but continues small. Inescapably, the hypothesis presents itself that Posto remained small because it could not compete for the best land (be it in the *ager* or on the hills) with the estates whose owners had located their residences on the San Rocco hill, i.e., that small-scale independent farming could compete with only limited effectiveness against larger entities organised, at least insofar as the grouping of villas on the San Rocco hill attests, in a spirit of social and economic cooperation among owners of similar, and similarly high, social status.

However, none of the evidence from the San Rocco villa, from the Posto villa or from the other villas on the hill allows us to say anything very precise about the social status of the owners, either because the size of the holding cannot be determined, or the income from it, or both. At San Rocco, for example, since it is not known *how much* oil could be made and stored, it is not possible even to guess *how much* land there was under olive cultivation or what component in the total income of the estate it represented. For an excellent general account of these problems, see White, 1970, 390-92. Furthermore, in the absence of inscriptions and other means of knowing, the San Rocco and Posto villas do not permit any definite statement as to the inner social differentiation — the precise relationship of free, slave and hired labour — of the larger *familiae*, or the precise social class of the *paterfamilias*. On villa economy in general, see Percival, 1976, 145-65 and relevant articles in *Dialoghi di archeologia*, iv-v, 1970-71.

Chapter III. The Period I Villa

(Pls. III–VI and Figs. 3–4)

Five seasons of work were undertaken during the summers of 1962–66 in all parts of the principal terrace and in limited areas beyond it. The excavations revealed that both the *domus* and the *villa rustica* were built in two stages (Periods I and II) and that both had subsidiary stages of construction, namely, a change of plan in the Period I *domus* (Period IA), and the addition of a bathing establishment and tile- and oil-making facilities in the Period II villa (Period IIA). The initial establishment (Period I), built on a previously uninhabited site, *c.* 100–90 B.C., was by no means a pioneering venture. The villa comprised at least ten rooms of which one (A) was decorated with a beautiful mosaic pavement *(op. mus.* 1, p. 85) and of which another (D) seems to have been a displuviate *atrium* of some architectural distinction. In Period II, the enlargement of the villa with terracing which more than tripled the area available for the *domus* and *villa rustica* attests to the viability of the initial establishment; within a generation it was possible to transform a ten-room house and farm into a mansion of some 40 rooms with an agricultural and industrial area of about 20 *vani.* Later, in Period IIA, the agricultural activities were diversified by adding a permanent *oletum* for processing olives and a *figlina* of three kilns for making tiles. For summaries of these building phases and their dating, see pp. 24, 33, 57 and 76. The orientation of the villa is roughly north-east/south-west. But in the text, 'north-east' has, for convenience, been called 'north', and 'south', 'east' and 'west' have been used likewise.

PERIOD I (Pls. IIIb–VI and Figs. 3–4)

The Period I villa was built *c.* 100–90 B.C. on two terraces of which the upper, northern terrace, was occupied by the *domus* and the lower, southern terrace by the *villa rustica.* This arrangement is unusual and is known only in a few other instances; the 'split level' plan served to emphasize the separation of residential and agricultural areas, and this separation was the dominant planning idea of the Period II villa as well.[1]

The structure of the Period I villa was very poorly preserved. The construction of the Period II villa, which entailed filling in over the earlier structure, new terracing and re-use of earlier wall lines, in large part destroyed the Periods I and IA villa; indeed, the builders of the later villa destroyed the earlier structures, especially the floors, rather thoroughly when they could not re-use them, with the result that less is known of the initial establishment than might be desired. This problem is compounded by the fact that the Period I *domus* underwent a radical remodelling, in Period IA, which also destroyed many of the original features of the house.

---

[1] The 'split-level' design on two terraces, requiring artificial terracing and special water-storage arrangements, was a deliberate choice made by the builders of the villa. The design seems to be rare — there are analogies for the *domus* plan itself (see n. 5 p.24) — but no close ones for a double terrace separating residential and agricultural areas. When multiple terracing is found, it corresponds not to differences in function but to a desire for variety and picturesqueness in a residental context, or to accommodate buildings sited on a sloping terrain, for example, cf. Noack and Lehmann-Hartleben, 1936, 195 ff. and Maiuri, 1947, 50-2, on the Villa dei Misteri.

The closest rural analogies are the terraces of a large unexplored villa at Boscoreale, where the agricultural rooms were apparently separate from the upper *domus;* and a small villa off the Sorrentine coast, cf. Della Corte, 1929[2], 178-89, and also Mingazzini and Pfister, 1946, 153-4, a terrace villa of Republican date on Isca (Galluzzo), off Sorrento. In the Naples area the small terrace villa, perhaps with a separate terrace for agricultural activities, may be an analogy; cf. Chianese, 1938, 81-7.

The Period I building technique consisted, in general, of walls in well-built *opus caementicium* faced with *opus incertum;* the limestone blocks used were larger than those used in Period II, and the mortar is a uniform medium-grey colour without much sand.[2] The walls, except where noted, were of a uniform width of between 0 · 49 and 0 · 50 m. In the cisterns of the northern and southern terraces the construction technique was of tufa in a mortar of the same recipe as that used in the *opus caementicium,* the tufa stones were used in much the same way as the limestone ones in the walls. The contrast between the building techniques of the Period I villas at Posto and San Rocco is striking. When Posto I was built, after *c.* 120 B.C. but before *c.* 80 B.C., the technique used was *opus quadratum,* whilst *after c.* 80 B.C. a new technique prevails, that of *opus caementicium* faced with *opus incertum.* By contrast San Rocco began early on as an *opus caementicium* and *incertum* structure, *c.* 100–90 B.C.

The Period I villa is described in two parts:
I. *The upper or northern terrace.*
II. *The lower or southern terrace.*

I. *The upper or northern terrace.*
The Period I features are:
A. The north, south, east and west retaining walls and the terrace fill.
B. The cistern and water-supply system.
C. The rooms (A-F) of the *domus.*

A. *The north, south, east and west retaining walls and the terrace fill.* (Pl. III*b* and Figs. 3–4)
The north wall of the northern terrace (1 · 00 m. wide), standing to a height of almost 2 · 00 m. along its entire length, was a substantially built structure of *opus caementicium* faced with *opus incertum* with a uniform medium-grey mortar. This north retaining wall defined the alignment of the walls of the Period I *domus* and was re-used in Period II, its orientation following the line of the limestone and clay which is the geological formation of the hillside. The wall was founded on a rough shelf of rock irregularly hacked out (*c.* 1 · 00 m. deep × 0 · 70 m. high) in a method still used at Francolise; the large irregular pieces of limestone, which is remarkable for its even texture and whiteness, can be broken into smaller pieces and used as part of the *opus caementicium* of the walls. The builders were not, however, entirely bound by the line of the limestone formation: in one area (in room 10 of the Period II villa), where there was a natural fissure in the rock too deep to fill, an arch (0 · 40 m. wide and 0 · 80 m. high) was built over the geological fault. The arch ran all the way through the wall's width; it was 'rediscovered' when a low-level kitchen floor was laid in Period II and the area under the arch was cleared to provide a little extra storage space. The eastern limit of the north wall is to be found in the area of room 11 of the Period II villa where there is a distinct change from the medium-grey mortar of Period I to the sandy-grey mortar of Period II. Although this point is slightly beyond the east retaining wall of the northern terrace itself (see below, p. 41) it probably marks the easternmost extent of the Period I

[2] Cf. Lugli, 1957, 470-4 and pl. CIX, 2 (for the villa walls, Via Setina); and Blake, 1947, 241-9. The terrace walls of the villa at San Rocco di Capodimonte, described by Chianese, 1938, 81-7, bear some resemblance to the *opus incertum* at San Rocco. Specifically, the Period I walls are very similar to the *opus incertum* of the Sullan walls of the sanctuary at Loreto in Teanum Sidicinum: see Johannowsky, 1963, 140. See also Coarelli, 1977, 9-19 and Appendix 2.

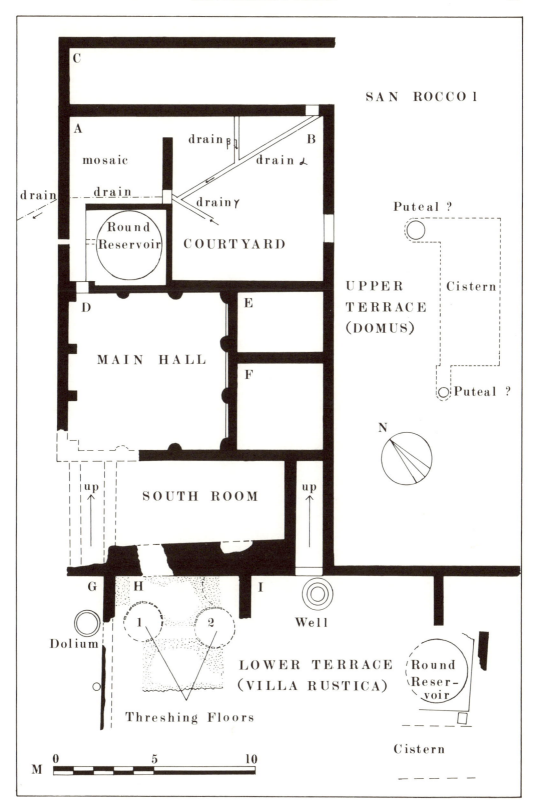

Fig. 3. Plan of the Period I villa

villa. The north side of the north wall was left unrendered and an earth fill was packed against it. The south side was brought to a smooth, rendered surface, probably intended for plastering. The method of construction was visible, the Periods II and IIA plaster and thermal jacketing having fallen away, so that the successive stages of surface could be seen. The wall was thus built in the familiar 'planking' method by which successive horizontal 'courses' of *opus incertum* can be set and allowed to dry between planks *c*. 0 · 30 m. wide.

The south retaining wall of the northern terrace, also of *opus incertum* and 0 · 50 m. wide in the area of rooms H and I, was made wider by 1 · 00 m. than the other retaining walls because it supported the downhill weight of the fill under the *domus*. On the north side of room G and in room I, just north of the well, walls of ordinary width continued the line of the retaining wall: they may have been terrace walls supporting a fill for the upper terrace, or, alternatively, the lower ends of a ramped fill connecting the *villa rustica* to the *domus*. In either case, assuming that only the wider part of the south retaining wall supported the northern terrace to its full height, the suggested shape of the Period I *domus* is that of a rectangular block with a projecting room or platform on the south, not as wide as the rest of the house, and perhaps with steps or ramps on either side of the projection. As in the case of the north retaining wall, the south retaining wall was founded directly on a shelf of limestone cut out of the hillside. The wall was dismantled to a height of *c*. 0 · 60 m. when the Period II terrace was built.

The east and west retaining walls are represented by the *opus incertum* footings (0 · 60 m. wide) of the east walls of rooms B, E and F and the west walls of rooms A and D, respectively. Both walls were built on the unworked natural limestone along its slope, and they bonded with the south walls projecting from the wider part of the south retaining wall. The east wall was dismantled down to its footings when the Period II terrace was built, but the foundations and part of the walls of the west retaining wall were long-lasting and solid enough to be reused as the west walls of rooms 27, 28 and 29, when these rooms were remodelled from the earlier structure.

The terrace fill of the northern terrace (Fig. 4, level 5) was much disturbed when the Period II terrace was built, mainly because the wider part of the south retaining walls was systematically dismantled, and the fill behind it was spread over it, thus providing a stone and compacted earth base for the Period II fill. This destruction can be clearly seen in section ABCD (Fig. 4). On either side of the north retaining wall, the Period I fill was removed for the construction of cisterns on the north side and for the Period II kitchen (rooms 9, 10 and 11) and the Period IIA *balineum* rooms 8, 9 and 27). Where the Period I fill was visible in an undisturbed state (in rooms B, E, and F), it was a homogenous, generally unlayered mass of dark clay and stone, much of it probably obtained from the excavations of hillside for the terracing. The Period I floors (see below, pp. 85–88) were laid directly on this fill, the *rudera* of the floors being spread directly on the compacted surface between the walls. The fill was evidently put in after the walls of the rooms had been built, since there were no wall trenches or trench-laid foundations; in this way, the fills were contained securely against slipping, in a method implied by Vitruvius (vi 7) in his discussion of terracing.

Outside the west retaining wall of the Period I villa, a deep trench was cut (see section EF, Fig. 6), to recover material associated with the occupation of the Periods I and IA villa. In a débris layer, much pottery associated with these periods was found (see below, p. 254–5).

B. *The cistern and water-supply system.* (Pls. IV *b–c* and Fig. 3).

The limestone matrix of the hillside, while suitable for many kinds of cultivation, did not really conserve the amount of water needed to make the villa fully habitable. For this reason, the collection of water, and its storage in a secure, clean and accessible location, were necessities carefully anticipated at all periods of habitation. Three different means of storing and supplying water were used in Period I: the first in the form of large vaulted cisterns, in the northern and southern terraces, in which the water, being covered, was protected from dust and would have remained cool, clean and suitable for drinking. The second means of storing and supplying water took the form of round reservoirs, with water-proofed walls but probably open to the sky, one on the northern and another on the southern terrace, which would have provided bathing, laundry, washing-up water and such water as was needed in agricultural processes or for watering animals. Finally, a well on the southern terrace may have provided water suitable for drinking. The cistern and the round reservoir on the northern terrace are described here: for the other cistern and round reservoir, see pp. 19–20.

The cistern. The Period I cistern, which lay on the east side of the *domus* and at a distance of 5 · 20 m. away from it, was a substantially built barrel-vaulted structure of irregularly-shaped pieces of blue-grey tufa set in a limey mortar and rendered, on the interior, with a fine coating of marble-dust and lime 0 · 01 m. thick. The walls and vault of the cistern were *c.* 0 · 60 m thick and the structure was evidently laid in an excavation specially dug for it in the clay and limestone of the hillside. The interior dimensions are 7 · 15 m. × 2 · 95 m. with a minimal capacity of 38,400 litres; it was at least 3 · 00 m. high from floor to the crown of the vault. On the south and west sides, U-shaped passages (1 · 70 m. long) extended outwards from the walls of the cistern. Both passages had bases for round *puteals* (*c.* 0 · 60 m. in diameter) which gave access to the water; their openings were later covered with the curb-stones and mosaics of the Period II peristyle.

The round reservoir. The principal source of water for immediate use in the Period I villa was a large round reservoir (1 · 10 m. deep and 3 · 35 m. in diameter). The reservoir occupied a separate room with wall of *opus incertum* (0 · 29 m. thick) on the north, south and east; the west wall was the west terrace retaining wall described above. The reservoir room was approached through doors communicating with rooms A and D and giving on to a corridor (0 · 90 m. wide) on the west side of the reservoir itself. The reservoir was at floor level: the border and sides were founded directly on hewn limestone which also supported the floor. The waterproof covering of the floor and sides was a compound of mortar and marble-dust (0 · 03 m. thick). An overflow channel, 0 · 05 m. below the edge of the reservoir on the west side, led to a drain with mortared tufa walls covered with tiles which ran through the west retaining wall. Since no supply channel led into the reservoir, the water was probably collected from the roofs of rooms A and D through drain pipes for rain water. The absence of a supply channel for the reservoir, and the consequent inference that it was filled by rain water, are two of the reasons for reconstructing room D as a displuviate *atrium* (see below, p. 18), and the room in which the reservoir stood as open to the sky. The capacity of the reservoir was 9,260 litres.

C. *The rooms A–F of the domus.* (Pls. IV *a* and V *a*; Fig. 3.)

The *domus* of the Period I villa consisted of a rectangular block with a courtyard (room B)

in the northeast corner and four covered rooms (A, D, E and F) in an L-shaped arrangement on the south and west sides. On the north side of the main block, along the north
retaining wall, there was a yard (room C) or perhaps a portico. On the west side, the natural
declivity of the hill was not terraced in any way, but on the east side a fill was laid on the
limestone at the level of the Period I floors, and a strip of land connected the house with the
puteals of the cistern. On the south side there was a terrace, or perhaps a covered room,
overlooking the *villa rustica* on the lower terrace, and this projection from the main block
of the house may have had ramps or steps on either side leading from the *domus* to the
lower terrace (see above, p. 14).

Room A (4 · 20 × 4 · 65 m.). The initial plan of room A was much obscured by later
rebuilding and re-use of the space. In its original state, room A was almost square. The
north wall, whose footings (0 · 60 m. wide) were uncovered below the later walls built on
the same line, was founded on the limestone rock and was well built in *opus incertum* with
the medium-grey mortar characteristic of the Period I walls all over the site. The south wall
separated room A from the room with the round reservoir: this wall (only 0 · 29 m. wide)
was much narrower than the other walls, probably because it supported roof-beams on one
side only. The east and west walls, also of *opus incertum*, were 0 · 50 m. wide. None of the
walls had offsets, probably because their foundations were rather shallow due to the high
level of the natural limestone rock in this area.

Room A had a beautiful mosaic pavement (*op. mus.* 1, p. 85 and Pl. XXIV) which was
very well preserved in the area of its original construction. This floor was re-used throughout the life of the villa, receiving additions on the south when the round reservoir went out
of use in Period IA, and repairs on the north side when the north wall of the room was dismantled, redesigned and rebuilt in Period II.

Nothing remains of the original mural decoration or finish of the Period I room. Access
to the reservoir was through a narrow door (0 · 65 m. wide) in the south wall near the
southwest corner. The courtyard (room B) was reached through two doors in the east wall,
at the northeast and southeast corners, 0 · 80 m. and 0 · 70 m. wide respectively. The door
jambs were quoined with limestone blocks (*c.* 0 · 30 m. high) set in courses. The arrangement of these two doors in symmetrical positions implies that the room was designed with a
view to achieving a certain formality or architectural dignity.

Room A may have had either a pitched roof running east to west or a roof slanting southwards to direct rain water into the reservoir. Drains passed under the floor of the room
along the north and south walls; these features entered the room under the thresholds of
the doors in the northeast and southeast corners and ran out through the west wall; traces
of the north drain were found at an angle following the natural slope of the hill under the
floor of the Period II portico (room 39). Their exact construction could not be determined,
because they were much destroyed in the area west of the villa and could not be investigated under the floor of room A in the interests of preserving the mosaic (*op. mus.* 1 and
27, cf. pp. 85 and 120).

Room B (7 · 90 × 7 · 90 m.). The enclosed courtyard of the Period I house occupied the
entire northeast corner of the main residential block. It was an exact square and did not
have porticos or internal divisions. The foundations of the walls, built of *opus incertum*
(0 · 60 m. wide) were laid directly on the limestone rock. A fill of dark mixed earth and
stones was then put in between the walls, and the *rudus* of the *opus signinum* floor (*op. sig.*

1, p. 87) tamped down on it. The level of the *opus signinum* floor was 0 · 08 m. lower than that of the mosaic of room A.

It could not be determined whether the walls, preserved only as foundations later reused, were plastered or decorated or how high they stood. The hard, smooth and waterproof floor indicates that the area was not used as a farm-yard; most likely it was used for storing and protecting from theft such vehicles or tools as were in daily use in the *villa rustica*, and it may therefore be assumed that the courtyard walls stood up to a good height for added security.

The main outside door of the courtyard was in the east wall, directly facing one of the *puteals* of the cistern. This door (1 · 30 m. wide) was supplemented by a second door (0 · 65 m. wide) giving onto the area between the *domus* and the north retaining wall (room C). There was probably an entrance into the living rooms (rooms D and E) on the south side, as there was on the west side into room A, but the walls were not preserved to a height sufficient to indicate this.

Three trench-laid drains, contemporaneous with the *opus signinum* floor, facilitated the evacuation of water from the courtyard itself and from the area to the north of it (room C). A main drain (marked α on Fig. 3) entered under the threshold of the narrow door in the north wall and crossed the courtyard diagonally; it passed under the threshold of the south door of room A and under the floor of that room. The main drain was supplemented by subsidiary channels (marked β and γ on Fig. 3) of which one (β) flowed from room C under the north wall of the courtyard and the other (γ) from the south side of the courtyard itself. All the drains were built of unmortared tufa slabs (0 · 50 m. long, 0 · 30 m. wide and 0 · 08 m. thick) with a rough mortar floor and tiles of tufa slabs for the cover. The *opus signinum* floor was moulded around the side of the drains to fit neatly against the cover-slabs which were evidently exposed.

Room C. The area to the north of the main residential block was virtually obliterated by the Periods II and IIA building. The space may have formed a second courtyard area (6 · 50 m. wide) supplementing the enclosed courtyard of room B. The evidence of the drains in the courtyard, two of which (α and β) drained from room C, indicates that some activity, possibly bathing and laundry but more probably some agricultural process, which required the quick evacuation of water or other liquids, was the use to which the space was put. Otherwise, nothing is known of this area in Period I except that it was evidently not part of the residential quarters of the house since it communicated only with the courtyard and not with room A.

Room D (7 · 60 × 7 · 80 m.). Its large size and its internal buttressing indicate that room D was the main hall of the house and the one room with any pretension to architectural magnificence.

As in the case of most of the other Period I walls, only the *opus incertum* foundations or, at most, the lower parts of the walls (0 · 50 m. thick) were found. Excavation revealed, however, that internal buttresses or pilasters existed on the north, south, east and west walls in a pattern which allowed the destroyed or unexcavated parts of the walls (in the southwest corner and along the north wall) to be reconstructed in a symmetrical arrangement of supports for the roof.

On the north wall, there were two half-round buttresses (0 · 60 m. in diameter) which were 2 · 00 m. apart (interaxial distance) and 2 · 00 m. from the buttresses at the corners of the room. The buttresses on the north wall corresponded to similar ones on the south wall.

On the east wall, there were half-round buttresses of similar size but set 1 · 60 m. apart and about the same distance from the corner buttresses (Pl. *Va*). On the west wall, there were square buttresses (0 · 44 × 0 · 44 m.) which were bonded into the wall. At the northeast and southeast corners of the room, approximately quarter-round buttresses (with a radius of about 0 · 30 m.) corresponded to square ones in the northwest and southwest corners, of which only the northwest one was preserved.

It is unfortunate that the Period I floor of room D was entirely eliminated in Period IA when the room was redesigned; only a thin spread of builders' material remained. However, inspection of the walls on their outer and inner surfaces revealed that there were no drains or water channels piercing the walls, and no traces of an *impluvium* or cistern, such as might be found in an impluviate atrium, were found. The absence of such features, together with the necessity of collecting water in the round reservoir on the north side of the room, suggests that an outward-sloping roof, of the type built on displuviate *atria*, was the method used to cover the room. No evidence for internal supports was found in the room, which further suggests that a self-supporting, outward-sloping roof covered the space rather than an inward-sloping one. The maximum span of the roof from buttress to buttress would have been 7 · 00 m., not an impossible span. Furthermore, the buttresses along adjacent walls may have been spanned diagonally and tenons or uprights raised on them for the corners of the pitched part of the roof. In either case—whether as a roof raised from beams spanning the room between opposite walls or as a structure raised on beams linking adjacent buttresses—a clerestory could have been part of the roof's structure[3].

The only evidence for a door into room D is on the north side from the room containing the round reservoir. There must have been other doors leading into the courtyard (room B) and into the two small rooms on the east (rooms E and F). An entrance in the south wall, perhaps leading down to the *villa rustica,* may also have been part of the room's plan.

Room E (2 · 90 × 4 · 20 m.) Only the foundations and lower parts of the walls of this small room were preserved, and those to a height insufficient to indicate where the doors and internal divisions of the room, if any, might have been. The *opus incertum* masonry of the walls was similar to that of other Period I walls, and as in the other rooms a separate fill was laid against the walls after their construction. The small size of the room and its proximity to room D indicate that it was part of the residential quarters of the *domus,* but otherwise nothing is known of its function or disposition. As in room D, the Period I floor had been removed completely; the floor was evidently untessellated since its débris, part of which was incorporated into the Period IA floors in this area, consisted mainly of mortar and *opus signinum* material.

Room F (4 · 20 × 4 · 20 m.). As in room E, almost nothing is known of this room except the outline of its walls in Period I. Its relatively large size, and its square shape, indicate that it was not a *cubiculum,* and its proximity to the terrace wall separating the upper from the lower terrace indicate that it was possibly connected by a ramp or stairs to the southern terrace and served as an antechamber to the *atrium* (room D).

[3.] The ancient source for displuviate roofs is Vitruvius (vi, 3, 2). For a review of Etruscan examples, see Boëthius and Ward-Perkins, 1970, 73. It should be noted, however, that room D does not conform fully either to Vitruvius' description or to the few known examples of displuviate *atria* in Etruscan tombs and on cinerary urns. First, in Period I at San Rocco, there is not the kind of symmetrical plan which Vitruvius assumes is the case in the houses he is describing. Second, there is no evidence that the walls of rooms E and F rose *above* those of room D; their small size indicates that they were roofed at a lower level. Vitruvius assumes that adjacent rooms will be higher than the ceiling of the displuviate *atrium.* Third, an *atrium* should have an *impluvium,* which room D did not have. Therefore, it is termed 'main hall' and its displuviate roof has been reconstructed without citing it as an example of a displuviate *atrium* as such.

South Room (5 · 00 × 8 · 50 m.) To the south of rooms D and F there appears to have been a projecting terrace, portico or room, bounded on the north by the south wall of the *domus* and on the south by the wide retaining wall of the northern terrace. On the east side a wall (0 · 50 m. wide) bounded the room and lay parallel to another wall of the same width: these two walls may have framed a staircase or ramp (1 · 30 m. wide) connecting room F with room I. On the west side of the projecting area, a wall-scar in the south retaining wall indicated that there had been a west wall which was destroyed when the Period II terrace was built. Between the west end of the south retaining wall and the west façade of the *domus* there was just enough space for a staircase or ramp as wide as that which may have existed on the east side, and the presence of such a feature would explain why the south retaining wall in this area is less wide that it is elsewhere. Such a connecting structure would have linked rooms D and G.

II. *The lower or southern terrace.*
    The Period I features are:
    A. The retaining walls and the terrace fill.
    B. The cistern, the round reservoir and the well.
    C. The rooms G to I of the *villa rustica.*

A. *The retaining walls and the terrace fill.* (Pl. VI *a* and Fig. 4).
Because the Period II terrace fill covered the area to a depth of almost two metres, only a small part of the southern terrace was excavated. The perimeter of the *villa rustica* was not precisely determined, and except for the partial excavation of three rooms and part of the water-supply system, the exact size and scope of the agricultural area was not fully elucidated. However, the survey of the site for traces of walls which defined the Period II terrace on the south side indicated that there were no terrace retaining walls further south than the line of the Period II wall. Therefore, the Period I retaining wall for the southern terrace was either north of the later wall or else was built on the same line. The latter hypothesis is preferable in that the builders of the Period II villa frequently reused major wall foundations and wall lines of the Period I structures for their own walls. It is thus reasonable to assume that the southern terrace was about 18 · 60 m. wide and afforded at least 400 square metres of work area for the activities of the *villa rustica.*

The east and west perimeters of the south terrace are also not defined precisely. On the east side, the extension of the terrace may have been considerable. On the west side, the absence of early walls west of the Period II structures leads to the conclusion that, as on the south side, the Period II retaining wall was built on the line of the Period I west terrace wall.

The terrace fill below the floors of the Period I rooms (level 6 of Fig. 4) was a solidly compacted single layer of dark earth and stone, sterile of datable material as might be expected from a fill of new earth on a previously uninhabited site. (Section ABCD of Fig. 4).

B. *The cistern, the round reservoir and the well.* (Fig. 3)
The means by which the water-supply on the southern terrace was assured were planned as carefully as those on the northern terrace. The presence of a cistern and a round reservoir indicates that the activities of the *villa rustica* needed not only permanent storage of water but also a considerable quantity easily accessible for immediate use. The cistern and reservoir were supplemented by a well in room I which would have provided a permanent

source of water, not only for the activities on the lower terrace, but also for the needs of the *domus.*

The cistern. The crown and part of the haunches of a vaulted cistern below floor level to the southeast of room I and to the south of the round reservoir were uncovered. The crown of the vault ran north to south on a line similar to that of the cistern of the upper terrace; the structure and materials of both cisterns were similar. A stretch (*c.* 2 · 00 m. long) of the crown of the vault was excavated, but the cistern itself was not sectioned or exposed, with the result that its size and the means of access to the water are not known. However, its solid construction indicates that the cistern of the lower terrace may have been equal in size and capacity to that of the *domus,* holding about 38,400 litres.

The round reservoir. The fragmentary remains of a round reservoir (3 · 05 m. in diameter and of undetermined depth) on the southeast side of room I indicated that the activities undertaken on the lower terrace required an easily accessible supply of water. The proximity of the cistern and the reservoir would have facilitated supplying the latter, but eaves' drip water may also have been collected.

The foundations of the reservoir were set directly on the hewn limestone of the hillside in a construction procedure exactly similar to that used for the round reservoir on the northern terrace. On the south side, beside the southeast corner of the square parapet which surrounded the tank, there was a limestone base supporting either a porch, or perhaps a beam supporting a cover, or the props for a block-and-tackle arrangment which would have facilitated the use of the reservoir. The water was accessible from room I and from whatever room or working area lay to the east of the excavated portion of the *villa rustica:* the wall dividing room I from the rooms to the east evidently ran up to the north wall of the reservoir.

The well. The well, and the area around it including the floor of the room in which it stood (room I), were much damaged by a collapse of the Period I *puteal* which caused the Period II fill above it to fall into the well. The well was evidently covered in a hasty and insecure way with either a stone or a wooden cover which in turn was used to support part of a wall in rooms 19 and 20 of the later villa. The cover collapsed, causing a cascade of Period II terrace fill and material into the well, together with the fill which lay under the Period I floor, and most of the Period I floor itself. The mixing of material from the two major periods of construction, clearly visible in section, adds to the difficulty in dating the features of the Period I southern terrace.

The well itself (1 · 45 m. in diameter) was at least 3 m. deep from the floor of room I. Traces of a series of hand-and-foot niches (1 Roman foot wide and about 0 · 15 m. high and deep at intervals of 0 · 50 m.) were observed on the south side. The total depth of the well could not be accurately determined since the limestone through which it was driven tended to crumble easily when not supported by the fill which had fallen into it.

The inconvenient location of the well, near the bottom of the ramp or staircase leading to the northern terrace, was probably mitigated by the presence of a *puteal* allowing passage around the well room: in fact, the well would have been located in a way which allowed it to be used with as much ease from the northern terrace as from the southern, thus providing well water for both the *domus* and the *villa rustica.*

C. *Rooms G to I of the villa rustica.* (Pls. V *b,*VI *b* and Fig. 3)

The remains of three rooms, used in the agricultural processes which were the main economic activity of the villa, occupied that small area of the southern terrace which was uncovered. The arrangement of the rooms, their relationship to one another, their roofs and their coordination with the rest of the *villa rustica* could not be determined exactly since in no case were the south walls of the rooms excavated. However, since all three rooms were at least 6 m. in depth, and in view of the fact that the southern terrace itself was not more than 18 · 60 m. wide, we may assume that the rooms opened to the south and gave onto an open passageway or terrace. Such an arrangement would have allowed the *area* or threshing floor (room H) to be left uncovered, while the room to the west (room G), and the well room (room I), could have been roofed individually. This disposition would conform to the usual design of *areae* in which the *opus signinum* floor was open to the sky to facilitate the threshing and winnowing of the grain.[4]

Room G. This room was evidently the westernmost room of the southern terrace. It was at least 6 · 00 m. long and of undetermined width. On the north it was bounded by the narrower portion of the retaining wall, and its east wall (0 · 50 m. wide) separated it from the *area* (room H). Traces of a beaten earth floor were found set on the dark earth and stone fill which underlay the Period I floors elsewhere. Against the east wall, and under a Period II wall, a *dolium* (1 · 60 m. in diameter at the rim and 0 · 72 m. deep) was found; it was uncertain whether the *dolium* (Pl. VI *b*) was part of the room's original equipment. If so, then the room could very well have been a warm, dry room suitable for the storage of finished grain.

Room H. The *area* of the *villa rustica* (6 · 20 m. wide and at least 6 · 00 m. deep) was bounded on the north by the wider portion of the northern terrace retaining wall which was roughly rendered and left unplastered. On the east a similarly unplastered wall separated it from room I. The threshing-floor was well built of *opus signinum* (*op. sig.* 2 cf. p. 88) made of mortar and crushed tile-chips and dust set on a thin *rudus* of crushed limestone and very carefully laid in order to seal the angle of the walls and floor and the corners of the room. The surface of the floor was not brought to the smooth finish which characterised the *opus signinum* floor for residential use on the northern terrace but was left slightly rough. In order to facilitate the threshing, two round raised areas of *opus signinum* with a slightly rougher surface supplemented the main area. These features were 1 · 95 m. (on the west, marked "1" on Fig. 3) and 2 · 10 m. (on the east, marked "2" on Fig. 3) in diameter and provided a slightly convex working surface about 0 · 04 m. higher than the rest of the floor. Their edges were made of pieces of broken tile (0 · 03 m. wide) firmly set in mortar.

At the same time that the Period II terrace was planned trenches were dug through the threshing floor of the *area* into the Period I fill for some undetermined reason. The room with its floor went out of use when the Period II terrace fill was put in.

Room I (9 · 10 m. wide and at least 6 · 00 m. deep). The north wall of this room was finished with a cream coloured plaster containing some marble dust; the plaster was broken off at the point at which it met the floor, which was probably dug out with the Period I fill below it to provide material with which to fill the well in the northeast corner of the room. The east wall was not preserved to a height sufficient to determine whether or not it was plastered, but the west wall was. On both the north and west walls, a square niche (0 · 30 m. wide, 0 · 30 m. high and 0 · 20 m. deep) was let into the wall through the plaster

---

[4.] For *areae* similar to those of San Rocco, see Della Corte, 1929[2], 178-9 and fig. 1, and also Della Corte, 1929[3], 191-9 and fig. 1. On grain economy, see Moritz, 1958, 210-15.

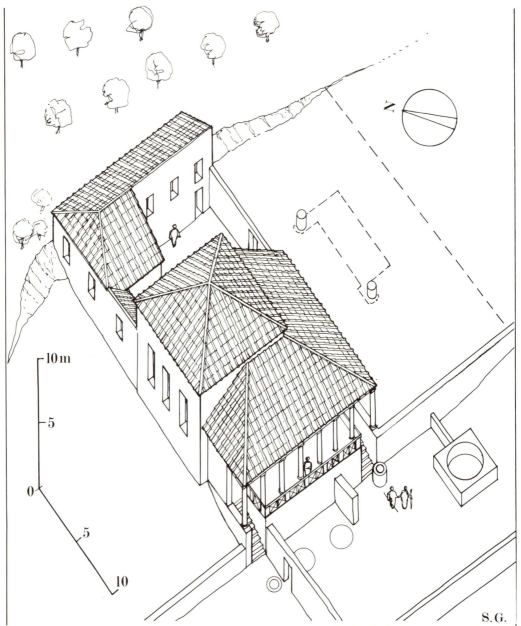

Fig. 3a. Axonometric reconstruction of the Period I villa. *By Sheila Gibson.*

at the level of the floor. The niches evidently held the ends of beams on which were mounted laths or board-ends affixed to the wall, above the niches, in grooves in the plastered surface of the wall: the remains probably represent part of the structure surrounding the Period I well, or a bin or storage chest, set into the corner of the room.

In the southeast corner of the room, the cistern and round reservoir (see above, pp. 19–20 completed the equipment of the *villa rustica* as far as it was excavated. The use of room I is uncertain; it may, however, have been the main room of the *villa rustica* since it stood at the bottom of the stairs or ramp leading to the *domus* and had access to the principal source of water. The rooms to the east of room I were not excavated.

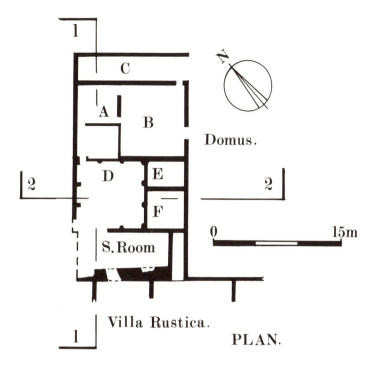

C

A

B

Domus.

N

D

E

F

S. Room

0   15m

Villa Rustica.   PLAN.

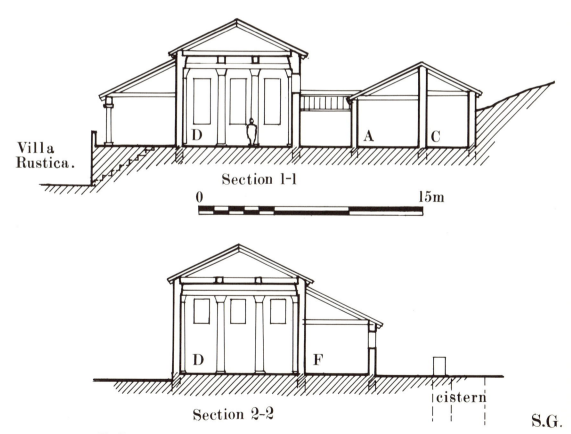

Villa
Rustica.

D

A   C

Section 1-1

0   15m

D   F

cistern

Section 2-2

S.G.

Fig. 3b. Plan and reconstructed sections of the Period I villa. *By Sheila Gibson*

PERIOD 1. SUMMARY AND CONCLUSIONS (Fig. 3a)

The Period I or first construction at San Rocco was a combined residential dwelling (*domus*) and farm (*villa rustica*) both of modest proportions. The *domus*, with the rooms disposed in an L-shape around a courtyard, was simple but distinguished by some architectural pretensions (room D) or by mosaic embellishment (room A). *Opus incertum* facing was used throughout.

As the cisterns and reservoir attest, care was taken to assure a permanent water supply, but insofar as it was preserved the *domus* of Period I was a simple but solidly built structure suggesting a small holding comfortably, but not luxuriously, set up for a small family and *familia*. Only two separate *cubicula* were present. The *villa rustica*, rather small insofar as it was excavated, was equally simple and straightforward. The only agricultural activity represented with any certainty is the threshing of grain; other activities may have been undertaken but could not be documented.

The external aspect and internal plan of the Period I villa, together with the character of its *opus incertum*, its mosaic pavement (*op. mus.* 1, p. 85) and the finds associated with level 6 of Fig. 4, should give a context and date for the structure. As excavated, the design in two terraces, one residential, the other agricultural, with emphasis on compactness and functionality on the exterior, is unusual but has analogies in the exterior aspect of other small villas around Pompeii, Sorrento and elsewhere (see n. 1 p. 11). The internal plan of the *domus* — an L-formation of residential rooms around a courtyard in the northeast quadrant, with a main hall (room D) in the southeast quadrant toward which the other rooms converged, the whole overlooking the *villa rustica* from a terrace — is also unusual. The plan does not correspond precisely to any of the kinds of houses found in the urban context at Pompeii, nor to the larger and more complex *villae rusticae* nearby. The asymmetry of the plan, the absence of any axial relationships among the rooms and the prominence given to the main hall and courtyard make the Period I villa analogous to certain small houses of the late second century and early first century B.C. For example, the L-shaped plan has analogies with two small villas of the Late Republic at Albano Laziale and others around Rome. Near Sorrento, the Republican villa on Isca, very fragmentary, may have had something of the same disposition. All are small, five-or six-room villas, like that of San Rocco in Period I.[5] For the problem of dating Period I to *c.* 100–90 B.C. see p. 253.

GRAIN OR WINE?

It will be observed that the built circular floors found in room G in Periods I and IA, and in courtyard 2 in Period II, have been interpreted as threshing floors. The authors are indebted to Professor K. D. White for this discussion of such an interpretation.

He pointed out that their size (1 · 95 m. and 2 · 10 m. in diameter in room G, and *c.* 2 · 00 m. in courtyard 2) was inconsistent with Varro's discription of a Roman threshing floor.

[5.] For the villas of Albano Laziale, see Lugli, 1946, 77-83. The following plans, very fragmentary, may have had something of the Period I plan: Tamaro, 1928, 412-14, at Isola; De Rossi, 1967, 133, no. 97; De Rossi, 1970, 71-4, no. 122; and Mingazzini and Pfister, 1946, 153-4.

For the material associated with level 5, see pp. 252-253, and with Periods I/IA débris level, pp. 254-6.

Varro (*De re rustica*, i 51–2 — Loeb ed., 1960, translation by W. D. Hooper, revised by H. B. Ask) wrote of it:

51. 'The threshing-floor should be on the place, in a somewhat elevated spot, so that the wind can sweep over it; the size should be determined by the size of the harvest. It should preferably be round, with a slight elevation at the centre, so that, if it rains, the water will not stand but be able to run off the floor in the shortest line — and of course in a circle the shortest line is from the centre to the circumference. It should be built of solid dirt, well packed, and especially if it is of clay, so that it may not crack in the heat and allow the grain to hide, or take in water and open the door to mice and ants. For this reason it is customary to coat it with amurca, which is poison to weeds, ants and moles. Some farmers build up the floor with stone to make it solid, or even pave it. Others, such as the Bagienni, go so far as to build a shelter over the floors, because in that country rain-storms frequently occur at the threshing time. When the floor is without a roof and the climate is hot, a shelter should be built hard by, to which the hands may go at midday in hot weather.'

52. 'On the threshing floor the largest and best ears should be placed apart, to furnish the best seed, and the grain should be threshed on the floor. This is done in some districts by means of a yoke of steers and a sledge. The latter is constructed either of a board made rough with stones or iron, which separates the grain from the ear when it is dragged by a yoke of steers with the driver or a heavy weight on it; or of a toothed axle running on low wheels, called a Punic cart, the driver sitting on it and driving the steers which drag it — a contrivance in use in Hither Spain and other places. Among other peoples the threshing is done by turning in cattle and driving them around with goads, the grain being separated from the beards by their hoofs. After the threshing the grain should be tossed from the ground when the wind is blowing.'

It is obvious that floors with the small dimensions of those at San Rocco would not lend themselves to any procedure which involved large animals walking around them. The question arose, therefore, as to whether or not these floors had not served for treading grapes or as wine presses. The dolium found in the adjoining room in Periods I and IA, into which the wine could be put for fermentation, seemed to support such a view. However, two points argue against such an interpretation. It is uncertain at which point the dolium was put there (it is only attested in that position at the time that the Period II wall was built over it); and the fact that the floors themselves have no surrounding channels or groovings for the collection of any liquids.

It seems reasonable, therefore, to retain the original interpretation, with the proviso that these floors could only be used for threshing the grain by hand, using flails. Varro's point that the size of the floor should be related to the harvest would suggest a small harvest suited only to the needs of the residents of the villa.

Chapter IV. The Period IA Villa

(Pls. VII and XXIV–XXV and Figs. 4–6)

The internal modifications of the Period I *domus* on the upper terrace some years after it was built radically changed its residential character. The number of bedrooms or possible bedrooms was doubled, and, in general, the spaces were made smaller but were differentiated as to their use in a way that had been less emphasised in the original design. Architectural clarity and distinction were sacrificed in favour of comfort and privacy. The Period I villa had two 'good' rooms (A and D) and two rooms which may have been bedrooms (E and F); the Period IA remodelling resulted in the enlargement of room A, which doubled in size (room A1) and in the subdivision of the old main hall (D) into an L-shaped room (D1) with two bedrooms (D3 and D4). A long narrow corridor (D2) marked the axis connecting the rooms to major entrances on the east and west and communicating with an antechamber or bedroom (E1) which in turn led to two small rooms (E2 and F1) which may also have been used as *cubicula*. The corridor, which would have reduced draughts and ensured privacy for the residential and sleeping quarters, is a new usage of space in the *domus*, which was not present in the earlier house.[1]

The Period IA remodelling occurred sometime between *c.* 100–90 B.C. and *c.* 30 B.C., a period of 60–70 years. Datable material was virtually non-existent (see below, p. 254), but two pavements put in at the time of the remodelling, *op. mus.* 3 (Room D1; see p. 90 below) and *op. mus.* 4 (Room D4; see p. 91 below) can be assigned a date in the time of Caesar, *c.* 50 B.C.

Many reasons can be suggested for these modifications. It may be surmised that the increased need for privacy and the addition of bedrooms was the result of a growing family. On the other hand, it may also be that the house came to be used as a long-term residence to a greater extent than before: it may well have become an often-used summer residence, for example, whilst before it had only been used for occasional visits. In either of these cases, the transfer of the *domus* and its farm to new ownership could have occurred. Furthermore, the increased use of the *domus*, resulting in the need for a greater diversity of spaces, evident from the new plan of the building, may well indicate a growth in the returns on agricultural enterprise which justified a closer and quotidian supervision of the *villa rustica* by an overseer or proprietor. Finally, it is possible that the remodelling of the *domus*, whether as an occasional residence or for perennial use, is the result of an attitude analogous to the pastoral modes of the poets, notably Vergil and Horace, who popularised in literature a taste for country living for which this villa would have been most suitable.[2] The connection in pastoral poetry between ancient virtue and the blessings of modern peace is verified at San Rocco insofar as productivity, stability and good returns on investment in agriculture can be inferred from the development of the building itself.

Except for a single instance of the use of quasi-reticulate masonry (in room A1) all the new Period IA walls and door-blockings were in *opus incertum*, indistinguishable in execution from the Period I *opus incertum*. The only difference was in the character of the mortar which was lighter in colour and had a greater sand content than Period I mortars. The walls of Period IA were all 0·49 to 0·50 m. wide, as in Period I.

---

[1] On the Period IA wall construction, see n. 3, p.34.
[2] See n. 11, p.7.

I. *The upper or northern terrace.*

The Period IA features are:

A. Room A1. The enlargement of room A and the suppression of the round reservoir.

B. Rooms B1 and B2. The modifications in the courtyard (room B).

C. Rooms C1 and C2. The modifications of the area north of the residential block (room C).

D. Rooms D1, D2, D3 and D4. The suppression of the main hall (room D) in favour of a corridor and small rooms.

E. Rooms E1, E2 and F1. The redesigning of the southeastern corner of the residential block.

A. *Room A1. The enlargement of room A and the suppression of the round reservoir.* (Pl. XXIV and Figs. 4–5)

Room A1 (7 · 90 × 4 · 65 m.). The enlargement of room A towards the south occurred when the round reservoir went out of use. Why the decision was taken to do without this source of water in the *domus* is not clear; it may be that there was some inefficiency in collecting the water, or perhaps the main cistern, which continued in use, was found to have an adequate supply for domestic purposes. The south wall of room A was dismantled along its entire length, the reservoir was filled with earth and rubble, and the pavement of room A was extended across this fill. The seam between the Period I floor (*op. mus.* 1, p. 85) and its Period IA extension (*op. mus.* 2, p. 88) was made carefully and the two pavements were laid in slightly different ways and with different beds (p. 89). The clean, accurate and careful way in which the original floor was preserved and 'matched' in the extension over the reservoir is an indication of the value, both utilitarian and aesthetic, which was attached to this floor, for this room and the floor came to be permanent features of the house in Period II, and the floor justified its careful preservation by withstanding nearly 200 years of use with only minor repairs.

The south and east walls of the reservoir room, which had been only 0 · 20 m. thick because the room had been open to the sky, were now brought to standard thickness (0 · 50 m.) by the addition of a lining of tufa stones set in a quasi-reticulate pattern. The tufa stones have squarish surfaces (0 · 10 × 0 · 10 m.) and backs cut to points; these were set into a heavy backing of mortar. The lining of the south and east walls of the reservoir room represents the only appearance of quasi-reticulate tufa masonry on the site. The west wall of the reservoir room was re-used without modifications, except perhaps for internal plaster or decoration suitable to its new use.

The enlargement of the room southwards, which almost doubled its size (room A = 19 · 53 m.²: room A1 = 36 · 73 m.²) was accompanied by a reorientation toward the north and south rather than toward the west as had been the case for room A. The old door in the northeast corner in the east wall continued in use to provide access through to the courtyard (room B1), but the other door in the east wall was blocked up. In the middle of the south wall, a door (1 · 10 m. wide) was opened in the old narrow *opus incertum* wall, thereby destroying one of the half round pilasters in room D. This door in the south wall was provided with limestone quoins. At the same time, the old door in the southwest corner of the reservoir room into room D was blocked with limestone *opus incertum*. The new south door led into the main corridor of the remodelled *domus* (room D2). Thus, in view of its large dimensions, its pavement and its wide door on axis, room A1 appears to have been one of the principal residential rooms of the house.

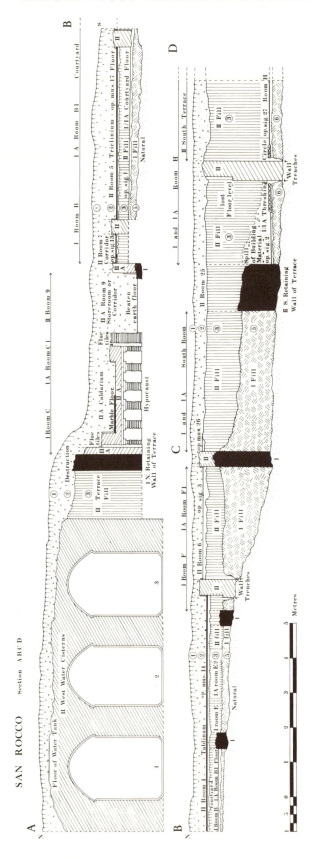

Fig. 4. Section ABCD through the north and south terraces

Nothing is known of the mural decoration of room A1. It could have been lighted by windows in the east or west walls; doubtless windows were now necessary since the size and length of the room would have made the light coming from the doors inadequate for good illumination. The roof needed to be completely modified from the previous structure: a pitched roof running north to south was probably substituted for it.

B. *Rooms B1 and B2. The modifications in the courtyard (room B).* (Fig. 5)
Little change occurred in the courtyard of the *domus* in Period IA. Evidently the walls and floor were reused in their old state, except for the occlusion of one of the doors which had led into room A. The area of the courtyard was subdivided by a wall-end ($2 \cdot 50$ m. long) off the west wall; this served to divide the space into northern and southern parts (rooms B1 and B2, respectively), though why this division was necessary is not clear. The doors in the north and east walls continued in use as did the main drain (α) running diagonally across room B1 and under the floor of A1. The drain coming from C1 (β) also remained in use, but that coming from room B2 (γ) was blocked with a stone at its west end and was taken out where the wall-end lay across it.

C. *Rooms C1 and C2. The modifications of the area north of the residential block (room C).* (Fig. 5)
The area to the north of the main residential block was subdivided into rooms C1 and C2 by a wall running east to west, of which a scar is preserved where it was hacked into the old Period I west retaining wall (in room 28 of the Period II villa). The wall was of *opus incertum* ($0 \cdot 50$ m. thick). It is not known whether it was upstanding along the entire length of the area since subsequent construction resulted in its dismantling.

D. *Rooms D1, D2, D3 and D4. The suppression of the main hall (room D) in favour of a corridor and small rooms.* (Pls. VII, XXV and Fig. 5)
The reasons for the dismantling of the main hall (room D) are not entirely clear. The re-modelling created a series of small rooms and a corridor where one large room had been before; evidently the need for privacy and convenience had a stronger claim on the inhabitants of the house than the desire for architectural distinction. It is also possible that the walls of room D were unsound, since only the north and west walls and a small section of the south wall were actually reused, the others being completely demolished and the floors removed. Furthermore, the result of the remodelling in the area of room D, in parti-cular the construction of the long corridor (room D2) running through the residential block, changed the plan of the *domus*, in providing a clearly defined main axis with a series of subsidiary spaces at right angles.

Room D was replaced by a corridor (D2), a large L-shaped room (D1) and two *cubicula* (D3 and D4). The walls of these rooms, except where noted, were in a masonry style little different from that of Period I, *viz.*, well-built limestone walls ($c. 0 \cdot 50$ m. wide) faced with *opus incertum* in a grey mortar somewhat sandier than that of Period I. The main dif-ference between the walls of the two periods was that the Period IA walls had trench-laid foundations dug into the Period I fills and usually had offsets ($c. 0 \cdot 07—0 \cdot 10$ m. wide) on one side.

Room D1 (L-shaped; $39 \cdot 96$ m^2). Room D1 was the largest roofed room in the house and, with room A1, constituted the complement of 'good' residential rooms. The long arm of

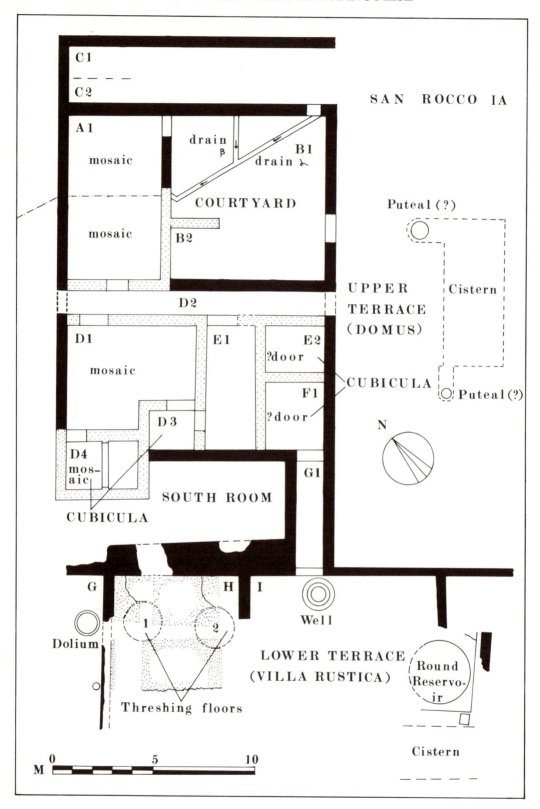

Fig. 5. Plan of the Period IA villa

the L running east to west was 3 · 60 m. wide and 6 · 30 m. long, the short arm running north to south was 3 · 60 m. wide and 4 · 80 m. long. The north, south and east walls, and the L-shaped wall between the south and east walls, were trench-laid in the Period I fill, while the west wall was reused, after the square buttresses of the old room D had been hacked off. Since the level of the mosaic floor of room A1 (*op. mus.* 1 and 2, p. 89) was still the determining level for the Period IA house, the floor of room D was completely dug out and replaced, in the area of room D1, with a terrazzo floor of white limestone chips with rows of large black *tesserae* (*op. mus.* 3, p. 90) running parallel to the walls. This resulted in a curious stratification; a fill of Period I date with a floor of Period IA resting directly upon it. This superimposition was, in general, the stratification found for the entire Period IA house, and it is for this reason that very few Period IA fills (level 4 of Fig. 4) could be distinguished. The Period IA plastering and decoration of room D1 were also completely destroyed when the room was remodelled in Period II.

On the north, room D1 communicated with the main corridor of the house (D2) through a door (1 · 30 m. wide) fitted with limestone quoins. This was the main entrance to the room. In the southwest corner, a narrower door (1 · 00 m. wide) led to a *cubiculum* (D4) and in the southeast corner a second, smaller *cubiculum* (D3) was reached through a door (1 · 30 m. wide); these *cubicula* may have been the master-bedrooms of the establishment.

Room D2 (1 · 20 × 13 · 65 m.). This is an axial corridor running through the house linking the major living rooms (A1 and D1) with each other and with a suite of three rooms in the southeast corner of the *domus* (E1, E2 and F1). The north wall of the corridor was largely a reuse of the south walls of room A and B of the Period I villa, with the following modifications: the round half-buttresses which had supported the roof of room D were dismantled to the level of the Period IA floors, the old door leading from room D into the reservoir room was blocked up; and a new door leading into room A1 substituted for it. On the east and west ends, the corridor terminated in doors as wide as itself; these doors may have had thresholds in Period IA but, if so, they were destroyed in the Period II remodelling.

Room D3 (1 · 90 × 2 · 20 m.). Although suitable in size and situation for use as a *cubiculum*, room D3 may also have served as a daytime passage between the suite of rooms in the southeast corner of the house and room D1. Two adjacent doors in the north and east walls (1 · 30 m. and 0 · 90 m. wide respectively) afforded access to rooms D1 and E1; the rest of the space (4 · 18 m.²) could have been used for a bed. The room may have been lighted by a window in the south wall.

Room D4 (2 · 30 × 3 · 60 m.). The west and south walls of the Period I villa were dismantled at the southwest corner of the building to provide space for a large *cubiculum* whose walls are entirely of Period IA construction (see above, p. 29). The deliberate extension of the room into the South Room (see above, p. 19) may indicate that the builders wished to illuminate the room through a window in the east wall, above the bed. Such morning light is recommended for *cubicula* by Vitruvius (vi 4.). The room was divided into two parts by pilasters projecting 0 · 10 m. into the room which may have supported a curtain rod or folding doors hiding the sleeping alcove. This architectural treatment was co-ordinated with the decorative treatment of the floor (*op. mus.* 4, p. 91) which had a tessellated threshold between the two pilasters (see below, p. 91). The architectural and decorative embellishment of the room indicates that it was the principal bedroom of the Period IA *domus*. The importance of this room, and perhaps the piety associated with the memory of its inhabitants, caused it to be reused, in a slightly modified form, in the Period II remodelling (see below, p. 52). The Period IA plaster of the room was removed on remodelling, with the result that, like room A1 and the other Period IA rooms, nothing is known of its mural decoration.

E. *Rooms E1, E2 and F1. The redesigning of the southeast corner of the residential block.* (Fig. 5)
The arrangement of these rooms suggests a suite of two bedrooms preceded by an antechamber. The site was entered through a door between Rooms D2 and E1; the bedding for a threshold block was visible.

Room E1 (5 · 90 × 2 · 40 m.). Room E1 probably served as an antechamber to two small *cubicula* (E2 and F1); the Period IA thresholds were removed in Period II, as was the north threshold, but doors in the east wall can be reasonably surmised from the plan. The north, west and east walls of room E1 were entirely of Period IA construction (see above, p. 26). The west wall had a new door leading into room D3. Room E1 was presumably lighted by a window or door on the south giving on to the Period I South Room (see above, p. 19). Nothing of the floor or mural treatment of room E1 survived the Period II remodelling.

Rooms E2 and F1 (2 · 20 × 2 · 90 m. and 3 · 20 × 2 · 90 m. respectively). These two small rooms were of suitable size and situation to be used as *cubicula*. They communicated with room E1, and it is doubtful whether rooms of this intimate size would have opened directly on to the area outside the house itself. The north and west walls of both rooms are of Period IA construction (see above, p. 26), whilst the east wall of room E2 and the east and south walls of room F1 were the old Period I exterior walls. The rooms may have been lighted through windows in the east wall providing the recommended southeastern morning light. Room F1 may also have communicated with the staircase or ramp leading to the southern terrace.

South Room. Whether or not the terrace or room of the Period I house was remodelled as extensively as the other rooms in Period IA, is uncertain. On the west, room D4 encroached on the area by *c.* 2 · 00 m. The stairs or ramp on the east side may have been remodelled to turn into the raised area, bypassing the *cubiculum* of room F1 and entering the *domus* in the south wall of room E1. The dismantled state of the wall in this area, due to the Period II terracing, does not permit further speculation.

II. *The lower or southern terrace.*
The equipment, cisterns and rooms of the lower terrace, to the extent that they were explored, do not appear to have undergone any remodelling comparable to that of the *domus*. The utilitarian nature of the area, and its continuous use, suggest that the *villa rustica* retained its basic plan, but rooms may have been added and features of equipment changed in accordance with need. The core of the area, rooms G, H and I, was not

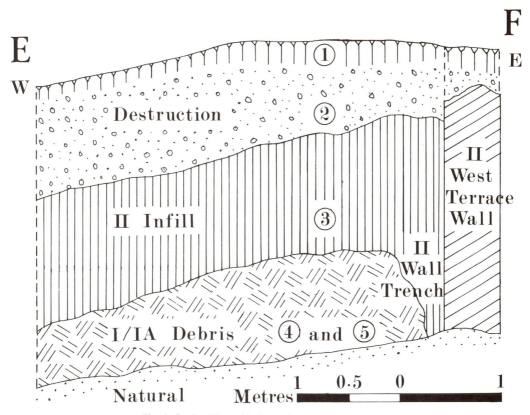

Fig. 6. Section EF outside the Period II west retaining wall

changed; this permanence suggests that the normal agricultural activity in the *villa rustica* generated, over the years, sufficient income to remodel the *domus* in its new, more complex and intimate form. A pattern of long-term growth is suggested as the financial basis for the Period IA modifications; it will be seen that new money, from outside sources, involving a complete transformation of *domus* and *villa rustica*, is indicated for the Period II villa.

PERIOD IA SUMMARY AND CONCLUSIONS.

In Period IA, the changes effected in the Period I structure modified the residential rather than the agricultural elements of the villa. The new construction in the *domus* took the form of subdivision of spaces into *cubicula* at the expense of large public rooms, but room A, the best paved room of the Period I *domus,* was enlarged. In the new plan, a concern for axial symmetry and grouping of rooms in unified suites is evident. *Opus incertum* construction was used, the surfaces being dressed in a manner virtually the same as those of Period I; only a small piece of quasi-reticulate masonry can be associated with Period IA. Architectural arrangements apart, little substantive change, either in domestic or in agricultural organisation, affecting the building itself took place. Since the changes of Period IA took place at some time during the 60–70 years between the initial construction of Period I and *c.* 30 B.C., when the Period II changes were made, the building at no time was 'old' or worn out, and in this sense the Period IA changes represent modifications according to internal needs—changes in use, in family size, in taste—rather than to external needs.

The outside aspect of the villa, its disposition on two terraces, did not change in Period IA. In the internal plan of the *domus* a new architectural conception is manifest, namely the notion of unifying the L-shaped plan by the axial corridor. In itself, the corridor does not create the familiar axial sequence (*fauces — atrium — tablinum*) which we associate with the urban houses of Pompeii, and the design is unusual. It may be that the plan was arrived at as much by accident as by intention, and its analogies are few: two *villae rusticae* of Late Republican date (?) at Pompeii have a long axial corridor, and the late second-century B.C. Villa Sambuco near Veii is also similarly designed. None of them belongs precisely to the period between *c.* 100–90 B.C. and *c.* 30 B.C. when the Period IA changes were made.

Datable construction is also difficult to come by for Period IA, and close analogies can only be found for the anomaly, namely the small stretches of quasi-reticulate masonry used to fill the south and west walls of room A1. Apart from examples from Rome and Latium, an analogy for the quasi-reticulate filling can be found at Cales, in the baths and theatre, to which Johannowsky has assigned dates from 90–70 B.C. at the earliest. This, together with analogies for the floors (*op. mus.* 3 and 4, pp. 90–91) are consistent with a date *c.* 50 B.C., but more precise dating is not possible. Period IA should be looked upon, therefore, as a modification of, rather than a complete change from, the Period I villa.[3]

The material from the contemporary layers was insignificant (see p. 254). On the other hand, the material derived from the Periods I/IA débris layer (see p. 254 and Fig. 6) does help to indicate the upper and lower brackets for the combined I/IA phases of the villa. This occupation, it is suggested, lasted *c.* 100–90 B.C. to *c.* 30 B.C. A more precise dating of the Period IA modifications, within this bracket, is not apparent, except for the date of *c.* 50 B.C. provided by the floors.

---

[3] For the Pompeian *villae rusticae* with axial corridors, see Della Corte, 1929[3], 191-9 and fig. 1, and Della Corte 1921, 1922 and 1923. See also a small *villa rustica* in Naples, Rocco, 1954, 37-8 and fig. 6. The Villa Sambuco is published in Poulsen, 1960, 313-20 and in White, 1970, 103-4 and figs. 36-7.

For the appearance of quasi-reticulate at Cales, see Johannowsky, 1961, 261-3. See also Lugli, 1957, 493 (Pompeii) and 495 (Ostia), and Blake, 1947, 251-3. For the finds associated with level 4, see pp. 254-6.

Chapter V. The Period II Villa

(Pls. VIII–XVII and XXVII–XXXV and Figs. 4, 7, 12, 12a–b)

The Periods I/IA San Rocco villa, comprising its small *villa rustica* and its newly reno-vated *domus,* was completely transformed, *c.* 30 B.C., into a residential and agricultural establishment quite different and much larger in scope. The earlier *domus,* always a simple and familial structure, was completely remodelled and, with the addition of many rooms and a peristyle, came to serve as the subsidiary spaces of an establishment of considerable architectural pretension and noteworthy decorative embellishment. It is a curious element in the design of the residential part of the new villa that certain rooms of the old *domus* (now designated the *domus vetus*) were preserved with minor changes, namely rooms A1, D4 and the corridor D2. The corridor came to be the determining axis of the new house, the *domus nova.* The element of continuity by which the *domus vetus* and the *domus nova* were combined architecturally is offset, however, by a new sense of space and a totally dif-ferent conception of the domestic environment. The intimacy and simplicity of the old house with its many bedrooms and its two dignified living rooms, was replaced by a large and more complex structure, centred around a formal peristyle, which implies by its plan an imposing, hierarchic and carefully regulated manner of living.

The *domus nova* was made possible by the same large outlay that went into the land and the farm buildings and equipment of the *villa rustica.* This 'capitalisation' was co-ordinated with an improvement in the transportation and water facilities which assured the accessibility and continuity of the villa as a functioning economic unit.

The *domus nova* and the *villa rustica* were reached by a new road, at least partially paved, running up to, through, and beyond the villa: this road provided the means by which goods and people could be efficiently and conveniently transported to and from the house. The road, to the extent that it can be traced, seems to run up the hill beyond the San Rocco area toward the other villas at the top, and it may very well be that it was built as a convenience-in-common paid for by several property owners in the district.

An enormous water catchment, storage and supply system, several times the capacity of the old one (from *c.* 38,400 to *c.* 1,100,000 litres) was built to service both parts of the villa. The new system comprised five cisterns in two groups of interconnecting barrel-vaulted structures situated to the north of the main western and eastern terraces, with water-catchment or settlement and purifying tanks on an upper terrace. It is noteworthy that the new water system was divided between the *domus nova* and the *villa rustica;* evidently the residential requirements for drinking, bathing, gardening and laundry water were as important in the design as the water needs for the agricultural establishment.

The old terraced area of the Period I villa was vastly expanded for the *domus nova.* The new buildings fronted on the road which separated the residential part of the establishment from the *villa rustica.* The terraced area of the farm was thus a new addition; its size and complexity were in their way as considerable as the sumptuous new *domus.* The *villa rustica* was built around two courtyards and in Period II included a pair of suites of rooms of a residential character, a 'commons', and other large spaces for agricultural activities. These additions to the 'working' parts of the villa suggest a variety of possibilities in the economic history of the estate: there may have been an increase in production and diver-sity in the use of the villa's lands or a diversification through new types of planting, or purchase or inheritance of new property, or perhaps increased productivity on the existing land. In all of these cases, money became available, justifying new residential and agricultural building, and the presence of new available 'capital' implies that the financial returns on agriculture in the district were good enough, *c.* 30 B.C., to encourage investment in either purchase or mortgage form. Moreover, profit and pleasure seem to have been mutually dependent, as can be illustrated by comparing the size of the *domus* (*c.* 1,335 m.^{2}) to that of the *villa rustica* (*c.* 898 m.^{2}): the house is larger than all the farm buildings taken together. The owners evidently felt no qualms about the productivity of, or the actual returns on, the land supporting the villa, even though the returns may have been supplemented by other income to staff, furnish and keep up the *domus*. Furthermore, throughout its history the *domus* was never encroached upon by the *villa rustica*. It was built to last.

Profitable diversification, a growth in yield by enlarging and organising the agricultural processes, an increase in personnel, a rising status for the owners conferred by sumptuous new quarters and an increasing social complexity in the functioning of the villa — all these phenomena seem to be present in the rebuilding of the late Republican period at San Rocco. Many of these phenomena are visible from the plan and rooms of the establishment or from the way in which the site as a whole was developed.

As it now stands, the broad terracing on two levels of the San Rocco site is due to the Period II building campaign. The ruins of the building were covered with a natural accretion of topsoil over the mosaic floors and wall stumps, and tough wild brambles effectively hid the terrace walls and cisterns from view. A few of the larger limestone blocks — thresholds, mainly — were built into the walls of the chapel of San Rocco near the site. In the 1930's, however, a sanatorium or hospital was planned on the main terrace of the villa, and ground broken to the extent that a triangular terrace projecting from the Roman south terrace was built and filled with earth. An access stairway from the lane below the site to the main terrace was also built, and three shallow wall foundations running at about a 45° angle to the Roman walls were put in with crosswalls linking them. At some point the contractors cut through into the cisterns, and work was stopped on the authority and through the representations of the Soprintendenza alle Antichità di Campania. The wall foundations, in some cases, cut through parts of mosaic floors, and evidently the surface of the main terrace had been flattened to make way for the modern structure. The sanatorium construction, while it led to the preservation of the site, destroyed or buried certain of its features in such a way as to make complete excavation very difficult. The construction of the access stairway cut through part of the south terrace wall and a modern fill (level 2 of Fig. 4) covered the south edge of the terrace, making it impossible to dig effectively for more of the Period I southern terrace than was revealed (see above, p. 19). The main entrance to the villa in Period II, and almost the entire length of the road running through the villa, were deeply buried at the south end and much cut away on the north when the site was flattened. It seems certain that the sanatorium contractors were aware of the Roman remains well before they were stopped, and the destruction of the Period II structures was considerable with the result that some features of the plan and design are unclear. Further destruction in the form of 'regulation' latrine and garbage burying pits was made in the area of the *domus nova,* probably by a unit of Allied soldiers during World War II. These two instances of disturbance made it difficult, in some places, to excavate the Period II structure, but wall lines projected on the plan can be justified.

The construction techniques of Period II consisted entirely of *opus caementicium* faced with *opus incertum* with, relative to the Period I limestone blocks, a smaller grade of stones set in a pinkish mortar with a high lime and sand content. In general, the surfaces were loosely rendered and fewer stones were used, proportionate to the mortar, than had been in Periods I and IA. The wall width at floor level was the same in Period II as previously (0 · 49 to 0 · 50 m.).

On the west side of the Period II villa, in room 39, a deep trench was cut directly to the west of the Period I west terrace wall (section EF, Fig. 6) to recover material associated with the construction of Period II walls. In a fill layer corresponding to level 3, much pottery associated with the Period II construction was found (see below, pp. 256–8).

The Period II villa is described under the following headings:

I. The main and back entrances and the road running through the villa.

II. The cisterns and the water-catchment and supply systems, to the north of the east and west terraces.

III. The western terrace, the *domus nova* and the *domus vetus*.

IV. The eastern terrace and the *villa rustica*.

I. *The main and back entrances and the road running through the villa.* (Fig. 7)

A road ran up to and through the main entrance to the Period II villa. This main entrance was on the south between the terrace walls which, in the area of the gate, were founded at the level of the road. Below the main entrance, the road, visible as a slight depression in the ground, takes a turn (*c.* 20°) to the west and probably continued down the hill to the *ager* below. It is visible for not more than about 10 m. in the field to the south of the south terrace walls: beyond that a grove of olive trees obscures its trace.

Between the main entrance and the back entrance, the road rises at an angle of *c.* 35° and continues up the hill following the natural contour. In the excavated portions of the road (see below, p. 57), the surface was a rough conglomerate of the natural limestone of the hillside cut to grade with a thin packing of limestone chips spread over it. Some attempt at smoothing the surface with flagstones may have been made in the areas near the doors (see below), but otherwise the roadbed was rough, providing good traction for the uphill climb.

At the main entrance, part of a triangular room, very deeply buried, was found. This room was let into the eastern terrace of the *villa rustica*: a door opened to the right of the main entrance and led into a room whose back wall was set at an angle across the corner of the western and southern terrace walls. This small room (*c.* 20 · 00 m.²), in view of its location, probably served as a porter's lodge. Another small room, similarly used, may have opened to the left of the main entrance; the presence of this room is indicated by the wall-end, perhaps a door-jamb, partially revealed in plan.

The first opening on the east, beyond the porter's lodge, was a gateway into the *hortus* which occupied the entire southern half of the *villa rustica* terrace. The gateway was paved with use-worn limestone flags irregularly shaped and 0 · 70 m. broad at the most, set into a hard mud packing. A rectangular limestone block with a pivot-hole (0 · 06 m. in diameter and 0 · 08 m. deep) on the north side indicated the presence of a heavy single-leaved gate of wood or metal barring the entrance to the garden. The level of the flagged threshold was 0 · 60 m. lower than the general level of the floors in the *villa rustica;* evidently the area of the *hortus* was lower than the rest of the terraced structures.

The surface of the road was much destroyed in the area of the entrance to the *domus nova,* but it is likely that there was a smooth flagging or some other level step. The T-shaped *vestibulum* (room 1) gave on to the road through a large door (3 · 00 m. wide) flanked symmetrically with narrower doors (2 · 30 m. wide).[1] This triple entrance was evidently reserved for formal receptions and for the more distinguished members of the villa, since there was a servant's entrance leading to a service corridor (room 15) to the north of the *vestibulum*. This door (1 · 30 m. wide) also gave on to the road and faced courtyard 1 of the *villa rustica*. The precise relationship between the road and courtyard 1 is not known because of the modern levelling of the site. There may have been a wall separating courtyard 1 from the road, or the courtyard may have been a U-shaped *piazza* open on one side.

At the back entrance, wall ends projecting from the superstructure of the cisterns on the west, and the wall of room 40 on the east, framed a gateway 2 · 90 m. wide. This gateway had a limestone threshold block (0 · 60 m. wide) which had evidently been repaired or patched with smaller limestone blocks on the west side, perhaps to hang a door or gate in the opening. In the wall of room 40, a door (0 · 88 m. wide) gave on to the road; this room may also have been the porter's lodge for the back entrance.

Above the villa, the road, represented as a slight depression in the ground and partially visible in section on the sides of a modern track, takes a slight 20° turn to the right and can be followed for about 40 m. up the hill, following the contour and running towards the other Roman villas (see below p. 42). The surface of the road visible in section has a surface similar to that portion excavated in the villa proper.

II. *The cisterns and the water-catchment and supply systems.* (Pl. VIII and Fig. 7)
The water supply of the villa was assured by two sets of cisterns, one for the *domus* on the west and another for the *villa rustica* on the east. Of the two sets, only that to the north of the *domus* could be fully explored; the cisterns for the *villa rustica* were deeply buried by débris from the tufa quarry to the northeast of the site and could not be cleared. The system of which the cisterns were a part comprised three elements: a channel or aqueduct bringing water to the western cisterns, a waterproof tank built on top of the vaults of these cisterns, which received the supply from the channel (and which could be used to catch rain-water and eaves' drip), and the cisterns themselves. The system is described as follows:
A. The water channel or aqueduct.
B. The tank above the cisterns of the western terrace.
C. The cisterns.

A. *The water channel or aqueduct.*
On the west side, water was supplied to the *domus* by a channel (0 · 45 m. wide) set into a rubble and mortar base (1 · 00 m. wide and 0 · 50 m. high). The channel was evidently not buried in earth but ran parallel to the north side of the villa, bringing water from a spring or watershed on the western flank of the hill. The sides and floor of the channel could be traced for about 13 m. along the north: a 90° turn near the northeast corner of the cisterns brought the water down to the tank. To the north and west, all traces of the channel were covered by the foundations of the chapel of San Rocco.

B. *The tank above the cisterns of the west terrace.*
The tank covered almost the entire area above the western cisterns. The structure was

---

[1] No precise analogy to the three doors, defined by wall-ends at the entrance to a *domus*, has been traced, unless the curving wall defining the back verandah of the Villa dei Misteri is allowed: cf. Maiuri, 1947, 57–8. The entrance would have been more like the *atrium* entrance, Mauri, 1947, 47-8 and fig. 11. The reconstruction drawing of the door as a wide opening framed by wall-ends and defined by two columns, as published in Boëthius and Ward-Perkins, 1970, 321 and fig. 124, and in Percival, 1976, 57 and fig. 10, is incorrect; the doors are separated by wall-ends defining three separate openings.

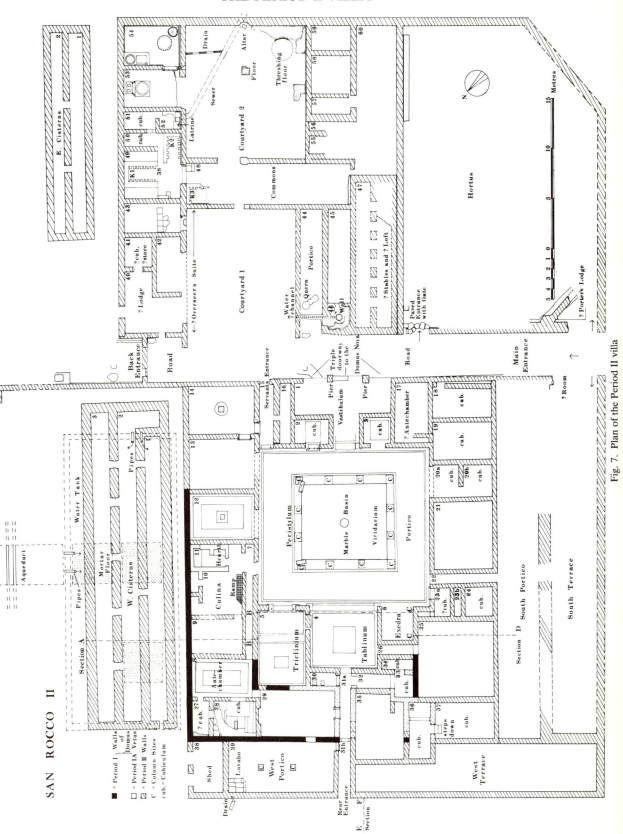

Fig. 7. Plan of the Period II villa

much destroyed, but traces of its walls (0 · 50 m. thick) were found on the north, south and east sides, and its floor, a finely mixed layer of mortar and marble dust (0 · 07 m. thick) laid on a bed of yellow clay and limestone gravel above the cistern vaults, could be seen in several places. The tank was at least 11 · 60 × 28 · 65 m. in area and, while its depth could not be determined, it must have been at least as deep as the preserved height of its south wall, 0 · 70 m., with a minimum capacity of 232,600 litres. It may have served as a cleaning or filtering system through which the water could have passed before being let into the cisterns.

C. *The cisterns.*

The cisterns on the west were carefully built of limestone rubble in lime and mortar. The walls were dug deeply into the natural rock of the hillside from an old topsoil level which can be seen in section between the north wall of the Period I villa and the south wall of the tank (section ABCD, Fig. 4). The walls were uniformly 1 · 00 m. thick, except for the west wall, which was 0 · 80 m. thick. The three cisterns were all 31 · 20 m. long, 1 · 74 m. wide and 2 · 81 m. high from the floor to the crown of the barrel vaults (2 · 10 high to the springing of the vaults). The vaults themselves were set back from the edge of the walls by 0 · 10 m., probably to leave room for the heavy waterproof coat which protected them. The angles of the walls and floor were sealed with a quarter-round moulding, and the interior surfaces were covered with a layer of mortar, marble dust and lime (0 · 07 m. thick) which in turn was protected by a fine lime and marble dust waterproofing coat. Between the southermost cistern and the central one, two low arched passages (1 · 20 m. high and 0 · 60 m. wide) running through the wall at floor level assured free flow of water; five such passages connected the central and northernmost cisterns. The central cistern was L-shaped, its short arm on the east side. It is not entirely clear how the water was piped or bucketed into the *domus,* since the openings in the cistern vaults appear to be later intrusions. The capacity of the three cisterns, if filled to the springing of the vaults, is 565,000 litres.[2]

The cisterns on the east were of similar construction to those on the west and were similarly dug into the rock of the hillside. The line of the walls (all *c.* 1 · 00 m. thick) could be observed after partial clearing of the undergrowth. There appear to have been two parallel cisterns (both 2 · 40 m. wide and 23 · 90 m. long), and they were vaulted in the same way as those on the west. Assuming that their height was comparable to the other cisterns (2 · 81 m.), their capacity was about the same, *c.* 565,000 litres. It is not known exactly how the stored water was brought into the *villa rustica.*

[2.] For cisterns, see Vitruvius (xiii 6, 14–15). No mention is made of how cisterns are to be roofed or vaulted. The closest analogies to the San Rocco cisterns are those of the other villas on the hill and those at Posto; see Cotton, 1979, 25–7. It should be noted that the cisterns at San Rocco are part of a general development in the history of Roman structural understanding. The construction of parallel barrel vaulted structures in which the vaults both support each other and rest on the same wall, and in which there are interconnections from space to space laterally through the doors in the wall is characteristic of the *porticus Aemilia;* see Boëthius and Ward-Perkins, 1970, 106 and 553, n. 7, and the remarks on dating by Richardson, Jr., 1976, 58–9. Similar types of construction occur in the Sullan buildings at Tibur and Terracina as terracing; see Fasolo and Gullini, 1953, 353–89. In Campania, the use of this type of construction can be found in cisterns, notably that of the Piscina Mirabile and the Cento Camerelle in the Phlegrean Fields; see Lugli, 1957, 491–3. Specifically, cisterns of similar construction and size to those of San Rocco can be found in documented Late Republican and Augustan villas near Sorrento and Rome: see Mingazzini and Pfister, 1946, 130–1 (Villa del Capo di Sorrento), and 94–5 (Cisternone degle Spasiani); De Rossi, 1967, 49 and fig. 91 (cisterns); and Muzzioli, 1970, 43–8 and fig. 37 (a villa with cisterns under an upper terrace). Many cisterns associated with villas are recorded in Lazio by Quilici, (*Forma Italiae, Collatia*) *passim.*

III. *The western terrace, the domus nova and the domus vetus.*
The main features of the Period II *domus* on the western terrace are:

A. The terrace retaining walls on the northern, southern, eastern and western sides and the terrace fill supporting the platform on which the *domus* was built.

B. The *domus nova*, comprising those new rooms (1–26 and peristyle) which were entirely of Period II construction.

C. The *domus vetus*, comprising those rooms (27–39) which had been part of the Periods I and IA *domus* and which were reused in a modified form in the new building.

A. *The terrace retaining walls on the northern, southern, eastern and western sides and the terrace fill supporting the platform on which the domus was built.* (Pl. IX and Fig. 7)
The terrace walls of the Period II *domus*, as well as the walls of the house itself, are of compact and careful construction in *opus caementicium* faced with *opus incertum*, almost all 0 · 50 m. thick, made of limestone rubble of a slightly larger grade than that of Periods I and IA and with a higher component of sand in the mortar than in the earlier walls. In general, the lower parts of all Period II walls were trench-laid with an offset, sometimes in two stages (*c.* 0 · 10 m. wide), between the foundation and the upper part of the walls. The upper parts were of 'planked' construction, built before the terrace fill was put in and resulting in sporadic layers of mixed building materials in the Period II fills.

The northern terrace wall (north wall of rooms 11, 12, 13 and 14), which supported the fill between the *domus* itself and the south wall of the cisterns, was a continuation of the north wall of the Period I villa. The foundation and part of the wall have survived, but it is significant that most of it has collapsed southwards into the adjoining rooms in contrast to the Period I portion which is still mostly upstanding; the quality and solidity of Period II construction were inferior to that of Periods I and IA. The eastern terrace wall (east wall of rooms 1 and 14–18) was in large part destroyed or eroded except for a section in rooms 1 and 17–18. The line of the south retaining wall, faced in *opus incertum*, could be followed for almost its entire length but was so deeply buried by the fill behind the modern hospital retaining wall that it could not be exposed. A portion of it is visible to the left of the modern steps leading up to the site; since it supported the weight of the fill, it was thicker (0 · 80 m.) than the other walls of the *domus*. It is suggested above (p. 19) that the Period II south retaining wall followed the line of the Period I retaining wall, but its foundations could not be uncovered without endangering its stability. Towards the bottom, weep-holes framed by limestone blocks running through the wall allowed for seepage of water percolating through the fill. The various stages of the 'planked' construction can be seen in the illustration (Pl. IX): the wall was evidently built in sections about 1 · 00 m. high, and there was some variation in the size of rubble used in each section. On the west side, most of the terrace wall (west walls of rooms 38, 39 and the western terrace wall) has collapsed, but the construction of its foundations corresponded to that of the north, east and south walls.

The terrace fill (level 4 of Fig. 4) laid between the terrace walls entirely covered the Period I southern terrace; the old *villa rustica* completely disappeared, even its well being inexpertly capped with fill laid over it. For the most part, the Period II fill (level 3 of Fig. 4) was of the heavy dark brown earth of the hillside, mixed with building materials from the earlier building (see section ABCD, Fig. 4). Many of the Periods I and IA walls and floors were destroyed; for example, the old south retaining wall of the northern terrace was dismantled almost to its foundations. The Period II retaining walls and room walls were carefully bonded, both at the level of the foundations and above, and this method divided the terrace fill into self-contained compartments, thereby reducing the downhill thrust of the fill. This method of making self-contained compartments of fill is suggested by Vitruvius (vi 7). The fill directly underlay the *rudera* of the floors in the *domus nova,* but in those rooms in which the Periods I and IA floors were not removed, the level was raised *c.* 0 · 60 m. by fills laid directly on the floors and between earlier walls whose doors were blocked.

B. *The domus nova.* (Fig. 7)
The site of the Period I villa was recognised as well-suited for a residence altogether different in character from the old. The views were fine ones, as evidently also was the water supply; the breeze is still healthful, descending from the mountains to the northeast in the hottest part of the afternoon and mitigating the heat until a cool breeze rises from the plain in the evening. The angle of the platform, facing south-south-west, in full view of the rising and setting sun, would have helped to warm the rooms in winter. The new *domus* was elaborate and large; it seems that the site justified its cost. Moreover, the district was becoming sufficiently wealthy to warrant the development of fine residences, thus requiring a certain pretension in the kind of spaces and types of rooms which were to be built in the villa, as well as a high standard of decorative embellishment. The impression of cultivated ease in dignified surroundings and a certain formality of life were the social images which the owners wished to project to their neighbours; the many bedrooms and the close proximity of the agricultural quarters suggest a well-organised, hospitable and familial life with a largish circle of relatives, servants, slaves and associates. The traces of other villas, as large as San Rocco, and presumably as well-decorated, together with the communal road and the mutual interest in agricultural pursuits, attest to social contacts in the district among owners and servants which must have been lively and continuous. The affinities among land-owners created by the communal need to safe-guard their land and houses must, at the outset at least, have forged a bond of concord and co-ordinated activity which itself would have been an investment. The region was safe enough to permit a display of wealth and sophisticated taste, and such goods, services or diversions as were unavailable in the country could be had conveniently at Cales, Teanum or Capua, or in the cities and resorts of the Bay of Naples, or at Formiae, using the Via Appia.

The new walls were uniformly built of *opus incertum* in limestone rubble of a sandy pinkish-grey mortar and were, with few exceptions, 0 · 49–0 · 50 m. thick at floor level and above, with an offset or offsets (0 · 10 m. wide) on one side for the foundations. In general, the walls of rooms on the south side of the peristyle, where the thrust of the fill would have been greatest, are more deeply founded than elsewhere. An example is the west wall of room 25, founded to a level of 1 · 80 m. below the Period II floor in three stages: a foundation trenched into the fill, an offset 0 · 10 m., then a second offset foundation of 'planked' construction, on which the wall itself was built. The process suggests that the terrace walls were built first and that filling had begun before this plan of the rooms was established, or in any case before the position of the room-walls had been determined. Separate contracts, one for the terracing work, another for the building itself, may have been undertaken.

The walls in the north part of the villa were shallowly founded, usually directly on the floors of the earlier building or directly on the foundations of earlier walls, and the fill was laid between them. The building procedure suggests that, once the terrace area had been established, the whole plan of the villa was a single unified conception in which all the rooms were designed for specific functions embodying the precisely predetermined needs of the inhabitants. The success of the conception is attested by the fact that the plan and use of the building was maintained almost unchanged for at least 250 years.

The rooms of the *domus nova* can be divided into three groups:
1. *Rooms 1−6 and the peristyle.*
The first group (rooms 1−6, the peristyle and *viridarium*) are arranged along the axis of the *domus* and constitute a formal sequence: a *vestibulum* (1) flanked by *cubicula* (2 and 3) leading to a peristyle with *viridarium*. Directly opposite the *vestibulum,* there was a *tablinum* (4) flanked by a *triclinium* and an *exedra* (5 and 6). These three rooms are the formal reception rooms of the house, in which the ceremonies of home-coming and the formalities of hospitality, dining and *symposium* would have taken place.
2. *Rooms 7−16.*
The second group consists of nine rooms (7−16) on the north side of the peristyle, of which two (7 and 15) were corridors, two were storerooms (9 and 16), two were kitchen rooms (10 and 11) and the rest (8, 12, 13 and 14) were large residential rooms finely paved and decorated.
3. *Rooms 17−26 and the southern terrace.*
The third group on the south side of the peristyle comprised large rooms (17, 18, 19, 21 and 25), *cubicula* (20?, 23, 24) and corridors (22 and 26); some of these rooms may have faced both inwards to the peristyle and outwards to the southern terrace.

The description of the *domus nova* follows the sequence of the three groups of rooms outlined above.

1. *Rooms 1−6 and the peristyle.* (Fig. 7)
Room 1, vestibulum (9 · 80 × 3 · 20 m. with the narrow arm 2 · 70 × 3 · 40 m.). The entrance to the *domus nova* was dignified by a façade of three doors separated by piers; the side doors were 2 · 30 m. wide while the central one, probably higher than the others, was fully 3 · 00 m. wide. The thresholds of the doors have not survived. The *vestibulum* lay immediately behind the façade, a large T-shaped room with the top part of the T at right angles to the axis of the plan and the long arm of the T constituting a kind of *fauces* on axis. The mosaic pavement (*op. mus.* 5, p. 92) was co-ordinated with the shape of the room, and the walls were plastered with several layers of progressively finer and finer plaster, 0 · 05 m. thick and painted bright red. The door into the peristyle was as wide as the room itself and had a limestone threshold, a central block with side-pieces fitted into the wall ends, with pivot holes on which were secured gates or doors. The T-shaped design of the *vestibulum* reflects the sequence of axial and cross axial volumes embodied in the relationship between *tablinum* and peristyle.[3]
Rooms 2 and 3, cubicula (3 · 40 × 2 · 45 m. and 2 · 80 × 2 · 45 m. respectively). Two small rooms on either side of the *vestibulum* but entered from the peristyle had mosaic pavements (*op mus.* 6 and 7, p. 94) whose geometric 'mats' suggested a decorative subdivision typical of *cubicula.* The couches could have been placed along the north walls of the rooms, which were screened by doors pivoting inwards on the limestone thresholds and secured by vertical bolts. These rooms were lighted from the peristyle through the doors, and traces of wall plaster were found, indicating that the *cubicula* were part of the residential decorative ensemble and not allocated to servants or porters.

[3.] No analogies for the T-shape of the *vestibulum* at San Rocco, in a villa of this size and situation, have been traced.

The peristyle and viridarium (17 · 40 × 15 · 80 m.). (Pls. X–XI). The peristyle and the *viridarium* were the centralising features of the plan of the *domus nova* and, together with the axial sequence of formal rooms, its dominating components. The squarish *viridarium* (8 · 60 × 7 · 60 m.) was surrounded on four sides by roofs sloping inwards and covering the porticos. The axis of the plan is suggested in the unequal depth of the porticos: on the east side, the portico is narrowest (only 3 · 60 m. deep), on the north and south sides the porticos are both 4 · 40 m. deep, while on the west, in front of the *tablinum,* the portico is deepest, 4 · 60 m. The centralising function of the peristyle is thus co-ordinated with a graduated spaciousness along the axis providing an elaborate processional introduction to the main room of the *domus nova.*

The walls of the peristyle were plastered and painted red along the baseboard in the small fragments which survived. The doors on the east, north and south had stone thresholds, though most of these had been robbed. Limestone blocks, two of them *in situ* in the northeast and northwest corners, set flush with the pavement, provided the stylobate for twelve columns, four on each side, separating the porticos from the *viridiarium.* The columns themselves stood on square or L-shaped limestone blocks (0 · 96 m. square), seven of which were found *in situ* on the north, south and west sides. Two of the limestone blocks were scored with a round raised surface (0 · 85 m. in diameter) intended to secure the column bases, and since the blocks themselves were flush with the stylobate blocks and the pavement, it appears that the columns had no plinths. Part of the plaster remains of one of these columns was found in the *viridarium:* the columns evidently had brick cores finished with plaster moulded in Ionic flutes (0 · 035 m. wide and 0 · 03 m. deep), with fillets 0 · 01 m. wide. The fragment found indicates that the column was c. 0 · 60 m. in diameter. Using Vitruvius' prescription for the Ionic order (iii,5,1–11) an Ionic column with an Ionic base 0 · 85 m. in diameter, as these are, should have a lower diameter of c. 0 · 605 m., which agrees well with our fragment. There would thus have been twelve flutes, half the usual number. A lower diameter of c. 0 · 605 m. for the columns, in a ratio of 1:8, gives a total height of 4 · 84 for the shaft, to which we may add 0 · 20 m. for the height of the base, 0 · 32 m. for that of the capital, and at most 0 · 83 m. for the entablature (probably less, since the entablature was of wood); thus the height of the porticos from stylobate to the top of the entablature would have been 6 · 19 m. Granting an angle of some 30° for the pitch of the roofs, the height of the back wall of the peristyle would have been c. 7 · 12 m. at the point at which the walls and the roof intersected. This would also have been the approximate height from floor to rafters of the surrounding rooms, since the ceilings would have lowered the rooms by c. 1 · 00 m., making them c. 6 · 12 m. high. In the case of the *triclinium,* this height corresponds approximately to the desired height of oblong rooms (half the width plus the length) in Vitruvius' calculation (vi,3,8).

The interaxials of the columns vary: on the north and south sides the middle interaxial is 2 · 85 m. and the two side ones 3 · 03 m. while on the east and west the interaxial is regular, 3 · 32 m.. The intercolumnar proportion is thus 1:3 and 1:4 with the diameter of the column. The cornice was crowned with terracotta lions' head antefixes, some of which were found in the *viridarium* topsoil (see below, p. 168).

The design of the mosaic pavement was co-ordinated with the spaces between the columns. The intercolumnar areas from the edge of the stone stylobate to the edge of the *scutulatum pavimentum* (*op. mus.* 8, p. 96) were decorated with 'mats' of geometric patterns (*op. mus.* 9–12, p. 97) of which a few fragments have survived. The *scutulatum pavimentum* of the peristyle was evidently intended to recall that of room A in the Period I house (*op. mus.* 1, p. 85).

In the *viridarium* itself, the Period I northern terrace cistern was covered with topsoil: a *puteal* may have been for use during Period II, but the disturbance and destruction caused by robbers obscured any features original to the garden. The remains of a shallow basin of Pentelic marble (about $0 \cdot 95$ m. in diameter and $0 \cdot 20$ m. deep) were found in the centre. Careful horizontal clearing of the topsoil layer did not reveal the characteristic mottling which post-holes and tree-trunk and root sections leave, as at Pompeii, but a garden of this size ($65 \cdot 36$ m.^{2}) might be expected to have extensive planting which the conditions of the villa's abandonment have not preserved in reconstructible form.[4]

All the major rooms of the *domus nova* opened on to the peristyle. In addition, there were corridors linking the peristyle with the road and the *villa rustica* (14), bypassing the *vestibulum*, a corridor to the kitchen area and the rooms in the northwest corner of the building (6), and one leading to the southern terrace (22). The centralising function of the peristyle is thus supplemented with radiating passages giving the design of the spaces a 'pin-wheel' configuration which is combined with the axis and cross-axes of the whole plan.

The peristyle was built outside the limits of the Periods I and IA villa. However, in the area west of the peristyle, the new rooms (4, 5 and 6) were built following the dismantling of rooms B1, E1, E2 and F1.

Room 4. The tablinum ($6 \cdot 90 \times 6 \cdot 35$ m.). The *tablinum* completes the axis of the *domus nova* in a manner suggested by Vitruvius. Its east side facing the peristyle was completely open; the threshold was paved in mosaic (*op. mus.* 13, p. 100) and was framed with limestone quoins projecting from the *antae*. The floor of the *tablinum* proper was also in mosaic (*op. mus.* 14, p. 104), enclosing in the centre an *emblema*, now lost. The walls were plastered. The height of the *tablinum* can be inferred from the height of the peristyle porticos ($c. 7 \cdot 12$ m. with a lower ceiling) which, with its width and depth ($6 \cdot 90 \times 6 \cdot 35$ m.), would have resulted in an almost cubic volume, adding a geometric formality to the room's decoration. On axis with the plan, a corridor (31a) linked the *tablinum* with the *domus vetus*: its threshold was decorated with the mosaic representation of an arched city-gate with towers and ramparts which may have formed some part of the villa's iconography (*op. mus.* 15, p. 105). On the south side, a corridor (26) led to a large room (25) giving on to the south terrace, and on the north, the *tablinum* communicated with the *triclinium* (5) through a door with a limestone threshold. The walls of the *tablinum* are entirely of Period II construction, with the exception of the foundations of the west wall to the south of the door, which were of Period IA construction.

Room 5. The triclinium ($4 \cdot 95 \times 7 \cdot 50$ m.). A doorway ($2 \cdot 70$ m. wide) fitted with limestone quoins supporting a double door of wood and a mosaic threshold (*op. mus.* 16, p. 107) linked the peristyle with the *triclinium*, whose function is denoted by the bipartite arrangement of its floor (*op. mus.* 17, p. 108). The width and length of the room ($4 \cdot 95 \times 7 \cdot 50$ m.), added together and divided by half, suggest a height of $c. 6 \cdot 12$ m., entirely commensurate with the approximate height of the rafters ($c. 7 \cdot 12$ m.) with a ceiling below.

The *triclinium* communicated with the *tablinum*, but the arrangement of the threshold suggests that a door opening inwards separated them: the whole room could be closed off from the surrounding area for greater warmth in winter and coolness in summer. The walls were plastered and painted with a red baseboard. The large size of the room could have accommodated four or six couches for dinner-parties of eight to twelve people. It is uncer-

---

[4.] On gardens, the contributions of Jashemski are decisive for their scientific and exemplary character. See, amongst others, her publications on a market garden orchard at Pompeii, Jashemski, 1974, 391–404, and on a large vineyard in Pompeii, 1973, 826.

tain how the *triclinium* and the *tablinum* were roofed, but in view of their size the drainage of rainwater from a flat roof would have been impracticable, and so we may plausibly assume that their roofs were pitched.[5]

Room 6, An exedra (3 · 25 × 3 · 35 m.). Flanking the *tablinum* on the south, an almost square *exedra* completed the suite of formal rooms on the west side of the peristyle. The room was an extension of the peristyle space, completely open on the east side and equipped with a utilitarian floor (*op. sig.* 3, p. 123) indicating that its use was less 'noble' than that of the *tablinum* and *triclinium*, even though its position was an honourable one. The *exedra* may have been used by the women of the house for activities such as spinning, weaving and dying cloth, which might have come under the supervision of the *matrona*. The room was plastered and painted blue.

2. *Rooms 7–16.* (Fig. 7)

The suite of rooms in the *domus nova* to the north of the peristyle consists of corridors (7 and 15), formal rooms (8, 12, 13 and 14) and a kitchen area with dependencies (9, 10 and 11).

Room 7. A corridor (0 · 78 × 11 · 45 m.) A door with a limestone threshold, now robbed, led from the north peristyle portico into a corridor (0 · 85 m. wide) running between the *triclinium* and the kitchen area and leading to room 8. The kitchen was entered from the corridor through a door giving onto a ramp. The floor of the corridor (*op. sig.* 13, p. 127) was relaid during Period IIA when the north wall of the passage was dismantled and rebuilt: no trace of the Period II floor was found.

Room 8 (6 · 15 × 3 · 80 m.). This room stands in a position which links the *domus nova* with the *domus vetus*. It occupied the position of room C of Period I, and its south wall was the Period I north wall of room B, its north wall the old Period I retaining wall. The magnificent mosaic floor (*op. mus.* 18, p. 113) indicates that room 8 was part of a formal ensemble of three rooms in the northwest corner of the *domus*: through doors in the west wall it communicated with a small room (27), perhaps a *cubiculum*, and with a larger room (28). These two rooms intercommunicated with one other, suggesting a suite of two *cubicula* with an antechamber. Room 8 further communicated with room 29, the principal room of the *domus vetus*. Since the Period II floors are *c.* 0 · 20 m. higher than those of Period I, the passageway paved in mosaic (*op. mus.* 19, p. 114) was slightly ramped.

The area of room 8, 27 and 28 was much transformed in Period IIA when the bath house was put in. The floor of room 8 was cut neatly in half, its south part was walled off and changed into a *frigidarium* with the door into room 28 blocked with a low wall adapted for a cold plunge (Pl. XII). The north part of room 8 became a *sudatorium* (see below, p. 64).

Rooms 9, 10 and 11. The culina. (Pls. XIII–XIVa) These three interconnecting rooms, entered from the corridor (7) constituted a large and comfortable kitchen area. The size of the rooms, and their separation from the *villa rustica*, indicates that there was some distinction maintained between the house servants and the agricultural workers of the estate.

The floor level of the kitchen rooms was lower by 0 · 40 m. than that of the *domus nova*. Why this should have been so is difficult to explain: it may be that a Period I room in this area preordained the level, or perhaps it was felt that the lower level provided a protection for the roofs of the *domus* against sparks from the kitchen hearth. Rooms 10 and 11 seem

---

[5.] The cubic proportions of the high *tablinum* and *triclinium*, as reconstructed here, and the height of the peristyle portico roofs, are characteristic of the major public rooms of nearly all the Pompeian houses insofar as they can be reconstructed. See, for example, Mau, ed. Overbeck, 1884, 301–6 and 353–6; and Spinazzola, 1953, 318–34.

to have been open, with a shed roof or a lean-to along one or two sides: the lower level and correspondingly lower roofs would have been discontinuous with the roofing system of the rooms on either side and directly below the tank sited above the cistern, making for easy fire fighting. The open-air space of rooms 10 and 11 would also have lessened the danger of fire, and considering the absence of any evidence of scorching or destruction by fire in the villa, such a 'fire-proof' design was evidently successful.

Room 9(5 · 30 × 3 · 70 m.) was evidently a storeroom of some kind, with a single entrance in the east wall. Originally, its south wall was of limestone-faced rubble construction like that of the rest of the Period II walls: this was visible in foundations only, since the wall was dismantled and rebuilt in the Period IIA remodelling. Traces of a Period II beaten earth floor were found, much disturbed, at the level of the rest of the kitchen. The arrangement of the door in Period II is not known, nor is that of the roof, but the room's position *in fondo* of the kitchen area possibly indicates that it was roofed separately from the others.

A limestone threshold, fitted with pivot holes for securing a door, led from the corridor (7) on to a platform (0 · 85 × 0 · 85 m.), very roughly built of building débris and faced and paved with tiles 0 · 60 m. square. The platform was in room 11, and a ramp, of construction similar to that of the platform, sloped down along the south wall into room 10. The ramp suggests that sledges or small carts were used to bring goods into the kitchen for storage and use.

Room 10 (5 · 30 × 4 · 30 m.). This room was completely floored in *opus spicatum* (*op. spic.* 1, p. 125) except along its north end. There, a T-shaped wall end extended 1 · 20 m. from the north wall and framed a beaten earth floor. The T-shaped wall end, and an *anta* projecting from the east wall, were of very loose construction (rubble and brick in mud): they evidently stood to no great height and probably supported a 'counter' with possibly a shed roof above and storage space below. The area next to the north wall was dug out, revealing a supporting arch of Period I construction, and this recess was evidently used for storage as well (see above, p. 12).

Extensive remodelling of room 10 was undertaken during Period IIA (see below, p. 65) when a seat for the *testudo* of the *caldarium* was put in.

Room 11. The wall between rooms 10 and 11 was strongly built and evidently stood up to some height. The arrangement of the floors (*op. spic.* 1 and 2, p. 126) was the same in the two rooms: on the north side the *opus spicatum* was substituted by a beaten earth floor extending 0 · 90 m. from the wall. In room 11, along the east and north walls, an L-shaped arrangement of loosely-constructed wall-ends, carefully plastered, supported a cooking table standing to a height of about 1 · 00 m.. Between two wall-ends on the east wall in room 11, an apron 1 · 10 m. high of tufa blocks and limestone rubble set in mortar served as the basis for a hearth: the wall above this area was heavily burnt. Holes for beams (0 · 09 × 0 · 09 m.) in the north wall of room 11, 2 · 60 m. above the floor, suggested that some kind of shed roof covered this area, but at a height much lower than that of the adjacent residential rooms.

Rooms 12, 13 and 14 (6 · 60 × 4 · 50 m., 6 · 60 × 4 · 90 m. and 6 · 60 × 4 · 90 m. respectively). (Pl. XIV *b*). In the northeast corner of the *domus nova* there were three imposingly large rooms, two of which were entered from the north peristyle portico. The exact arrangement of the doors of rooms 12 and 13 cannot be determined since the threshold blocks, and part of the south walls, were robbed. Room 12 had a beautiful mosaic floor (*op. mus.* 20, p. 115) with an *emblema,* now lost. Rooms 13 and 14, which were connected by a door with a plain limestone threshold, were paved in decorated *opus signinum* (*op.*

sig. 4 and 5, p. 123). Room 14 had, in the centre of the floor, a square limestone base set flush with the floor which was laid neatly around it: the base may have supported a statue or small domestic altar. A door in the south wall of room 14 provided access to a corridor (15) leading to the road and the *villa rustica* across the way. All three rooms were plastered. The size and the quality of their floors indicate that they were part of the formal ensemble of dignified residential rooms, but their exact use is not clear.

3. *Rooms 17–26 and the south terrace.* (Fig. 7)

The rooms to the south of the peristyle were much destroyed, possibly by shallow plough-ing of the terrace but mainly by the leveling undertaken for the sanatorium construction. In most cases, the walls were destroyed to a level below that of the floors and thresholds with the result that the relationship of the rooms could not be accurately determined. In general, however, it seems that most of the rooms were plastered and paved, either in mosaic or in *opus signinum* and that most opened on to the peristyle rather than on to the south terrace. The alternation of small and large rooms suggests that this area of the house combined living rooms with *cubicula* in a series of separate suites.

Room 17 (3 · 40 × 5 · 95 m.). This room was paved in mosaic, traces of which were found along the south wall (*op. mus.* 21, p. 118). It was equipped with a subdividing wall end on the west side which extended 1 · 90 m. into the room providing a narrow space similar to those in rooms 23a and 35. The wall-end may have been a screening wall for a *lavabo* or the seating for a bath; unfortunately the floor was destroyed below the level at which a drain would have appeared. It is not known how this room was entered; it may have opened into the peristyle, or into room 13 through a door in the south wall.

Room 18. A cubiculum (?6 · 10 × 3 · 40 m.). The size of this room, long and narrow, is not incompatible with its having been used as a bedroom. Its east wall was buttressed by a double-thick wall because the road sloped down in this area and the terrace fill needed shoring up securely.

Room 19. A cubiculum (?6 · 10 × 3 · 20 m.). This small room and the preceding one, together with room 17, may have formed a group of two bedrooms with an antechamber like that of the suite of rooms 8, 27 and 28. Traces of white mosaic (*op. mus.* 22, p. 119) and plaster were found along the east wall of room 19, but the position of the doors is not known because the walls were destroyed to the top of their foundations.

Rooms 20a and 20b. A cubiculum. Both rooms were entered through a narrow door (1 · 00 m. wide) in the south peristyle portico. The sub-division of the space into two rooms (the northernmost 2 · 55 × 3 · 20 m., the other 3 · 10 × 3 · 20 m.) suggests that it was a double *cubiculum*. Both rooms were paved in mosaic (*op. mus.* 23, p. 119) and plastered.

Room 21 (6 · 10 × 6 · 70 m.). Room 21 was the second largest room of the villa. Its size and its location in the middle of the south façade of the *domus* give it a particular dignity. Its exact orientation is not known, since the wall on the peristyle and the south terrace sides have been destroyed to a level below which door blocks would have appeared.

Room 22. A corridor. The peristyle and the south terrace were linked by a corridor (0 · 95 m. wide) paved in *opus signinum* (*op. sig.* 7, p. 124) traces of which were found along the west wall. The corridor bypassed the *cubicula* and residential rooms on either side, allow-ing communication between the peristyle and the south terrace portico in winter, when the roofed rooms would have been shut and heated.

Rooms 23a and 23b. A cubiculum (2 · 80 × 2 · 90 m.). A small *cubiculum*, paved in mosaic (*op. mus.* 24, p. 119), was entered from the peristyle across a threshold equipped with pivots for a door opening inwards. The room was plastered and had, in the northwest corner, a narrow space between the west wall of the peristyle and room 25. The space may have been used as a closet, storeroom or perhaps a *lavabo* of some kind, and it was separated from the *cubiculum* itself by a low wall 0 · 24 m. high.

Intervening between rooms 23a and 24, a narrow space between the walls may have served a similar function to the feature described above; its walls were too damaged to tell if a door or window had existed there at some time.

Room 24. A cubiculum (2 · 80 × 2 · 80 m.). The position of the entrance to this small room could not be determined. Its mosaic floor (*op. mus.* 25, p. 120) was damaged by the collapse of the Period II terrace fill into the inadequately capped well beneath it. Much of the blue painted plaster of this cubiculum, together with fragments of its floor, were found in the sondage made in the well (see above, p. 20).

Room 25 (7 · 90 × 7 · 50 m.). This room was by far the largest room in the villa, but one whose function and decoration are obscure. On the north, it communicated with the *tablinum* by means of a corridor (26); in the south it opened onto the portico of the south terrace. Its north door had a limestone threshold, but otherwise the doors of the room are destroyed. The room was paved in mosaic (*op. mus.* 26, p. 120) and was therefore roofed. Its very large size and squarish shape might suggest that it be interpreted as a winter dining room facing south, but its exact function is not obvious.

Room 26. A corridor. This narrow corridor (0 · 35 m. wide) linked the *tablinum* with room 25. It was plastered and painted red and paved in decorated *opus signinum* (*op. sig.* 8, p. 124). The limestone threshold at its south end was equipped with door pivots.

The south terrace. A terrace, with a portico, ran the full length of the south façade of the villa along rooms 18–25 and 37. The portico (4 · 25 m. wide) was generously proportioned and possibly had brick, masonry or wooden columns, founded on a shallow wall (1 · 10 m. wide), traces of which were found. There were doubtless doors and windows opening on to the portico from the *cubicula* and residential rooms behind, and access to the peristyle was provided through a corridor (22).

A large open terrace (4 · 60 m. wide), spacious enough to have been planted with trees and shrubs, overlooked the plain; there was probably a stone or wood parapet on top of the south terrace wall itself. We imagine that, from below, the view of the villa with its terrace and portico would have had a 'hanging garden' aspect, giving much the same effect as the ruins have at present. The terrace commands a majestic view of the plain and, on most days, the sea, providing a vantage point for the type of scenes associated with the sceno-graphic villas of Stabiae and elsewhere.[6]

C. *The domus vetus.*

The size, lavish decoration and dignified spaces of the *domus nova* indicate a desire for rich display. The owner was evidently anxious to have a modern and tasteful environment for himself and his family, but his ostentation was tempered by a thrifty, and perhaps pious, desire to preserve, insofar as possible, the old dwelling and some of its floors. The Periods I and IA *domus* was adapted to serve as the rear quarters of the house, less elaborate, perhaps, but pleasant and useful nonetheless, and having an orientation westward to the hills and mountains which was more 'Arcadian' and quieter than the dramatic view from

[6] As has been pointed out by Johannowsky, 1970–71, 491–3, and by Percival, 1976, 57–8, the San Rocco villa is designed with an emphasis on the peristyle as the centralising focus rather than an *atrium*. See n. 8, p.58 for the 'scenographic' effects of the exterior.

the south terrace. The reasons for preserving some of the old *domus* may have been that it was an ancestral home made worthy of regard by long use; reasons of economy and expedience may also have entered in. Whatever the reason, some thought and money were spent to adapt the spaces and floors to the new plan.

The Periods I and IA villa, here called the *domus vetus*, was adapted in three ways: by subdividing existing areas with new walls (rooms 27, 28, 32, 33 and 35); by remodelling or enlarging old rooms (numbers 29, 30, 31b, 35 and 36), and by adding new rooms to complete the plan of the existing ones (rooms 37, 38, 39 and the west portico and west terrace).

The rooms of the *domus vetus* can be divided into three groups:

1. *Rooms 27–30.*

This is the group of rooms to the north of the Period IA corridor (31a), comprising two *cubicula* (27 and 28), a large residential room (29) and a staircase or ladder room (30) providing access to the eaves.

2. *Rooms 32–37.*

To the south of the corridor (31a) there were two suites of small rooms (32–34 and 35–37), presumably *cubicula*.

3. *The west portico and west terrace.*

Two porticos were added (38 and 39) together with the west terrace.

1. *Rooms 27–30.* (Fig. 7)

Rooms 27, 28 and 29 of the *domus vetus*, and room 8 of the *domus nova*, formed a unified intercommunicating suite of two *cubicula* with an antechamber adjacent to a large residential room (see above, p. 46). All four rooms were in the area of rooms A/A1 and C/C1 of the Periods I and IA *domus*.

Room 27. A *cubiculum* (2 · 65 × 3 · 50 m.). This narrow room had a narrow door (0 · 65 m. wide) through to room 8. Its north and west wall were of the original Period I construction, its east and south walls of Period II, carefully bonded into the earlier walls. Remains of plaster were visible on the north wall down to the level of the Period II floor of room 8, but both the Period II and Periods I and IA floors were taken out when the room was converted into the furnace room of the Period IIA bath house. The south wall was dismantled to its foundations at that time.

Room 28. A *cubiculum* (4 · 40 × 3 · 50 m.). This bedroom was larger than room 27 and had a larger door. Its west wall was of Period I construction, but its north, east and south walls were new. Excavation in the south part of the room revealed the foundations of the north wall of room A of the Period I *domus*, dismantled to its base and replaced by a thin wall (0 · 40 m. wide) separating it from room 29. As in room 27, the extensive remodelling in Period IIA, for the cold plunge bath, and the subsequent use of the room as a storeroom, obliterated its Period II decoration and pavement. Its door into room 8 was blocked at that time.

Room 29. This room is room A1 of the Period IA *domus*, preserved almost intact but with some remodelling. The vicissitudes of the room in Periods I and IA have been described above (see p. 27). In Period II, the north wall of room A1 was dismantled, care being taken to preserve the floor insofar as was possible (*op. mus.* 27, p. 120). In place of the dismantled wall, a thin wall founded at a higher level was built, bonded into the Period I west wall and brought across into room 8 at its east side. This wall was provided with a niche (0 · 20 m. deep and 1 · 60 m. wide) placed slightly off the axis of the room. The niche may have served as the architectural respond for a statue or a piece of furniture, though no bases were found; it is more likely to have enclosed a cupboard or shelves of some kind. The niche was, in any case, a distinctive part of the desired design of the Period II room.

The door in the northeast corner of the old room A1 was blocked, and the east wall extended to the east side of the door in the old north wall, making the passage narrower than before. The floor in the north part of the room was carefully repaired (*op. mus.* 27, p. 120) and since the Period I floor level was lower than that of Period II by 0 · 30 m., the mosaic floor in the passage between rooms 8 and 29 was ramped (*op. mus.* 19, p. 114). Otherwise, the west, south and most of the east walls of room A1 were left unchanged except for replastering. A new limestone threshold block was dropped into the door in the south wall, and the floor repaired around it. There may have been windows in the east wall overlooking the new portico (39).

Room 30 (2 · 50 × 1 · 30 m.). A door with a limestone threshold, fitted with pivots for a door opening outward, provided access to this narrow room. Traces of a beaten earth floor were found at the level of the Period II floors, and the room had a masonry support or console at its north end. The arrangement of the room, and the fact that it was not lighted, suggest that it was a shaft between the walls of the *domus vetus* and *domus nova* in which a steep wooden staircase or ladder could have been built to provide access to the eaves between the rafters and ceilings of the *tablinum* and *triclinium*. It is unlikely that there was a full second storey anywhere in the villa, since a more adequate staircase would probably have been provided, but the obvious advantage of being able to reach the eaves for repairs, cleaning and firefighting would have been achieved by a ladder room of the kind suggested.

Rooms 31a and 31b. A corridor (1 · 20 × 12 · 95 m.). The corridor of the Period IA *domus* (D2) was maintained in Period II; its line determined the axis of the *domus nova*. It served to link the *tablinum* with the *domus vetus* and the rear entrance to the house. The old corridor was shortened by 1 · 40 m. on its east end by dismantling the walls to accommodate the new *tablinum*, and doors into rooms 30, 32 and 35 were added. The new room (31a) was replastered and repaved in mosaic (*op. mus.* 28, p. 121). As elsewhere in the villa the Period IA floor was removed and the new floor ramped at an angle of *c.*6° to coordinate the Period II level with the level of the reused floor of room 29. On the west, a limestone threshold crossed the corridor and led to its extension (31b), which ran between the west portico (39) and the west terrace and on to the rear entrance. The walls and floors in this area of the corridor were damaged and only the lines of the walls could be determined. A high stepped threshold of limestone, with door pivots, provided access to the west portico (39).

2. Rooms 32–37

Two sets of *cubicula* (33–34 and 36–37) brought up to twelve the number of possible bedrooms in both the *domus vetus* and the *domus nova*. Their embellishment varied widely, and it is by no means certain that 'full occupancy' of the *cubicula* indicates the size of the family in residence. Some may have been used for favoured household servants, some for guests, and so on.

Rooms 32–34. A corridor and cubicula. A door was cut through the portion of the Period IA corridor wall where it met the west wall of the *tablinum:* the sides of the door were fitted with limestone blocks. The walls of rooms E1, E2 and F1 were demolished, and new walls were built to make the corridor (1 · 35 × 4 · 45 m.) which was plastered and paved in *opus signinum* painted red and strewn irregularly with white tesserae (*op. sig.* 9, p. 124). At its south end a door with a limestone threshold led to a *cubiculum* (room 33: 1 · 80 × 2 · 30 m.) also paved in *opus signinum* (*op. sig.* 10, p. 125). A yet smaller room, just big enough for a bed (3 · 30 × 1 · 10 m.) adjoined it (34). The walls of room 33 are those of room D3 of

Period IA, with the pavement dug and replaced, and the roof presumably rebuilt, but with the doors remaining in the same position. The walls of room 34 are entirely of Period II construction. It is not known how these rooms would have been lighted.

Room 35 (4 · 95 × 6 · 50 m.). The large size of this L-shaped room indicates that it was a residential room of some kind, with perhaps an alcove for a bed. It is room D1 of the Period IA *domus,* shortened on its east side and extended on the west. Its north and south walls are of Periods I and IA construction, with the exception of the door blockings, which were put in to adapt the room to the Period II design. The Period IA floor of this room (*op. mus.* 3. p. 90) was covered with a fill supporting a mosaic floor (*op. mus.* 29, p. 121), traces of which were found. The east wall was carefully bonded into the Periods I and IA construction in the northeast and southeast corners of the room, but the old west wall was demolished to floor level and the room was extended westwards by 1 · 75 m. into the west terrace. In the southeast corner of the room, a wall end (extending 1 · 10 m.) concealed a *lavabo* or closet of some kind. Since the walls were poorly preserved, it is not known how room 35 was entered: there may have been a door in the corridor (32) on the east side.

Room 36 (2 · 30 × 5 · 35 m.). Room D4 of the Period IA *domus* was evidently usable or had to be preserved for some reason, so it and its floor (*op. mus.* 4, p. 91) were kept almost intact. The door in the north wall was blocked, and a new door was cut through the south wall and, as in room D1/35, an extension (1 · 75 m. wide) was built on to the west terrace. The extension necessitated both the dismantlement of the old Period I west terrace wall, and the completion of the room by adding an inferior imitation (*op. sig.* 11, p. 125) to the earlier fine floor (*op. mus.* 4, p. 91). The room was replastered and the roof was probably rebuilt, but otherwise it retained its Period IA appearance.

Room 37. A cubiculum (?6 · 10 × 3 · 55 m.). The *cubiculum* reused from Period IA communicated with this new room set in the southwest corner of the villa. The east and west walls of the room were bonded carefully into the Period IA north wall, but otherwise the room was entirely of Period II construction. The level of the floor, which itself was completely destroyed, was that of Period II, so that two steps of tufa blocks leading down to the door were needed, a rather clumsy arrangement made necessary because the floor in room 36 was reused.

3. *The west portico and the west terrace.*

The *domus vetus* was equipped in Period II with porticos and a terrace. One of the porticos (38) was a shed in the northwest corner of the villa and was connected with the nearby cisterns. The west portico (39) was, with the west terrace, part of the residential area of the villa.

Room 38. A portico or shed (2 · 90 × 5 · 10 m.). The west end of the cisterns faced an open area flanked, on the south, by a service or storage room which was completely separate from the rest of the villa. The north wall of this room had a masonry pier flanked by wall ends. The walls were not plastered and the remains of a beaten earth floor were found in the northwest corner.

Room 39. The west portico (5 · 00 × 10 · 70 m.). (Pl. XV). The west portico flanked rooms 28 and 29, was open to the west and was entered through a door, with a limestone sill, from the corridor (31b). Two piers remained on which pillars had stood. Part of one still lay in the area; it was of quarter-round bricks covered with fluted stucco. In the north-west corner of the portico, a small paved area had been walled off. It had probably housed a *lavabo,* for it was connected with the exterior of the terrace retaining wall by a substantial drain which penetrated that wall.

IV. *The eastern terrace and the villa rustica.* (Pl. XVI *a*).

The eastern terrace was built on two levels, the upper level, that of the *villa rustica* proper, with two courtyards surrounded by various rooms arranged in groups for various purposes; and the lower level, on the south side, a garden or *hortus*. The terrace walls, the fill and the room walls are entirely of Period II construction, their fabric and the building techniques being similar to those in the *domus nova*.

The main features of the east terrace are:

A. The terrace retaining walls and their fill supporting the platform on which the *villa rustica* was built.

B. The *villa rustica*.

C. The *hortus*.

A. *The terrace retaining walls and their fill supporting the platform on which the villa rustica was built.*

The line of the *opus incertum* of the terrace walls could be followed everywhere except along the south, where it was deeply buried under modern fill. As in the west terrace, the exterior walls were $0 \cdot 80$ m. thick, and the system of progressive filling as construction proceeded was observed also in section. The north terrace wall was built against the fill south of the east cisterns (see above, p. 40): its north side was trenched, but its south side was 'planked' in a fashion similar to that of the north retaining wall in the western terrace. The east wall was visible for almost its entire length: it was founded directly on the limestone of the hillside and followed the natural slope. The southeast corner of the *hortus* was 'bevelled': the line of its diagonal wall was cleaned almost to its connection with the south wall. The western terrace bounded the road and ran along the west side of the *hortus* and the *villa rustica;* in the area of courtyard 1 it was interrupted, but it reappears in the area of the back entrance.

B. *The villa rustica.* (Fig. 7)

The *villa rustica*, in Period II, was large and roomy, covering a total area of *c.* $8 \cdot 50$ m.[2] with suites of rooms facing on to two courtyards. There were residential and utilitarian areas around courtyard 1 (40–47) with a 'Commons' (48) separating it from courtyard 2. At the north end of the 'Commons', there were three rooms (49–52) which were probably residential in character, since they were furnished with a latrine. Courtyard 2 was partially paved and was surrounded with groups of rooms (53–54, 58–60) intended probably for agricultural uses and care of animals.

Erosion and levelling in the *hortus*, and the south part of the *villa rustica*, have destroyed the features of the rooms down to the foundations of their walls, with the result that their precise function cannot be determined. For example, the oil separation vats added in Period IIA, in rooms 57 and 58, are well preserved only because they were below the level of the Period II floors. In the north part of the *villa rustica* the rooms were well-preserved but were remodelled considerably in Period IIA.

The *villa rustica* is described as follows:

1. Courtyard 1 and the rooms to the north (40–43) and south (44–47).
2. The 'Commons' (48) and the rooms to the north (49–52).
3. Courtyard 2 and the rooms to the north (53–54) and south (55–60).

1. *Courtyard 1 and the rooms to the north (40–43) and south (44–47).*

Courtyard 1 (11 · 10 × 12 · 80 m.) was a large area probably open to the road along its west side and flanked by a portico on the south. Soundings revealed traces of a beaten earth floor, but no structures were found. On the north, four large rooms served as residential rooms: they were paved with *bipedales* tiles set in earth, most of which had been removed but whose impressions could be seen on excavation. The north wall of the courtyard (the south wall of rooms 40 and 42) was almost entirely robbed.

Room 40 (5 · 90 × 3 · 50 m. with an arm 2 · 75 × 2 · 60 m.). This room was L-shaped and communicated with the courtyard through a door in the south wall, now lost, and with the road through a limestone-quoined door (0 · 90 m. wide) in the west wall. The room may have served as a lodge to supervise the back entrance of the villa. In the north wall, a similarly quoined door (1 · 10 m. wide) may have led to an open area like that north of room 38 in the *domus vetus*. In the east wall of the L, a door (1 · 10 m. wide) gave access to room 41. The traces of a beaten earth floor carried impressions of *bipedales* tiles such as were noted in room 43.

Room 41 (2 · 75 × 2 · 90 m.). This small room was plastered and would have been suitable for use as a *cubiculum* or as a store-room.

Room 42 (2 · 50 × 5 · 50 m.). The size and position of this room indicate that it was a residential room of some kind. The door entering from the courtyard had a limestone threshold, now robbed.

Room 43 (5 · 70 × 2 · 90 m.). This large room was equipped with a limestone threshold at the door and with a tiled floor. The threshold block, and most of the *bipedales* tiles were missing, but four *bipedales* and some fragments were found *in situ* in the middle of the room.

These four rooms (40–43) are clearly defined as a unit north of the courtyard and suggest an overseer's suite with a south exposure for year-round living. The space provided (*c*. 66 m.^{2}), would be ample for an overseer with a small family, and there would have been plenty of room for such activities as spinning and weaving, perhaps the duty of the overseer's wife, who may have acted also as the *concierge* of the back entrance.

Room 44. A portico (2 · 70 × 12 · 75 m.). On the south side of courtyard 1 there were traces of a rubble stylobate for a portico, very shallowly founded, extending all along the south wall: this portico, probably of wood, provided an especially cool refuge since it faced north. Traces of a beaten earth floor, at the same level as that of the courtyard, were visible, and the tufa footings of a round quern with a kneeling platform were found on the west side.

Rooms 45 and 46 (2 · 25 × 9 · 45 m. and 2 · 25 × 2 · 50 m., respectively). Behind the portico stood a long narrow room (45) with, at its west end, a small area (46) separated from the larger room by a low narrow wall (0 · 60 m. high). The small area enclosed a well, the top of which was found, together with a water channel (0 · 21 m. wide and 0 · 32 m. deep) of loosely mortared tufa blocks draining northwards. The channel ran from the edge of the well through the north wall of room 46 and across the portico into courtyard 1. The well head itself (0 · 65 m. in diameter) was excavated along its limestone rubble and mortar edge but could not be investigated to a depth greater than 0 · 30 m.

Room 47 (3 · 75 × 14 · 50 m.). This oddly shaped room overlooked the *hortus*. Its walls were very badly damaged but the wall lines could be defined: there were five roughly constructed piers (0 · 55 × 0 · 95 m.), between wall-ends, extending from the west and east walls, dividing the room into two narrow but interconnecting spaces (each 1 · 60 m. wide).

At first, this shape suggested that the room was a cistern of the same type as those to the north of the *domus* and *villa rustica*, and it has been published as such. However, further investigation by this author indicated that the floor of the room was of beaten earth at the same level as that of courtyard 1, and that nowhere was there the characteristic multi-layered plaster associated with the water-proofing of cisterns.[7] Furthermore, the walls are the same width as those of the residential rooms, and the piers were so roughly built as to suggest that they did not rise to any great height. The shape of the room suggests that it was a stable or loft building of some kind. Animals could have been accommodated in stalls entered between the piers, and some mucking-out arrangement in the south wall might have existed to provide fertilizers for the *hortus*. A loft, either for storage or sleeping, may have been built over one or other sides of the piers or, alternatively, the piers may have supported water-troughs and grain bins.

2. *The 'Commons' (48) and the rooms to the north (49–51).*
Room 48. The 'Commons' (16 · 75 × 4 · 00 m.). Room 48 was the largest room in the *villa rustica*. It separated the two courtyards and opened on to rooms on the north and south. Its position, central to the *villa rustica*, defines it as some kind of all-purpose room in which the diverse activities of the inhabitants might have taken place: sleeping, working, gathering for meals and festivities and so on. Its long narrow shape suggests that it had a pitched roof running north to south. Doors to courtyards 1 and 2 were placed in the east and west walls, and on the south a narrow door (0 · 60 m. wide) led out into room 60. At the north end, a door (1 · 90 m. wide) led to rooms 49–52. In the northwest corner of the room, the remains of some *bipedales* tiles, set in beaten earth, indicated that it was at least partially paved.
Rooms 49–52. The plan of the four interconnecting rooms between the north terrace wall and the 'Commons' (48) suggests that of a small self-contained residential suite with a largish living room (49), two *cubicula* (50 and 51) and a latrine (52). The decoration and embellishment of these rooms in Period II could not be determined because they were subsequently changed in Period IIA for use as a *figlina*.
Room 49 (5 · 70 × 4 · 60 m.). Room 49 was a large squarish space entered through a door from the 'Commons'. In the northwest corner a wall-end subdivided the space for a long narrow *cubiculum* or closet (50). In Period II, room 49 was doubtless plastered and roofed, and the floor was of beaten earth mixed with limestone pebbles and mortar.
Rooms 50, 51 and 52 (3 · 40 × 1 · 40 m.; 3 · 20 × 1 · 70 m.; 2 · 10 × 1 · 70 m. respectively). These three small rooms were paved in *opus spicatum* (*op. spic.* 3, 4 and 5, pp. 125–6) set in mud sprinkled with a little mortar. Rooms 50 and 51 were connected through a door with a limestone threshold. In the southeast corner of room 52, (Pl. XVI *b–c*) there was probably an aperture in the floor to house a latrine which drained into a sewer crossing courtyard 2 (see below, p. 56). The Period II features of the latrine were removed when the room became part of the *figlina* in Period IIA.

3. *Courtyard 2 and the rooms to the north and south.*
Courtyard 2 (12 · 25 × 13 · 20 m.) was a little smaller than courtyard 1 and was not equipped with a portico on the south side. On the north it was bounded by two large rooms (53 and 54), on the west by the 'Commons' (48), and on the east by the eastern terrace wall

[7.] Room 47 is incorrectly identified as a cistern in the published plans: Boëthius and Ward-Perkins, 1970, fig. 124 and Percival, 1976, fig. 10.

of the villa. Its east and south sides were at least partially paved with a smooth terrazzo surface of limestone pebbles set in mortar (*c.* 0 · 06 m. thick). This floor covered an earlier floor of lozenge-shaped bricks (0 · 12 long × 0 · 08 wide × 0 · 04 m. thick) set in mud and mortar, patches of which were found. In the southeast corner, near the intersection of the walls, there was a round raised *area* for threshing grain bounded by tiles up-ended in the floor, similar to the *area* found in the Period I *villa rustica* (Pl. XVII). The floor extended almost to the middle of the courtyard and was also found along the south wall.

A sewer crossed the courtyard. It originated at the aperture in the south wall of room 52 and was cut into the limestone of the hillside. It was covered with limestone rubble set in mortar and was evidently arched in some way. The sewer ran through the east wall at a slight angle.

Near the intersection of the channel and the east wall, on the axis of the courtyard and placed symmetrically on the wall, a shallow rounded niche (1 · 15 wide and 0 · 45 m. deep) cut into the wall framed a limestone base (0 · 49 × 0 · 39 × 0 · 82 m. high). The base may have served as a domestic altar or as the support for a small statue of a divinity such as might be worshipped appropriately in a setting of this kind.

Rooms 53 and 54 (5 · 70 × 3 · 75 m. and 5 · 70 × 4 · 05 m. respectively). These two large rooms bounded courtyard 2 on the north. There was probably a door, narrower than the preserved opening, in the middle of the north wall of the courtyard leading to room 53; in the east wall of the room a door (1 · 25 m. wide) led into room 54. Both rooms were probably paved at the level of the courtyard, but in the interest of preserving the Period IIA *oletum*, which later occupied the area, no attempt was made to uncover the original Period II floors. The use of these two rooms in Period II is not known.

The rooms to the south of courtyard 2 were destroyed to a level below that of their original Period II door and floors, in part by modern light ploughing in the area, in part by the installation, in Period IIA, of two oil separation vats in rooms 57 and 58.

Rooms 55 and 56 (3 · 90 × 3 · 75 m.). These rooms were probably a single large room with a partition wall in the northeast corner. The exterior walls are all well built and deeply founded, whilst the west wall of room 56 was shallowly founded and was built with loose sandy mortar.

Rooms 57, 58 and 59 (3 · 90 × 1 · 60 m.; 3 · 90 × 3 · 75 m.; 3 · 90 × 2 · 60 m. respectively). These rooms were originally separate rooms and their use is unknown. The Period II floors are all destroyed. Rooms 57 and 58 were later converted into oil separation vats, at which time the floors were dug out and the walls lined with an extra coat of *opus reticulatum.*

Room 60 (4 · 20 × 14 · 85 m.). This large rectangular room abutted room 47 on the west and separated rooms 55–59 from the *hortus,* which it overlooked. It may have been an unroofed terrace area or a pen for animals, but its features were too destroyed to define its use with any certainty.

C. *The hortus*

The *hortus* or garden (20 · 80 × 30 · 80 m.) occupied the entire lower southern half of the *villa rustica* terrace. The level of the topsoil was about 0 · 60 m. below the level of the *villa rustica* floors. The line of its walls could be followed along the north, east and west sides, where they were *c.* 0 · 60 to 1 · 00 m. thick. The line of the south wall was too deeply buried to be investigated fully, but it probably ran along the line of the south terrace wall of the *domus.* Entrance to the *hortus* was provided through the gate described above (p. 37). In the southwest corner there was a small room, probably a porter's lodge, also described above (p. 37). The southeast corner of the terrace was 'bevelled' and a section of the angled wall connecting the east wall to the line of the south wall was found. Sondages determined that no structures existed over the whole area, but traces of planting were not preserved.

PERIOD II. SUMMARY AND CONCLUSIONS

The San Rocco villa in Period II took on an architectural and decorative lavishness which was combined with a certain conservatism, expressed in the careful retention of certain original features. The expansion of the residential quarters was coordinated with an expansion of the agricultural facitilies. The distinction between the *domus* and the *villa rustica*, which was already present in the Period I villa, was maintained, but on a much larger scale. A well graded and surfaced road connecting the villa with the plain, and with the other villas on the hill, divided the *domus* from the *villa rustica*, both of which were built on vastly extended terraces and were made viable by new cisterns. The method of construction used was that of *opus caementicium* faced with *opus incertum* in the interior walls and foundations, and *opus incertum* for the exposed surface of the south terrace wall.

In the *domus* on the west terrace, an axially planned villa converging on a central peristyle was built with, however, outward-looking 'scenographic' terraces with porticos on the south and west; there were mosaic floors in almost every room. The *domus nova*, with its triple-doored T-shaped *vestibulum*, its peristyle, *tablinum*, *triclinium* and *exedra* was an elaborate *enveloppe* for the Periods I and IA *domus vetus*, of which certain rooms were reused after some rearrangement and redecoration.

In the *villa rustica* on the east terrace, there were two large courtyards separated by a 'Commons' and surrounded by suites of rooms suitable for habitation by a *familia*. The *villa rustica* overlooked a large *hortus* terraced at a lower level. Apart from a threshing floor, the exact nature of the agricultural activities which took place in the *villa rustica* could not be determined (see n.4 p. 21).

The Period II villa is a *villa suburbana* comprising a *domus* and a *villa rustica*. All parts of the structure were designed to blend and stand out against the landscape silhouettes of the San Rocco hill. On the one hand, the road leading up the hill provided a convenient access to a building designed to be both inviting and impressive; on the other hand, the *basis* or terrace of the *domus* provided a stage for an impressive display of man-made *amoenitas*. Approached from below, the *domus* on the left would have stood forward prominently, while the *hortus* and *villa rustica* on the right would have shelved backwards into the hillside. For the development of impressive terraced villas in the Late Republic, especially in the immediately pre-Augustan period, there are many examples, both near Rome and especially on the Bay of Naples. The examples range from the very large and grand villas, which that of San Rocco emulated, to smaller ones of which this is one of many. Near Rome, the terraced villa 'dei Centroni', of Late Republican date and with terraces of very similar *opus incertum*, is a well known example, but there are other Late Republican ones at Grottarossa, Praeneste and Tibur. Near Sorrento, the villa at Minori, though larger than San Rocco, must have had a similar aspect.

The internal design of the *domus* corresponds to the development of other *villae suburbanae;* the house is inward-looking as well as outward-looking, centred on the peristyle but facing views framed by porticos. For the development of the house plan centred on a peristyle, the Villa di Diomede at Pompeii is the most familiar example, and villas at

Grottarossa, near Cora and at Sorrento are analogous; all of these are Late Republican or Augustan. Finally, the conception, intrinsic to the Period II design, of creating an axially planned space (*vestibulum*-peristyle-*tablinum*) ending in the long corridor leading to the *domus vetus* (or the reused rooms of the Periods I and IA house) is an interesting example of an architectural *enveloppe* for which there is a later analogy in the villa of Hadrian at Tibur.

The plan of the *villa rustica,* an H-shaped structure of rooms with two courtyards, has a somewhat similar analogy in the plan of the later villa at Castel Giubileo. Like the disposition of the rooms in the *domus,* the rooms in the *villa rustica* were grouped in suites: two groups north of the courtyard and 'Commons', working rooms to the south of them.

The method of construction, in *opus incertum,* has Late Republican and even Augustan analogies at Rome and elsewhere. For the foundation walls with deep offsets, the terrace wall of the early Augustan villa on Capri may be cited as a parallel. On terrace IV of the sanctuary at Loreto in Teanum Sidicinum, *opus incertum* with Late Republican or early Augustan *opus reticulatum* was used, but the dates of *opus incertum* are not definitive in themselves. A better basis for dating is the style of the mosaics, which in Period II have the crisp patterning and execution, sharp colour contrasts with almost no tonal effects, distinctly 'architectural' look and geometric motives associated with pavement designs of the years just before Augustus (see mosaic catalogue, pp. 92–127). The finds in level 3 of Fig. 4 confirm the dating of the Period II villa to these years, *c.* 30 B.C. (see below, pp. 256–8).[8]

[8.] For the development of the *basis* villa, see Swoboda, 1924, *passim,* and for their external look, Rostovtzeff, 1911, 1 ff. and *passim.* Other terraced villas which provide a context for the exterior aspect of San Rocco in Period II are: Cozza, 1952, 257–83 ('Centroni Grotte'); Stefani, 1944–45, 52–72 (a Late Republican villa near Grottarossa); Brandizzi Vitucci, 1965, 116, no. 37 and 181, no. 200; Muzzioli, 1970, 43–8, fig. 37, no. 15 (a villa on the slopes of Colle Cappalle); Giuliani, 1970, 315–36, no. 209 (the villa of Quintilio Varo); and Schiavo, 1939, 129–33 (the villa of Minori).

For the plan of the *domus,* see Maiuri and Pane, 1947, *passim,* on the House of Loreio Tiburtino and the Villa di Diomede at Pompeii. For other villas centred around a peristyle, see Stefani, 1944–45, 52–72; Brandizzi Vitucci, 1968, 116, no. 37 and 181, no. 15; and Boëthius and Ward-Perkins, 1970, 160.

The Republican villa at Tibur is published by Lugli, 1927, and 1965. The *villa rustica,* perhaps part of an early Imperial estate, at Castel Giubileo, has an H-shaped plan like the *villa rustica* at San Rocco, cf. Quilici, 1976, 263–79 and figs. 11 and 12.

For the terrace walls with offsets, see Maiuri, 1938, 127 and pl. XI, 1, on the Augustan villa of 'Palazzo a Mare' at Capri; the Teanum walls are published in Johannowsky, 1963, 142; but see also Lugli, 1957, 478–80 and Blake, 1947, 250–1.

For the associated finds of level 3, see pp.256–8.

Chapter VI. The Period IIA Villa

(Pls. XVIII–XXIII and Figs. 8–13)

The Period II *domus* and *villa rustica* at San Rocco were used, without substantial modification, for 80 or more years. After *c.* A.D. 50, however, three new features—a bath-house (*balineum*) in the *domus* and, in the *villa rustica*, tile kilns (a *figlina*) and an olive oil processing unit (an *oletum*)—were added, probably all at once in a single building campaign. These new constructions are characterised by an extensive use of tufa *opus reticulatum* and by using brick in the walls and floors (see below, p. 61). While brick had been used in Period II in floors (*op. spic.* 1 and 2, p. 125) none had been used in the construction of walls; the Period IIA brick floor (*op. spic.* 6, p. 128) is of a different style.

The contemporaneous construction of the three new features is indicated by the similarity in their technique. The walls of the bath-house—both the upstanding walls dividing rooms and the low walls surrounding the plunge-baths and the footings for the *testudo*— are very similar to the brick walls of the basins in the *oletum* and parts of the revetment walls and stairs in the oil separating vats. Moreover, the use of brick in the *figlina*—even though parts of the kiln may have been rebuilt from time to time—indicates a coeval date with the bath-house and *oletum*. In both the bath-house walls and the oil separating vats there is an occasional use of tufa *opus reticulatum* very similar in treatment.[1]

The Period IIA features are described separately below because their implications for the two parts of the villa are different.

The Period IIA features are:
I.   The *balineum* or bath-house in the *domus*.
II. The *figlina* or tile factory in the *villa rustica*.
III. The *oletum* or oil-factory in the *villa rustica*.

I. *The balineum or bath-house in the domus.* (Pls. XVIII–XIX and Fig. 8)
The construction of the bath-house, adding a note of luxury, if not of architectural distinction, to the *domus* was effected by taking over the storage room (9) off the *culina*, thus reducing the kitchen area by about a third, and by converting the suite of rooms (8, 27 and 28)—the antechamber with *cubicula*—in the northeast corner of the villa (see above, p. 50). The conversion of these rooms and the construction techniques used are curious in that, like the *fornax* and *oletum* in the *villa rustica*, the 'technical' aspects—the *suspensurae* of the hypocaust, the thermal jacketing of the walls and so on—are excellently and carefully done. In contrast, the decorative aspects and the 'finish'— the truncation of the mosaic in room 8, the floor treatment in the *sudatorium* and *caldarium* and so on—are quite ugly and are unimaginatively, if carefully, done, without much sense of architectural dignity. It could be suggested that, at the same time that the contracts were established for the *figlina* and the *oletum*, the same builder was asked to do the bath-house. His *forte* was evidently 'technical' building of a utilitarian sort: when it came to decoration and 'finish' he did the best he could.

The plan of the bath-house—really a small complicated sauna—is clear. There were service areas, namely a storage yard behind the cold plunge-bath in room 28, a *praefurnium* or furnace room in room 27 and a service corridor, perhaps used as a woodshed

---

[1.] See n. 3, p. 61 for analogies to the Period IIA construction.

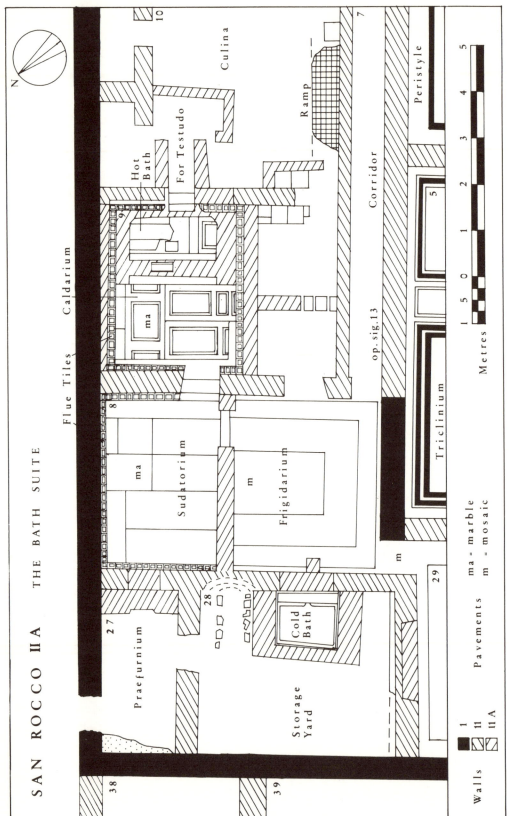

Fig. 8. Plan of the Period IIA bath wing

for the fuel used under the *testudo* in room 10. The bath-house or *balineum* itself was approached from the peristyle along the corridor (7) leading to room 8, or through the door between rooms 8 and 29. The south part of room 8, together with the plunge-bath opening off its east wall, was the *frigidarium*, an unheated cold room. The north part of room 8, its floor supported on *suspensurae* and its walls flued, was a hot dry room, designated a *sudatio* (*sudatorium*) or *Laconicum* (?) by Vitruvius (v 10). The north part of room 9 was a *caldarium*, also with a hypocaust and equipped with a bath supplied with hot water. The group of rooms—*frigidarium* with cold plunge-bath, *sudatorium* and *caldarium* with bath—were intended to be used *en suite*, and are so described.

Construction of the bath-house necessitated dismantling the Period II roofs of rooms 7, 8, 9, 27 and 28 and possibly the upper part of their walls. How the rooms were re-roofed is difficult to say. In the service areas (storage yards and *praefurnium*) in rooms 27 and 28, shed roofs or other light coverings might have been used, the *praefurnium* itself being uncovered. The south part of room 9 may also have been open or lightly roofed. The *frigidarium* and the plunge-bath may have had separate flat or pitched roofs. For the *sudatorium* and the *caldarium*, Vitruvius (v 10) assumes that they would have been domed, but this was probably not the case here, since the south wall of the *caldarium* is unusually narrow, only $0 \cdot 25$ m. wide, not enough to support a dome or vault over the room. Alternatively, two separate barrel vaults, their haunches running north to south, could have covered the two rooms, the flues emerging from the base of the vaults on four sides. Such a structure would not have have been difficult to build, and it has been so reconstructed (Fig. 12), though a flat roof covered with *opus signinum* could also have been used.[2]

The characteristic building technique of Period IIA is *opus reticulatum* and brick. The *opus reticulatum* walls are, except where noted, all the same: the tufa blocks were $c. 0 \cdot 10 \times 0 \cdot 10$ m. and about $0 \cdot 12$ m. deep, with pointed ends set in thick sandy mortar. The *opus reticulatum* was used in conjunction with brick, laid in regular courses with sandy mortar from $0 \cdot 02$ to $0 \cdot 03$ m. thick between them. The bricks varied in size: many were broken, some were *tegulae*, but most often they were a characteristic triangular brick, moulded and

[2] For bath-houses in villas, see Carrington, 1931; Drerup, 1959, 157–67; and especially Koethe, 1940, 43 ff. and Staccioli, 1958, 273–8.

The incorporation of the bath-house into previously built rooms of the villa precludes its being associated with the 'types' of plan proposed in Staccioli, 1958, and Koethe, 1940. And because the plan of the *balineum* at San Rocco is due more to the use of existing rooms than to an independent design, it cannot be associated with the *villae maritimae* of the Sorrento coast.

However, the construction, during the first century A.D., of small luxurious bath-houses is well documented. Of the Pompeian examples, the best is that of the Villa di Diomede, see Maiuri and Pane, 1947, 350 ff. The *villae rusticae* published by Carrington, 1931; Day, 1932; and Crova, 1942; and also by Rostovtzeff, 1957, 551, n. 26, and most recently by Skydsgaard, 1961 and 1970, 92–105, had bath-houses in some of them; but for the best descriptions see the original publications by Della Corte, 1921, 415–67; 1922, 459–85; and 1923, 271–87. At Boscoreale, small and large villas had bath-houses like those at San Rocco, but these are much better preserved: see Pasqui, 1897, 446–63 (della Pisanella) and Paribeni, 1903, 64–7 (in Contrada Centopiedi). Further afield, one can cite the *villae rusticae* with bath-houses at Tricarico and Fondi as being of similar size to that at San Rocco; see Di Cicco, 1903, 350 and Lissi Caronna, 1971, 330–63.

A small bath was added to a villa on the Via Tiberina near Rome, see Felleti Maj, 1955, 212. A four-room bath-house, undated but similar in size to that of San Rocco, was found at Formia; cf. Spano, 1927, 434–43. These examples are usually additions, in the first century A.D. and usually after the middle of the century, to existing buildings. The remarks by Seneca, of this date, on the austerity of Scipio's life compared to the modern conveniences of luxurious bath-houses give a clue to the motivation for making these additions (*Epistulae*, 86, 10). Note also that the position of the *balineum* of San Rocco, beside the kitchen, is recommended by Vitruvius (vi, 2, 1).

For a parallel with the marble revetment re-used as a pavement in the *caldarium*, see the middle section above the dado in the plaster example published in Laidlaw, 1975, 42–3.

[3] The small size of the triangular bricks and their thickness have close analogies in Claudian and Neronian buildings in Rome and elsewhere, cf. Lugli, 1957, 591, pl. CLXI, 1 (*Domus Aurea*) and Blake, 1959, 65–70 and 81–3 (Acqua Claudia and others); but as Lugli, 1957, 521, points out, the dating of *opus reticulatum* with brick is difficult in Pompeii because its widespread use began only a few years before the city was destroyed. It can be noted, however, that for bath buildings and other waterproof structures, it became usual to build entirely of brick only in Flavian times; before then, some combination of brick and *opus reticulatum* was usual. See the comments in Jacopi, 1936, 21–50.

sometimes stamped, with a front edge 0 · 23 m. long, all *c.* 0 · 035 m. thick.[3]

The effect of the *balineum* construction on the *domus* was to reduce the number of *cubicula* by two, but adding a feature which would have greatly enhanced the *amoenitas* of living at San Rocco.

The main parts of the *balineum* of Period IIA in the *domus* are:

A. The service areas, comprising the storage yard, *praefurnium* and hypocaust, *testudo* and corridor or shed.

B. The *balineum,* comprising the *frigidarium* with plunge-bath, *sudatorium* and *caldarium* with bath.

A. *The service areas, comprising the storage yard, praefurnium and hypocaust, testudo and corridor or shed.*

The floor levels of the service areas around the bath-house and hypocaust were *c.* 0 · 60 m. lower than those of the Period II villa. The lower level was effected by removing the Period II floor fills of rooms 27 and 28 and the north part of room 8, and by shoring up the exposed fill with walls of brick. In many places the excavation of the floor fills exposed the natural limestone rock of the hillside, leaving an irregular rough surface, especially in room 28. At the same time, the Period II doors between room 8 and rooms 27 and 28 were blocked up with brick and a rough opening cut through the north terrace wall to provide a passage between the *praefurnium* and the open area to the west of the cisterns (see above, p. 52). The Period II door between rooms 27 and 28 was retained, but the threshold was taken out and the level lowered.

In room 8, the floor in the north part of the room was taken up and the fill removed to open up a space for the hypocaust. This involved truncating the beautiful mosaic floor (*op. mus.* 18, p. 113) in about half, retaining the south part to serve as the floor for the *frigidarium* but removing it entirely in the north part. The exposed fill was shored up with a brick wall, and a door was left in the north wall of the *frigidarium* at the northeast corner to provide access to the *sudatorium.* At the same time, a door in the east wall of the *frigidarium* was cut to open into the south part of room 9, and another door was cut into the east wall of the *sudatorium* to provide access to the *caldarium.*

In room 9 in Period IIA no excavation of the floor was necessary since the floor of the *culina* in Period II (rooms 9–11) was already at a lower level. However, the room was divided by a narrow wall, of tufa *opus reticulatum* with brick, running east to west. The south part of the room became a kind of shed or corridor linking room 10 to the *frigidarium;* the north part became a *caldarium* with a floor raised on a hypocaust.

The storage yard. The area of room 28, probably unroofed or lightly roofed, surrounded the new cold plunge-bath off the *frigidarium.* The walls of the bath projected into the space, and a drain, much destroyed, could be seen crossing the floor east to west from the middle of the west wall of the plunge-bath to the west wall of the room. At the west wall, the drain turned a 90° angle southwards, running along the west wall; it passed under the south wall through a roughly cut opening to connect with the Period I drain under the floor of room 39 (see above, pp. 17, 52). The area could have been used to store fuel for the *praefurnium* in room 27.

The praefurnium. The *praefurnium* in room 27 communicated with the storage yard and with the open area west of the cisterns (see above, p. 52) through a door crudely hacked into the north terrace wall. As in room 28, the floor fill was removed and an opening to the hypocaust cut through the natural limestone. The opening was roughly square (0 · 50 m. wide and *c.* 0 · 60 m. high): above it the Period II door between room 27 and room 8 was blocked with a brick wall on a footing of *opus caementicium*.

The hypocaust. The suspended floor or hypocaust of the *sudatorium* and *caldarium* was extremely well built, very nearly to the recipe of Vitruvius (v 10, 2–3). The limestone rock was evidently broken up and smoothed down, and *bipedales* tiles were laid down on it in sandy, light mortar. Quarter-round *suspensurae* of wedge-shaped bricks (0 · 03 m. thick with a radius of 0 · 11 m.) were placed in the corners, and half-round *suspensurae* (0 · 22 m. wide) lined the walls, four along each wall in both rooms. The free-standing round *suspensurae* (0 · 22 m. in diameter), 16 in each room, were nine courses high with a large square *abacus* of bricks on top. Mortar (0 · 03 m. thick) separated each course of wedge-shaped bricks. The *suspensurae* supported *bipedales* tiles which in turn supported the floor. The height of the hypocaust at the mouth of the *praefurnium* is 0 · 70 m., with the lower floor sloping upwards to give a height of *c.* 0 · 60 m. at the east end of the *caldarium*, in the manner prescribed by Vitruvius. Between the half-round *suspensurae* lining the walls, the ends of the flues of the thermal jacketing of the *sudatorium* and *caldarium* were exposed: they allowed heat to circulate not only horizontally under the floor but vertically through the walls as well. There was evidence of considerable burning on all surfaces of the hypocaust.

The testudo. In the *culina* (room 10), arrangements were made for a metal *testudo*, the seating for which was found. In the northwest corner of the room, a section of the Period II *opus spicatum* floor (*op. spic.* 1, p. 125) was taken out and edged with a limestone curb (0 · 20 m. wide); a beaten earth floor replaced the brick one. A similar curbing was put in in the southeast corner of the room in front of the door leading to the corridor or shed. The two parallel wall ends for the *testudo* were of triangular bricks very roughly built, 0 · 30 m. wide and extending out 0 · 65 m. from the west wall of room 10, 0 · 65 m. apart and standing at least 0 · 95 m. high. Between them a low fire could be built in a brazier to heat the water in a metal vessel: a pipe would have extended through the wall into the bath. The proximity of the cisterns and the tank on the upper terrace would have facilitated filling the *testudo* by siphon and regulating its level.

At the same time that the footings for the *testudo* and the limestone curbings were set into the floor, the entire east face of the west wall of room 10 was covered with tufa *opus reticulatum*. The tufa blocks (0 · 10 × 0 · 10 m., with triangular ends) were set in thick sandy mortar. At the edges of the doors, and next to the wall ends supporting the *testudo*, there were quoins of triangular bricks (0 · 23 m. wide) also set in a thick layer of sandy mortar.

The corridor or shed. The south part of room 9 was completely rebuilt. The north wall dividing the corridor or shed from the *caldarium* was a new wall of *opus reticulatum* in tufa (0 · 30 m. wide). The Period II south wall of room 9 was dismantled to its foundations and was replaced by a similar wall of *opus reticulatum*, mainly in tufa but with an occasional course of limestone blocks of the same dimensions as the tufa ones (0 · 10 × 10 m.). Both walls were roughly bonded into the existing *opus caementicium* west and east walls. In the east wall, the Period II door between rooms 9 and 10 was retained but was made narrower with quoins of triangular bricks (see above), whilst in the west wall a door providing access to the *frigidarium* was roughly hacked through. Since the level of room 9 had always been lower than that of room 8 by 0 · 60 m., a step would have been necessary to provide access to the bath-house from the *culina*. It is not known whether or not this shed or corridor was roofed. It could have been used to store fuel and other equipment for both the kitchen and the bath-house areas. At no time were its walls plastered or its floor anything but beaten earth.

B. *The balineum, comprising the frigidarium with plunge-bath, sudatorium and caldarium with bath.*

The frigidarium (3 · 15 × 3 · 72 m.) (Pl. XVIII*a*). The *frigidarium* was built into the south part of room 8. The mosaic floor (*op. mus.* 18, p. 113) was carefully preserved and reused where it was not dug out completely. Access to the *frigidarium* from the rest of the *domus* was through the door from room 29 in the south wall and the corridor (room 7) leading to the peristyle. The Period II door into room 28 was blocked with a low wall (0 · 60 m. high) finished with a rounded top in *opus signinum:* the wall allowed the bather to sit on it to swing his legs over and step into the plunge bath comfortably. The north wall of the *frigidarium* partitioning the Period II room was built of bricks — whole and broken square and triangular ones — set in the same sandy light tan mortar as that used in the hypocaust and the Period IIA *opus reticulatum* walls. The wall ends around the door were completely quoined in brick, and the threshold was covered with a slab of white marble, but otherwise the arrangement of the door — moveable panels or a hinged partition of some kind — is not known. In the east wall, a door was hacked through the Period II wall to communicate with the corridor or shed. The south wall, originally of *opus incertum* in Period II, was dismantled to floor level and was rebuilt in tufa *opus reticulatum* like that of the *caldarium:* part of the wall of the corridor (room 7) was also rebuilt in the same way, and the Period II floor was replaced with one of decorated *opus signinum* (*op. sig.* 13, p. 127).

There was a thorough replastering in several layers of fine plaster in room 8; along the north wall, the plaster hid the broken edge of the mosaic floor. The *frigidarium* may have been lighted by a transom window above the plunge-bath in the west wall, or by a window in the plunge-bath walls. For the roof of the *frigidarium*, see above, p. 61.

The plunge-bath walls (0 · 45 m. thick), (Pl. XVIII*b*) of unfaced *opus caementicium*, were roughly bonded into the Period II west wall of room 8. A step (0 · 22 m. wide) ran along the low wall separating the bath from the *frigidarium*: the bath itself was 0 · 80 m. deep and, comfortably filled, had a capacity of *c.* 1,475 litres. The walls and floor were lined with fine *opus signinum*, and a quarter-round moulding ran round the angles. A hole in the middle of the west wall ran through the moulding and into the drain (see above, p. 62). The walls of the plunge-bath may have been lower than those of the *frigidarium*, in which case a transom window in the upper wall could have lighted the *frigidarium*. Alternatively, there may have been windows in the plunge-bath walls themselves. It is not known how the plunge-bath was filled: water could have been siphoned in from the tank on the upper terrace, or bucketed in through the *praefurnium* and storage yard areas, or perhaps bucketed in from the *culina* through the corridor in the south part of room 9.

The sudatorium (2 · 37 × 3 · 50 m.) (Pl. XVIII *c*). In the north part of room 8, the hypocaust provided heat irradiation from the floor of a room evidently intended as a sweating room or *sudatorium (sudatio, Laconicum)* as described by Vitruvius: a hot dry room sealed off from the *frigidarium* and *caldarium*, in which the heat would have been very intense, not only from the floor nearest the *praefurnium* but also from the thermal jacketing in the walls. The north, east and west walls were completely lined with flue tiles set in walls made of lumps of mortar and large pieces of broken brick of various kinds. The flue tiles were rectangular (0 · 145 × 0 · 10 m. and *c.* 0 · 45 m. long), and they were arranged in single rows 0 · 03–0 · 04 m. apart; they were covered with a layer of *opus signinum* about 0 · 03 m. thick. It is not known exactly how much heat would have been produced by the thermal jacketing of flue-tiles: here, as elsewhere, the flue tiles may have served more to equalise the distribution of heat over the floor and to prevent condensation on the walls than to actually heat the room.

No added lining of mortar and brick was interposed between the flue tiles and the north terrace retaining wall in the area of the *sudatorium*, to isolate the atmosphere of the room from the existing structure. The builders probably did not think that the hot dry atmosphere here would endanger the wall, but, in the area of the *caldarium*, a wetter atmosphere prevailed, and this necessitated a thick lining being placed between the terrace wall and the flue tiles.

The floor of the *sudatorium* was robbed, leaving only the *opus signinum* basal levelling set with occasional pieces of broken marble. Along the north wall, a section of white marble slab (0 · 11 m. wide) set in *opus signinum* indicated that there was a marble border running round the edges of the room. It is possible that the whole floor was made of reused marble slabs, as in the *caldarium*. A white marble slab (0 · 20 m. wide) was preserved *in situ* beside the door to the *caldarium*.

The caldarium (2 · 80 × 3 · 08 m.). (Pl. XIX). The *caldarium*, with its bath, was built in the north part of room 9. The north terrace wall was lined with an added wall (0 · 22 m. thick) of tufa *opus reticulatum* like that of the south wall of the *frigidarium* and the other Period IIA walls. The east and west walls were similarly built, and the door leading to the *sudatorium* had tile quoins. The south wall (0 · 32 m. thick) was built of triangular bricks similar to those used in other Period II walls. All four walls were lined with flue tiles, set in *opus signinum* with pieces of broken brick in it; the walls and sides of the bath were finished with a layer of fine *opus signinum*.

The floor of the *caldarium* was carefully, if unattractively, finished with slabs of marble revetment reused from another context. Along the north, west, and part of the south walls, a border of plain white marble slabs (0 · 15 m. wide and 0 · 015 m thick) was set, in *opus signinum* with a top coat of fine white plaster. Inside this border, three sections of a panelled dado of Carystian marble (*cipollino*), white with a few bluish veins, were set; a fourth piece was used as the floor of the bath. All four sections were from the same decorative context: the slabs were all 0 · 018 m. thick and 0 · 79 m. wide except where they were cut down. The edges were bevelled and the back left slightly rough, indicating that they had been used to cover a wall. The panels, alternating large horizontal rectangles (0 · 54 × 1 · 01 m.) and small vertical ones (0 · 54 × 0 · 32 m.), were defined by *cyma recta* mouldings cut into the surface: the borders and centres of the panels were on the same level. In all, sections of four large and four small panels are present, making a total length of 6 · 76 m. of dado, long enough, for example, to have covered the west wall of the *triclinium* if the decoration were to be reconstructed as having had small vertical panels at the ends next to the corners of the room with four large and three small panels between them (a total length of 7 · 24 m. — the wall was 7 · 50 m., and the borders at the corner might have been a little wider). The *triclinium* must, indeed, have been redecorated when its north wall was partially rebuilt in Period IIA, but whether the panels came actually from there, or from another room, is impossible to say.[4]

In the east part of the *caldarium*, occupying nearly half the room, there was a small bath for hot water, heated from a *testudo*, for which the footings were found in room 10 (see above, p. 47). There was a step (0 · 29 m. wide and 0 · 36 m. high) used both for getting into the bath and for sitting on: this was finished with *opus signinum*. A low wall and a step into the bath itself allowed the bather to 'ease into' the hot water. The floor of the bath was made up in part of a section of the marble panelling described above, and in part from

[4] For the revetment, see Laidlaw, 1975, 42–3.

broken pieces of other types of white marble. The whole bath was *c.* 0 · 63 m. deep and had a capacity of *c.* 600 litres if comfortably filled.

II.   *The figlina or tile-factory in the villa rustica.* (Pl. XX and Fig. 9).
The Period IIA *figlina*, or tile-factory, in the *villa rustica* is indicative of the diversity of land, personnel and habitation at San Rocco and its environs. The making of tiles, and their sale, in a volume large enough to justify the expense of the equipment and personnel needed, are themselves indications that industrial or manufacturing activities supplemented agricultural activities and revenue; there must, moreover, have been a market for these specialized building materials. Thus the Period IIA additions to the villa — bathing, tile-making and oil-producing facilities — may have been part of a more general refurbishing of buildings and land in the area, or a growth in population and housing in such towns as Cales and Teanum nearby, or both. Tile-making is a specialised, year-round activity which probably required specifically skilled personnel, either brought to San Rocco from elsewhere or trained from the existing *familia.* Finally, the presence of tile-making facilities indicates that the land held or leased was newly diversified: not only were there lands in the Ager Falernus or hillside plots for wheat, olive trees and other produce, but clay beds as well, probably to be found in the valleys and streams to the west of the site. The clay beds may have always been available, but it is only in Period IIA, *c.* A.D. 50, that they came to be exploited commercially.

Erosion and levelling in the area of the *villa rustica* destroyed many features of the tile kilns, in particular the upper part of their walls, with the result that is is impossible to determine accurately the size of the firing chambers and thus their capacities. It is their large size, the absence of any significant quantity of pottery sherds in or around the kilns, and the presence of tiles of all forms and sizes (see below, p. 164) which allow the identification of them as tile-kilns rather than pottery kilns. Even more serious for the understanding of the *figlina* is the disappearance of its refuse dump. The pile of misfired tiles, broken samples and other scrap associated with the kilns was probably outside the *villa rustica* in the area of the modern tufa quarry to the northeast and has now been dug away.

Fornaces or kilns were found in two rooms: in the 'Commons' (room 48) and in room 49. Rooms 50, 51 and 52 which, together with room 49, had in Period II formed a residential suite, with a latrine in room 52 (see above, p. 55), were now given over to tile-making, just as in the *domus, cubicula* were replaced by bathing facilities.

The remains of a small *fornax*, very badly preserved, were found in the northwest corner of the 'Commons' (room 48), set directly against the northwest walls. The kiln's walls were of broken tile laid in courses and set in mortar (0 · 03 to 0 · 05 m. thick). The fire was evidently lit at floor level, and the indented north and west sides supported the tiled floor of the upper firing chamber. The small size of the firing chamber (1 · 55 × 1 · 55 m. maximum, height unknown) would have made this *fornax* suitable as a drying oven, in which tiles would have been initially treated before final firing in the larger *fornaces* in room 49. Alternatively, the small *fornax* in room 48 might have been used for making moulds which did not require so intense a heat as the tiles themselves; it is in this kiln that the fragments of a mould for a figured antefix showing a ship were found (see below, p. 158). Whatever its precise function in the *figlina*, the *fornax* in room 48 might also have served as a source of heat in winter, or as a bread-baking oven serving the needs of the *domus* inhabitants and the *villa rustica* workers. How the kiln would have been flued through the roof of the 'Commons' is an unanswered question.

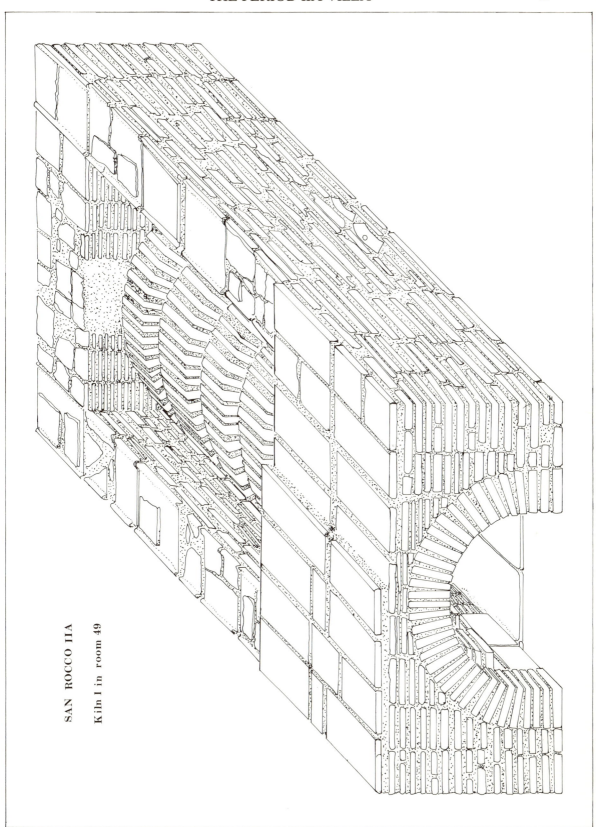

SAN ROCCO IIA

Kiln 1 in room 49

Fig. 9. Reconstruction of the Period IIA kiln in the *figlina. By G. Sansbury*

The fornaces. The two large kilns were located in room 49. Both were built on the Period II floor of the room, and both were roughly the same size: the firing chambers were both *c.* 3 · 00 m. long × 1 · 60 m. wide.

Kiln 1 faced the entrance to the room and backed against the north terrace wall. Its exterior walls on the north, east and west (0 · 70 m. thick) were built of limestone blocks, broken roof tiles and flanged *bipedales* tiles set in very irregular courses with about 0 · 03 to 0 · 05 m. of sandy mortar between them. Engaged piers (0 · 22 × 0 · 22 m.) extended from the east and west walls, on the inside, eight along each wall, to support the floor of the firing chamber; there were probably arches connecting them. The height of the lower chamber, where the fire would have been lit, could be determined from the kiln's arched door: the arch, built of brick (1 · 02 m. in diameter and 1 · 12 m. high) was probably secured by a door or grill. Between the east and west walls of the room and the kiln walls there was a rough packing of mud and broken tiles, set in irregular courses, to provide insulation around the lower chamber; it is not known how high this insulation stood. There may have been a platform around the sides and behind the kiln for the operation of vents.

Kiln 2 was built against the south wall of room 49 at right angles to the entrance and to kiln 1. Its walls were less thick (0 · 60 m.) and it was not as massively insulated as kiln 1, but otherwise its construction was the same. The structure of its door and lower chamber could not be determined since it was destroyed almost to floor level. Five engaged piers extended from the walls on the south and north sides; they too may have supported arches for the floor of the firing chamber above. The lack of insulation and the narrower walls indicate that kiln 2 was not fired to the temperature of kiln 1: it may have been a drying kiln for the initial parching of the moulded clay previous to the final firing in kiln 1.[5]

It is in the nature of such kiln structures that they be partially built and rebuilt several times. The kilns presently preserved probably had upper structures which were frequently replaced, and the foundations of the kilns might have replaced earlier ones. However, the need to preserve the present structures for exhibition precluded investigation of the room for evidence of earlier structures.

The work area. The three small rooms (50, 51 and 52) adjacent to room 49 were converted to use as the working areas of the *figlina*. The Period II floors were retained (*op. spic.* 3–5, p. 126), but like room 49, the three rooms were probably open to the sky or had awnings for protection when needed. In room 52, the floor was roughly trenched through along the south wall to form a trough or basin (0 · 49 m. wide); the Period II latrine went out of use. Evidently some part of the tile-making or moulding process required large amounts of water, probably in the mixing of the clay and in smoothing it into the moulds. The water could have been stored and drained from the trough and drain in room 52. Water was easily obtainable from the cisterns north of the eastern terrace and could have been bucketed in from above.

III. *The oletum or oil-factory in the villa rustica.* (Pls. XXI–XXIII and Figs. 10–11)
The construction of permanent facilties for the processing of olive-oil reflects the diversity of the agricultural and human organisation at San Rocco in much the same way as does the *figlina*. It seems that tile-making and oil production were not present in Periods I and IA,

---

[5.] For the *fornaces*, close analogies are listed in Cuomo di Caprio, 1971–72, 439–45 and 452–3. The San Rocco kilns correspond to type II/b of the author's classification and rather closely to the example which she describes. Although there are many difficulties in accurate dating, it can be noted that of the more than ten examples listed, the two dated ones are Tiberian and mid-first century A.D.

but whether they were features of the Period II *villa rustica*, now obscured by the Period IIA developments, is impossible to say. *Mutatis mutandis*, it is possible to say that the three Period IIA constructions — *balineum, figlina* and *oletum* — reflect the desire for convenience and luxury made possible by wealth and, in the *villa rustica*, the shrewd investment in equipment tending towards the productive diversification of land, also made possible by wealth. Moreover, in the *oletum*, a third motivation may be evident: that of producing and storing a large quantity of oil to await upward fluctuations in price. Finally, the size and efficient design of the *oletum* equipment may indicate that it was built to process not only the olives of the property belonging to the villa but those of other villas as well; like the *figlina*, the *oletum*, if indeed it was rented or used by other landlords in the environs on a contract basis, may represent as much a commercial adjunct to the *villa rustica* as an agricultural one. Naturally, some combination of internal use and external contract for use by others may also have existed.[6]

Relative to the other features of the *villa rustica*, the *oletum* — both the pressing equipment in rooms 53 and 54 and the oil separation vats in rooms 57 and 58 — is well preserved. This good state of preservation is due to the fact that the pressing equipment was protected by the spill from the northern terrace over the area; the oil separation vats were below pavement-level in the southern part of the main terrace overlooking the *hortus*, and so were preserved.

The main parts of the *oletum* of Period IIA in the *villa rustica* are:

A. The *oletum* proper with its pressing equipment and sedimentation system in rooms 53 and 54.

B. The oil separation vats in rooms 57 and 58.

A. *The oletum proper with its pressing equipment and sedimentation system in rooms 53 and 54.*

The two big rectangular rooms (53 and 54) in the northeast corner of the *villa rustica* were set aside for the processing of olives into olive oil. The two rooms face south. Room 53 was completely paved in *opus spicatum* set in mortar (*op. spic.* 6, p. 128) at a level 0 · 40 m. above that of courtyard 2, whilst room 54 was paved with a smooth *opus signinum* (*op. sig.* 14, p. 128). The walls of both rooms were plastered and were thus roofed, a necessary precaution, as pressing and sedimentation were done in late autumn. The rooms were connected by a door with a limestone threshold. The walls, floors, doors and processing equipment are all of a piece, built together and used without modification for some time. The unit was neatly self-contained: all the equipment was located in these two rooms so that the

---

[6.] An account of the processing of olives is available in Cotton, 1979, 63–9. In general, the problems associated with the olive oil economy stem from a difficulty which the San Rocco *oletum* also poses, namely, that of estimating the amount of oil produced in a given season. The separation vats, which are part of the *oletum*, have a capacity of *c*. 31,920 litres or about 1,238 *amphorae* (1 *amphora* = 25 · 78 litres), but this does not represent the oil content since much of the bulk consisted of water, *amurca* or other material. But the size of the surface area, from which the oil was skimmed off, did affect the time it took to separate and to collect the remaining oil. Seasonal changes, time of harvest, ripeness and variety of fruit introduce variables on which information is short, and, moreover, the price of oil in Campania in the first century A.D. is uncertain. Whilst the production of oil was a significant part of the villa's economy, it was only a part, with the result that the determination of its precise contribution to the over-all 'return' on investment in equipment, buildings and personnel cannot be calculated. These problems, of which the San Rocco *oletum* is an example, contribute to making the over-all picture of olive oil economy very murky indeed.

A general review for Italy appears in White, 1970, 225–9 and 390–2; and for some of the problems associated with estimating amounts of oil produced, see Camps-Fabrer, 1953, *passim*, and Oates, 1953, 86 ff. See also the remarks in Day, 1932, 172 and Percival, 1976, 108.

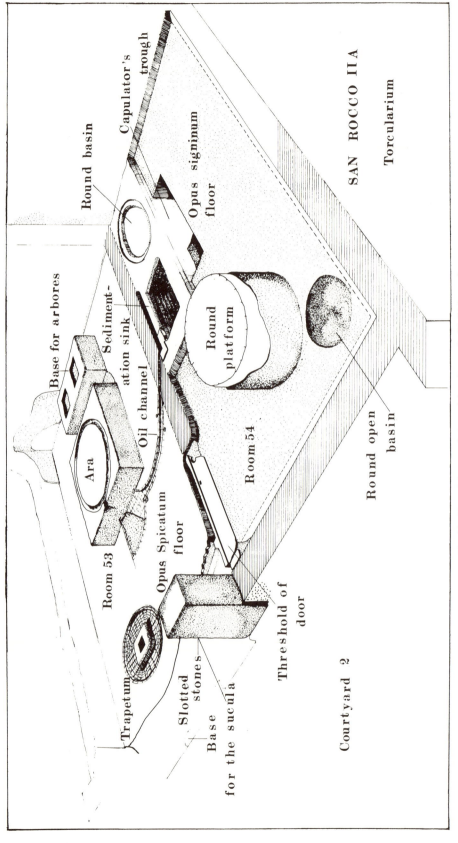

Fig. 10. Plan of the *torcularium* of the *oletum*. By H. Richmond

work there could be an uninterrupted sequence of activities from separation to preparing the product for storage.

The *oletum* was divided into two areas. One of them (in room 53) was reserved for the pressing process—by milling (the *trapetum*) and by crushing (the *torcularium*): the other (in room 54) was for two kinds of finishing—an initial sedimentation of oil from its *amurca* and pulp, so as to obtain fine edible oil (the *olio vergine*) from the fruit crushed in the *torcularium*, and another stage of separating oil of a second quality from the residue of *amurca* and the solid matter of the pulp. A third procedure, requiring long-term separation in still conditions, is represented in the oil separation vats. The separation of the working areas indicates that the work was specialised to some degree: the operation of the machines was reserved for some of the personnel, that of sieving, separating and preparing the product for storage for others. Cato's distinction between olive-pickers (*strictores* and *leguli*), the oil-maker (*factor*) and the oil-drawer (*capulator*) is preserved archaeologically in this *oletum*.

The equipment, except for wood or metal parts, was largely built-in. The advantages are obvious; for equipment under pressure, the structure of the walls and floors would help stabilise moving parts under stress, and there were space-saving advantages in having fitted basins and containers. Moreover, this design simplified the construction, use and maintenance of certain parts and also allowed for the easy replacement of such moving parts in wood or metal as tended to deteriorate.

The description of the *oletum* below follows the sequence of the oil making process from the reception of the fruit to the preparation of its product for storage.[7]

The milling or crushing of the olives was the first step, after they had been harvested, to separate the pips from the pulp. For this, the *trapetum* was used. This initial separation took place in room 53. The fruit, received at the door of room 53 from courtyard 2, could be stored anywhere in either room, temporarily, because the press or crushing equipment (the *torcularium*) would not be in operation while the fruit was being milled.

The trapetum. The base of the crushing mill or *trapetum* was found in room 53, next to the door. The base is essentially a round depression built into the *opus spicatum* floor. The lip and bottom of the depression (0 · 595 m. or 2 Roman feet in diameter, 0 · 12 m. deep) were built of square tiles (0 · 10 × 0 · 10 m.) set in mortar. In the centre of the depression, there was a rectangular limestone block (0 · 20 × 0 · 22 m.) raised 0 · 05 m. from the bottom, firmly mortared in. This block was pierced with a square hole (0 · 12 × 0 · 12 m.) running through it and down into the fill below. It was evident that the round depression and the block were not themselves used for milling as there was no evidence of wear or stress on them. Rather, they were the support for a removable superstructure, the *mortarium* or *trapetum* basin itself.

The design of the base of the *trapetum*, as preserved, allows a reconstruction of the other parts. Like most *trapeta* found elsewhere, the *mortarium*, presumably of stone, would

---

[7.] In the description of the *oletum* equipment, four sources have been followed: Juengst and Thielscher, 1954, 32–93 and 1957, 53–126; White, 1975, 225–33; and the essential descriptions in Drachmann, 1932 and Thielscher, 1963, *passim*; a good reconstruction exists in Pasqui, 1897, 496–503.

Good parallels for the *oletum* at San Rocco exist at Pompeii and elsewhere. The *villae rusticae* near Pompeii cited in n. 2, p. 61 had *cellae oleariae*, as did the Villa dei Misteri, described in Maiuri, 1947, 86 ff.; and a villa at San Sebastiano al Vesuvio, cf. Cerulli-Irelli, 1965, 161–78, though this last post-dates 79 A.D. Close parallels exist elsewhere: at Tivoli in the first century A.D. (Facenna, 1957, 148–53); at Capena in Augustan times (Pallottino, 1937, 20–2); and at Guidonia (Caprino, 1944–45, 45–9), also in the first century A.D. There is another first century A.D. example at Orbetello, cf. Maetzke, 1958, 34–41.

For the separating vats to the south of courtyard 2, precise parallels cannot be found at Pompeii but do exist in two examples of Late Republican and first century A.D. date on the Via Tiberina and the Via Latina, see Felletti Maj, 1955, 214–15 and fig. 7 and Paribeni, 1924, 423–4, respectively.

have had a round base, with curving sides, both inside and outside, and a round *miliarium* or central raised projection. The round base would have been mortised around the square central block still preserved, with the advantage that the *mortarium* would thus have been secured from slipping while the mill was being turned. The *miliarium* would have been perforated with a square hole for a fixed post into which an iron pin (*columella*) would have been driven to attach the round wooden part called the *cupa*. The handles (*modioli*) of the *trapetum* would have been driven into the *cupa*. The stone hemispheres or *orbes*, perforated with holes for the handles, would then be put in place, and the *trapetum* would be ready for use.

The advantages of this design—a built-in base and post support for moveable *mortarium, modioli* and *orbes*—are obvious. Because the *mortarium* is securely supported and mortised, the torque or circular motion of the *orbes* is not impeded. Moreover, the position of the *orbes* themselves is separated from the *mortarium* and secured by the block set in the base: this provided greater stability and also allowed the height of the *orbes* to be changed by adding washers between the *miliarium* and the *columella*. Since the *mortarium* was secured by the mortise over the block, rather than by its own weight, it could be lighter and easily removable when the *torcularium* was in operation. Finally, the lighter *mortarium*, and the fixed post into which the *columella* was set, would have stabilised the position of the *orbes* in such a way as to simplify, radically, the design of the *modioli* or handles. The *modioli* supporting the *orbes* were subject to both lateral stress and torque from the motion of the mill, with the result that, when attached by *cupa* and *miliarium* to the *mortarium* itself, they wobbled and tended to turn unevenly. To correct this defect, Cato (xxxi 2) recommends the use of a complex series of flanged washers (*cupiedines*) set between the *modioli* and the *orbes*. However, in this *trapetum*, with its completely stable fixed post, *columella* and *cupa* set in the floor, and a separate *mortarium* mortised over the supporting block, these washers would not have been necessary, since the two structures would have been independently secured. The device of stabilising both *mortarium* and axis of this *trapetum* separately is a simplification and an improvement on the evidently vexed problem of *trapeta* design, that of positioning the *orbes*. The farm-tool engineer, if one may call him that, solved the problem. By providing a fully built-in base, which could be used for a long time, he bypassed the need for expensive complex carpentry which might have to be repaired or replaced frequently.

The torcularium. The same rationale of design — fixed elements built-in for permanent use in order to by-pass carpentered parts — is evident in the *torcularium*, or press, as it was in the *trapetum*. The wooden bin (*galeagra*) in which the olive pulp would ordinarily be housed, was bypassed by the design of the press-stone (*ara*) itself, and the winch-frames (*stipites*) were replaced by built-in stone elements.

The milled olives from the *trapetum* were ready for crushing in the *torcularium* in room 53. The design of the *torcularium* is in three parts: the fulcrum-frames (*arbores*) supporting the lever (*prelum*) and press-board (*orbis*), the press-stone itself (*ara*) and the winch-frames (*stipites*) supporting the rope-drum (*sucula*) and handspakes (*vectes*) for tightening the lever. All three parts are represented in our *torcularium*.

A rectangular limestone block (0 · 595 m. or 2 Roman feet × 1 · 19 m. or 4 Roman feet and 0 · 64 m. high), with two square mortises (0 · 36 × 0 · 24 m. and 0 · 145 m. deep, 0 · 295 or 1 Roman foot apart) was preserved between the press-stone (*ara*) and the north terrace wall: the block was set in the fill below the floor, which was built up to it. The block supported the two fulcrum-frames (*arbores*). Between the *arbores* the 'tongue' (*lingula*) of the wooden lever (*prelum*) would have been hung. The *prelum* was at least 6 · 00 m. long, extending through the door of room 53 and out into courtyard 2. Next to the base block for the *arbores*, there was a square limestone press-stone or *ara* set into the floor. A round channel (1 · 45 m. in diameter, 0 · 05 m. deep) with sloping sides and a groove on the south side of the *ara* allowed oil to collect and drip off the stone when the round press-board (*orbis*) crushed the olive pulp. The surface of the *ara* was 0 · 02 m. lower inside the round channel than its surface outside: thus, there was no need for a low wooden bin (*galeagra*) to hold the pulp in place, since the pulp squeezed by the pressure of the mechanism would have collected in the channel. A sieve interposed at the mouth of the groove would have prevented the pulp from dripping off with the oil.

Leverage on the *prelum* was maintained by a winch at its south end. On the east side of the door of room 53, a rectangular stone (0 · 62 × 0 · 73 m. and 0 · 89 m. high) set into the wall end had, on its west side, a straight slotted cut-away connected to a round cut-away above it, in an L-shaped configuration, for the introduction and lifting of a round rope-drum or winch (*sucula*). This stone corresponded to another just like it, now lost, on the west side of the door. The two stones together acted as the weights for the wooden winch which was slipped through the slots and raised into the round cut-aways: on this *sucula* would be wound the rope connected to the *prelum* to operate the press. The slotted stones are a built-in substitute for the more usual free-standing *stipites* found at other sites and described by Cato (xviii, 4–5). They provide absolute security for the *sucula* (which, when roped to the *prelum*, tends to raise the *stipites*) but also allow it to be removed, repaired or replaced. The slotted stones fulfill the double function of supporting the *sucula* and adding counterweight to the *prelum*, something that Cato's recommendations do not do. By this ingenious design, the 'farm-tool engineer' of our *torcularium* allowed for the maximum flexibility and accessibility in the handling of carpentered parts while firmly fixing the various supports, bases and weights needed for the action of the press.

The *sucula* with its handspakes (*vectes*) was housed in a wooden or stone frame, now lost. The impression of this frame can be recognised along the south edge of the *opus spicatum* floor of room 53 which ends along the south door. A wooden or stone frame supported the floor fill behind the *sucula* and between the slotted stones: it would have been *c.* 0 · 40 m. high, corresponding to the difference of level between the raised floor of room 53 and that of the courtyard 2.

The olive pulp, once crushed by the action of the *prelum* tightened by the ropes of the *sucula*, released its oil into the drip-groove of the *ara*. A sieve was probably interposed, but oil would have dripped down the stone into a funnelled channel set into the floor. The channel was built of tile mortared into the *opus spicatum* floor and was *c.* 0 · 02 m. deep. It had a triangular funnel just below the drip-groove in the *ara*; the channel then narrowed to a width of 0 · 02 m. and ran along the floor eastward to the wall dividing rooms 53 and 54. The wall itself had, at the level of the channel, a small, tile-enclosed hole running through it to a sedimentation system in room 54. Thus the oil, by being channelled across the floor and through the wall, could be collected for separation in a spot out of the way of the activity round the *torcularium* itself.

The sedimentation and separation systems. There were two systems in room 54 in which the oil could be finished, that is to say, allowed to stand for a while until the residue of *amurca*, débris, water or fragments of pulp sank and clear oil was drawn off by the oil-drawer, the *capulator*. The first sedimentation or finishing system for the *olio vergine* was in the nothwest corner of the room and consisted of three parts: a trough for the *capulator* to stand in below floor level, a rectangular sedimentation sink and a round covered basin, from which the oil was collected before final storage or sale. The second separation or finishing system for the treatment of the pulp was in the southeast corner of the room and consisted of two parts: a round raised platform and a round open basin. The two systems are described separately.

The capulator's trough, sedimentation sink and covered basin. The oil pressed from the pulp in the *torcularium* dripped off the *ara* and was fed by a flat funnel to a channel which ran through the east wall of room 53 and emerged into the sedimentation sink in room 54, at floor level. Because the sedimentation sink and the covered basin were at the level of the *opus signinum* floor, the process of allowing the residual *amurca* and bits of pulp to separate was facilitated by a stepped trough (2 · 46 × 0 · 77 m. and 0 · 83 m. deep) in which the *capulator* could stand with the sedimentation sink at about the level of the middle of his thigh. The sides, floor and step of this trough were of the same *opus signinum* as the floor itself, and the whole feature allowed one person to stand comfortably without having to squat.

On the *capulator's* left side, a tile-walled sedimentation sink (1 · 03 × 0 · 77 m. and 0 · 75 m. deep) was let into the floor. The sink had a rounded edge (0 · 05 m. wide) raised 0 · 03 m. from the floor. On the west side, the channel bringing oil from the *torcularium* through the wall was let in under the raised edge and allowed the liquid to drip into the sink. On the north side, there was a hole in the wall of the sink (0 · 02 m. in diameter) set 0 · 05 m. below the edge. This hole led to the round basin on the *capulator's* right. The process is clear: the *capulator* would allow the oil from the *torcularium* to fill the sink whilst the drain leading to the round basin was stoppered with a cork or rag. Then, once the residual *amurca* and débris had sunk to the bottom, the *capulator* would unstopper the drain and allow the pure oil to pass into the round basin. Whatever oil then remained in the separating sink could be skimmed by hand into the round basin. The *amurca* and solid matter could then be flushed by hand from the sedimentation sink.

The round basin itself (0 · 73 m. in diameter, 0 · 60 m. deep) was built of rubble set in mortar coated with *opus signinum*, some of which still remains. Its edge had a depressed rim (0 · 05 m. wide × 0 · 01 m. deep) for a round cover made of wood or tile: this cover protected the pure oil from dust and débris before it was transferred to permanent storage or to *dolia* for sale and transport.

The round platform and open basin. In the southeast corner of room 54, a second separating system was built. It is possible that the pulp from which the *olio vergine* had been extracted was re-treated in some way. Churning of pulp and *amurca,* perhaps treated with hot water, would have released more oil, doubtless of a second quality. The system for this re-treatment was different from the sink and basin described above in that the oil from the *torcularium* did not reach it directly. Rather, the churned or re-treated pulp, perhaps re-pressed, was transferred to the round platform. This round platform (1 · 54 m. in diameter, c. 1 · 00 m. high), very roughly built of broken tiles, mortar and building débris, was large enough for three or four workers to stand or sit around. The platform was very carefully covered with *opus signinum* on the sides, and, evidently, on the top. Although the angle of the working surface cannot be determined, it probably sloped toward the round basin (1 · 01 m. in diameter, 0 · 62 m. deep) set into the floor in the southeast corner of the room. The round basin, also carefully covered in *opus signinum*, may have been used to skim oil into, or used to hold *amurca* flushed from a container on the platform, or, most probably, used to hold a *dolium* into which either oil or *amurca* could be poured. It is not known pre-

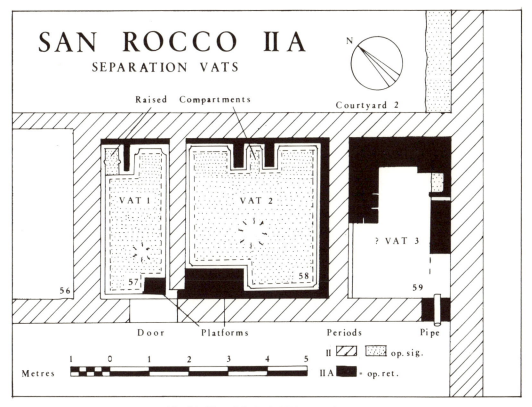

Fig. 11. Plan of the Period IIA separating vats

cisely how the platform and round basin were used, but they seem, by their association with the sedimentation sink and covered basin in the northwest corner of the room, to be one part of the finishing processes; this time, perhaps, the need arose to separate water from the oil, unlike the first sedimentation process in which no water was involved.

B. *The oil separation vats in rooms 57 and 58.*
Rooms 57 and 58 were set aside for a third procedure in which two large separating vats were used, which were intended to hold large quantities of liquid in still conditions for some time, for by now the bulk of the fluid consisted of water, with only residual oil.

Both vats were approached through a doorway (1 · 15 m. wide) cut into the south wall of room 57 and now preserved only as the impression of a limestone threshold block. The wall dividing the two rooms was probably dismantled in part, with a door cut into it leading into room 58. The floors of both rooms were dug out to a depth of *c.* 1 · 90 m. below that of the floor of courtyard 2, and the north, west and south walls of room 57 and the north, east and south walls of room 58 were lined with a coat of *opus reticulatum* (0 · 20 m. thick). The wall between the two rooms was left intact, though its offset and foundations may have been trimmed to uniform thickness. Once the excavation and walling work was completed, a thick uniform layer of *opus signinum* (0 · 06 m. thick) was applied to the floor and walls. There was a quarter-round moulding at the intersection of the walls and floor and in the corners, and both floors were inclined toward the centre where there were round basins into which water would collect as it separated from the oil. This oil, the result of a third treatment in the *oletum,* may have been used as grease, leather- or wood-treating oil, or lamp oil. The smaller of the two vats on the east had a platform built of tufa in the southeast corner. The platform probably supported steps leading from the door down to the floor of the vat and it could be used as a place for a worker to stand when skimming and ladling off the surface oil. Like the walls and floor, the platform was covered with a thick coat of *opus signinum.* In the northwest corner, a wallend (0 · 40 m. wide) extended into the vat; it, too, was coated with *opus signinum* and was married to the floor of the vat with a quarter-round moulding. On its inner face, a groove (0 · 06 m. wide and 0 · 04 m. deep) corresponded to a similar groove in the wall. Evidently a wooden door, or a series of boards, were fitted into the grooves down to the floor of this raised compartment (0 · 60 × 0 · 39 m. raised 0 · 09 m. from the floor of the vat) which was separated from the vat itself.

The large vat on the west had a platform of tufa in the southwest with two steps still *in situ* (risers 0 · 43 × 0 · 20 × 0 · 30 m. high), providing access from the door down the floor of the vat. In the middle of the north wall, there were two projecting wall ends (0 · 40 m. wide) on either side of a raised platform (0 · 60 × 0 · 45 m., raised 0 · 09 m. from the floor of the vat), also grooved on their inner sides allowing the raised compartment to be separated from the vat itself with boards or a shutter.

The suggested use of the vats is as follows: the raised compartments, defined by wall ends, would have been separated from the vats by the introduction of a sliding door or boards secured and waterproofed with rags or pitch. The vats themselves would then be filled to the level of the door or boards and the contents allowed to separate over a long period of time. Water, residual *amurca* and solid particles, if any, would settle in the bottom of the vats and in the round basins. When the oil was ready for storage, containers, probably *amphorae,* could have been lowered into the compartments on ropes from apertures in the north wall. Oil could be easily skimmed and ladled into the containers or ladled in through funnels. When full, the containers would be hoisted up into courtyard 2, stoppered and packed. As the level of the vats' contents went down, holes could have been opened through the door or boards taken out in order to make the skimming easier. Finally, when all the useable oil had been removed, the sides and floor of the vats could have been cleaned. There was easy access through the door on the south side and via the steps leading down to the vats' floors.

PERIOD IIA. SUMMARY AND CONCLUSIONS

Period IIA represents a coordinated reorganisation of the Period II *domus* and *villa rustica,* one in which walls of tufa *opus reticulatum* or of brick, or of a mixture of the two, were built as subdividers of existing spaces or as parts of permanent installations. In the *domus,* a *balineum* or bath-house was added, small but luxurious, somewhat lacking in architectural distinction but ingenious and contributing to comfort. The *balineum,* built into the existing structure in the northwest, consisted of a *frigidarium* with a cold bath, a *sudatorium,* a *caldarium* with a hot bath, service areas (*praefurnium,* storage yard) and a seating for a *testudo.*

The most significant Period IIA additions were in the *villa rustica,* and there residential or living areas were apparently sacrificed to put in the industrial equipment associated with a *figlina* or tile-kiln, the *fornaces* of which were found. In courtyard 2, an *oletum* or oil processing factory was installed: it consisted of a mill, press and sedimentation and separating facilities on the north side and of two large separating vats on the south side. Period IIA, in the *villa rustica,* represents either a continuation and expansion of existing agricultural activities or a new departure; in either case, permanent new structures for tile-making and oil processing were required.

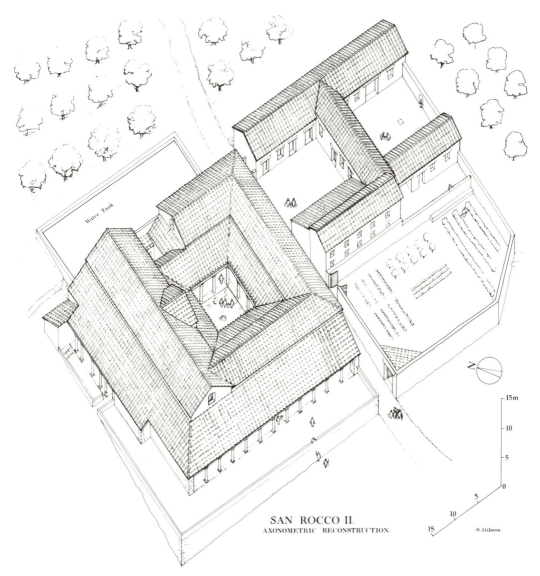

Water Tank

SAN ROCCO II.
AXONOMETRIC RECONSTRUCTION.

15m
10
5
0

N

S. Gibson.

Fig. 12. Axonometric reconstruction of the Period II villa. *By Sheila Gibson*

The Period IIA additions to the *domus* and the *villa rustica* are significant in that they add notes of new luxury and productivity to the history of the San Rocco estate in the first century A.D., indicating a past prosperity and perhaps new uses for the villa and the land. No structural changes in the plan occurred, but diversity of activities in both leisure and work must have resulted from the putting in of the *balineum*, the *figlina* and the *oletum*.

The date of construction, based on the use of *opus reticulatum* and brick, can be assigned to the third quarter of the first century A.D., when the use of small triangular bricks begins in Campania, but before the widespread adoption of brick construction occurred in late Flavian times (see n. 3 p. 61). The pavements put in during Period IIA are of no help in dating (see the mosaic catalogue), and the date of construction could not be confirmed from material associated stratigraphically with the Period IIA features because they had to be preserved for exhibition. However on the basis of the method of construction and the stamped tiles, a date in the late Julio-Claudian period or early Flavian period can be postulated.[8] A reconstruction of this villa is suggested in Fig. 12, which was drawn by Miss Sheila Gibson, F.S.A.

PERIODS I–IIA. SUMMARY AND CONCLUSIONS
The San Rocco Villa at Francolise, *c.* 100 B.C. to A.D. 200

The San Rocco villa at Francolise represents a microcosm of larger phenomena in the history of the Roman landscape in Italy and in Campania, in the development of domestic architecture and of the social and economic processes of the late Republic and Empire. The pattern from an early simplicity to a greater complexity is clear; what must also be emphasised is the remarkable durability and stability of the natural and man-made environment for a period of nearly three hundred years. The region evidently remained viable environmentally and agriculturally for this period, and the changes which the villa underwent reflected as much the permanence of the Ager Falernus as a durable residential and agricultural locale as the modifications of use which the Romans undertook in it.

The villa was founded in the first decade of the first century B.C. on a previously uninhabited site, near the well-established towns of Cales and Teanum Sidicinum, in the southern part of the Ager Falernus. Its siting on a hill is compatible with the Roman architectural and agricultural practice as known from wall-paintings and agricultural manuals such as those of Cato, Varro and Columella. The region had been, or soon was, centuriated, there were established market-days or *nundinae* in the region, and the Via Appia was close by. In addition, there was another villa less than half a kilometer away, that of Posto.

The first phase of the villa's existence (Period I) is represented by two artificial terraces, connected by stairs, of which the northern or upper terrace was the residential area primarily, and the southern or lower terrace was the *villa rustica*. The upper terrace, comprising about 400 m.[2] of space and having a cistern with a capacity of at least 38,000 litres, had a simple, dignified *domus* with a square paved courtyard in the northeast corner (room B) and an L of residential rooms (rooms A, D, E and F) around it, at least one of which was paved (*op. mus.* 1) and one of which was a large room with elaborate interior articulation of the walls and an elaborate roof (room D). It was not possible to assign the function of *cubiculum* to any of the other rooms, though rooms E and F may have been *cubicula.* Evidently the residential use of the rooms was undertaken in close association with the economic life of the villa, since the round reservoir and rooms to the north of the residential block (room C) together with the courtyard, indicate that the activities of living and working went hand-in-hand. The *domus* had a room or portico (the South Room) which overlooked the lower terrace.

The lower terrace itself seems to have been given over to the *villa rustica*, also about 400 m.[2], and with its own cistern, round reservoir and well. The plain floor of room H and its special arrangement (*op. sig.* 2) indicate that the threshing of grain was one activity undertaken here; the other rooms (G and I) seem to have been arranged along an open terrace facing south.

The first construction at San Rocco is characterised by a simplicity and compactness of design reflecting an establishment in which owner, servants, slaves if there were any,

---

[8.] For parallels for the *balineum*, see n. 2, p.61: for the *fornaces*, n. 5, p.68; for the *oletum*, nn. 6, p.69 and 7, p.71. The method of construction is described in n. 3, p.61 and the stamped tiles can be found on pp. 164–7.

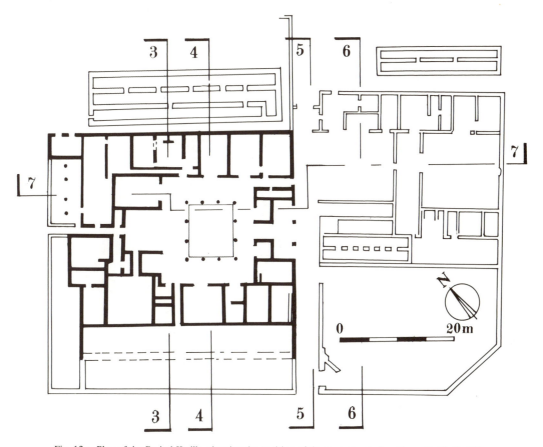

Fig. 12a. Plan of the Period II villa, showing the position of the reconstructed sections. *By Sheila Gibson*

animals and land were closely bound in a life of agricultural activity not unmarked, however, by an appreciation of fine things such as a 'good' mosaic floor. The space for work and the space for living were about equally allocated, but at least one room must have been impressively designed, even though only four or five rooms can certainly be denoted as residential, i.e., clearly unassociated with agricultural activities. The whole structure suggests a small estate with a *paterfamilias* or steward living in close functional association with the rudiments of farm life. Although the L-shaped plan of the *domus* is unusual, such small establishments have analogies with other *villae* of the same period, *c.* 100–90 B.C., and the use of *opus incertum* throughout is usual for the period.

Within about forty years or less, around 50 B.C., the *domus* (but apparently not the *villa rustica* on the lower terrace) was quite considerably changed, and changed in the direction of providing a greater number of residential rooms (Period IA). Why? The period after the Sullan campaigns in the area to the Caesarian period, a time in which the stability of Italy, *mutatis mutandis*, was slowly secured, may well be reflected here: the family of the owner or steward may have been growing, longer residence in the countryside may have become fashionable, and the returns on agriculture may have justified, over two generations or so, the rewards of privacy and comfort. Although the basic structure remained the same, at least four *cubicula* were pieced out of previously existing rooms, and the finely paved room of the first villa was enlarged and had its pavement extended (room A1 and *op. mus.* 2).

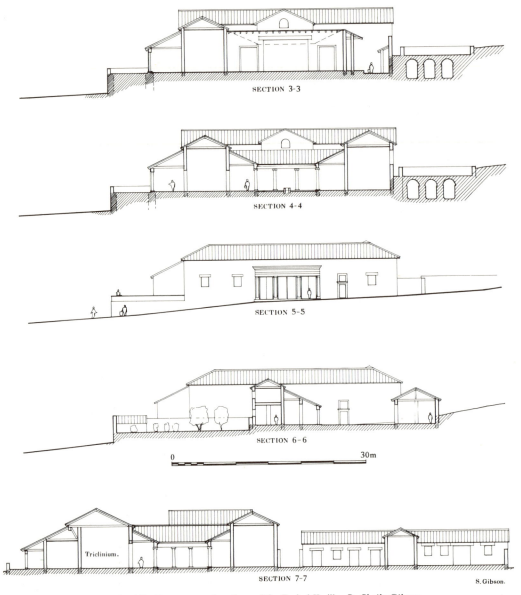

SECTION 3-3

SECTION 4-4

SECTION 5-5

SECTION 6-6

0   30m

Triclinium.

SECTION 7-7

S. Gibson.

Fig. 12b. Reconstructed sections of the Period II villa. *By Sheila Gibson*

The plan changed; a long narrow corridor became the dominating axis of the subdivided house, and pavements were added to some of the new rooms (*op. mus.* 3 and 4). The one large and architecturally impressive room of the first villa (room D) was dismantled in favour of smaller, more intimate and 'liveable' spaces, but all these changes were modifications upon a structure whose exterior did not change much and whose economic life seems to have remained the same: the courtyard of the first villa remained the space toward which all the other rooms converged, and it itself received only minor changes (room B1). There is nothing to indicate that between *c.* 100–90 B.C. and *c.* 50 B.C. (Periods I and IA) there was any major change in the character or size of the estate or its use and management: the changes were changes in taste and a slightly more comfortable manner of living insofar as the floors and spaces are indications.

The major change in the character of the villa occurred within a very few years after the villa was modified, sometime between *c.* 50 and 30 B.C. And when the change did occur, it transformed the villa radically (Period II). Accessibility and viability were assured by the construction of a road with a hard surface and paving stones around the entrances; this road ran up from the *ager* and bisected the terraces of the new villa, emerging on a slope above and continuing toward the other villas at the top of the hill. The road, indeed, seems to have served to connect the San Rocco villa both with the *ager* and with other villas of similar size and date on the hill, and the impression is that of a group of large villas sharing conveniences such as the road. The proximity of other villas besides the one at Posto indicates that the lands of the estates were not necessarily contiguous with the residential and agricultural structures, but separate from them.

Viability was further ensured by the construction of two sets of very large barrel-vaulted cisterns, one above the west terrace, another above the east terrace, with a total capacity of at least 1,100,000 litres, equipped with a water channel feeding water into them and at least one very large open tank.

The distinction between the *domus* and the *villa rustica*, already present in the design of the first villa, was emphasised in the design of the villa of *c.* 30 B.C. (Period II). The western terrace was vastly extended, covering up the old lower terrace, and a lavish new house, the *domus nova*, was built, in part as an *enveloppe* for certain rooms of the old house, the *domus vetus*, to which additions were made but one of which (room A/A1/29) was slightly modified but also preserved in a manner suggesting ancestral pride and piety, or perhaps mere thrift. The new residential quarters, all built of *opus incertum*, comprised some 1,335 m.^{2} and 40 rooms or *vani* (including terraces and corridors), and were designed in the most up-to-date manner, comparable in many ways to the Villa of the Mysteries at Pompeii in its later stages, the villa at Oplontis and the villa at Sette Finestre (see Carandini and Settis, 1979). From the south and west, the aspect of the villa was that of a grandly picturesque *basis-villa* with terraces and porticos affording views to the mountans and the plain and sea. An impressive entrance from the road on the east side of the *domus nova* led to a T-shaped *vestibulum* which in turn gave on to a peristyle and *viridarium* with a garden; twelve columns supported the peristyle roofs on four sides, and there were antefices with lions' heads and a marble basin in the middle of the garden. Ranges of rooms, most of them finely paved in polychrome mosaic with geometric patterns, gave on to the peristyle on the north and south sides, and there were corridors linking the peristyle with the west terrace and with the road and *villa rustica*, and a separate 'step-down' for entrance into the *culina* and adjacent rooms. The peristyle thus acted as the centralising element in the plan, an aspect of the design which is further emphasised by the absence of an *atrium*. At the same time, slight adjustments in the width of the porticos—narrow on the east side, slightly wider on the north and south, widest on the west—maintained in the peristyle the axial progression set up by the T-shaped *vestibulum*.

The axis led to the *tablinum*, a large magnificently paved room, flanked by an *exedra* and an equally lavishly decorated *triclinium*. A corridor from the west wall of the *tablinum*, grafted on to the *domus nova* design from an earlier phase of the villa (Period IA) but modified and repaved, led to the reused, remodelled and added-on-to rooms of the first villa, the *domus vetus*, and to a back entrance flanked by porticos and terraces.

There was a total of 12 possible *cubicula* in the new house, and there was access to the eaves of the building as well. The atmosphere of lavishness in the mosaic pavements, in the traces of painted wall-plaster, in the possible marble dado in the *triclinium* was borne out by the dignity and consequence of the size and number of the rooms; at the same time, the grafting on of certain of the old rooms (at much effort to equalise their lower levels with ramps) gives the house a certain environment of conservatism and continuity, emphasised by the continuing use in the *domus nova* of mosaic patterns copied from the first floors (*op. mus.* 1, 2 and 8). The impression is of an up-to-date *amoenitas* and *otium*, emphasised by interior luxury and picturesque exterior views and aspect, but of reserve, care and reverence for certain old spaces and for the site of the villa itself.

By contrast, strict functionality and compactness of design characterised the *villa rustica* on the eastern terrace. The south part of the eastern terrace was a *hortus* at a lower level; it was a good size, some 600 m.^{2}, and its design is like the lower-level *hortus* at the villa at Sette Finestre, though it was without decorative architectural embellishment. The *villa rustica* itself was an H-shaped series of rooms with two courtyards; the ranges of rooms on the north and south were linked by a long narrow 'Commons'. A small residential suite on the north side of courtyard 1 may have been for an overseer or steward; there was a building which may have been a stable and storage rooms or dormitories around courtyard 2. The whole design, and the amount of space (some 850 m.^{2}, smaller than the *domus*) allocated to the *villa rustica,* is direct and without particular distinction, an impression emphasised by the utilitarian floors. The only mitigation of this almost industrial design is a small niche in the east wall of courtyard 2 which may have framed a statue or altar, but this itself was next to a threshing floor, with the result that the consolations of prayer were in proximity to the necessities of work.

In this second villa—*domus nova, domus vetus, villa rustica*—there is an order, dignity, luxury, careful class distinction, interior differentiation of space and function, conservatism, clarity and productivity which sum up, architecturally and materially, the highest ideals of the propaganda of Augustus, with whose Principate the villa is virtually contemporary. There is an atmosphere of intensive and productive agricultural work in a peaceful, welcoming environment in the *villa rustica.* The *domus* is another matter. To keep such an establishment going, the hypothesis presents itself that the villa was owned by a non-resident *paterfamilias* of high status and sound, if indeterminable, income, occupied only partially with his agricultural estates and engaged in politics or war primarily. His *otium* was in part the rest which a period of residence—whether short or long is unknown—at his villa in the Ager Falernus would afford him and his family. The estate would be run by a high servant in permanent residence who oversaw the management of the lands which may have been nearby but were not contiguous with the building. Furthermore, there was at no time any sense of social isolation: the *domus* was built and enjoyed for what it was: a country house with a healthy climate, breezes and lovely views, but it was at the same time very close to other villas belonging to families of similar social class. The heads of households would have had much to talk about, not least of which must have been the rational commercial use, purchase, exchange and co-operative exploitation of the very valuable agricultural properties in the *ager* and on the hills. The mutual up-keep of the road, the loan of water, slaves and farm equipment at various times of the year, as well as gossip and covenants of marriage and political alliance, could have filled many hours of productive talk. That done, the family and the *familiae* could have gone their separate ways, some to the Bay of Naples, others to local towns or cities such as Capua, others yet again to Rome, leaving behind a supervised work force with clearly scheduled duties and instructions as to where the income from sales of agricultural goods was to be sent. There was privacy, comfort and luxury at San Rocco, to be sure, but productive work, planning and efficient strategies for co-operative exploitation of manpower and land as well.

What had been true of the second phase (Period II) of the San Rocco villa built around 30 B.C. was further emphasised about 80 years later, in the middle of the first century A.D., by additions to the plan (Period IIA) in the new styles of masonry, *opus reticulatum* in tufa and brick construction. In the *domus,* a small but well-planned (if somewhat carelessly built and decorated) *balineum* was built in a taste and design comparable to other bath-suites in similar villas (see Fabbricotti, 1976). The *balineum* had a *frigidarium* with a cold-plunge bath, a *sudatorium* and a *caldarium* with a bath as well as service and storage areas. No significant change of aspect to the exterior of the *domus* was involved in the construction of the *balineum,* and what was sacrificed in terms of rooms for the hypocaust and *praefurnium* was made up in efficient design (the *testudo* for the bath in the *culina*) and added luxury.

It was another matter in the *villa rustica.* There, one large room was converted to use as a *figlina* or tile-making factory, of which at least one of the products was decorated ante-fixes. Two large *fornaces,* very well designed and laid out in proximity to a water-supply for storing and moulding clay, were built. In addition, a complicated *oletum* or oil-making and storing factory was set up in courtyard 2; there was a large press-room and the entire panoply—*trapetum* for milling , *torcularium* for pressing, sedimentation and separating systems, and separating vats—of equipment for the virtually industrial processing of olives from fruit to oil and axle-grease. As with the *figlina,* the *oletum* was superbly designed with a view to efficiency and economy.

These additions of *balineum, figlina* and *oletum* indicate that around A.D. 50 or later, secondary uses of the space and land had occurred. Although the villa may have had, from the beginning, some aspect of its life in the form of olive-culture, this was intensified in the middle of the first century A.D. and the returns on olives justified big investment in equipment and, presumably, more land for it. There was also enough local building going on, and clay-beds available as well, to justify construction of the *figlina.* The impression is of growth, diversification and new investment in processes of production secondary to, but consequent upon, the ownership or new acquisition of land. This resulted in the investment in equipment, and thus, of course, in further specialisation and interior differentiation of space and function of the physical and social resources of the villa. The consequence was that greater luxury could be had in the form of a very comfortable *balineum.* If the villa in its second phase (Period II) embodied the ideals of Augustus, the villa toward the end of the Julio-Claudian or the beginning of the Flavian periods (Period IIA) embodied, with its additions, the greater complexity of economic life of the period: investment in equipment to make finished products (tiles and oil) on a small but factory-organised scale supplemented, perhaps even substituted for, investment in manpower and property to produce agricultural goods. The impression is one of greater productivity and shrewd exploitation in the *villa rustica,* and greater selfishness and epicene comfort in the *domus.*

About a century and a half later, but certainly no later than the last years of the second century A.D. in the Antonine period, the villa was beginning to fall into ruins. Why it should have done so is not clear. It was certainly still accessible, though the construction of the Via Domitiana along the coast may have made it more of a back-water place than it had been when it was on the Via Appia. There is no reason why its water supply should have failed. It can be speculated that some change in land-use may have made it impossible for the owner to compete effectively with better organised owners of larger properties; in addition, falling-off of construction in the area may have terminated the *figlina's* usefulness, and imports of oil from North Africa may have ended the viability of the *oletum*. The concentration of power around a peripatetic emperor may have made the *domus* a burden and an unwanted responsibility rather than a periodically enjoyed country house, and some other form of income may have replaced the prestige and profits which an agricultural estate would have conferred. Still, by the end of the second century A.D., it is to be expected that the long history of human associations and the social, economic and physical infrastructure of the Ager Falernus, of which the San Rocco villa was a part at its initial occupation and construction *c.* 100–90 B.C., would have worn out in many ways. A record of durability and stability over three centuries represented by the various phases of the San Rocco villa's development, is, after all, a tribute to the pleasures and productivity of the Roman use of the rural environment.

Chapter VII. Mosaic and Pavement Catalogue

The mosaics and pavements in the villa at San Rocco constitute a partially datable series of floors associated with its four periods (I,IA,II,IIA); the major part of the mosaics, however, belong to Period II. Because some of the mosaics are datable, and because the study of mosaic pavements now requires separate treatment in archaeological publication, the San Rocco floors are presented in catalogue form. The catalogue is organised according to the construction periods of the villa, then broken down according to the types of floor, namely, *opus musivum* (= *op. mus*), *opus signinum* (= *op. sig.*) and *opus spicatum* (= *op. spic.*). In order to facilitate reference, the floors are numbered in sequence and according to the order of description of the rooms themselves (see Chapters III–VI). Thus, the floors of Period II are *op. mus.* 5–30, *op. sig.* 3–12 and *op. spic.* 1–5 and they are numbered according to the order in which the rooms in which they appear are described.

Each floor is presented as follows:-

1. *Type of floor,* catalogue number, location with room number, size of room (where necessary), illustration reference (where necessary; small fragments of plain mosaics and other plain floors are not illustrated).
2. *Bed.* Description of bed (where necessary), e.g. *statumen, rudus, nucleus,* and *supranucleus.* In the description of the beds, the ratios of mortar, lime, sand and so on are based on visual analysis. For the *supranucleus,* see Moore, 1968, 57–68.
3. *Tesserae.* Colour, material, type and size of *tesserae* and *scutulae* used in each floor.
4. *Description.* Description of patterns and analysis; includes description of underscoring with laying out and guide lines where necessary. Every attempt has been made to conform to the descriptive vocabulary of the *Association internationale pour l'étude de la mosaïque antique* (AIEMA), but the multi-lingual handbook of pattern names was not available at the time of writing.
5. *Dimensions.* Dimensions of the entire floor and of its decorative elements.
6. *Condition.* Condition of floor upon excavation, after lifting or repair, present condition or location (*in situ,* lifted and replaced in position, removed from original position, lost).
7. *Parallels.* Parallels in the published literature are given for all floors except those in too fragmentary condition to determine the pattern. Parallels are not given for plain floors or for *opus signinum* floors without decoration.
8. *Conclusion.* Date of the floor where appropriate.

As in Chapters III-VI, the dimensions, unless specifically stated, are given NS first, EW second.

PERIOD I. MOSAICS AND PAVEMENTS
Opus musivum

Op. mus. 1. *Room A* (4 · 20 × 4 · 65 m.). Pls IV*a–b.*, XXIV *a–b.*

Bed: Statumen and *rudus* not visible, *nucleus* at least 0 · 03 m. thick, composed of light grey mortar and lime in a ratio of *c.* 4:1. *Supranucleus* of lime and cream-coloured marble dust.

Tesserae: Three types of stones compose the floor: large *scutulae* of red, light and dark green, yellow and black limestone and of white and cream coloured marble, small *scutulae* of red, green, yellow and black limestone and of terracotta, and rectangular *tesserae* of white limestone. The large *scutulae* are 0 · 0075 to 0 · 01 m. thick and are between 0 · 045 and 0 · 065 m. long. They are roughly trapezoidal, the narrow side between 0 · 033 and 0 · 039 m. and the wide side between 0 · 04 and 0 · 049 m. Some of the marble *scutulae* are square, between 0 · 06 and 0 · 07 m.[2]. The small *scutulae* of limestone and terracotta are on the average between 0 · 018 and 0 · 025 m. long and 0 · 015 m. wide and thick. The white *tesserae* are 0 · 018 m. long, 0 · 01 m. wide and thick. Cf. *op mus.* 8 and 17.

Description: Op. mus. 1 is a *scutulatum pavimentum* (what previously has been termed a *lithostroton*) filling room A in Period I and subsequently reused and added on to (see *op. mus.* 2 and 27). The 'pattern,' very expertly randomised according to colour, is as follows: the large *scutulae* lying EW are generally alternated with two other ones lying NS on one side and EW on the other, with the result that the *scutulae* form squarish 'grounds' between them which are filled in with white rectangular *tesserae* lying two-by-two in a basket-weave arrangement with occasional small *scutulae* taking the place of a white *tessera*. The ratio of large *scutulae* to small ones is about 1:4. Naturally, there are variations and irregularities in the placement of the *scutulae* and *tesserae*. The borders on the E and W are made up of large *scutulae* lying lengthwise with one, two or three *tesserae* or one or two small *scutulae* between them: all the *scutulae* in the pavement lie parallel to the line of the walls of the room on their long axis, about half of them EW, half NS.

The borders on the N and S are missing because they were broken up in Period IA when *op. mus.* 2 was 'married' to the earlier mosaic to continue the floor southwards into room A1, and in Period II when *op. mus.* 27 was 'married' to *op. mus.* 1 when room 29 was created in the space. The edges of the mosaic on the N and S between the borders and the wall are of white *tesserae* lying two-by-two in a basket-weave arrangement. Occasionally three *tesserae* are placed side by side, but the alternating NS/EW placement of the groups is maintained throughout.

The mosaic has a crispness and sharp definition of colour and pattern in the arrangement of the *scutulae* which is emphasised by the animation and visual texture of the rectangular white *tesserae* linking the large and small *scutulae*. The effect is at once sponteous and sober, lively and dense. Cf. *op. mus.* 8.

Dimensions: Originally the pavement was the size of room A, 4 · 20 × 4 · 65 m., but the edges and borders on the N and S were lost when the S wall of room A was dismantled in Period IA. *Op. mus.* 1 was then chopped back about 0 · 30 m. on its S side; the same happened in Period II when the N wall of room A was dismantled—*op. mus.* 1 was chopped about 0 · 40 m. and *op. mus.* 27 added on.

Edges: W edge: 0 · 275 m. EW
　　　　 E edge: 0 · 245 m. EW

Field: border of *scutulae* and *tesserae* merging with field, 4 · 08 m. EW and at least 3 · 70 m. NS.

Other: The large *scutulae* are set on the average 0 · 07 to 0 · 095 m. apart, measuring from approximate centre to approximate centre.

Condition: As excavated, *op. mus.* 1 was broken at the edges and borders on the N and S and was cracked in the areas of subsidence around the drain running under the floor. Many *scutulae* and *tesserae* were missing, allowing the *nucleus* and *supranucleus* to be seen. The mosaic was left *in situ* and consolidated with cement in the cracks, *lacunae* and perimeter after cleaning.

Parallels: Morricone, 1980, 44, 71–3, no. 38, pl. IV, 38 (Rome, house between the *Scalae Caci* and the foundations of the temple of the Palatine Apollo, 100–90 B.C.) Morricone's catalogue of the *scutulata pavimenta* in and near Rome is definitive both for the nomenclature (*viz.* the setting aside of the old term *lithostroton*) and the higher dating (*viz.* the assignment of pre-Sullan dates) of this type of pavement. None of the examples cited in her appendix, 89–91, on the *scutulata pavimenta* outside Rome resemble *op. mus.* 1 at San Rocco as closely as her no. 38 which is associated with quasi-reticulate masonry and is securely dated to the first decade of the first century B.C. The arrangement of the small and large *scutulae* parallel to the borders and walls, the ratio of large and small *scutulae* (*c.* 4:1) and their colours, and the dimensions of the 'pattern' and elements are virtually the same in the Roman example and in *op. mus.* 1. The major difference is in the setting-off of the field in the Roman example with a border of black tesserae; this was probably due to the Roman mosaic filling a room larger than room A at San Rocco. See also Morricone Matini, 1967, 44 ff. and Blake, 1930, 53, 59–60, pl. 11, 4 (Praeneste and Pompeii); in these last two, however, from Praeneste and the Villa dei Misteri, neither example has both the basket-weave background and the two sizes of *scutulae*, and the Sullan date to which Blake had assigned the mosaic floors which had been called *lithostrota* must be corrected with Morricone, 1980, 9–14.

The date of the parallel from Rome is important for the dating of the Period I villa at San Rocco. Although the Roman example was found in association with quasi-reticulate masonry, and the walls at San Rocco are of *opus incertum* (see above, p. 12), the dissimilarity of masonry styles, due perhaps to variations in local practice, cannot obviate the close stylistic similarity of the pavements themselves. None of the examples of *scutulatum pavimentum* from Rome associated with either *opus quadratum* or *opus incertum* (either in limestone or tufa) so closely resemble Morricone's no. 38 from the Palatine or *op. mus.* 1 at San Rocco. As Morricone herself points out (1980, 72), the Roman example is stylistically quite different from others to which the same or similar date can be assigned. In view of the similarity of the two pavements and because assigning accurate dates based on masonry in Rome to structures of walls in Campania presents numerous difficulties (see F. Rakob in Coarelli, 1976, 32–3 and Rakob, 1976, 370–2), it seems appropriate to follow the date of the Roman example in the first decade of the first century B.C. and assign a similar date to *op. mus.* 1. An earlier dating based on the association of *op. mus.* 1 with *opus incertum*, which according to the *Roman* examples catalogued by Morricone, 1980, 26–42 would give it a date in the second half or in the last years of the second century B.C., is improbable in view of the relative elasticity of masonry techniques in this period; mosaic styles appear to change more rapidly, and it is this last which makes the date 100 to 90 B.C. appropriate for *op. mus.* 1 on the basis of its close stylistic similarity with its Roman parallel.

Conclusion: A date in the first decade of the first century B.C. is suggested for *op. mus.* 1 on the basis of the closest parallel. This date, which must give a date for the construction of the Period I villa, is borne out by other evidence (see below, p. 253).

Opus signinum

Op. sig. 1. *Room B, courtyard* (7 · 90 × 7 · 90 m.). Not illustrated.

Bed. A thin *rudus*, 0 · 02 m. thick, of limestone gravel in mortar and lime (ratio 1:4) underlay the pavement.

Tesserae. None.

Description. The pavement was 0 · 02 m. thick and had a smooth undecorated surface of well-mixed tile chips, tile dust and mortar, light brown in colour. The surface is thicker where it is moulded around the tufa cover-slabs of drains α, β and γ of Period I.

Condition. The surface of *op. sig.* 1 seemed to have been subject to some weathering, and it was broken up in patches. It was covered with a Period II fill (layer 3). Left *in situ.*

Conclusion: The presence of a floor in the courtyard (room B) of the Period I villa indicates that the space was reserved for pedestrian traffic, light vehicles and light storage; heavy storage and the sheltering of animals would have occurred elsewhere because *op. sig.* 1 could not have withstood hard use. It was for residential and pedestrian use rather than utilitarian to withstand rough wear.

Op. sig. 2. Room H, area (6 · 20 × 6 · 00 m.). Pl. V*b.*

Bed. A *rudus,* 0 · 05 m. thick, of limestone gravel in mortar and lime (ratio *c.* 4:1) underlay the pavement.

Tesserae. None.

Description. The pavement was 0 · 04 m. thick and had a somewhat rough surface of well mixed tile chips, tile dust and mortar, light brown in colour. In the two threshing circles themselves, the surface was made rougher than that of the floor by adding to the *opus signinum* a greater proportion of tile chips as well as a little limestone gravel: the surface would have been used for breaking up the grain components.

Condition. Op. sig. 2 was in good condition when excavated; it had, however, been broken through with large round trenches, probably for drainage, when the Period II terrace was built. The floor was covered by the terrace fill (layer 4). Left *in situ.*

Parallels. See note 4, p. 21, for the *areae.*

Conclusion. The thickness of the bed and floor indicate that heavy use was made of the surface; this room may have been unroofed.

PERIOD I MOSAICS AND PAVEMENTS. CONCLUSION

The simplicity of both the *domus* and the *villa rustica* in Period I at San Rocco is underscored by the *opus signinum* floor of the courtyard (*op. sig.* 1). Only one room apparently had a mosaic floor, a *scutulatum pavimentum* of fine construction and composition (*op. mus.* 1). This floor can be dated to between 100 and 90 B.C. (see above, p. 87).

PERIOD IA MOSAICS AND PAVEMENTS

Opus musivum

Op. mus. 2. Room A1 (7 · 90 × 4 · 65 m.). Pl. XXIV*a−b.*

Bed: A *statumen* of limestone gravel 0 · 02 m. thick underlies a *rudus* 0 · 035 m. thick of limestone gravel in mortar and lime (ratio *c.* 4:1). The *nucleus* contains more mortar in relation to lime (ratio *c.* 5:1) than *op. mus.* 1 and is 0 · 03 m. thick. The *supranucleus* is of lime and white marble dust, more friable and powdery than the *supranucleus* of *op. mus.* 1.

Tesserae: Three types of stones compose the floor: large *scutulae* of red, pink, light and dark green, yellow, ochre and black limestone and of white, cream-coloured and blue-veined marble, small *scutulae* of red, pink, light and dark green, yellow, ochre and black limestone (none of terracotta) and square white tesserae 0 · 01 m.[3] of limestone. The range of colours is greater than in *op. mus.* 1, having tonal variation (pink, ochre) which the earlier pavement did not have. The large *scutulae* are 0 · 0075 to 0 · 01 m. thick and are between 0 · 05 and 0 · 07 m. long. They are roughly trapezoidal, the narrow side between 0 · 03 and 0 · 035 m. and the wide side between 0 · 04 and 0 · 055 m. The small *scutulae* are on the average between 0 · 018 and 0 · 025 m. long and 0 · 015 m. wide and thick. The white *tesserae* are 0 · 01 m.[3]. Cf. *op. mus.* 8 and 17.

Description: Op. mus. 2 is an extension, in a slightly different style, of the *scutulatum pavimentum op. mus.* 1 of Period I; it was 'married' to the earlier mosaic when the S wall of Room A was dismantled and the room extended southward to make room A1. The 'pattern' is similar in composition to that of *op. mus.* 1; large *scutulae* lying EW are generally alternated with two other ones lying NS on one side and EW on the other, with the large *scutulae* forming squarish 'grounds' between them filled with white *tesserae* and small *scutulae*. The differences between *op. mus.* 1 and *op. mus.* 2 are these: in *op. mus.* 2 there are a greater number of tones (pink, ochre) resulting in a more diffuse and rosier colour effect, the white *tesserae* are square rather than rectangular, giving a less textured, flatter appearance, the ratio of large *scutulae* to small ones is about 1:5 rather than 1:4, and, finally, the large *scutulae* are set further apart. The result is that *op. mus.* 2 has a greater complexity of colour but has a flatter, looser look than the sharp definition, density and crispness of *op. mus.* 1. It is clearly intended to imitate the earlier mosaic. Cf. *op. mus.* 8, 17 and 27.

Dimensions: The size of *op. mus.* 2 was determined by the dimensions of the extension to room A; room A1 was all of room A plus an extension 3 · 70 m. southwards. The S edge and border of *op. mus.* 1 was broken up and part of the Period IA *op. mus.* 2 laid on its bed, but a new bed was made for the extension. Thus, the EW measurement is 4 · 65 m. and the NS measurement at least 4 · 00 m. along a ragged edge.

Edges: W edge: 0 · 275 m. EW
       S edge: 0 · 31 m. NS
       E edge: 0 · 245 m. EW

Field: border of *scutulae* and *tesserae* merging with field 4 · 08 m. EW and at least 3 · 70 m. NS.

Other: The large *scutulae* are set on the average 0 · 08 to 0 · 10 m. apart, measuring from approximate centre to approximate centre.

Condition: As excavated, *op. mus.* 2 had subsided into the filled Period I round reservoir which it covered. Apart from this deep subsidence and a few small *lacunae*, the mosaic was in good condition. It was lifted for purposes of excavation after cleaning and has been replaced in its original position on a cement foundation.

Parallels: As might be expected, none of the examples of *scutulata pavimenta* in or near Rome catalogued by Morricone, 1980, are stylistically comparable to *op. mus.* 2, whose closest parallel, in fact, is *op. mus.* 1 of which it is an imitation. The reason is that, in the Roman examples cited by Morricone, the introduction of square white *tesserae* (as opposed to rectangular ones in a basket-weave arrangement) results in the replacement of the rectangular *scutulae* with black or grey *tesserae* and in the disposition of the axes of the *scutulae* to a 45° angle running obliquely to the walls of the room rather than parallel to them. By contrast, in *op. mus.* 2, the *scutulae* are set parallel to the walls and the two sizes, large and small, of *scutulae* are retained even though the basket-weave background was replaced with square white *tesserae*. In Rome, *scutulata pavimenta* with square white *tesserae*, but with only one size of *scutulae* and all set obliquely to the walls of the room, and in any case quite different from *op. mus.* 2 (see Morricone, 1980,

77–9), can be dated to the first half of the first century B.C., one of them to about 50 B.C. (Morricone, 1980, 54, no. 55, pl. XXIII).

See also Blake, 1930, 60–3, pl. 12, 2 (Tivoli) though see discussion of oblique background, 64. Pernice, 1938, 15, pl. 4, 3 (Solunto, first century B.C.)

Conclusion: The pavement is structurally later than *op. mus.* 1 but its date cannot be determined precisely from parallels. *Op. mus.* 2 must be dated in association with *op. mus.* 3 and 4 with which it is contemporary.

Op. mus. 3. *Room D1, cubiculum* (L-shaped, 39 · 96 m. square). Pls. VII*a*, XVI*a* and XXV*a*.

Bed. A *statumen* of limestone gravel, 0 · 03 m. thick, underlies a *rudus*, 0 · 035 m. thick, of limestone gravel in mortar and lime (ratio *c.* 4:1). The *nucleus* contains mortar and lime (ratio *c.* 5:1) and is 0 · 02 m. thick, and the *supranucleus* is of lime and cream-coloured marble dust.

Tesserae. Large black and white limestone *tesserae* 0 · 015 m³ are set in white limestone chips.

Description. Op. mus. 3 is not, strictly speaking, a mosaic, but rather a *terrazzo* pavement with mosaic cubes set into it and a white mosaic strip bordered with black bands separating the main floor from the alcove for the bed. The *terrazzo* in the large part of the room, made of limestone chips, between 0 · 005 and 0 · 009 m. long, set in lime and cream-coloured marble dust and carefully smoothed down to a hard, flat surface, was set with large black *tesserae* aligned parallel to the walls, 43 rows NS, 77 rows EW. The white mosaic strip consisted of a row of white *tesserae* and three rows of large black *tesserae*, the same size as those set into the *terrazzo*, on either side of a broad strip of white limestone *tesserae*, also the same size, set at a diagonal to the walls. The alcove for the bed was paved with plain white *terrazzo* undecorated with black *tesserae*. The whole floor is simple, sharp and clear.

Dimensions. The *terrazzo* decorated with black *tesserae* was the same size as the long part of the L: 3 · 60 × 6 · 30 m., and the black *tesserae* were set 0 · 08 to 0 · 09 m. apart from centre to centre. The mosaic strip separating the main part of the room from the alcove had exterior dimensions of 0 · 37 × 3 · 54 m. (the width of the alcove opening). On the E and W ends, the centre strip and the black and white borders apparently ran up to the walls without N and S borders. The N border consisted of a white band one *tessera* wide, 0 · 015 m. wide, a black band of three *tesserae*, 0 · 04 m. wide; the S border was the same but in reverse order. The strip of white *tesserae* which the borders framed was 0 · 25 m. wide, 3 · 54 m. long. The white *terrazzo*, undecorated, in the alcove was 0 · 96 × 3 · 54 m.

Condition. A general subsidence of the fill under the floor caused much cracking and breaking up of the surface and bed. Many *lacunae* of *tesserae* and cracking were noted in the strip between room and alcove. The floor was cleaned and edged with cement around the cracks but otherwise left *in situ*.

Parallels. Blake, 1930, 38 and 73, and pl. 2,2 (Pompeii, second century B.C.?) though in this example the black *tesserae* are set obliquely to the line of the walls rather than parallel to them as in *op. mus.* 3. Morricone Matini, 1971, 16, no. 70, and pl. V (Rome, Caesarian); this example is the best parallel

Conclusion. A date in the middle of the first century B.C. may be advanced for *op. mus.* 3.

Op. mus. 4. *Room D4, cubiculum* (2 · 30 × 3 · 60 m.). Pls. VII *b*, XVI *a* and XXV *a–b*.
    Bed. Same as the bed in *op. mus.* 3.

    Tesserae. Same as in *op. mus.* 3.

    Description. As with *op. mus.* 3, *op. mus.* 4 is a *terrazzo* floor with *tesserae* and a mosaic strip. The room is divided into two parts by pilasters which correspond to a strip of black and white mosaic running NS between them. In the W part of the room, the same large black limestone *tesserae* as were used in *op. mus.* 3 were set parallel to the walls, 35 rows EW, 38 rows NS, more closely spaced, however, than in the previous floor. The same white limestone chips in marble dust constituted the rest of the floor. The strip between the pilasters separating the alcove from the room was a white stepped zigzag on a black ground, with white borders on all sides. In the alcove at the E end of the room, there was a plain white *terrazzo* as in *op. mus.* 3. As in *op. mus.* 3, the clarity of the contrast between the black *tesserae* and the white *terrazzo* gives a pleasing sharpness to the simple design. For the Period II additions to this mosaic, made when the room was extended westward, see *op. mus.* 30 and *op. sig.* 11.

    Dimensions. The white *terrazzo* decorated with black *tesserae* in the W part of the room was 2 · 30 × 1 · 72 m. The black *tesserae* were between 0 · 03 and 0 · 04 m. apart. The mosaic strip between the pilasters was 2 · 10 m. long × 0 · 34 m. wide. The strip was edged with a single row of large white *tessserae* on the E and W sides and by two rows on the N and three on the S along the edges of the pilasters. The black ground was thus 2 · 01 m. long and 0 · 31 m. in exterior dimensions. A border of three black *tesserae* 0 · 045 m. wide blended with the zig-zag steps successively 7,5,3 and 1 black *tesserae* wide (corresponding to the same stepped rows of white *tesserae)* which made up the ground of the white zig-zag figure. At the four corners, a single white stepped zig-zag defined two black steps with a diagonal row of white *tesserae* between them. The plain white *terrazzo* in the alcove was 2 · 30 × 1 · 54 m.

    Condition. The floor was in good condition except for a large amount of subsidence in the SW corner of the room. After cleaning, the floor was edged with cement and was left *in situ.*

    Parallels. Pernice, 1938, 38–39 and pl.10,7 (Pompeii, associated with First Style) for the *terrazzo* surface only. Morricone Matini, 1975, 33–34, no. 16 and pl. IV (Anzio, late second to early first centuries B.C.) for the *terrazzo* surface only. No good parallel for the strip between the pilasters could be found. This mosaic is mentioned and illustrated in McDonald, 1966, 130–131 and pl. 67.

    Conclusion. Because *op. mus.* 4 is associated with the laying of *op. mus.* 3, a date in the middle of the first century B.C. can be advanced for it, even though no good parallel for its decorated portion could be found. Parlasca dated the decorated part as *c.* 60–50 B.C. or even a little later (personal communication).

PERIOD IA MOSAICS AND PAVEMENTS. CONCLUSION

The simplicity of Period I at San Rocco is replaced by a greater elaborateness of the floors in Period IA. The expert matching and extension of *op. mus.* 1 with *scutulatum pavimentum* (*op. mus.* 2) was done with a concern for economy and continuity, but a certain luxurious disposition is evident in the paving, in *terrazzo,* of two new *cubicula* (D1 and D4; *op. mus.* 3 and 4). These *terrazzo* floors have close parallels of Caesarian date in Rome: they may therefore be dated to about the middle of the first century B.C. (*c.* 50 B.C.).

PERIOD II MOSAICS AND PAVEMENTS

Opus musivum

Op. mus. 5. Room 1, vestibulum (T-shaped, 40 · 54 m.²). Pl. XXVI*a*.

Bed. A *statumen* of limestone rubble and gravel, 0 · 05 m. thick, underlies a *rudus*, 0 · 05 m. thick, of limestone rubble, gravel and lumps of mortar in mortar and lime (ratio *c.* 4:1). The *nucleus* is very thick, 0 · 09 m, of poorly mixed mortar and lime (ratio *c.* 5:1). The *supranucleus* is of lime and white marble dust.

Tesserae. The mosaic is composed of black, white, pink, purple, red, bluish-black, green, yellow and ochre limestone *tesserae*, 0 · 01 m.³.

Description. Since all of the mosaic in the E part of the room was destroyed due to the construction, on the diagonal NW to SE, of one of the hospital walls, only the extant fragments in the W part of the room, namely the edges, borders and part of the field of the short arm of the T and the threshold between the limestone blocks framing the door leading from room 1 into the peristyle, can be described. It is not known how the rest of the pavement was designed, but fragments of the bed dug into by the hospital walls do indicate that the whole room was embellished with mosaic. The mosaic is described as:-

A. The *cancellum* in the E part of the short arm of the T.

B. The threshold between room 1 and the peristyle.

A. The *cancellum.* The field in the short arm of the T-shaped *vestibulum* is surrounded on the N, E and W with diagonally placed white edges and is bordered with bands of eight black and three white *tesserae*. It is a *cancellum* or grid made of three white *tesserae* set parallel to the walls. At every *other* intersection, the white *tesserae* are replaced by black ones, and from these intersections radiate bands composed of a row of black *tesserae* flanked by white ones; the *tesserae* are set parallel to the walls and thus make zig-zag edges to the bands. These diagonal bands separate the areas enclosed by the white *cancellum* which are filled with *tesserae* of complementary colours. Thus, of the fragments still left, the one remaining square at the N side of the W end is pink on the SW side of the diagonal band, purple on the NE. In the next group, five squares remain; the westernmost is yellow in the NW, ochre in the SE, and in the squares moving eastwards, purple in the SW, pink in the NE, then black in the NW, green in the SE, then purple in the SW, pink in the NE, then purple in the NW, pink in the SE. The next group, also moving from the W to the E with five extant squares, begins with a square which is green in the SW, black in the NE, then one which is ochre in the NW, yellow in the SE, then pink in the SW, purple in the NE, then black in the NW, green in the SE, then one which is ochre in the SW, yellow in the NE. Next to the last group, two squares remain, beginning at the W border; the first is purple in the NW, pink in the SE, and the one next to it on the E was green in the SW, black in the NE. A final fragmentary square remaining next to the border on the W and just S of the last group described was pink in the SW, purple in the NE. The principle of the colour arrangement in the pattern is clear: squares divided diagonally with complementary colours — pink/purple, black/green and yellow/ochre — in the opposite triangles. The dominant combination, however, is pink/purple, of which there were twice as many squares as the other two, with the result that, in every group of four squares, two were pink/purple. On the N side, a fragment of diagonal edge, between the border and the wall, allows us to reconstruct the field as having had seven squares NS, and at least seven (probably more) EW.

B. *The threshold.* The threshold between the *vestibulum* and the E portico of the peristyle was a double row of interconnecting white meanders in coloured isometric perspective on a black ground flanked by lozenges on the N and S. Between the *cancellum* and the threshold there was an edge of diagonally set white *tesserae*. The threshold itself was bordered with a band of three white *tesserae* (except on the S side where there were six white *tesserae* to fill in the mosaic up to the limestone block), and an inner border of four black *tesserae* running around both the lozenge and the meanders. On the S side the lozenge is framed by a border of four green *tesserae;* the lozenge frame is 0 · 25 × 0 · 48 m. without the border. The background for the lozenge is white, with the triangular spaces in the four corners filled with green right-angled triangles on the W, yellow ones on the E. The lozenge itself is made of bands of *tesserae* in twos or threes set on the diagonal. Beginning at the outside and counting inward, the sequence of bands making up the lozenge is: two pink, three yellow, two white, two green, two white and the central part of the lozenge is green. By contrast, on the N end, the framed lozenge is larger (0 · 275 × 0 · 56 m.) because it has no border: the white exterior bands defining the lozenge touch the outer edges of the rectangle. The ground is composed of black *tesserae;* the triangular spaces in the four corners are filled with white right-angled triangles. The outermost band of the lozenge is made of two white *tesserae*; the next band in is of white *tesserae* set parallel to the walls on a black border, making a zig-zag band. The next bands in are of two white, two green and two pink *tesserae,* and the central lozenge is white. The two lozenges, while different in composition and size, are not different in construction or date: they have the same bed and the *tesserae* are of the same size, and there is no visual evidence of patching or repair. Their asymmetry is intentional but subtle and corresponds to the asymmetry of the *cancellum* pattern described above, which was slightly off the axis of the room. Between the lozenges, and separated from the S lozenge by a band of three purple *tesserae,* was a double row of interconnecting meanders in coloured isometric perspective, four complete swastikas to each row. The swastikas 'roll' alternating northward and southward in opposing pairs. They are made of bands of two white *tesserae.* The background, which can only be seen in those corners in which the 'receding' planes of the perspective do not come up to the white bands, is black. The perspective is meant to 'recede' from the SE to the NW, and the colour scheme is this: as in the triangles in boxes of the *cancellum,* adjacent 'receding' planes are always arranged to be pink/purple, bluish-black/green and yellow/ ochre. All the dark colours (the purples, bluish-blacks and ochres) are on the S 'receding' planes, all the light colours (the pinks, greens and yellows) on the W 'receding' planes, with the result that, whilst the perspective 'recedes' from the SE to the NW, it is 'lit' (by the lighter colours) from the W — from the light coming in between the peristyle portico columns. Colouristically, all the shorter receding planes near the centres of the swastikas are bluish-black/green or yellow/ochre, leaving the pink/purple to be the colour of the larger planes at the sides and top and bottom of the figure. Thus the rose tone of the colour composition of the *cancellum* (which had twice as many pink/purple boxes as any in other colour combinations) was maintained in the threshold between the *vestibulum* and the peristyle. The regular spacing of the centre of the swastikas and the unequal length of their arms together with the neat straight edges of the white *tesserae* indicate that the white *tesserae* were laid first from predetermined measured centres. The 'receding' planes, usually three *tesserae* wide, have some clipped or irregularly shaped *tesserae* adjusted for their size and position to fit between already laid bands of white *tesserae.* A construction from the centres of the swastikas outward must be supposed: first the swastikas, then the background and 'receding' planes, then the lozenges of which the unusual size was a result of the slight variations of the meanders, finally the borders.

Dimensions. A. *The cancellum.* The entire mosaic occupied the short arm of the T between N and S walls and from the diagonal edge of white *tesserae* on the W to the E part of the room: it must therefore have measured at least $2 \cdot 70 \times 2 \cdot 76$ m. Excluding the diagonal border, the outer band of three white *tesserae*, $0 \cdot 03$ m. wide, and the inner band of eight black *tesserae*, $0 \cdot 08$ m. wide, framed at least $1 \cdot 75 \times 1 \cdot 75$ m. The *cancellum* measured at least $1 \cdot 60 \times 1 \cdot 60$ m; it was made of bands of three white *tesserae*, $0 \cdot 03$ m wide, and the coloured boxes were $0 \cdot 195$ m. $\times 0 \cdot 195$ m.

B. *The threshold.* Without the diagonal borders on the E and W, the exterior dimensions of the threshold between the N wall and the limestone block on the S side and the E and W bands of three white *tesserae* are $2 \cdot 04 \times 0 \cdot 70$ m. The S lozenge rectangle with its border of four green *tesserae* is $0 \cdot 36 \times 0 \cdot 56$ m., but $0 \cdot 25 \times 0 \cdot 48$ m. without the border. The N lozenge in its black rectangle is $0 \cdot 275 \times 0 \cdot 56$ m. The exterior dimensions of the double row of meanders are $1 \cdot 15 \times 0 \cdot 56$ m. The centres of the swastikas, which were determined first, were all $0 \cdot 25$ m. apart. The lengths of the arms of the swastikas in each meander were irregular, adjusted to meet at the centres.

Condition. The condition of this mosaic was poor. In the E part of the room, all of the surface and most of the bed were dug away by the hospital construction. In the short arm of the T, part of the field and some of the borders remain. The threshold, however, is almost intact. The mosaic was cleaned, consolidated with concrete and was left *in situ.*

Parallels. For the threshold in coloured isometric design, see *op. mus.* 17 and 18. For the *cancellum,* the best parallel is a floor in the villa on the Via Nomentana of Sullan (?) or Late Republican date, cf. Lugli, 1930, 534–5 and pls. XX and XXI, 3. See also Blake, 1930, 74–5 and pl. 17,4 (Pompeii, Late Republican or early Augustan). Cf. Becatti, 1961, 204–5, no. 389 and pl. IX (Ostia, Augustan) though the colours are not the same. Cf. also Morricone Matini, 1967, 23, no. 8 with fig. 7 and pl. II (Rome, Sullan) for pattern only; 35–6, no. 24 and pl.XXVII (Rome, Sullan) for pattern and colours.

Conclusion. Around Rome, the *cancellum* pattern began in Sullan times, but at Pompeii it is Late Republican or early Augustan. For this reason, and because it is associated with a coloured isometric threshold, a Late Republican date can be advanced for *op. mus.* 5.

Op. mus. 6. *Room 2, cubiculum* ($3 \cdot 40 \times 2 \cdot 45$ m.). Pl. XXVI*a–b* and XXVII*a.*

Bed. A *statumen* of limestone rubble and gravel, $0 \cdot 05$ m. thick, underlies a *rudus*, $0 \cdot 05$ m. thick, of limestone rubble, gravel and lumps of mortar in mortar and lime (ratio *c.* 4:1). The *nucleus* is 0.04 m. thick, of mortar and lime (ratio *c.* 5:1). The *supranucleus* is of lime and white marble dust.

Tesserae. The mosaic is composed of purple, black and white *tesserae* $0 \cdot 01$ m.[3].

Description. A major part of this floor was destroyed, on a diagonal line running NW to SE, with the construction of a hospital wall. Enough remains, however, to reconstruct the pattern of the mosaic in its entirety. A central mat of purple and white lozenges in rows set with their points E and W was framed with an outer border of three white, a middle border of six black and an inner border of six white *tesserae.* On the N and S sides, purple half-lozenges (cut lengthwise) and, on the E and W sides, purple half-lozenges (cut widthwise) define the sides of the mat. As a result, the pattern appears as purple lozenges on a white ground, with seventeen lozenges (including the two half-lozenges) NS and eleven lozenges (including the two half-lozenges) EW. The lozenges are made as follows; the NS and EW sides of both white and purple lozenges are made of two rows of *tesserae*, neatly laid with straight edges and with triangular *tesserae* at the points. Between these rows, on the opposite NW and SE sides, two rows of *tesserae*, purple or white, were laid, apparently freehand as the edges are not quite straight. Then the centres of the lozenges, with *tesserae* laid in rows running diagonally NE to SW, were laid. To the E, between the borders of the central mat and the E wall, and to the W, between the mat and the limestone threshold, strips of diagonally laid white edging fill in the room. To the N and S, the white diagonal edging was decorated with black *tesserae*. On the N side the crosslets were made of four black *tesserae* around a white centre set diagonally to the line of the walls. The rows of crosslets are alternated from row to row rather than set in parallel lines to maintain the diagonal movement of the white *tesserae*. On the N side, there were 23 rows of crosslets NS and room for 45 rows EW. By contrast, on the S side, the same kind of crosslets were set in parallel rows of single black *tesserae*, also set on the diagonal; there was room for 17 rows of crosslets and single *tesserae* NS, 45 rows EW. The bold central mat would have provided the decorative focus of the room while the beds of this double *cubiculum* would have stood on either side.

Dimensions: The whole mosaic had the dimensions of the room, 3 · 40 × 2 · 45 m. The exterior dimensions of the central mat with its borders were 1 · 66 × 2 · 10 m. The borders of three white, six black and six white *tesserae* were 0 · 03, 0 · 055 and 0 · 055 m. wide respectively. The field of lozenges was 1 · 36 × 1 · 81 m. The lozenges were 0 · 18 m. long and 0 · 09 m. wide. On the N side, the diagonally laid edge with crosslets formed a bed alcove, 0 · 90 × 2 · 45 m.: the S bed alcove was 0 · 84 × 2 · 45 m. The white centres of the black crosslets on the N were set 0 · 10 m. apart in alternating rows; the white centres of the crosslets and the single black *tesserae* in parallel rows on the S were 0 · 09 m. apart.

Condition: The conditon of *op. mus.* 6 was poor. A large part of it was dug away by the hospital construction. Portions are missing in the NE and SW corners. The mosaic has been consolidated *in situ* with cement.

Parallels: Although the rows of coloured crosslets are not unusual (see *op. mus.* 14) the mat of white and purple lozenges is; no good parallel could be found.

Conclusion: Op. mus. 6 was laid at the same time as the other Period II mosaics, in Late Republican times.

Op. mus. 7. *Room 3, cubiculum* (2 · 80 × 2 · 45 m.). Not illustrated.

Bed. The bed of *op. mus.* 7 is virtually identical to the composition of the bed of *op. mus.* 6.

Tesserae: The small fragments of the mosaic still extant are of white *tesserae* 0 · 01 m.[3] only.

Description: Two small fragments of diagonally laid white edging, too narrow to retain any of the floor's pattern, were preserved along the N wall. Sections of the bed are preserved in different parts of the room indicating that originally it was completely floored in mosaic.

Condition: This mosaic has been completely destroyed except for the fragments and bed mentioned above.

Conclusion: Because the bed is the same as that of *op. mus.* 6, this floor is of the same date. (Cf. *op. mus.* 6).

Op. mus. 8. *Peristyle* (209 · 56 m.²). Pls. XXVII*a–b*.

Bed: A thin *statumen* of limestone chips 0 · 02 m. thick underlies a *rudus* 0 · 04 m. thick of limestone rubble, gravel and lumps of mortar in mortar and lime (ratio *c.* 4:1). The *nucleus* is also thin, 0 · 03 m. thick, of mortar and lime (ratio *c.* 5:1). The *supranucleus* is of lime and white marble dust, very friable. The exceptional thinness of the bed of *op. mus.* 8 must be due to a desire to cut building costs when covering a large surface; its result is the poor condition of the mosaic.

Tesserae: The mosaic is composed of black and white limestone *tesserae* 0 · 01 m.[3]. In addition, there are coloured limestone and marble *tesserae* and *scutulae* in three categories of size and colour:

1. Small square limestone *tesserae*, *c.* 0 · 015 × 0 · 015 m.² and about 0 · 01 m. thick, a little bigger than the ordinary *tesserae*. Most of these small *tesserae* are equally divided among green and black; occasionally there is a yellow one.

2. Medium rectangular limestone *scutulae*, 0 · 025 × 0 · 0175 m.² and about 0 · 01 m. thick. The colours are about equally divided among pink, purple, yellow, green and black.

3. Large, roughly trapezoidal limestone and marble *scutulae* *c.* 0 · 04 to 0 · 075 × 0 · 035 to 0 · 055 m.² and about 0 · 005 m. thick (thinner than the *tesserae* and other *scutulae*). Those of limestone are about equally divided among green, black, yellow and beige; there are a very few pink ones. There are occasional beige marble *scutulae*.

The ratio among the coloured *tesserae* and the medium and large *scutulae* is approximately 2:2:1; there are about twice as many coloured *tesserae* and medium *scutulae* as there are large *scutulae*.

Description: Op. mus. 8 is a *scutulatum pavimentum* of unusual size and sustained composition. At the outer edges along the walls, there is a diagonally laid plain white edging in square *tesserae*. The outer borders are made of bands of three white, seven black and seven white *tesserae*; these borders framed the *scutulatum pavimentum* proper. The inner borders around the *viridarium* lie beside the stylobate of the columns. From the *scutulatum pavimentum* to the stylobate, the inner borders are bands of three white, nine black, nine white and four black *tesserae*; this last black border lies beside the limestone stylobate blocks or beside the mosaic mats (*op. mus.* 9–12) between the columns.

The *scutulatum pavimentum* itself is made of three sizes of stones aligned parallel to the walls in a background of diagonally-set white *tesserae*. In general, the large *scutulae* are set with two medium ones in alternating alignments on two sides, and one medium *scutulatum* and two coloured *tesserae* at the two other sides. The setting of the *scutulae* in a diagonally-set background is different from the method used in the other *scutulata pavimenta* of Periods I and IA (*op. mus.* 1 and 2) and of Period II (*op. mus.* 17). Moreover, because the *scutulae* are more closely set (about 0 · 05 m. apart centre to centre) than in the others, the surface seems flatter and denser. The ratio among the *tesserae* and the medium and large *scutulae* (*c.* 2:2:1) creates a contrast of sizes less bold, more modulated, than that of *op. mus.* 1, where the ratio of large and small *scutulae* was about 1:4. The effect in *op. mus.* 8 is thus flatter and looser, more like *op. mus.* 2 and 17. In addition, because of the greater number of coloured *scutulae* and *tesserae* relative to the white background, a continuous surface is emphasised in the composition of *op. mus.* 8, appropriate to the large spaces it embellished. There were medium *scutulae* in a greater range of colours (including pink and purple) than the other *scutulae* and the coloured *tesserae*, with the result that pinkish tones balance the generally dark or neutral tones of the other *scutulae*.

Finally, the wider borders around the *viridarium*, wider than those along the walls, balance the architectural focus of the space: by underscoring the inner borders, the passage to the uncovered area is equalised with the passage through doors into other rooms along the outer borders.

Dimensions: The entire area of the peristyle floor, 209 · 56 m.², was covered with mosaic. The other dimensions are as follows:

Diagonally laid white edging along walls:
>N side: 0 · 19 m.
>E side: 0 · 26 m.
>S side: 0 · 32 m.
>W side: 0 · 35 except along *tablinum* threshold (*op. mus.* 13)

Outer borders: The band of three white *tesserae* is 0 · 03 m. wide, the band of seven black and seven white *tesserae* 0 · 17 m. wide.

Scutulatum pavimentum: The width of the *scutulatum pavimentum* is as follows:
>N side: 3 · 75 m.
>E side: 2 · 88 m.
>S side: 3 · 62 m.
>W side: 3 · 79 m.

Inner borders: The inner border from the *sculutatum pavimentum* to the stylobate is as follows: the band of three white *tesserae* is 0 · 03 m. wide, then the band of nine black *tesserae* 0 · 10 m., nine white *tesserae* 0 · 10 m. The innermost band of four black *tesserae* is 0 · 04 m. wide.

Condition: The condition of *op. mus.* 8 is poor. Large sections have been destroyed from both ancient and modern intrusions. The *tesserae* do not adhere well to the bed, which itself is much buckled and sunk. The floor has been repaired with cement *in situ*.

Parallels: Blake, 1930, 63, pl. 12, 2 (Tivoli, late Republican or Augustan) but this is not a good parallel as the three sizes of *scutulae* and *tesserae* used in *op. mus.* 8 are not similar. The same absence of good parallels for *op. mus.* 8 obtains in the Roman examples catalogued in Morricone, 1980; stylistically, *op. mus.* 8, while it fits in with Morricone's second type of *scutulata pavimenta* with plain white backgrounds (78–9), is unique in its design with graded sizes of *scutulae* and variously coloured *tesserae*. A geographically close parallel is in W. Johannowsky, 1961, 261 for the late Republican *scutulatum pavimentum* (termed *lithostroton*) in the *apodyterium* of the central baths at Cales.

Conclusion: Johannowsky's late Republican date for pavements of *scutulatum* type at Cales, together with the generally later dating of such pavements with obliquely set backgrounds in white *tesserae* (see *op. mus.* 2 parallels and conclusion) gives a late Republican date for *op. mus.* 8.

Op. mus. 9, 10, 11 and 12. *Peristyle 'mats'.* Pl. XXVIIIa–d.

Between the columns supporting the portico roofs of the peristyle were mosaic mats decorating the stylobate; the mats occupied the area between the inner borders of *op. mus.* 8 and the limestone curbs which separated the covered area from the ground of the *viridarium*. Originally, it is probable that all twelve openings between the columns had mosaic mats; only four have survived in a fragmentary condition. The patterns used in the mats were intended to reproduce, on a smaller scale, the patterns used elsewhere in the villa. Thus a scale, a stepped triangle, a coloured checkerboard and a *cancellum* pattern were used, recalling *op. mus.* 5, 6 and 16. Whilst some of the mats may have had the same pattern, the four remaining ones all had different ones, suggesting that the composition of the mats was intended to add decorative variety and complexity to the peristyle.

The lengths of the mats would have varied with the interaxials of the columns, but their width would have been $0 \cdot 85$ m. from the inner black border of *op. mus.* 8 to the edge of the *viridarium*. The mats were separated from the topsoil of the garden by a border of limestone blocks such as the two found *in situ* in the NE and NW corners.

The position of the mats is:— *op. mus.* 9, E side of peristyle between the column at the SE corner and the southernmost column, in the sourthernmost opening: *op. mus.* 10, S side of the peristyle, between the central columns: *op. mus.* 11, S side of the peristyle, between the column at the SW corner and the westernmost column, in the westernmost opening: *op. mus.* 12, W side of the peristyle between the column at the NW corner and the northernmost opening.

For mats between columns, see the Pompeian examples: in the Casa del Labirinto, Pernice, 1938, 36 and pls. 8 and 9—and in the Casa di Meleagro, Blake, 1930, 100 and pl. 32, 3.

Op. mus. 9. *Peristyle mat, E side.* Pl. XXVIII*a*.

   Bed: Same as that of *op. mus.* 8.

   Tesserae: Op. mus. 9 is composed of pink, purple, black, green, yellow, ochre and white limestone *tesserae*, $0 \cdot 01$ m.[3]

   Description: A *cancellum* of rows of two white *tesserae* set diagonally to the line of the walls. The squares between the rows of white *tesserae* were divided NS into triangles of similar colours. Only four squares survived, coloured black and green, yellow and ochre, pink and purple. The half-square next to the border of *op. mus.* 8 was purple.

   Dimensions: The rows of two white *tesserae* were $0 \cdot 02$ m. wide and framed squares $0 \cdot 095$ m.[2] divided into triangles $0 \cdot 135$ m. at the base.

   Condition: This fragment was in poor condition on excavation. In 1965, when some mosaics were lifted, this fragment was lost.

   Parallels: There are no good published parallels for this type of coloured *cancellum*.

   Conclusion: For suggested date, see *op. mus.* 10 and 12.

Op. mus. 10. *Peristyle mat, S side.* Pl. XXVIII*b*.

   Bed: Same as that of *op. mus.* 8.

   Tesserae: Op. mus. 10 is composed of pink, purple, black, green, yellow and ochre limestone *tesserae*, $0 \cdot 01$ m.[3]

   Description: Op. mus. 10 is a scale ('fish-scale' or imbricated) pattern like *op. mus.* 16. It had an exterior border of four black *tesserae* and a fillet of two *tesserae* alternately black and white creating a checkerboard band. The scale pattern was made of spade-shaped scales bisected lengthwise with a row of white *tessserae* so that half of every other scale on the S side was white and half of every other scale on the N side was in coloured *tesserae*. The coloured scales were set in diagonal rows with the result that the pattern could be 'read' horizontally, vertically or diagonally. Of the remaining two and a half rows of scales (five half-rows), there were only four remaining in the SW corner of the mat. The colours of the diagonal rows, beginning in the SW corner and moving NE, were ochre, green, purple and pink, colours also found in *op. mus.* 1 and in other mosaics at San Rocco.

Dimensions: The border of four black *tesserae* was 0 · 04 m. wide; the inner border of black and white checkerboard was 0 · 02 m. wide. The scales themselves were 0 · 135 m. long from the top of one scale to the top of the next; they were 0 · 08 m. wide at their widest (two half-scales).

Condition: Only a small section of the SW corner remained on excavation. In 1965, when some mosaics were lifted, this fragment had disappeared.

Parallels: Pernice, 1938, 36–37 and pl. 8, 6 (Pompeii, associated with First and Second Styles); see also 86 and pl. 39,2 (Pompeii, associated with Second Style).

Conclusion: As the parallels for this pattern can be dated with Second Style painting, a late Republican date like that for *op. mus.* 8 can be advanced.

Op. mus. 11. Peristyle mat, S side. Pl. XXVIII*c*.

Bed: Same as that of *op. mus.* 8.

Tesserae: Op. mus. 11 is composed of pink, purple, green, black and white limestone *tesserae*, 0 · 01 m³.

Description: Op. mus. 11 is a multicoloured checkerboard with an effect of dark zig-zag bands on light ones. The checkerboard was framed by a black border at least four *tesserae* wide. The squares were set up in rows: white triangles on the S side, then a row of purple squares, a row of pink ones, a row of white ones, then a fragment indicating that the next row was a row of green squares. Since the white squares 'read' as a background, the pattern on the whole has the effect of zig-zag bands of pink/purple and black/green on a white ground.

Dimensions: The black border was at least 0 · 04 m. wide. The coloured squares were all 0 · 07 m².

Condition: Only fragments of six rows of the mat were found, in poor condition. In 1965, when some mosaics were lifted, this mosaic had disappeared.

Parallels: While multicoloured checkerboards exist, no good published parallels for one with this kind of zig-zag effect could be found.

Conclusion: For suggested date, see *op. mus.* 10 and 12.

Op. mus. 12. Peristyle mat, W side. Pl. XXVIII*d*.

Bed: Same as that of *op. mus.* 8.

Tesserae: Op. mus. 12 is composed of pink, purple, yellow, ochre, black and white limestone *tesserae* 0 · 01 m³.

Description: Op. mus. 12 is a stepped triangle pattern in which rows of coloured triangles alternate with white ones. The small fragment which has survived in the SW corner of the mat was framed by a border of seven white and four black *tesserae*: sections of these bands were found on the S and W sides. The stepped triangles were made of a 'base' of seven *tesserae*, then with rows of five, three and one *tesserae* of the same colour. Every other triangle was white: the southernmost row of coloured triangles was green, the next black, then pink, purple, yellow, ochre and pink. All the coloured triangles 'pointed' northward, on a background of white triangles which 'pointed' southward.

Dimensions: The outer white band in the border was 0 · 08 m. wide, the inner black band 0 · 04 m. wide. The base of all the triangles was 0 · 07 m. wide: each was 0 · 04 m. long.

Condition: Only a small fragment in poor condition was found on excavation. In 1965 when some mosaics were lifted, this mosaic was lost.

Parallels: Pernice, 1938, 15 and pl. 4, 2 (Solunto, first century B.C.) and the Pompeian examples, 56, 68–9, 86 and pls. 22, 1, 29, 1 and 38, 6 (Pompeii, associated with Second Style).

Conclusion: As the parallels for this pattern can be dated with the Second Style painting, a Late Republican date like that of *op. mus.* 8 can be advanced.

Op. mus. 13, 14 and 15. *Room 4, tablinum* (6 · 90 × 6 · 35 m). Pls. XXIX, XXX, XXXI*a* and Fig. 13*a–c*.

The mosaic floor of the *tablinum* consisted of three sections: the threshold on the E side into the peristyle (*op. mus.* 13), the main floor area (*op. mus.* 14) and the narrow W threshold depicting a city gate (*op. mus.* 15). There was originally a fourth section, an *emblema* of separate manufacture, now unfortunately lost, in the middle of the main floor area. These three sections of essentially the same floor are described separately. As might be expected, the greater part of decorative and, indeed, figurative richness was expended in the main living room of the house: not only was there a special *emblema* in the middle of the floor, there were also small hexagonal *emblemata* with rosettes in the threshold. The floor of the *tablinum* is also unusual in that the threshold (*op. mus.* 13) still bore the marks of laying-out and guide-lines to help the mosaicist in laying his *tesserae*. These preliminary lines should be compared to those of *op. mus.* 20.

Op. mus. 13. *Room 4, tablinum threshold.* Pl. XXIX*a–d* and Fig. 13*a–c*.

The threshold of fifteen hexagons with rosettes, each of them an *emblema* of separate manufacture, incorporates unusual features. It is set off from the borders of the peristyle, *scutulatum pavimentum* (*op. mus.* 8) by a narrow white marble border with two little sections of *opus sectile*; it also incorporates two sizes of limestone *tesserae* in the hexagons. The hexagons themselves were probably manufactured separately in a workshop elsewhere and incorporated into borders laid around them. The positioning of the hexagons and of the surrounding borders was effected by scoring the still wet *nucleus* with lines for the laying of the *tesserae*, in a system like that of *op. mus.* 20 but not preserved in quite the same way at other sites. The special character of *op. mus.* 13 thus involves its construction and consequently its bed, its *tesserae* and its pattern.

Bed. A *statumen* of limestone rubble and gravel 0 · 05 m. thick, indistinguishable from that of *op. mus.* 8 and 14, underlies a *rudus* 0 · 05 m. thick of limestone rubble, gravel and lumps of mortar in mortar and lime (ratio *c.* 4:1). In the stratum of the *nucleus*, the fifteen hexagons (but *not* the half-hexagons at the N and S ends of the threshold) had *nuclei* and *supranuclei* distinctly different from the *nucleus* and *supranucleus* of the surrounding borders. The differences were marked as much by the material composition of the two kinds of *nuclei* as by the different ways they have decayed; the *nuclei* of the fifteen hexagons were much more friable, in part because the ratio of mortar to lime was *c.* 5:2 and was mixed with some sand, in part also because the *tesserae* were set in a very adhesive *supranucleus* which broke off the surface of the *nucleus* when the *tesserae* came off. The result is a series of hexagonal depressions of the hexagons' *nuclei* in the harder *nucleus* of the rest of the pavement. The *supranucleus* of the hexagons is of lime and white marble dust, very friable. The *nucleus* under the limestone *tesserae* of the rest of the threshold was like that of *op. mus.* 5, of poorly mixed mortar and lime (ratio *c.* 5:1) but a little thinner, only 0 · 07 m. The top surface of this part of the *nucleus* was left to cure partially, and was then scored with guide-lines for the setting of the *tesserae*. The *supranucleus* was of lime and marble dust, harder and whiter than that of the hexagons. *Tesserae.* Two sizes of *tesserae* exist, a larger size in the borders and the outermost parts of the hexagons, and a smaller size in the inner parts of the hexagons and rosettes. The borders and the outer parts of the hexagons are composed of pink, purple, black and white *tesserae* $0 \cdot 01$ m³. From the inside out, the borders of the hexagons consist of five rows of black, five rows of pink and two rows of white *tesserae;* the position of this last row was scored on the *nucleus* outside that of the prefabricated hexagons. The borders were all of the larger size of *tesserae*. The triangular borders outside the double rows of white *tesserae*, also of the larger size, were purple, green and black. On the *nuclei* for the hexagons with rosettes, there was an innermost hexagonal edge of either white or purple *tesserae* of the larger size ($0 \cdot 01$ m.³). The rosettes themselves, however, were of smaller pink, yellow, purple, black and white *tesserae* $0 \cdot 005$ m.³ to $0 \cdot 0075$ m.³. It is possible that there were a few glass *tesserae* of a similarly small size in the rosettes — none were found *in situ*, but a few were found loose in the surrounding soil (they may have been used in repairs).

Description. The threshold of the *tablinum* can be divided into five parts: 1. The marble border. 2. The mosaic hexagons. 3. The scoring of the *nucleus*. 4. The borders of the hexagons. 5. The borders framing the entire threshold.

1. *The marble border.* A marble border separated the peristyle from the *tablinum*. The marble was a fine-grained bone-white one, cut into slabs $0 \cdot 145$ m. wide, $0 \cdot 05$ m. thick and varying between $0 \cdot 65$ and $0 \cdot 95$ m. in length. All four surfaces had been given a smooth finish, and the marble slabs were set into the *nucleus* of the rest of the pavement. On the axis of the room, there were two small panels ($0 \cdot 10 \times 0 \cdot 10$ m.) with raised fillets $0 \cdot 02$ m. wide cut into the marble slab; these had raised squares on edge and the corners were evidently intended to be filled with small triangles of coloured limestone or marble. This is the only appearance of *opus sectile* at San Rocco. The decorative marking of the *tablinum* axis and thus of the axis of the *domus nova* is an instance of the architectural 'eye' with which the mosaicists were working at San Rocco.

2. *The mosaic hexagons.* The difference between the *nuclei* of the fifteen mosaic hexagons and their borders indicates that the hexagons themselves with their rosettes were made separately from the rest of the threshold as special *emblemata*. Where they were made is not certain: they were, in any case, made of smaller *tesserae* and had a detail and finesse absent in those other parts of the mosaic laid *in situ* on the site. Like the *emblemata* in *op. mus.* 14 and elsewhere, they were probably laid in *nuclei* set in cloth or wood supports and brought from a bench or workshop, set in position, then cemented in with the *nucleus* of their borders. The hexagons were $0 \cdot 20$ m. wide. Their exterior sides were made of either pink or black *tesserae* in three rows, $0 \cdot 03$ m. wide. The rosettes at their centres were set in circles $0 \cdot 14$ m. in diameter or in hexagons $0 \cdot 14$ m. across. Of the rosettes themselves, only three, the centremost and the one next to it on the N and an almost complete one at the northernmost end beside the final half-hexagon, were complete enough to reconstruct. The centremost rosette was framed in a circle made of white *tesserae* with a black background. It had six sharp-pointed oval petals alternately purple and white with no centre. Next to it on the N, the hexagon had a border of three white *tesserae* framing a purple hexagon. The rosette was set in a black circle and had six scalloped petals outlined with a single row of white *tesserae*. The petals themselves were made with rows of pink and purple *tesserae* and converged on a black centre sur-

rounded by a triple row of black *tesserae*. The hexagon on the north next to the half-hex-agon was of exactly similar design to the pink/purple scalloped petal hexagon just described. It would seem that the hexagons framed circles with alternating sharp-pointed and scalloped rosettes and had a predominantly pink and purple tone. At either end, next to the limestone slabs framing the *tablinum* door opening, there were half-hexagons whose *nuclei* were part of the *nucleus* of the rest of the pavement, quite unlike the *nuclei* of the other hexagons. The S half-hexagon had a small, very crudely laid rosette of four (rather than six) scalloped petals. The half-hexagons were slightly longer (by $0 \cdot 05$ m.) than the others in order to fill the space in which they stood; evi-dently the fifteen pre-fabricated hexagons did not quite fill up the space provided, so the half-hexagons had to be 'stretched'. The half hexagons appear, from the evidence of their *nuclei*, to have been laid along with the rest of the threshold once the prefabricated hexagons had been laid in place.

3.   *The scoring of the nucleus.* The *nucleus* of *op. mus.* 13 was scored to provide lines for the laying of the hexagonal border around the prefabricated hexagons once they were in place. The simplest possible method was used, one which required no measurement as such but merely the transfer, to the still wet mortar, of the position of strings or of edges marked off on a card or board. The method must have been one in which the divisions were made of simple halves or quarters of the threshold's width to determine the correct angle of the hexagonal borders: the method needed no measuring. Furthermore, the scoring could be done independently of the hexagons already in place; the sequence seems to have been as follows:—
  1. Spreading of *rudus* and *statumen*.
  2. Positioning of prefabricated hexagons with their own *nuclei*.
  3. Spreading of *nucleus* around hexagons.
  4. Scoring of still wet *nucleus* with laying-out and guide-lines.
  5. Laying of *tesserae* of the borders around the hexagons.
The scored lines could be seen in patches all over the cleaned *nucleus* and, where the surface was worn, enough remained in other areas to reconstruct the rest. The scoring consisted of two sorts of lines: laying-out lines and guide-lines. The laying-out lines determined the position of the guide lines, and the guide-lines determined the lines along which the *tesserae* were laid. The laying-out lines were thus drawn to provide points from which the guidelines for the *tesserae* could be projected, a necessity because some of the guide lines had to be diagonal ones. The description of the scoring of the *nucleus* follows the distinction between the laying-out lines and guide-lines.
a.   *Laying-out lines.* the laying-out lines consisted of five parallel lines $0 \cdot 12$ m. apart running the entire length of the threshold, dividing it into four equal parts. The central line would have been a broken one, interrupted by the prefabricated hexagons already in place: the lines dividing the two halves would have just touched the prefabricated hexagons, whilst the outermost lines would have been continuous ones. In all probabil-ity the middle of the centre line (along its length) would have been determined by where the centremost prefabricated hexagon was placed; it would have been easiest to project the position of the other laying-out lines from that point. Evidence for projection from the centre is as follows: the half-hexagons at the north and south ends, which were not prefabricated, were a little bigger than the prefabricated hexagons, 'stretched' in order to fill up the end of a space in which the position of the rows of *tesserae* had for the most

part been determined geometrically. The first stage of the laying-out lines for a sample of three hexagons is illustrated in Fig. 13*a*. Once the centre had been determined, it was an easy matter to mark the position of the hexagonal borders by using strings or cards of standard length, in this case 0 · 20 m. The result is that neat regular lines crossed the original ones perpendicularly at intervals of 0 · 20 m. The second stage of the laying-out lines for a sample of three hexagons is illustrated in Fig. 13*b*. These constituted the laying-out lines for the whole threshold. Cf. *op. mus.* 20.

b.   *Guide-lines.* The guide-lines for the hexagonal borders consist of lines, some of them drawn diagonally, to mark the position of the rows of two white *tesserae* framing the hexagons. These scorings consist of centre lines drawn diagonally from the intersections of the laying-out lines to make hexagons in every other division. These centre lines were flanked (0 · 01 m. on either side) by parallel lines crossing the outermost laying-out lines and the perpendiculars. In addition, two lines parallel (0 · 01 m. on either side) to the perpendicular laying-out lines were drawn, thus completing the guide-lines for the rows of two white *tesserae* flanking the hexagons. A sample of three hexagons with both laying-out and guide-lines scored in the *nucleus* around the prefabricated hexagons is illustrated in Fig. 13*c*. The combination of laying-out lines and guide-lines was used to determine the final position of the *tesserae* in the borders which framed every hexagon. Cf. *op. mus.* 20.

4.   *The borders of the hexagons.* The guide-lines for the borders of the hexagons established the line of the double row of white *tesserae* framing every hexagon; the coloured bands inside and outside the rows of white *tesserae* were, however, laid without guide-lines. From the hexagonal sides of the inner prefabricated hexagons, all the hexagonal borders were composed of five black *tesserae* framed by five pink *tesserae*. These bands were enclosed by the rows of two white *tesserae* for which the guide-lines had been drawn. In the upper and lower triangular spaces between the hexagons, V-shaped bands of six purple, four green and three black *tesserae* completed the outside borders.

5.   *The borders framing the entire threshold.* On the E side next to the peristyle and on the W side beside the continuation of the *tablinum* pavement (*op. mus.* 14), black and white bands framed the threshold. On the E side, from the marble border toward the hexagons, there was a band of three white, six black and two white *tesserae*. On the W side, the same sequence framed the pavement: an outermost row of three white *tesserae*, then rows of six black and two white ones. On the N and S sides there were no framing bands: the half-hexagons were laid up aganst the white limestone slabs which defined the wall-ends of the door of the *tablinum*.

Dimensions: The entire threshold is 6 · 38 × 0 · 70 m. The framing bands on the E and W sides are, from the inside out, 0 · 20 m. (two white), 0 · 06m. (five black) and 0 · 03 m. (three white). The prefabricated hexagons are all 0 · 20 m. from side to side, 0 · 24 m. from point to point. The inner hexagonal borders of five black, five pink and two white *tesserae* are 0 · 05 m., 0 · 05 m. and 0 · 02 m. respectively. The V-shaped borders of six purple, four green and three black *tesserae* are 0 · 06 m., 0 · 04 m. and 0 · 03 m. wide respectively.

Condition: The condition of *op. mus.* 13 is poor. All but three of the prefabricated hexagons with rosettes have disappeared, as have most of their borders. The surface of the scored *nucleus* was also quite worn. The mosaic was lifted, repaired and replaced in its original location. The marble border was left *in situ* but was reinforced with cement.

Parallels: The pattern of hexagons in a long threshold strip seems to be unique; there are no good published parallels. For the scoring of the *nucleus*, there are two types of parallels: painted and grooved. For painted examples, see Robotti, 1973, 42–4 and figs. 1–5 and Alexander and Ennaifer, 1973, 34–5, no. 36 with pls. XIV and LXI. For the grooved examples, there is an example in Pompeii for an *opus sectile* pavement; Pernice, 1938, 34, pl. 7, 5, where, to mark the position of marble lozenges in a floor of isometric cubes, the angle of the lozenges was derived from a rectilinear grid. There is another example in Bologna: Bergonzoni, 1965, 63–4 and fig. 5.

Conclusion: The *tablinum* threshold appears to be of special construction and design, but its foundations are continuous with the foundations of *op. mus.* 8 and 14, and it therefore can be given a similarly Late Republican date.

Op. mus. 14. *Room 4, tablinum* (6 · 90 × 6 · 35 m.). Pl. XXXI*a* and Fig. 13*d*.

The main part of the tablinum floor, excluding both thresholds, (*op. mus.* 13 and 15) consisted of a large area of white diagonally-laid *tesserae* with coloured crosslets. This 'carpet' was framed by black borders and had, in the centre, a double frame of coloured chevrons (outside) and lozenges (? inside) surrounding a central *emblema* of separate manufacture, now lost.

Bed: A *statumen* of limestone rubble and gravel, 0 · 05 m. thick, indistinguishable from that of *op. mus.* 8, 13 and 15, underlies a *rudus* 0 · 05 m. thick of limestone rubble, gravel and lumps of mortar in mortar and lime (ratio *c.* 5:1) 0 · 07 m. to 0 · 08 m. thick. The *supranucleus* was of lime and white marble dust, very friable. In the area of the *emblema*, inside the frame of chevrons and lozenges, the *nucleus* was of a different composition: there was some sand and a greater proportion of lime, in this respect like the *nuclei* of the prefabricated hexagons in *op. mus.* 13.

Tesserae: The mosaic is composed of pink, purple, red, green, yellow, ochre, black and white *tesserae* 0 · 01 m.[3].

Description: The main floor of the *tablinum* was decorated with a 'carpet' of diagonally-laid white *tesserae* with rows of crosslets, framed with borders of black and white bands. At all four sides, between the borders and the walls, there were edges of plain white diagonally-laid *tesserae*. On the N and S, these ran up to the *tablinum* walls and under the wall plaster; on the E and W sides they were continuous with the construction of the thresholds. The borders were as follows from the outside inward: a band of three white *tesserae*, nine black, eight white, seven black and three white ones, the conception being that the bands of three white *tesserae* frame on the outside and inside black and white bands whose relative widths are determined by subtracting one row of *tesserae*: 9, 8, 7.

The 'carpet' was made of white *tesserae* very carefully laid on the diagonal so that there was no visual interruption in its continuity. Tiny coloured crosslets laid in diagonal rows decorated it; the crosslets were of four *tesserae* surrounding a central white one at intervals of 0 · 125 m., 45 rows of crosslets NS, 36 rows EW. The colour of the crosslets was determined by laying rows on the diagonal rather than on the horizontal or vertical axes, in the following order: diagonal rows running NE to SW with black, green, pink, purple, yellow, ochre, then black and a repeat of the same sequence of colours. After the densely patterned and coloured effects of the E threshold (*op. mus.* 13), the 'carpet' would have looked refreshingly simple and unpretentious. At the centre of the 'carpet', there was an ornate frame for a central *emblema* of separate construction. The frame, of which only a fragment in the SE corner survived, had two outer bands: one of three white and an inner one of six black *tesserae*. Next came a chevron border, then a black band of four *tesserae*. The innermost border may have been of lozenges, green on white. The chevron border was composed as follows: the S side, with the chevrons 'pointing' westward, came all the way down to the corner, whilst the E side, with the chevrons 'pointing' northward, came over only to the outer edge of the inner border, as illustrated in Fig. 13*d*. The chevrons themselves were of four types: pink and purple, all white, green and black, yellow and ochre. This was the colour scheme of complements used elsewhere in the pavements of Period II. Thus, a sequence of parti-coloured chevrons was separated by all-white ones, giving an agreeable chromatic succession mitigating the boldness of the design. In the S border, starting at the SE corner, the colours were as follows: pink/purple, followed by a white one, then green/black, pink/purple, all white, yellow/ochre, green/black. In every case the lighter colour was on the outside (S side). In the E border, starting at the SE corner, the chevrons were as follows: yellow/ochre, all white, pink/purple, green/black, all white, yellow/ochre, all white, green/black, a slightly different sequence from that of the S border. A fragment of an inner border made of white and green *tesserae* indicates that there was a border of lozenges (?) on a white ground used as a border around the *emblema*. The *emblema* itself with its separate *nucleus* had been destroyed.

Dimensions. The entire pavement excluding the thresholds (*op. mus.* 13 and 15) is 6 · 90 × 5 · 65 m. The edges of plain white diagonally laid *tesserae* are 0 · 24 m. wide. The outer borders are made of bands of *tesserae* of the following widths: three white 0 · 03 m. wide, nine black 0 · 10 m. wide, eight white 0 · 09 m. wide, seven black 0 · 08 m. wide, 3 white 0 · 03 m. wide. The central 'carpet', excluding the border, was 5 · 76 × 4 · 52 m; its crosslets were set at intervals of 0 · 125 m. centre to centre. The inner borders around the *emblema* were as follows: three white *tesserae* 0 · 03 m. wide, six black 0 · 06 m. wide, chevron border 0 · 095 m. wide, four black *tesserae* 0 · 04 m. wide. The width of the inner border and the dimensions of the *emblema* could not be determined accurately.

Condition. Most of the floor was in good condition except for the area at the centre. The mosaic was lifted and repaired, then relaid in its original location.

Parallels. For the rows of coloured crosslets: Pernice, 1938, 56 and pl. 22, 3 (Pompeii, associated with Second Style). For the coloured chevron border of the *emblema*, Blake, 1930, 72 and pl. 46,6 (Pompeii, Late Republican) and especially Lugli, 1930, 530–1, and pls. XX and XXI, 7 (Via Nomentana, Sullan).

Conclusion. A Late Republican date is consistent with the date of the parallels for *op. mus.* 14.

Op. mus. 15. *The threshold between room 4, the tablinum and room 31a.* (1 · 18 × 0 · 45 m.). Pl. XXX*a–b*.

The threshold between the *tablinum* and the rooms in the W part of the villa marked the separation between the *domus nova* and the *domus vetus*; the threshold was decorated with a handsomely designed and well executed arch flanked by walls or towers with arcades and crenellations at the top. This castellated design, an example of the *Zinnen-ornament*, 'faced' eastward and was intended to be viewed from the *tablinum*. It marked the axis of the house as the corridor (room 31a) leading to the rooms of the *domus vetus* was on the architectural axis of the *domus nova*.

Bed. A *statumen* of limestone rubble and gravel, 0 · 05 m. thick, indistinguishable from that of rooms 4 and 31a (*op. mus.* 14 and 28) underlies a *rudus*, 0 · 05 m. thick, of limestone rubble, gravel and lumps of mortar in mortar and lime (ratio *c.* 4:1). The *nucleus* was continuous with that of *op. mus.* 14 and 28 as well: poorly mixed mortar and lime (ratio *c.* 5:1) 0 · 07 to 0 · 08 m. thick. The *supranucleus* was of lime and marble dust, very fine and hard.

Tesserae. Op. mus. 15 is composed of yellow, black and white *tesserae* 0 · 01 m.[3].

Description. In the following description, for convenience, the 'bottom' is on the E side of the threshold, the 'top' on the W, 'left' on the S and 'right' on the N. The motif stands on a band of three *tesserae* which run between the walls of the doorway: the band is a checkerboard of black and white *tesserae.* The yellow I-shaped members—representing piers or pilasters—bracket the arch: they are made of rows of six *tesserae* with projections of three *tesserae* on either side at the top and bottom. The arch itself, from the inside out, is made of a single row of black, one of white, then one of alternating black and white, one of white, one of black and an outer row of black and white *tesserae.* The inside of the arch is filled in with white *tesserae:* the interior silhouette of the arch was outlined with a double row of white *tesserae* before the horizontal rows of white ones were set in. Flanking the arch, there were 'walls' of four 'courses' of ashlar masonry, represented by 'blocks' made of five horizontal rows of white *tesserae* separated by single rows of black ones.

Each 'block' was 15 or 16 white *tesserae* long: the bottom-most 'course' on both sides had two 'headers' flanking a 'stretcher', the next above it had two 'stretchers', the third two 'headers' flanking a 'stretcher', the topmost row had two 'stretchers'. This arrangement brought the wall up to about two-thirds the height of the arch. Above the sections of 'wall' there was a double row of white *tesserae* serving as the base for three arched windows on either side of the arch itself. These windows were filled in with white *tesserae* and their interior outlines were single rows of black *tesserae* with a band of alternating black and white *tesserae* next to them. Above the windows were four T-shaped crenellations on either side: the vertical part of the T was made of four black *tesserae*, the horizontal part made of two rows of the same. A triple row of black *tesserae* bounded the walls and windows on the left and right sides, merging with the outermost crenellations. The area above the central arch was flat. The representation at first glance looks like a crenellated wall with arched windows flanking a large arched entrance. However, because arched windows are almost exclusively features of towers rather than walls, one must for preference see a twin-towered gate. The representation is much schematized, of course, and it is depicted without perspective.

Dimensions. The entire threshold is 1 · 18 × 0 · 45 m. From side to side, the motif of the twin-towered gate is 1 · 05 m. wide. The central arch is, from the base to the inner crown of the arch, 0 · 29 m.; the curved bands are 0 · 23 m. in inner diameter and 0 · 32 m. in exterior diameter. The yellow I-shaped supports are 0 · 185 m. high. The ashlar 'blocks' are all 0 · 05 m. high, the 'stretchers' all 0 · 155 m. to 0 · 165 m. wide, the 'headers' all half that width. The arched windows are all 0 · 075 m. high from the bottom of the window to the inner crown of the arches and 0 · 095 m. high to the outer crown. The interior diameter of the arched part was 0 · 04 m. The T-shaped crenellations were 0 · 045 m. high.

Condition. The condition of *op. mus.* 15 upon excavation was very poor, the mosaic having sunk and buckled. It was lifted and restored completely and has been replaced in its original location.

Parallels. For the ornament in general, Parlasca, 1959, 129–31. The closest parallel for the type of treatment of arched bands, crenellations and frame is from a villa at Albano Laziale, of Sullan (?) date: Lugli, 1946, 78–9 and figs. 23 and 24.

Conclusion. This interesting representation, used here as a threshold rather than as a continous border as most examples were, can be dated with *op. mus.* 14 to the Late Republic.

Op. mus. 16 and 17. *Room 5, triclinium*: (4 · 95 × 7 · 50 m.). Pls. XXXI*b*–*d* and XXXII *a*–*b*.

The mosaic pavement of the *triclinium* has for convenience been given two separate numbers, one for its threshold (*op. mus.* 16), another for the floor of the main part of the room (*op. mus.* 17). *Op. mus.* 16 is a coloured scale ('fish-scale' or imbricated) pattern like *op. mus.* 10. *Op. mus.* 17 in the main part of the room consists of no less than three separate parts: a rectangular *scutulatum pavimentum* in the E part of the room, a 'runner' of interconnecting white meanders between boxes in coloured isometric perspective and, in the W part of the room, a squarish white 'carpet' with coloured crosslets framing a central white *cancellum*, also in coloured isometric perspective. The subdivisions of the space of the room by the design of its floor corresponds to its use as a *triclinium*; the 'runner' divides the square area set up with eating beds in the W part of the room from the serving and entertainment floor (the *scutulatum pavimentum*) on the E side, near the doors leading to the peristyle (which had access to the *culina*, rooms 10–11) and the *tablinum*.

Op. mus. 16. *Threshold, room 5, triclinium* (1 · 56 × 0 · 75 m.). Pl. XXXI*b*.

Op. mus. 16 stood between the large limestone blocks with square slots for door frames which separated the *triclinium* from the peristyle.

Bed: A thick *statumen* of limestone rubble and limestone chips 0 · 05 m. thick underlies a *rudus* 0 · 04 m. thick of limestone rubble, gravel and lumps of mortar in mortar and lime (ratio *c.* 4:1). Both the *statumen* and the *rudus* are continuous with that of the peristyle floor (*op. mus.* 8) and of the *triclinium* (*op. mus.* 17). The *nucleus* of both *op. mus.* 16 and 17 is thicker than that of *op. mus.* 8: 0 · 05 m. thick, but of the same composition of mortar and lime (ratio *c.* 5:1). The *supranucleus* is of lime and white marble dust.

Tesserae: The mosaic is composed of pink, purple, yellow, ochre, green, black and white *tesserae* 0 · 01 m.[3].

Description: On the E and W sides of the threshold, there are bands of white diagonally laid *tesserae* linking *op. mus.* 16 to *op. mus.* 8 and 17. The threshold itself is framed on all four sides by three rows of white *tesserae* and a band of four black *tesserae*; the three white *tesserae* lie next to the limestone blocks on the N and S sides.

The scale pattern was made of spade-shaped scales bisected lengthwise with a row of white *tesserae* so that half of every other scale on the W side was in colour. The coloured scales were set in diagonal rows with the result that the pattern, like *op. mus.* 10, could be 'read' horizontally, vertically and diagonally.

On the S side, the threshold pattern is finished with the rounded tops of the half-scales; on the N side, the pointed bottoms of the half-scales finish it. There were eleven scales NS, six scales (14 half-scales) EW. The colours of the diagonal rows of half-scales on the E side of each row, beginning in the SW corner and moving to the NE corner, were as follows: ochre, black, green, purple, pink, green, black, ochre, yellow, pink, purple, black, green, ochre, yellow. The asymmetry of the composition is unusual: the colours do not follow each other in regular order but in the order of chromatic intensity, the order of the pink and the purple rows reversed on either side of the ochre and yellow ones in order to 'fade' effectively into the black and the green ones.

Dimensions: The border of three white *tesserae* was 0 · 03 m. wide; that of four black 0 · 04 m. wide. The scales themselves were 0 · 125 m. long from the top of one scale to the top of the next; they were 0 · 08 m. wide at their widest (two half-scales).

Condition: Large patches of the threshold had been destroyed before excavation; enough remained, however, to reconstruct the colours of all the rows. The mosaic was lifted, repaired with some reconstruction and has been replaced in its original location.

Parallels: See *op. mus.* 10.

Conclusion: A late Republican date for *op. mus.* 16 is consistent with the parallels at Pompeii.

Op. mus. 17. *Room 5, triclinium* (4 · 95 × 7 · 50 m.). Pls. XXXI*c–d* and XXXII*a–b*.

Bed: A *statumen* of limestone rubble and limestone chips 0 · 05 m. thick underlies a *rudus* 0 · 04 m. thick of limestone rubble, gravel and lumps of mortar in mortar and lime (ratio *c.* 4:1). Both the *statumen* and the *rudus* are continuous with the *triclinium* threshold (*op. mus.* 16) and thus with the peristyle pavement (*op. mus.* 8). There is a *nucleus* of mortar and lime (ratio *c.* 5:1) 0 · 05 m. thick and a *supranucleus* of lime and white marble dust, very fine and hard.

Tesserae: *Op. mus.* 17 is composed of pink, purple, olive, green, yellow, ochre, black and white tesserae 0 · 01 m.[3]

The *scutulatum pavimentum* (see 'A' below) has limestone *tesserae* and limestone and some marble *scutulae* in three categories of size and colour.

1. Small square limestone *tesserae c.* 0 · 015 × 0 · 015 m. and about 0 · 01 m. thick, a little bigger than the ordinary *tesserae*. These *tesserae* are about equally divided among pink, purple, green, ochre and black; occasionally there is a yellow one.
2. Medium rectangular or trapezoidal limestone *scutulae c.* 0 · 025 × 0 · 02 m. and about 0 · 01 m. thick. The colours are about equally divided among pink, purple, yellow, green and black; there are no ochre or olive ones.
3. Large, roughly trapezoidal limestone and marble *scutulae c.* 0 · 04 to 0 · 075 × 0 · 035 to 0 · 055 m. and about 0 · 005 m. thick, thinner than the ordinary *tesserae* and the other *scutulae*. Those of limestone are about equally divided among green, yellow, beige and black; there are a very few pink ones. Occasionally a large beige or white marble *scutula* is present.

The ratio among small *tesserae* and medium and large *scutulae* is approximately 3:2:1, there being about three times as many small *tesserae* and twice as many medium *scutulae* as there were large ones.

Description: The description of *op. mus.* 17 is as follows:

A. The *scutulatum pavimentum* and its borders in the E part of the *triclinium*.

B. The 'runner' of white meanders and boxes in coloured isometric perspective.

C. The 'carpet' with its central *cancellum* and borders in the W part of the *triclinium*.

A. The *scutulatum pavimentum*. A rectangular *scutulatum* edged with diagonally laid white mosaic embellished the E part of the *triclinium*. It had three borders: an exterior band of three white *tesserae* setting it off from the diagonal white edging, then one of seven black *tesserae* and an inner one of seven white *tesserae*; this last defined the sides of the *scutulatum* itself. The *scutulae* were set in white *tesserae* laid parallel to the walls: the angle of laying was thus different from that of the peristyle (*op. mus.* 8). The result was that the *scutulae* are set perpendicular to each other but parallel to the alignment of the walls. In general, the large rectangular *scutulae* were set with their long sides running EW, with one medium *scutula* on one side and two on another, with the small *tesserae* in between them. There are subtle differences between *op. mus.* 17 and *op. mus.* 8. In *op. mus.* 17, there are relatively fewer large *scutulae* and more medium ones than in *op. mus.* 8, even though the spacing is about the same (*c.* 0 · 05 m. centre to centre). A flat effect is obtained because the surface is not as frequently interrupted by large *scutulae* as in *op. mus.* 8. Moreover, the colour range of the small *tesserae* in *op. mus.* 17 is greater than in *op. mus.* 8, closer to the range of colours in the medium and large *scutulae*, with the result that a much less bold contrast of colours is obtained. The whole effect was calmer and less bold than *op. mus.* 8, in that respect more favourable to a good digestion!

B. The 'runner.' The floor of the *triclinium* was decoratively divided by a long thin 'runner' set off from the diagonally laid edging on four sides by a band of three white *tesserae*; this band framed a background of black *tesserae* for the handsome band of white meanders and boxes in coloured isometric perspective. There were altogether five meanders, of which three (the central one and the ones at the N and S ends) were made of simple swastikas 'rolling' southward with their arms extended to frame the boxes on either side and to interconnect with the other meanders.

The two interconnecting meanders between the ones at the ends and the central one were fancier: they had extra returns to their arms, with the result that the swastikas 'rolled' northward.

Between the simple and fancy meanders there were boxes, six of them, made of two concentric squares with a square centre, framed by the arms of the swastikas making up the meanders.

From south to north, the sequence of the border was as follows: box, simple meander, box, fancy meander (with extra returns on the arms), box, simple meander at the centre, box, fancy meander, box, simple meander, box. Because the simple swastikas 'rolling' southward are alternated with northward 'rolling' fancy swastikas, the directional effect of the meander border is mitigated.

The meanders and boxes were made of bands of two white *tesserae*, and the coloured planes 'receding' on the diagonal were four *tesserae* wide. The black background was visible as a single band of black *tesserae* between the edges of the 'receding' planes and the next white band of a box or a meander; the black background was also visible at the 'top' along the E side and in triangles at corners of bands. The perspective was designed to 'recede' from the NW to the SE, in the opposite direction to the perspective of the threshold of *op. mus.* 5.

The colour scheme is more complex than in *op. mus.* 5 and less logical in terms of 'lighting,' though it is more repetitive from element to element. All the boxes are coloured as follows: the outside of the outer box is ochre on both the southward and eastward facing 'receding' planes, and yellow on both the southward and eastward facing inner planes of the same box. For the inner box, the outside southward and eastward facing planes are both of olive *tesserae*, but the inside southward facing plane is pink, whilst the adjacent inner eastward facing plane is purple. The square centre made of four white *tesserae* has a southward facing plane of yellow, an eastward facing plane of ochre. Thus, all the inner planes of the boxes are of lighter tone (either all yellow or adjacent pink/purple) and all the outer planes are darker

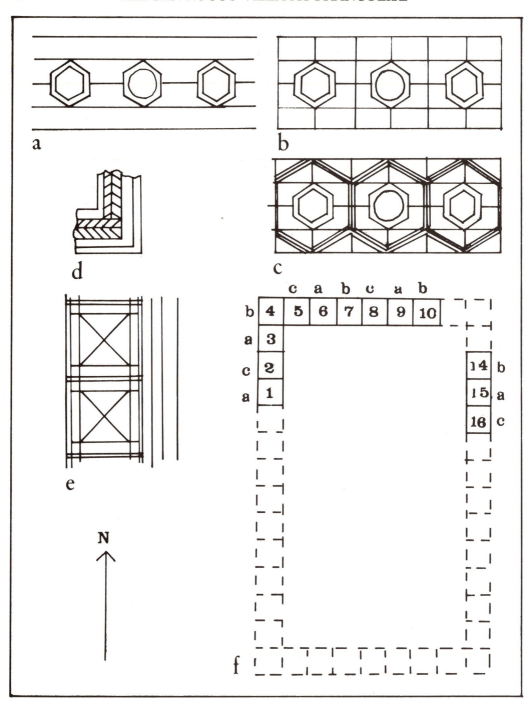

Fig. 13. Diagrammatic details of the mosaic floors
a–c. Op. mus. 13. *a.* Laying-out lines for hexagonal borders surrounding pre-fabricated hexagons. First stage.
b. Second stage. *c.* With added guide-lines for borders. Final stage.
d. Op. mus. 14. Pattern of chevron border at its SE corner.
e–f. Op. mus. 20. *e.* Guide-lines for mosaic pattern scored into *nucleus.*
f. Reconstruction sketch of coffers; numbered ones are extant. Letters a, b, c, outside them indicate framing patterns
described on p.117. (Scale: 1:20, except for *f,* not to scale).

(either all ochre, all olive or adjacent yellow/ochre). The result is that the inner planes of the boxes seem to be illuminated from the SE corner, with light falling on the southward and eastward facing planes.

For the meanders, another colour scheme for the 'receding' planes was used, one which depends on the contrast between olive and adjacent pink/purple.

The two fancy meanders with extra returns on their arms were coloured as follows: all the 'receding' planes facing either S or E which were beside the centre of the swastika were olive: the olive planes continued for two changes of direction. The third and fourth change of direction had adjacent pink and purple planes, all the pink planes facing S, all the purple planes facing E. The fifth and sixth change of direction was made of olive planes, by which point the arms of the meanders were interconnecting with the arms of other meanders. The result was that the fancy meanders with extra returns looked as if they were lit from the NE corner (the corner adjacent to that of the 'light' for the boxes) because all the pink planes faced E, all the dark ones S. The differences in angle of 'lighting' between the boxes and the fancy meanders further mitigates the directional effect of the swastika shapes.

The three simple meanders, those which did not have extra returns on the arms of the swastikas, were coloured as follows: all the 'receding' planes facing either S or E which were beside the centre of the swastika were either pink or purple, all the pink planes facing E, all the purple planes facing S (a reverse of the scheme of pink/purple in the fancy meanders). In the third and fourth changes of direction, the 'receding' planes were olive; those planes 'met' the olive planes of the fancy meanders. The result was that, because the lighter pink planes faced E, the single meanders seemed to be 'lit' from the SW corner, unlike the boxes and unlike the fancy meanders. The 'light' in the isometric perspective came from three different directions in this border: SE, NE and SW. The mosaicist was at pains to achieve the most complex illusion possible by alternating dark and light adjacent planes. As in *op. mus.* 5, 8 and others, the pinkish or pink/purple tones predominate.

The regular spacing of the centres of the swastikas and boxes and the unequal length of their arms, together with the neat straight edge of white *tesserae*, indicate that the white *tesserae* were laid first from predetermined, measured centres, whilst the *tesserae* of the 'receding' planes and background, some of them clipped or irregularly shaped, were adjusted for their size and position to fit between existing rows of white *tesserae* already laid.

A construction from the centres outward must be supposed: first the centres of the swastikas and boxes were determined, then the arms of the swastikas and the sides of the boxes, then the background and 'receding' planes, finally the borders.

C. The 'carpet.' The western part of the *triclinium* was set off by a squarish 'carpet' with a black and white border and a large white field with tiny black crosslets around a *cancellum*. Edges of diagonally laid white *tesserae* ran around the four sides of the 'carpet.' There were bands of three white *tesserae*, ten black, nine white, eight black and three white *tesserae*: these bordered the field of diagonally laid white *tesserae*. Crosslets formed of four black *tesserae* with a white centre embellished the field: the centres of the crosslets were 0·075 m. apart, and there were forty-four rows NS, thirty-four rows EW and, as they were set in a diagonally laid field, the rows were alternating ones.

In the middle of the carpet, a square frame of three white, five black and two white *tesserae* defined a white *cancellum* made of diagonal rows of two white *tesserae.* This *cancellum* was in coloured isometric perspective on a black background. The perspective 'receded' from S to N; the 'receding' planes faced NW and SW and were made of four rows of *tesserae.* The background was made of a square of four black *tesserae* in each square unit. The triangles at the four corners and along the sides (between the *cancellum* and the band of two white *tesserae)* were black.

The colours of the *cancellum* were as follows: beginning in the SW corner and going to the NE, the first two squares of the *cancellum* were yellow and ochre, the next four pink and purple, the next six green and olive and the next eight pink and purple. The eight squares after that were purple and yellow, with the purple facing NW and the yellow facing SW. After that, continuing from the SW to the NE, the 'receding' planes were green and olive, pink and purple, and the last two were yellow and ochre. In every case except that of the purple and yellow combination, the lighter coloured 'receding' planes (yellow, pink, green) faced NW whilst the darker ones (ochre, purple, olive) faced SW. The result was that the *cancellum* was 'lit' from the N: the chromatic intensity passed from light colours through dark ones to pink/purple tones, then through dark to light ones from corner to corner.

Dimensions:

A. The *scutulatum pavimentum.* The white diagonally laid edgings between the borders and the wall were 0 · 19 m. on the N, 0 · 22 m. on the S and 0 · 18 m. on the E side. The diagonal strip between the *scutulatum* border and the border of the 'runner' was 0 · 125 m. wide. The exterior border of three white *tesserae* was 0 · 03 m. wide; those of seven black and seven white were both 0 · 08 m. The *scutulatum* field was 3 · 96 × 1 · 92 m.

B. The 'runner'. The diagonal edges between the borders and the walls were 0 · 14 m. on the N and 0 · 15 m. on the S. The diagonal strip between the outer borders of the 'runner' and the *scutulatum* to the E was 0 · 125 m. wide; between the 'runner' and the borders of the 'carpet' to the W the diagonally laid white strip was 0 · 13 m. wide. The border of three white *tesserae* was 0 · 03 m. wide; the exterior dimensions of the black background were 4 · 29 × 0 · 60 m.

The four white *tesserae* making up the centres of the boxes and the centres of the swastikas were set 0 · 39 m. apart (centre to centre). In the boxes, the outer boxes' exterior dimensions were 0 · 32 m.^{2}; the inner boxes' were 0 · 18m^2. The 'receding' planes were all 0 · 05 m. wide.

C. The 'carpet.' The diagonal edges between the outer borders and the walls are 0 · 15 m. on the N, 0 · 19 on the S and 0 · 29 m. on the W. The borders are as follows, from the outside in: three white *tesserae* 0 · 03 m. wide, ten black *tesserae* 0 · 11 m., nine white *tesserae* 0 · 10 m., eight black *tesserae* 0 · 09 m. and three white *tesserae* 0 · 03 m. The field with crosslets is 3 · 73 × 3 · 29 m.; the crosslets are 0 · 075 m. apart (centre to centre), forty-four rows NS, thirty-four rows EW.

The frame of the *cancellum* including its borders is 1 · 00 × 1 · 00 m.; its border of three white *tesserae* is 0 · 03 m. wide; the four black and two white bands 0 · 04 and 0 · 02 m. wide respectively. The rows of two white *tesserae* making up the *cancellum* are 0 · 02 m. wide; each square is 0 · 12m.^{2}

Condition: Op. mus. 17 was in fair condition upon excavation, virtually intact except for some large round holes near the centre of the *cancellum* and some scuffed-up patches. The mosaic was lifted, repaired and has been replaced in its original location.

Parallels: For the *cancellum*, Pernice, 1938, 50, pl. 17, 3 (Pompeii, associated with the late First Style and the Second Style); for the swastikas with extra returns to the arms, Pernice, 1938, 91–2, pl. 42, 5 (Pompeii, associated with Second Style), Blake, 1930, 73, pl. 15, 3 (Faenza, late Republican or early Augustan) and Morricone Matini, 1967, 24–5, no. 9, fig. 8, pl. D, 2 (Rome, first half of the first century B.C.).

Conclusion: A late Republican date for *op. mus.* 17 can be advanced on the basis of the parallels.

Op. mus. 18. Room 8 (6 · 15 × 3 · 80 m.). Pls. XII and XXXII*c–d*.

The present aspect of *op. mus.* 18 differs from that of its original state. In Period II, the mosaic was almost exactly twice the size it is now because in Period IIA room 8 and this mosaic were cut in half, the N part of the room becoming a *sudatorium* with a new floor. Before that, however, in Period II, room 8 was paved with a floor which must have had a black and white central checkerboard 'carpet' with a border of white boxes and simple meanders in coloured isometric perspective. This beautiful floor, very well preserved where it was not entirely destroyed, has a special crispness of design and finesse of execution which distinguishes it from the other pavements of Period II. Its special character identified the original function of the room, before its S half was turned into a *frigidarium*, as having some particular importance: it had two *cubicula* giving on to it (rooms 27 and 28) and connected with the *domus vetus* (29) and the peristyle through a corridor (7). What the room was used for in Period II is unclear; it formed a special suite with the *cubicula* on the W side.

Bed. A *statumen* of limestone rubble and gravel 0 · 05 m. thick, underlies a *rudus*, 0 · 05 m. thick, of limestone rubble, gravel and lumps of mortar and lime (ratio *c.* 4:1). The *nucleus* is 0 · 07 m. thick of mortar and lime (ratio *c.* 5:1). The *supranucleus* is a lime and white marble dust, very hard and adhesive, which accounts for the good state of preservation of the mosaic.

Tesserae. Op. mus. 18 is made of pink, purple, bluish-black, green, yellow, ochre, black and white *tesserae* 0 · 01 m.[3].

Description. The main decorated part of the floor was edged in diagonally laid white *tesserae*. A border of black background originally ran around the four sides; part of the E and W and all of the S background border remain. On this black background there were simple interconnecting meanders alternating with boxes, both in coloured isometric perspective. The meanders and boxes were made of rows of three white *tesserae*, and the coloured planes 'recede' from NW to SE. All the boxes consisted of a square of white *tesserae* with a square centre of nine *tesserae*. All the boxes were coloured: on the outside boxes, the planes facing E were ochre, the planes facing S were yellow. All the centre squares were the same: the planes facing E were green, those facing S were bluish-black. The meanders were coloured a little differently: proceeding outward from the centre of each swastika, the planes were coloured so as to alternate between adjacent planes of either pink and purple or bluish-black and green. The result is that, whilst the boxes appear to be 'lit' from the S, the meanders are 'lit' from several sides. In the S part of the isometric border, there were four boxes and three meanders; in the E and W borders three meanders and four boxes are still visible. In the original design, if it is reconstructed symmetrically, there must have been six meanders and seven boxes in the E and W borders. All the swastikas in the meanders 'rolled' in a counter-clockwise direction. The central part of the pavement was a black and white checkerboard set at a

45° angle to the line of the walls; the sides of each square were made of eight *tesserae*. The checkerboard 'carpet' had, from the outside in, borders of five white, five black and four red *tesserae* separating it from the black background of the isometric border. As in *op. mus.* 5 and 17, the centres of the swastikas and boxes were regularly spaced; a construction from the predetermined centres of each element outward is suggested. Cf. *op. mus.* 5 and 17.

Dimensions. the diagonal edge on the S was $0 \cdot 46$ m. wide; in the E side, $0 \cdot 44$ m. and on the W side $0 \cdot 43$ m. wide. The white band of three *tesserae* was $0 \cdot 03$ m. wide. The black background for the meanders and boxes was $0 \cdot 59$ m. wide The borders of five white and five black *tesserae* framing the central 'carpet' were both $0 \cdot 05$ m. wide, that of the four red *tesserae* was $0 \cdot 04$ m. wide. Each square in the checkerboard was $0 \cdot 09$ m.^{2}; the whole checkerboard 'carpet' was $1 \cdot 30$ m. EW. In the border of meanders and boxes, the nine *tesserae* making up the centres of the boxes and the swastikas were set $0 \cdot 04$ m. apart (centre to centre). The exterior dimensions of the boxes were $0 \cdot 22$ m.^{2}. The 'receding' planes were $0 \cdot 06$ m. wide.

Condition. The condition of *op. mus.* 18 is good. Small patches are missing in the checkerboard 'carpet'. The mosaic was left *in situ* and was repaired, its edge being consolidated with concrete.

Parallels. There are numerous parallels for this type of isometric pavement, of which the best known is that of the Republican villa at Rabat on Malta: Pernice, 1938, 13 and pl. 4, 1 (Palermo, first century B.C.); 16 and pl. 5, 3 (Solunto, first century B.C.) and two examples from Pompeii, Pernice, 1938, 36 and pl. 8, 3; and 70 and pl. 36, 5 (associated with Second Style); Blake, 1930, 71–3, and pl. 16, 3–4; and 81–4 and pl. 17, 1 (Pompeii, Late Republican or early Augustan). The Sullan (?) villa on the Via Nomentana also has a similar floor: Lugli, 1930, 530–2 and pls. XX and XXI, 5.

Conclusion. A late Republican date, after Sulla but before Augustus, can be advanced for *op. mus.* 18 on the basis of its parallels.

Op. mus. 19. *Passage between rooms 8 and 29, threshold* $(0 \cdot 82 \times 0 \cdot 76$ m.$)$. Pl. XXIV*b*.
Bed. Same as *op. mus.* 18 of which it is an extension.

Tesserae. Op. mus. 19 is made of pink, purple, yellow, ochre, green, black and white limestone *tesserae*, $0 \cdot 01$ m.^{3}.

Description. Op. mus. 19 is a composition of coloured *tesserae* set in a white background laid diagonally to the alignment of the walls. The *tesserae*, instead of being used as elements in a measured design with straight, neat edges, are used to create a regular, unarticulated surface of seemingly randomly placed *tesserae*. The laying of the mosaic floor is in large irregularly aligned zig-zags: rows of alternately all white and coloured and white were laid, each row *c.* $0 \cdot 20$ m. long, with a 90° change of direction at the end. This method of laying the *tesserae,* together with a very expert randomising of the coloured *tesserae* set amongst the white ones, created an even surface effect appropriate to a corridor space. The proportion of the coloured *tesserae* (including black) to each other was about equal, with the result that no one colour dominated. *Op. mus.* 19 was virtually the same in pattern, in method of laying in large zig-zags and in colour as the mosaics in rooms 24 and 31a and 31b; cf. *op. mus.* 25 and 28. The pavement was laid without separate borders, the *tesserae* running under the wall plaster on the E and W and merging with the white diagonally laid edging of *op. mus.* 18 and with *op. mus.* 27. The floor was ramped to connect the lower level of the *domus vetus* (room 29) with that of the *domus nova* (room 8).

Dimensions. The mosaic covered the entire space in which it was set, 0 · 82 × 0 · 76 m.
Condition. Op. mus. 19 was found virtually intact. It has been repaired and edged in cement and left *in situ.*
Conclusion. Op mus. 19 was continuous in construction with *op. mus.* 18 and can be given the same date.

Op. mus. 20. *Room 12*(6 · 60 × 4 · 50 m.). Pls. XIV*b*, XXXIII and XXXIV and Fig. 13*e–f.*
Op. mus. 20, like *op. mus.* 18, has a specially designed border at the sides of the room which surrounds a central 'carpet'; in the case of *op. mus.* 20, the border is one of coffers rather than of meanders and boxes, and the 'carpet' has a frame in the centre around an *emblema.* The visual differences between this mosaic and the other mosaics of the San Rocco villa are due mainly to the different colours used in *op. mus.* 20, not to differences in construction or decorative conception. In fact, the bed, guide-lines and the presence of a central *emblema* with a specially decorated frame are similar to the pavement of the *tablinum* (*op. mus.* 14). The decorative conception, that of a fancy border around a central 'carpet', is like *op. mus.* 18. The colours, however, are very different: in *op. mus.* 20 the odd combination of green, yellow, a little ochre, pink, purple, black and white without the chromatic balance of ochre and either olive or bluish-black as in other mosaics makes the colour scheme unique. The predominant tones are green and yellow, with a green/red contrast built into the colour scheme. The coloured effect with three-dimensional sugges-tion in the design of *op. mus.* 20 is similar to the isometric perspective encountered in the other mosaics. Thus the similarity between *op. mus.* 20 and the others may be noted; the differences between them seem to be due to a matter of taste or decorative and colouristic coordination with the rest of the room rather than to any difference in date.

Bed. A *statumen* of limestone rubble and gravel 0 · 03 m. thick, underlies a *rudus,* 0 · 03 m. thick, of limestone rubble, gravel and lumps of mortar in mortar and lime (ratio *c.* 4:1). The *nucleus* of mortar and lime (ratio *c.* 5:1) is 0 · 03 m. thick, especially thin and more like that of *op. mus.* 8 in the peristyle than the *nuclei* of floors in other rooms. The *supranucleus* is of lime and white marble dust, very friable.

Tesserae. Op .mus. 20 is made of green, yellow, ochre, pink, purple, black and white limestone *tesserae,* 0 · 01 m.[3]. The frame of the *emblema* has a background of dark green limestone *tesserae* unique to this pavement, 0 · 01 m[3].

Description. Op. mus. 20 is composed of a fancy border of variously decorated coffers at the edge of a 'carpet' with a framed *emblema* at its centre. The floor was well preserved in the NW corner of the room and along part of the E wall, but the whole room was dia-gonally cut by the modern hospital wall construction in such a way that all of the NE corner and all of the S part of the room is missing. A fragment of *nucleus* preserved near the SE corner of the room revealed, upon careful cleaning, scoring with guide-lines similar to those of *op. mus.* 13. The description of the floor is as follows:-
1. The scoring of the *nucleus.*
2. The border of decorated coffers.
3. The 'carpet', frame for *emblema* and *emblema* base.

1. *The scoring of the nucleus.* A section of *nucleus* which had been skimmed of its *tess-erae* was found near the SE corner of the room. The scoring for the last two decorated squares from the corner in the E border were preserved, and their lines indicate how the mosaic border of coffers would have been laid out. In the first place, all the lines in *op.*

mus. 20 are guide-lines, that is to say, all of the lines scored on to the *nucleus* were used as edges for bands of mosaic. In this respect, the scored *nucleus* of *op. mus.* 20 is unlike that of *op. mus.* 13, which had laying-out lines (not used as edge indicators) from which the guide-lines were derived geometrically. This difference — laying-out and guide-lines for *op. mus.* 13, guide-lines only for *op. mus.* 20 — is due to the greater simplicity of design of the coffers which, unlike the hexagons in *op. mus.* 13, needed no projection of accurate angles or the complex spacing of the *tablinum* threshold. The guide-lines were scored as follows: for the outer borders, four parallel lines 0 · 08 m. and 0 · 05 m. apart from the outside in stood as the guide-lines for the edges of the bands of eight black, six white and five yellow *tesserae* which, with an outer band of three white *tesserae*, separated the border of coffers from the white edge of diagonally laid white *tesserae* which ran around the whole pavement. The coffers were framed and separated with two rows of white *tesserae;* the mosaicist was at pains, as in *op. mus.* 13, to score in the lines of these rows, both the ones running EW and those running NS, very carefully. A line parallel to the first four running 0 · 02 m. from the edges of the yellow border was scored in and, at a right angle, two parallel lines 0 · 02 m. apart crossed it to indicate the separating band between each coffer. These lines made large squares 0 · 38 × 0 · 38 m. as the two 'bottom' lines on the W side were also scored in. All the squares were then crossed by parallel lines 0 · 05 m. from the sides running through the square NS: these were the guide-lines for the exterior yellow and olive frames of five *tesserae*. Guide lines for the N and S parts of the frame were scored in, thus making an inner square 0 · 28 × 0 · 28 m. in which the centres of the coffers would be laid. The only other guide-lines scored in were diagonal lines used to determine the central point of each coffer: this was done by scoring in lines connecting the opposite corners of each inner square. These guide-lines allowed the mosaicist to lay the coffers free-hand whilst giving him both a central point from which to work and diagonal guide-lines for changing the direction of the framing bands. The whole guide-line system for the sample of two squares still preserved is illustrated in Fig. 13*e*.

2. *The border of decorated coffers.* On the N, E and W sides, edges of diagonally laid white *tesserae* connected the main part of the floor with the walls. From the outside in there were bands of three white, eight black, six white and five yellow *tesserae* : this border framed the whole mosaic. Bands of two white *tesserae* framed and separated each coffer. Originally, there must have been nine coffers (including the corner ones) on the N and S sides, fourteen (including the corner ones) on the E and W sides, a total of 42. Only 12 complete and two partial coffers are preserved: the one in the NW corner and the first, second and third ones S of it in the W border and the first to the sixth E of it in the N border, and three coffers and two halves in the E border. All the coffers shared certain repetitive frame elements. They all had exterior frames of five *tesserae* of which in all the preserved coffers the N and S sides were ochre, and the E and W sides were yellow. Inside the yellow/ochre frames, there was a single row of black *tesserae* setting off decorated bands of three types — zig-zags, diagonal bands, and simple meanders, described below. Inside these decorated bands, rows of four *tesserae* framed the central motifs, also described below. The rows of four *tesserae* were coloured on all three preserved sides: on the N side white, on the S side black, on the E green and on the W red. These inner bands, if read as 'receding' planes, were 'lit' from the S side where the door of the room was, the plane on the N side facing S being white, the opposite one black.

These inner frames and the yellow/ochre ones have a three-dimensional effect which gives the illusion of turning the squares into coffers. All the coffers had one of three types of decorated bands between the yellow/ochre and inner frames. These decorated bands were as follows:-

a. *Zig-zags.* The zig-zag band was made of a single row of white *tesserae* defining triangles — four outer triangles, three inner ones, on each side. The triangles are alternately green and red, or all green on the outside and all red on the inside, or haphazardly paired or alternated in green and red.

b. *Diagonal bands.* The diagonal bands are made of rows of single black, two or three purple or two or three green and two or three white *tesserae* set at a 45° angle to the squares. The arrangement is haphazard, but white always alternates with one of the three other colours: green, purple or black. The number of rows of *tesserae* in each coloured band may vary between two or three white, green or purple ones, but the black *tesserae* are always in a single row. There are white triangles at the corners. The bands on each side are set at 90° to each other, either running SW to NE or NW to SE.

c. *Simple meanders.* The third type of decorated band is a simple rectilinear meander made of a row of single white *tesserae* in groups of four—four 'over', four 'up', four 'across', four 'down', and so on, making rectangles three by four *tesserae* wide and deep. The colours of the rectangles were haphazardly arranged in the following colours: black, yellow, green or purple, in no particular order but no two of the same colour side by side.

The decorated bands appear in a haphazard order in the following way. In Fig, 13*f*, the extant coffers are in dark lines and are numbered 1–10 and 14–17; the destroyed coffers are in broken lines and are either numbered in parentheses or unnumbered. The letters a, b and c refer to the zig-zag, diagonal bands and simple meander frames respectively. Finally, all the coffers had decorated squares in the centres: each was framed by a single row of black *tesserae*, but every central motif was different and apparently laid freehand. The motifs in each extant coffer were as follows (see Fig. 13*f*).

Coffer 1. A quartered circle on a black background; the quarters were yellow and white in opposite quadrants.

Coffer 2. A sharp-pointed four-petalled yellow rosette on a ground with purple and black in opposite quadrants.

Coffer 3. A green and white volute or snail shell on a white and purple ground.

Coffer 4. A concave-sided yellow square on a white ground with a purple round-edged four-petalled rosette at the centre.

Coffer 5. A 'pin-wheel' of six triangles alternately green, white and purple.

Coffer 6. Another concave-sided yellow square on a white background with a black round-edged four-petalled rosette at the centre.

Coffer 7. A sharp-pointed four-petalled white rosette with a round black centre on a ground either green or purple in opposite quadrants.

Coffer 8. A quartered circle on a black background with pink/purple and white/yellow in opposite quadrants.

Coffer 9. A sharp-pointed four-petalled green rosette on a purple ground.

Coffer 10. A white circle on a black ground. The white circle has a black square in it; in the black square is a white sharp-pointed four-petalled rosette.

Coffer 11–13. These are missing.

Coffer 14. The central motif is missing.

Coffer 15. A white, sharp-pointed four-petalled rosette with a round black centre on a green ground.

Coffer 16. A white circle on a green ground with a quartered concave-sided square, green and purple in opposite quadrants.

The dominant colours of the border of the decorated coffers are yellow/ochre and purple/green with black and white. The combination, very bold and clashing, has none of the smooth chromatic transitions typical of the other San Rocco mosaics.

3. *The 'carpet' and emblema frame and base.* The 'carpet' has bands of six black, six white, six black and three white *tesserae* surrounding a large area of diagonally laid white *tesserae*. At the centre, the frame of the *emblema* was set off with bands of three white, four black and three white *tesserae*. The bands surrounded a field of dark green *tesserae* on which, in the NW corner, there were stalk and stems (made of single rows of small white *tesserae*) and the white heart-shaped leaves of a vine. So little of this was preserved that it was impossible to reconstruct it; it seemed, however, to be set on the diagonal, running from the corner towards the centre of the frame. The *emblema* of *op. mus.* 20 is lost. It was seated on a square limestone tray $0 \cdot 34$ m^2 and $0 \cdot 02$ m. thick set in the centre of the room: this tray probably was a substitute for a separately laid *nucleus* as the *nucleus* of the rest of the pavement was laid against it.

Dimensions. The diagonally laid white edge is $0 \cdot 3$ m. wide on the N side, $0 \cdot 27$ m. wide on the E and $0 \cdot 26$ m. wide on the W. The outer bands of three white, eight black, six white and five yellow *tesserae* framing and separating the coffers are $0 \cdot 02$ m. wide. Each coffer is $0 \cdot 38$ m.^{2}, the yellow/ochre frames are $0 \cdot 05$ m. wide, the decorated borders $0 \cdot 05$ m. wide and the inner frames $0 \cdot 03$ m. wide. The central squares with motifs were $0 \cdot 12$ m.^{2}. Around the 'carpet' the bands of five yellow, six white, six black and three white *tesserae* were $0 \cdot 05$ m., $0 \cdot 06$ m., $0 \cdot 06$ m. and $0 \cdot 03$ m. wide respectively. The 'carpet' was of undetermined size because its southern extent was not known. The borders of the frame around the *emblema*, of three white, four black and three white *tesserae* were $0 \cdot 03$ m., $0 \cdot 04$ m. and $0 \cdot 03$ m. wide respectively. The dark green frame with white vines must have been at least $0 \cdot 84 \times 0 \cdot 84$ m.; the central *emblema* was set on a base $0 \cdot 34$ m.^{2}.

Condition. The condition of *op. mus.* 20 is very poor. In the NW corner, some of the surface of the pavement had been subject to burning which caused changes in the colours of the limestone *tesserae*. The thin *nucleus*, where exposed, is pitted, indicating old damage to the pavement. The hospital wall crossed the room in two directions, and the entire S part of the mosaic, and all of its *emblema* and its frame, are missing.

Parallels. Pernice, 1938, 17−18 and pl. 6, 1 (Teramo, Augustan). The best parallel is with a coffered mosaic in the villa on the Via Nomentana: Lugli, 1930, 530−3 and pl. XX and XXI, 4, 8 (Sullan?). See also the article by Morricone Matini, 1965, 79−81 and pls. XXIII−XXIX; the San Rocco example fits best with the design of other coffered mosaics at the middle of the first century B.C. or a little later, as the analysis and dating suggest.

Conclusion. Op. mus. 20 is compatible in date with the other mosaics, Late Republican, before the time of Augustus.

Op. mus. 21. Room 17 ($3 \cdot 40 \times 5 \cdot 95$ m.). Not illustrated.

Bed. A *statumen* of limestone rubble and gravel, $0 \cdot 05$ m. thick, underlies a *rudus*,

0 · 03 m. thick, of limestone rubble, gravel and lumps of mortar in mortar and lime (ratio *c.* 4.1). The *nucleus* is 0 · 05 m. thick of poorly mixed mortar and lime and white marble dust. Traces of the bed were found *in situ* all over the room, indicating that in Period II the entire room was paved in mosaic.

Tesserae. Only traces of white limestone *tesserae*, 0 · 01 m.³, are preserved.

Description. A few traces of white diagonally laid edging were found *in situ* along the S wall.

Condition. Op. mus. 21 had been almost entirely destroyed before excavation.

Conclusion. The presence of mosaic bedding and mosaic *in situ* indicates that room 17 was roofed in Period II: the bed itself was similar to that of *op. mus.* 5.

Op. mus. 22. Room 19 (16 · 10 × 3 · 20 m.). Not illustrated.

Bed. A *statumen* of limestone rubble and gravel, 0 · 05 m. thick, underlies a *rudus*, 0 · 05 m. thick, of limestone rubble, gravel and lumps of mortar in mortar and lime (ratio *c.* 4:1). The *nucleus* is 0 · 05 m. thick of poorly mixed mortar and lime (ratio *c.* 5:1). The *supranucleus* is of lime and white marble dust. Traces of the bed were found under the extant *tesserae* next to the E wall and along the N and S walls, indicating that in Period II the entire room was paved in mosaic.

Tesserae. Only traces of white limestone *tesserae*, 0 · 01 m.³, are preserved.

Description. A few traces of white diagonally laid edging were found in situ along the E wall.

Condition. Op. mus. 22 had been almost entirely destroyed before excavation.

Conclusion. The presence of mosaic bedding and mosaic *in situ* indicates that room 17 was roofed in Period II; the bed itself was similar to that of other Period II mosaics.

Op. mus. 23. Rooms 20a and b (2 · 55 × 3 · 20 m. and 3 · 10 × 3.20 m.). Not illustrated.

Bed. The bed of *op. mus.* 23 was the same as those of other rooms on the S side of the peristyle (rooms 19, 23a, 24 and 25; see *op. mus.* 22–26). The bed was found *in situ* in fragments all over both rooms, indicating that in Period II they were paved in mosaic.

Tesserae. Only traces of white limestone *tesserae*, 0 · 01 m.³, are preserved.

Description. A few very small fragments of mosaic *in situ* were found along the walls of both rooms and inside them.

Condition. Op. mus. 23 had been almost entirely destroyed before excavation.

Conclusion. The presence of mosaic bedding and mosaic *in situ* indicated that rooms 20a and b were roofed in Period II; the bed itself was similar to that of other Period II mosaics in the rooms on the S side of the peristyle.

Op. mus. 24. Room 23a, cubiculum (2 · 80 × 2 · 90 m.). Not illustrated.

Bed. The bed of *op mus.* 24 was the same as those of other rooms on the S side of the peristyle (rooms 19, 20a and b, 24 and 25; see *op. mus.* 22–6). The bed was found *in situ* in fragments all over the room, indicating that in Period II the entire room was paved in mosaic.

Tesserae. Only traces of white limestone *tesserae*, 0 · 01 m.³, are preserved.

Description. A few traces of white diagonally laid edging were found *in situ* along the S wall.

Condition. Op. mus. 24 had been almost entirely destroyed before excavation.

Conclusion. The presence of mosaic bedding and mosaic *in situ* indicates that the room 23a was roofed in Period II; the bed itself was similar to that of other Period II mosaics.

Op. mus. 25. *Room 24, cubiculum* (2 · 80 × 2 · 80 m.). Pl. XXXV*a*.

Bed. The bed of *op. mus.* 25 was the same as those of other rooms on the S side of the peristyle (rooms 19, 20a and b, 23a and 25; see *op. mus.* 22–6).

Tesserae. Op. mus. 25 is made of pink, purple, yellow, ochre, green, black and white limestone *tesserae*, 0 · 01 m.[3]

Description. Op. mus. 25 is virtually identical in conception, construction and colour to *op. mus.* 19 and 18. It is a composition of coloured *tesserae* on a white diagonally laid background, presented without borders or separate edging. See description, *op. mus.* 19.

Condition. Room 24 was built in a location which placed it right over a poorly capped well of Period I and IA which had been buried when the Period II terrace covered this feature. At some point the capping of the well collapsed, with the result that the floor began to collapse into the hole in the terrace fill. As a consequence, the floor was found in large pieces at an angle to the walls on four sides, and larger fragments of it were found in the collapsed centre of the room. See pp. 20, 49.

Conclusion. See *op. mus.* 19.

Op. mus. 26. *Room 25* (7 · 90 × 7 · 50 m.). Not illustrated.

Bed. The bed of *op. mus.* 26 was the same as those of the other rooms on the S side of the peristyle (rooms 19, 20a and b, 23a and 24; see *op. mus.* 22–6). The bed was found *in situ* along the N wall of the room, indicating that in Period II at least part of the room was paved in mosiac.

Tesserae. Only traces of white limestone *tesserae*, 0 · 01 m.[3], are preserved.

Description. A few pieces of white diagonally laid edging were found *in situ* along the N wall.

Condition. Op. mus. 26 had been almost entirely destroyed before excavation.

Conclusion. The presence of mosaic bedding and mosaic *in situ* indicates that room 25 was roofed in Period II; the bed itself was similar to that of other Period II mosaics.

Op. mus. 27. *Room 29, edging.* Pl. XXIV*b*.

Room 29 in the *domus vetus*, in Period II, was paved for the most part with two *scutulata pavimenta* of the earlier periods (I and IA, *op. mus.* 1 and 2 in rooms A and A1). The earlier pavements were carefully preserved with a regard similar to the concern for preserving the rooms in which they stood which characterised the design of the house itself and the ensemble of rooms. For some reason, however, the N wall of the room was dismantled and rebuilt on the same line in Period II; the new wall was narrower. As a result of this rebuilding, the Period IA edging (*op. mus.* 2) was damaged or perhaps intentionally scraped off, and a new *nucleus* and edging laid at the same time that the nucleus of *op. mus.* 19 (threshold in the NE corner of the room) was laid. The relaying of the plain white edging was probably intentional: the new edging was laid along a straight line the entire length of the N side, 0 · 32 m. wide, in a space which may have been occupied by an earlier edging.

Bed. Only the *nucleus* and *supranucleus* were visible in small patches, the *nucleus* quite different in colour and texture from that of *op. mus.* 2 with which it joined along a straight line. The mortar-lime ratio (*c.* 5:1) was about the same, but the *nucleus* of *op. mus.* 27 was browner and flakier than that of *op. mus.* 2. The *supranucleus* was of lime and white marble dust, very fine and hard.

Tesserae. Op. mus. 27 was made of white limestone *tesserae*, 0 · 01 m.[3]

Description. Op. mus. 27 is an edge along the N side of the pavement of room 29 (*op.*

mus. 2); it was added after an earlier edging had been taken out. It is thus a Period II addition to a Period IA reused pavement. The white *tesserae* were set in rows running EW in a manner more regular and neater than the rows of white *tesserae* which were used as the background for the *scutulae* of *op. mus.* 2.

Dimensions. The strip along the N edge was $0 \cdot 32$ m. wide and ran the entire length of the room.

Condition. Op. mus. 27 is almost intact except for some scuffed patches. It was left *in situ.*

Conclusions. Op. mus. 27 is an example, in the commissions for the mosaics, of the thrift or piety or both with which the villa of Period II was built with regard to the earlier structure. Where possible, rooms and floors were reused; when they had to be changed in some way, as here, care was taken to replace as little as possible and to make additions in the most discreet way without disturbing the look of the earlier pavements.

Op. mus. 28. Rooms 31a and b, corridor. $(1 \cdot 20 \times 12 \cdot 95$ m.$)$. Pl. XXXV*b*

Bed. The bed of *op. mus.* 28, where it could be seen, appeared to have been identical with that of the *tablinum, op. mus.* 14, of which it was an extension.

Tesserae. Op. mus. 28 is made of pink, purple, yellow, ochre, green, black and white limestone *tesserae,* $0 \cdot 01$ m.^{3}.

Description. Op. mus. 28 is virtually identical in conception, construction and colour to *op. mus.* 19 and 28. It is a composition of coloured *tesserae* on a white diagonally laid background, presented without borders or separate edging. See description, *op. mus.* 19. The pavement was slightly ramped to connect the lower level of the *domus vetus* and the rear entrance of the villa with the level of the *domus nova* and the *tablinum* (room 4).

Condition. Op. mus. 28 was virtually intact except for some scuffed patches along the entire length of the corridor. It was edged in cement and left *in situ.*

Conclusion. See *op. mus.* 19.

Op. mus. 29. Room 35 $(4 \cdot 95 \times 6 \cdot 50$ m.$)$. Pls. VII*a*, XXV*a* and XXXV*c.*

Bed. A thin *statumen* of limestone chips, $0 \cdot 03$ m. thick, underlies a *rudus,* $0 \cdot 04$ m. thick, of limestone rubble, gravel and lumps of mortar in mortar and lime (ratio *c.* 4:1). The *nucleus* is also thin, $0 \cdot 03$ m. thick, of mortar and lime (ratio *c.* 5:1). The *supra-nucleus* is of lime and white marble dust, very powdery. Patches of the bed were found all over the room, indicating that a Period II floor was laid over the entire room.

Tesserae. Op. mus. 29 was composed of pink, green, yellow, black and white *tesserae,* $0 \cdot 01$ m.^{3}; there may have been other colours.

Description. Only a small fragment of the 'carpet' decorated with black crosslets on a white background surrounding an *emblema* or some other central motif survived. The 'carpet' was made of white diagonally laid *tesserae* with crosslets in alternating lines, $0 \cdot 125$ m. apart, centre to centre; the crosslets were made of four black *tesserae* around a white central one, like those of *op. mus.* 14 and 17. Near the centre of the room there was a small triangle framed, from the outside in, with three rows of white, five of black, five of green, two of pink, five of green and two of pink. The triangle itself had a black background with stems made of a single row of green *tesserae* and yellow pears or figs with sharp pointed green leaves. The precise relationship of this triangle to others, and of the whole central motif to the 'carpet', could not be accurately determined as the pieces of mosaic had been disturbed. No other traces of the original mosaic surface survived.

Dimensions. The triangle with the pears or figs had an interior dimension of 0 · 24 m. at the base, 0 · 16 along the sides; the rows framing it were: three white *tesserae* 0 · 03 m. wide, five black 0 · 06 m., five green 0 · 06 m., two pink 0 · 02 m., five green 0 · 06 m., and two pink 0 · 02 m. In the 'carpet', the crosslets are 0 · 125 m. apart centre to centre.
Condition. Op. mus. 29 had been almost completely destroyed before excavation, probably by displacement by the roots of a large fig tree which grew in the area.
Conclusion. The bed of *op. mus.* 29 closely resembles other Period II beds, especially that of *op. mus.* 8. The colours in the surviving patterns, which stress a pink/green contrast, are like those of *op. mus.* 20. Not enough of this mosaic remained, however, to reconstruct its pattern or to establish parallels for it.

Op. mus. 30. Room 36, cubiculum (2 · 30 × 0 · 46 m.). Pls. VII*b* and XXV*a–c.*
In Period II, room D4 of Period IA was extended westwards, with the result that the W wall of the room was dismantled and a new one, with wall ends linking it to the earlier N and S walls, was built. The dismantling of the wall and the reuse of the room in a larger form did not involve dismantling the Period IA floor (*op. mus.* 4), which continued in use during Period II. However, the scar or top of the dismantled wall had to be covered and the W extension of the room paved; on the wall scar *op. mus.* 30 was added, and the rest of the extension was paved in decorated *opus signinum* (*op. sig.* 11).
    Bed. There is no *statumen* or *rudus* because the mosaic was laid on the foundation of the dismantled wall. A thin *nucleus*, 0 · 01 m. thick, of poorly mixed mortar and lime (ratio *c.* 5:1) was used to level the wall, and the *tesserae* with a hard *supranucleus* of mortar and lime were laid on it.
    Tesserae. Op. mus. 30 is composed of black and white limestone *tesserae*, 0 · 015 m.[3], slightly larger than most other *tesserae* in Period II mosaics but approximately the same size as those in Period IA mosaics such as *op. mus.* 3 and 4. The mosaicist may have wished to continue the effects of the Period IA floor by using *tesserae* which more or less matched those of the earlier one.
    Description. Op. mus. 30 is a band of black interconnecting meanders and boxes on a white background. On the E and W sides, it is set off from *op. mus.* 4 and *op. sig.* 11 by a border of four black *tesserae.* In the band itself, the swastikas of the three meanders all 'roll' northward and alternate with four boxes made of a simple square centre of nine *tesserae.* Both the swastikas and the boxes are made of rows of three black *tesserae.* As in the other borders of meanders with boxes (*op. mus.* 5, 17 and 18), the centres of the swastikas and boxes are regularly spaced, the arms of the swastikas being adjusted to fill the space, and a construction from measured centres seems likely.
    Dimensions. The whole band is 2 · 30 × 0 · 46 m.; the centres of the swastikas and boxes are 0 · 31 m. apart (centre to centre) and are made of bands 0 · 04 m. to 0 · 045 m. wide. The rows of four black *tesserae* on the E and W sides are 0 · 06 m. wide.
    Condition. Except for a few lost *tesserae, op. mus.* 30 is intact. It was cemented and left *in situ.*
    Parallels. Pernice, 1938, 64 and pl. 27, 2 (Pompeii, associated with Late Second Style but, as Pernice notes, this pavement is unlike the others in the house which are definitely earlier). Blake, 1930, 84 and pl. 21, 1 (Pompeii, associated with Second Style but the pattern continues later).
    Conclusion. The precise dating of *op. mus.* 30 cannot be determined from the parallels, but it is not impossible that the strip was laid at some time in Period II.

Opus. signinum

Op. sig. 3. Room 6, exedra (3 · 25 × 3 · 35 m.) Pl. XXXV*d*.

Bed. A thin *rudus*, 0 · 03 m. thick, of limestone gravel in mortar and lime (ratio *c.* 4:1) underlay the pavement.

Tesserae. None.

Description. The pavement was 0 · 02 m. thick and had a smooth surface of well mixed tile chips, tile dust and mortar, light brown in colour.

Condition. Op. sig. 3. was much sunk and cracked and had been trenched along its W side in such a way as to expose the Period IA wall which had been dismantled on the construction of Period II. Left *in situ*.

Conclusion. The utilitarian surface of the floor of the *exedra* as opposed to the fine pavement of the adjacent rooms (*op. mus.* 13–17), indicates that the room was used for residential purposes more work-a-day in character than were the *tablinum* and *triclinium*.

Op. sig. 4. Room 13 (6 · 60 × 4 · 90 m.). Not illustrated.

The floors in rooms 13 and 14 were virtually identical in construction.

Bed. A *rudus*, 0 · 04 m. thick, of limestone gravel in mortar and lime (ratio *c.* 4:1) underlay the pavement.

Tesserae. None.

Description. The pavement was 0 · 02 m. thick and had a very smooth surface. It was composed of white limestone chips in white marble dust with some yellow tile dust as well; the floor was a *terrazzo* floor, not an *opus signinum* with tile, in the strict sense.

Condition. Op. sig. 4 was found in excellent condition with only a few lost patches. Left *in situ*.

Parallels. Morricone Matini, 1971, 10–11, no. 26 and pl. IX (Rome, early Sullan?).

Conclusion. The finely smoothed plain surface of *op. sig.* 4 denoted a residential use for room 13 in Period II.

Op. sig. 5. Room 14 (6 · 60 × 4 · 90 m.). Not illustrated.

Bed. A *rudus* 0 · 04 m. thick of limestone gravel in mortar and lime (ratio *c.* 4:1) underlay the pavement.

Tesserae. None.

Description. See *op. sig.* 4. In the centre of the room there was a square limestone base, 0 · 54 m.[2], set with its flat, slightly rough top flush with the pavement.

Condition. Op. sig. 5 was in excellent condition except for some worn areas. Left *in situ*.

Parallels. See *op. sig.* 4.

Conclusion. The finely smoothed plain surface of *op. sig.* 5 denoted a residential use of room 14 in Period II.

Op. sig. 6. Room 15, corridor (1 · 40 × 6 · 40 m.). Not illustrated.

Bed. A *rudus* 0 · 04 m. thick of limestone gravel in mortar and lime (ratio *c.* 4:1) underlay the pavement.

Tesserae. A small number of black and white limestone *tesserae*, in equal proportions, 0 · 01 m.[3], decorated the pavement.

Description. The pavement was 0 · 02 m. thick and had a smooth surface of tile chips, tile dust and mortar. The surface treatment was of large flakes of tile with black and white *tesserae,* randomly scattered but set in flat, *c.* 0 · 03 to 0 · 05 m. apart. There were no borders at the thresholds or along the walls of the room; the pavement was calculated to be continuous and without pattern.

Condition. Op. sig. 6 was in excellent condition except for a few lost patches. Left *in situ.*

Parallels. The closest parallel is in Morricone Matini, 1971, 14, no. 49 and pl. XIII (Palestrina, late second century B.C.?), but see also 8, no. 5, and pl. VIII (Rome, late second century B.C.), 10, no. 23 and pl. IX (Rome, early Sullan?) and 11, no. 29, pl. X (Anzio, mid second century B.C.).

Conclusion. Although the parallels for this mosaic are earlier than the mosaics and other pavements, a simple pattern of this type might have been repeated in Period II when the room was put in, in Late Republican times.

Op. Sig. 7. *Room 22, corridor.* (7 · 05 × 0 · 95 m.). Not illustrated.

Bed. A thin *rudus,* 0 · 03 m. thick, of limestone gravel in mortar and lime (ratio *c.* 4:1) underlay the pavement.

Tesserae. None.

Description. The pavement was 0 · 02 m. thick and had a smooth surface of well mixed tile chips, tile dust and mortar. Light brown in colour and virtually identical with *op. sig.* 3.

Condition. Op. sig. 7 was in fairly good condition on excavation. Left *in situ.*

Conclusion. The position and function of room 22 linking the peristyle and the S terrace make the utilitarian surface appropriate.

Op. Sig. 8. *Room 26, corridor* (3 · 65 × 0 · 95 m.). Not illustrated.

Bed. A *rudus,* 0 · 04 m. thick, of limestone gravel in mortar and lime (ratio *c.* 4:1) underlay the pavement.

Tesserae. A small number of black and white limestone *tesserae* in equal proportions, 0 · 01 m.^{3}, decorated the pavement.

Description. The pavement was 0 · 02 m. thick and had a smooth surface of tile chips, tile dust and mortar. The surface treatment was of large flakes of tile with black and white *tesserae,* randomly scattered but set in flat *c.* 0 · 03 to 0 · 05 m. apart. There were no borders at the thresholds or along the walls of the room; the pavement was calculated to be continuous and without pattern.

Condition. Op. sig. 8 was in excellent condition except for some lost patches. Left *in situ.*

Parallels. See *op. sig.* 6.

Op. sig. 9. *Room 32, corridor.* (1 · 35 × 4 · 45 m.). Not illustrated.

The pavements in rooms 32 and 33 (*op. sig.* 9 and 10) were virtually the same; they were evidently laid at the same time.

Bed. A *rudus,* 0 · 04 m. thick, of limestone gravel in mortar and lime (ratio *c.* 4:1) underlay the pavement.

Tesserae. A few white *tesserae* 0 · 01 m.^{3}, decorated the pavement.

Description. The pavement was 0 · 02 m. thick and had a smooth surface of tile chips, tile dust and mortar. The surface treatment was of large flakes of tile painted deep red with white *tesserae,* randomly scattered but set in flat *c.* 0 · 05 to 0 · 07 m. apart. There were no borders at the thresholds or along the walls of the room; the pavement was calculated to be continuous and without pattern.

Condition. Op. sig. 9 was in excellent condition except for a few lost patches and some pitted areas. Left *in situ.*

*Parallels.*This pavement is of the same type as *op. sig.* 6, see above.

Conclusion. The pavement can be dated to Late Republican times with the other Period II pavements.

Op. sig. 10. *Room 33, cubiculum* (1 · 90 × 2 · 30 m.). Not illustrated.
Op. sig. 10 is identical in construction with *op. sig.* 9; for description see above.

Op. sig. 11. *Room 36, cubiculum* (2 · 30 × 1 · 75 m.). Pls. VII*b* and XXV*a,b.*
Op. sig. 11 was the floor of the Period II extension, on its W side, of room D4 of Period IA. The Period IA pavement (*op. mus.* 4) was not disturbed, and the wall scar was covered with a mosaic band (*op. mus.* 30). See *op. mus.* 30.

Bed. A thin *rudus,* 0 · 02 m. thick, of limestone gravel in mortar and lime (ratio *c.* 4:1) underlay the pavement.

Tesserae. No *tesserae* were present but the pavement had *scutulae* 0 · 25 to 0 · 45 m. wide and roughly trapezoidal, in pink, green and black limestone 0 · 01 m. thick.

Description. The pavement was 0 · 02 m. thick and had a very smooth surface of well mixed limestone chips in white marble dust and mortar with some yellow tile dust mixed in; the floor was a *terrazzo* floor like those of *op. sig.* 4 and 5. The *scutulae,* set *c.* 0 · 10 to 0 · 12 m. apart, decorated the surface; there were no borders and the treatment was meant to be continuous and without pattern.

Condition. Op. sig. 11 was virtually intact on excavation.

Parallels. Morricone Matini, 1971, 11, no. 25 and pl. IX (Rome, early Sullan).

Conclusion. Op. sig. 11 represents an attempt on the part of the Period II mosaicists to add, in the cheaper medium of *opus signinum,* a section of pavement to an older one, which itself would have been in mosaic *scutulatum* (cf. *op. mus.* 1, 2 and 4).

Op. sig. 12. *Room 39, west portico* (10 · 80 × 5 · 10 m.) Not illustrated.
Bed. A thin *rudus,* of limestone gravel in mortar only underlay the pavement; the thickness of the bed varied between 0 · 01 and 0 · 03 m.

Tesserae. None.

Description. The pavement was made of poorly mixed chips, tile dust and mortar, roughly smoothed to a surface; the thickness of the pavement varies between 0 · 01 and 0 · 02 m.

Condition. Op. sig. 12 was much cracked, sunk and lost upon excavation due to the thinness of its bed and pavement.

Conclusion. Op. sig. 12 was very poorly constructed and very thin; evidently room 39 was either not much used or used for purposes which did not necessitate either a strong or a beautiful floor.

Opus spicatum
Utilitarian rooms in the Period II villa at San Rocco were paved either in *opus signinum* or in brick paving set in a herring-bone pattern, *opus spicatum.* The floors were of a remarkably consistent construction.

Op. spic. 1. *Room 10, culina* (5 · 30 × 4 · 30 m.). Pls. XIII and XIV*a.*
Bed. The bed of *op. spic.* 1 consisted of a crust of mortar and limestone gravel, 0 · 02 m.

thick, spread directly on the terrace fill itself. The bricks were set in a muddy mortar.
Description. The floor was made up of light red bricks, $0 \cdot 08$ to $0 \cdot 085$ m. long, $0 \cdot 03$ m. wide and $0 \cdot 05$ to $0 \cdot 055$ m. deep. They were set in a herring-bone pattern with a space *c.* $0 \cdot 005$ m. between the bricks for the mortar and mud to hold them together. The resulting surface is remarkable for its flatness and strength. Around the thresholds and at the sides of the room, the bricks were clipped to conform to their position.
Dimensions. Op. spic. 1 covered the entire room except for a section under the 'counter' along the N wall.
Condition. Op. spic. 1 was in good condition on excavation. It was left *in situ.*
Parallels. Lugli, 1930, fig. 5 (Sullan?). Pallottino, 1937, 20–1, (Capena, first century B.C.?). Zevi, 1970, 18–22 and figs. 12 and 13 (Ostia, first century A.D.?).
Conclusion. There are no standards for dating *opus spicatum* floors from parallels. *Op. spic.* 1 is of the same date as the other Period II floors, Late Republican, and should be seen as the utilitarian counterpart of the mosaic floors of the rest of the villa.

Op. spic. 2. *Room 11, culina* ($5 \cdot 20 \times 4 \cdot 45$ m.). Pl. XIII.
The construction of *op. spic.* 2 was continuous with that of *op. spic.* 1. For bed and description, see *op. spic.* 1.
Dimensions. Op. spic. 2 covered the entire room except for a section under the 'counter' along the N wall.
Condition. Op. spic. 2 was in good condition on excavation. It was left *in situ.*
Parallels and Conclusion. See *op. spic.* 1.

Op. spic 3, 4 and 5. *Rooms 50, 51 and 52* ($3 \cdot 40 \times 1 \cdot 40$ m.; $3 \cdot 20 \times 1 \cdot 70$ m.; $2 \cdot 10 \times 1 \cdot 70$ m. respectively). Pl. XVI*b*
These three floors were continous with one another and of the same Period II construction as the rest of the rooms of the *villa rustica.*
Bed and Description. See *op. spic.* 1.
Dimensions. These three floors evidently completely covered the rooms in which they were laid.
Condition. All three floors were in fair condition on excavation with some missing patches. All three were left *in situ.*
Parallels. See *op. spic.* 1.
Conclusion. See *op. spic.* 1.

PERIOD II MOSAICS AND PAVEMENTS. CONCLUSION
The mosaics of the Period II villa, especially those of the *domus nova*, orchestrate the environment of display and architectural magnificence which was achieved with the new plan of the villa. All the rooms surrounding the peristyle were paved either in mosaic or in decorated or undecorated *opus signinum*. The result was a quantity and consistency of paving unusual in country villas: such paving of all the rooms is more usual in a *villa suburbana* like the Villa dei Misteri at Pompeii or in a city house like the Casa dei Grifi in Rome.
    The mosaic decoration forms a unified composition throughout the whole house. Two principal elements — the use of coloured isometric perspective and the pink-purple tone — unify the scheme with few exceptions. The *vestibulum* (room 1; *op. mus.* 5) has both isometric perspective and pink-purple dominance, and either or both of these are continued

in the mats of the peristyle (*op. mus.* 9–12), in the *tablinum* threshold (*op. mus.* 13) and the *triclinium* threshold and floor (*op. mus.* 16–17). Both elements occur in what was perhaps the finest pavement of the *domus nova* in room 8, *op. mus.* 18. The only pavement which differs from the other extant ones in colour tones is the coffered pavement in room 12, *op. mus.* 20.

Another element unifying the pavements of major rooms would have been the extensive use of special *emblemata*, of which the three preserved prefabricated hexagons in *op. mus.* 13 are examples. The *emblemata* of *op. mus.* 14 in the *tablinum, op. mus.* 17 in the *triclinium* and *op. mus.* 20 in room 12 have been destroyed. They may have been figurative in character, as the frame with vines of *op. mus.* 20 suggests, or schematic, as the gate threshold suggests (*op. mus.* 15).

Every attempt was made by the mosaicists of Period II at San Rocco to blend the mosaic decoration of the reused rooms of the *domus vetus* with the pavements of the *domus nova*. *Op. mus.* 1 and 2 in room 29 was edged with *op. mus.* 27 to preserve it, and the *scutulatum pavimentum* pattern was used in the peristyle (*op. mus.* 8). In room 36, both mosaic and *opus signinum* of a character conforming to the Period I or IA designs were used in the remodelling of the floor (*op. mus.* 30 and *op. sig.* 11).

An exceptional element, very rarely preserved, is the underscoring for certain geometric patterns in *op. mus.* 13 and 20. These laying-out and guidelines indicate that the mosaicist carefully planned and directed the laying of the *tesserae;* copy-books of practical geometry for establishing these patterns may have been used.

Because of the large number and great variety of patterns, the parallels for the Period II mosaics and pavements are equally various. In general, however, the parallels at Rome and Pompeii establish a late Republican date for the mosaics, *c.* 50 B.C. to the pre-Augustan years; the wide variety of colours and the isometric perspective were in extensive use in this period.

PERIOD IIA MOSAICS AND PAVEMENTS
Opus signinum
Op. sig. 13. *Room 7, corridor* (0 · 78 × 11 · 45 m.). Not illustrated.
In Period IIA, when the *balineum* was put in rooms 8, 9, 27 and 28, the N wall of room 7, the corridor leading from the peristyle to room 8, was dismantled and rebuilt along the same line. Why this was done is not certain. At that time, whatever floor must have existed in Period II was taken out and replaced, once the wall had been rebuilt, with *op. sig.* 13.
    Bed. A *rudus,* 0 · 04 m. thick, of tile chips and limestone gravel in equal proportions in mortar and lime (ratio *c.* 4:1) underlay the pavement. The addition of tile chips to the bed distinguishes the bed of *op. sig.* 13 from those of Period II *opus signinum* pavements.
    Tesserae. Op. sig. 13 had *tesserae* of two types. The crosslets were made of black and white *tesserae* 0 · 01 m.[3]. Between them were green and black *tesserae,* 0 · 01 m. thick 0 · 01 m. wide and 0 · 02 m. long, a rectangular shape not found in the other pavements at San Rocco.
    Description. The pavement was 0 · 03 m. thick and had a smooth surface of tile chips, tile dust and mortar into which were set rows of alternate crosslets and single rectangular *tesserae.* The crosslets, made of four square white *tesserae* surrounding a square black one, were set diagonally to the walls in rows of which every other was of crosslets. The rows of rectangular *tesserae,* each of the rows alternately black and green, were set with

the *tesserae* running lengthwise NS. There were six rows NS, at least 126 rows EW. There were no borders at the thresholds or along the walls.

Dimensions. The alternating rows of crosslets and rectangular *tesserae* were set 0 · 09 m. apart (centre to centre) EW, 0 · 01 m. apart (centre to centre) NS.

Condition. Op.sig. 13 was virtually intact except at the E end of the room where the loss of the wall caused the loss of the floor. Repaired and left *in situ.*

Parallels. No precise parallels have been published; while *opus signinum* pavements with crosslets are not uncommon, the alternation of crosslets and rectangular *tesserae* is unusual. See, however, Blake, 1930, 28 and pl. 4,4 (Pompeii, associated with Second Style); Pernice, 1938, 63 and pl. 26,5 (Pompeii, associated with Second Style); Becatti, 1961, 95 and pl. LII (Ostia, late second century B.C.); Morricone Matini, 1971, 14, no. 46 and pl. IV (Ostia, second half of the second century B.C.).

Conclusion. The precise date of *op. sig.* 13 cannot be determined on the basis of its parallels; this type of design seems to have had a long life in Italy.

Op. sig. 14. *Room 54, oletum* (5 · 70 × 4 · 05 m.). Pls. XXI*a* and *c* and XXII*a.*

Bed. The bed in the floor proper of *op. sig.* 14 could not be observed because this part of the *oletum* was preserved for exhibition.

Description. Op.sig. 14 was a coat of tile chips, tile dust and mortar of an even buff colour, very carefully smoothed in the floor area. The surface of the floor was moulded around other features of the room such as the *capulator's* basin and steps and the round base in the SE corner of the room.

Dimensions. Op.sig. 14 covered the entire area of the room.

Condition. The floor was found virtually intact and was left *in situ.*

Opus spicatum

Op. spic. 6. *Room 53, oletum* (5 · 70 × 3 · 75 m.). Pls. XXI*a–b* and XXII*b–c.*

This Period IIA floor of the *oletum* differed in only a few respects from the *opus spicatum* floors of Period II (*op. spic.* 1–5).

Bed. The bed of *op.spic.* 6 was a thin spread of mortar and lime (ratio *c.* 3:1), 0 · 02 m. thick, laid directly on the Period IIA floor fill. The bricks were set in the same mortar and lime as the bed.

Description. The floor was made up of bricks of the same size and was set in the same pattern as that of *op.spic.* 1. The only difference was one of colour, the bricks of *op.spic.* 6 being more yellow or buff in tone than those of *op.spic.* 1–5. Because mortar and lime cemented the bricks in place, the surface was smooth, flat and quite waterproof as well. The bricks were clipped to fit around the *ara, trapetum,* and bases for the *arbores.*

Dimensions. Op. spic. 6 covered the entire room.

Condition. Except for a broken part along the S door, *op. spic.* 6 was in good condition on excavation. It was left *in situ.*

Parallels. See *op.spic.* 1.

Conclusion. As with *op. spic.* 1, no definite date could be assigned to *op. spic.* 6.

PERIOD IIA MOSAICS AND PAVEMENTS. CONCLUSION

Few new floors were needed in Period IIA, and the one decorated *opus signinum* floor (*op. sig.* 13) did not represent a decorative departure from the designs of the Period II floors. Specific dates from their parallels cannot be assigned to the Period IIA floors.

Chapter VIII. The Finds

1. COINS
Michael H. Crawford

(I wish to thank Mr. Michael H. Crawford most sincerely for the help he has given in identifying, dating and commenting on the coins. M.A.C.)

The 43 coins found at San Rocco were:

Greek coins

1 (791). A coin of ? Neapolis. Cf. *BMC Italy,* 114, no 209. *c.* 250 B.C.
2. (649). A coin of ? Paestum. *c.* 150 B.C.
3. (375). A coin of the Mamertini. *BMC Sicily,* no. 11. Third century B.C.
4. (174). A coin, indistinguishable, of Magna Grecia.

Provenance: Three of the four coins came from the original sub-soil; no. 1 from the south terrace platform in the area of the round reservoir, no. 2 to the east of the Period II villa, and no. 3 from the garden area. No. 4 was unstratified in the destruction layer over the south-western area of the platform.

None of these coins can be associated directly with the Period I villa and they seem to be stray finds which were lost there before this villa was built. They may thus reflect some local activity, when Greek coins were circulating in the region, between *c.* 250–100 B.C. or later, but they cannot be used to date the Period I building.

Republican coins

5. (148). A *sextans.* Anonymous post semi-libral. Crawford, 1974, 41/9. 215–212 B.C.
6. (718). *As.* Crawford, 1974, 110/2. 211–208 B.C.
7-10. (175b) (270) (686) (630). Four *As.* (only a quarter of 7 persists) Cf. Crawford, 1974, 56/2. After 211 B.C.
11. (175a). *As.* Crawford, 1974, 199/1. 169–158 B.C.
12. (311). *As* of BALBVS. Crawford, 1974, 179/1. 169–158 B.C.
13. (725). *As* of VALERIVS. Crawford 1974, 191/1. 169–158 B.C.
14. (313). *As* of Q.MARCIVS LIBO. Crawford, 1974, 215/2. 148 B.C.
15. (631). *As* of M.ATILIVS SARANVS. Crawford, 1974, 214/2b. 148 B.C.
16. (526). A *quadrans.* Anonymous. *c.* 135 B.C.
17. (632). A *denarius* of Q.LVTATIVS CERCO. Crawford, 1974, 305/1. 109 or 108 B.C.

Provenance: Three of these coins were found in the platform II make-up (nos. 9, 12 and 13). Two coins (nos. 15 and 17) came from the basal make-up of the Period II mosaic pavement of room 4 (the *tablinum*). All should have been derived from the Periods I/IA occupation, or even from the Period I building phase. The remainder were found in destruction layers or top soil.

The five stratified coins (nos. 9,12–13, 15 and 17) range in date from after 211 to 109/108 B.C. Crawford comments that these Republican coins could have continued in use beyond Periods I/IA, and he quotes the Bolsena hoard of bronzes, with its latest coin of A.D. 97, which contained 96 Republican pieces out of a total of 719 (see *MEFR,* 1964, 51); and the Uskub hoard of *denarii,* which, with the latest coin of A.D. 244–249, included 8 Republican coins (see *NZ*, 1968, 37). So these coins might be associated with the Periods I/IA or even the Periods II/IIA occupations. The *as* of BALBVS of 169–158 B.C. (no. 12) was in the débris thrown over the terrace wall of the Period I villa, over the Periods I/IA deposit, and the coins of the moneyers VALERIVS, M. ATILIVS SARANVS and Q. LVTATIVS CERCO were in layers associated with the building of the Period II villa. In view of the above evidence, these Republican coins cannot be used to date the building periods.

Imperial coins

18. (269). *As* of DIVVS AVGVSTVS. Worn. *M. and S.*, 6. After A.D. 22.
19. (634). *As*. Illegible. First to second century A.D.
20. (685). *Sestertius* of DIVA FAVSTINA I. *M. and S.*, 1128. After her death in A.D.141.

Seven coin hoard of silver denarii

The following seven silver coins, in fine condition, and all minted at Rome, are a small hoard found close together in the top of the tumble of the fallen west retaining wall of the Period II platform bounding the west portico (room 39). It consisted of:

21. (36). A *denarius* of TRAIANVS. *M.and S.*, 118 (an *aureus*). A.D. 106–111.
22. (37). A *denarius* of TRAIANVS. *M. and S.*, 337. A.D. 115 (Spring) — 116 (Spring).
23. (41). A *denarius* of HADRIANVS. *M. and S.*, 311. A.D. 134–138.
24. (42). A *denarius* of ANTONINVS PIVS. *M. and S.*, 165. A.D. 147–148.
25. (38). A *denarius* of ANTONINVS PIVS. *M. and S.*, 276. A.D. 157–158.
26. (39). A *denarius* of FAVSTINA II. *M. and S.*, 502(a). A.D. 145–161. Struck under ANTONINVS PIVS.
27. (40). A *denarius* of MARCVS AVRELIVS. *M. and S.*, 483. A.D. 159–160. This hoard was probably not assembled before the last third of the second century A.D.

28. (629). A *denarius* of IVLIA MARSA. *M. and S.*, 268. A.D. 218–222.
29-30. (644) and (633). Two *sestertii* of SEVERVS ALEXANDER. *M. and S.*, 635. A.D. 231–235.
31. (168). A *sestertius* of MAXIMINVS I. *M. and S.*, 78. A.D. 236 (January) — 238 (March/April).
32. (793). A *sestertius* of GORDIANVS. *M. and S.*, 303a. A.D.241–243, probably 242.
33. (635). A *sestertius* of PHILIP I. *M. and S.*, 184(a). A.D. 244–249.
34. (753). An *antoninianus* of DIVO CLAVDIO (Claudius Gothicus). *M. and S.*, 266. A.D. 270 or later.
35 (748). An *antoninianus* of PROBVS. *M. and S.*, 158. A.D. 276–282.
36. (122). A coin of CONSTANTINVS II (as Caesar). cf. Cohen, 1880–92, 9. A.D. 320–324.

Provenance: Excluding the small coin hoard, the 12 remaining coins of Imperial date were found in destruction layers or top soil. The seven-coin hoard of silver *denarii*, whose latest coin is one of MARCVS AVRELIVS of A.D. 159–160, was deposited at a time when the western platform retaining wall of the villa was no longer maintained and had fallen outwards, indicating that by the last third of the second century A.D. the residential part of the villa had lost its importance, though perhaps the use of the *villa rustica* may have continued until the end of the century, or even to the end of the first quarter of the third century A.D. The few coins of later date may be strays.

It is noteworthy that no coins were found that are dated between 110 B.C. and A.D. 22. It is during this hiatus in the coin list that the Periods I and II villas were probably built, so that the only two coins that are contemporary are nos. 18. and 19, the *as* of the first to the second century A.D. and the *as* of DIVVS AVGVSTVS of A.D. 22 or later. 'However,' Crawford writes, 'as has been pointed out, early Republican bronze still circulated in the late first century A.D. and Republican *denarii* even later. Much of the unstratified Republican bronze may therefore be associated with the life of the Period II villa. The coin finds from San Rocco should not be taken as indicating the absence of money from the villa, but rather as evidence for the persistence in rural areas of old issues to the exclusion of current coins.'

Medieval coins

37–38. (374) and (719). Two very worn illegible bronze coins, of late medieval date, were found in the top soil and the slip from the upper terrace. They may perhaps be associated with the use of the little chapel of San Rocco.

Modern coins

39–43. (312), (44), (400), (792) and (401). Five modern Italian bronze coins came from the top soil, one dated 182?, another 1918.

2. LAMPS
(Figs. 14-17)
Marie C. Keith, M.A.
(Institute of Fine Arts, New York University)

We are indebted to Mr. Donald M. Bailey, of the British Museum, for examining and dating the lamps marked +.

(i) *Lamps in black glazed wares. c. 50 B.C. to A.D. 1 or earlier* (Fig. 14, 1–6)

1. (732). A lamp, in light brown paste with scanty remains of a matt brown-black glaze. It lacks the handle. Of biconical form with a flat base, the small plain discus has a large oil hole. The nozzle is angular, with a large wick hole. The lamp was not glazed below the base. *c.* 150–100 B.C.

    Cf. Bernhard, 1955, Tabl. XIII, 81 (third-second century B.C.); Broneer, 1930, 148, fig. 75, 191, (Type XIII—Hellenistic); Deneauve, 1969, pl. XXX, 195 (Type XI—third-second century B.C.); Fabbricotti, 1969, pl. II, 11, 12 (Hellenistic); Leibundgut, 1963–64, Abb. 447, 11 (Greek and Hellenistic—from Pompeii); Lerat, 1954, pl. II, 13 (A93) (Hellenistic); Loeschcke, 1911, pl. LXXVII,1727 (Type I—third-second century B.C.—Italian); Mercando, 1962, pl. I, 2 (12) (Greek and Hellenistic); Ponsich, 1961, pl. III, 18 (Type IC—Hellenistic); Rolland, 1951, 258, fig. 164, right, (Hellenistic third-first century B.C.).

2. (8).+ The nozzle from a large lamp. In buff paste with a worn black glaze. First century B.C.?

3. (232). A ring handle from a large lamp. In soft buff paste. No glaze remains.

4. (24).[+] A lamp fragment, in light brown paste with a thick dull black glaze. Part of the body, with a projecting lug, survives, and part of the discus, with a bounding circle and moulded decoration. *c.* 50 B.C. to A.D. 1.

   Cf. Bernhard, 1955, Tabl. XLIII, 213 (first century B.C.-first century A.D.); Brants, 1913, pl. I, 147, 151, 153 (Type VI—first century B.C.—Italian); Carettoni, 1957, fig. 34b, c, d (Late Republican-early Augustan); Deneauve, 1969, pl. XXXIV, 272, 273 (Type III—last stage in evolution which led to Roman lamps of Augustan epoch); Dressel/Lamboglia, type 3 (Republican); Fabbricotti, 1969, pl. IV, 22 (end of first century B.C.-beginning of first century A.D.). pl. IV, 29; Heres, 1972, pl. 56, 521 (first half of first century A.D.) pl. 51, 480 (first-third centuries A.D.); Leibundgut, 1963–64, Abb. 448, 15 (Republican—probably from Baiae); Loeschcke, 1919, Abb. 8, 1 (Type VIIIA - mid first century A.D.—post Augustan and less frequent in last third of century—from Trier), Taf. XVI, 632 and Taf. XVII, 637 (Type V—post Augustan—second and third quarters of first century A.D.); Loeschcke, 1911, pl. LXXVII, 1869 (Type VIII—Rhineland); Menzel, 1969, Abb. 19, 9 (327) (Rome), Abb. 19, 6 (68) and 19, 2 (67) (lamp type—second half of first century B.C.), Abb. 19, 10 (163) (lamp type—first century A.D. beginning with Augustus and disappearing at the beginning of the third century A.D.); Mercando, 1962, pl. II, 1 (Republican), pl. IX, 1 and 2; Perlzweig, 1961, pl. 1, 3 and 5 (late first century B.C.); Ponsich, 1961, pl. III, 20 (Type IC—Hellenistic first century B.C.); Bailey, 1975, Q 725–6, Q 737–740 (*c.* 50 B.C.–A.D. 1).

5. (602). Part of a lamp in buff paste with a slightly irridescent thick black glaze. The surface of the lug is decorated with three impressed dot-and-circle motifs. The discus is demarcated by a deep groove. *c.* 50 B.C. to A.D. 1?

   Cf. Fabbricotti, 1969, 11, 13 (Hellenistic/Republican—first century B.C.); Lamboglia, 1950, 65, fig. 25, 2 (Strata VIa, revised dating 100/90–30/20 B.C.).

6. (47a-b).[+] Part of a lamp in buff paste with the remains of a dull black glaze. The discus has a moulded relief pattern of leaves. There is a three-ribbed lug on one side, and, at the base of the nozzle a small volute moulding. Augustan.

   For the shape of the lamp (the ear handles and the volute) cf. Broneer, 1930, 176, fig. 103, 453, (Type XXII—first century A.D.); Deneauve, 1969, pl. XLII, 370 (Type IVB—generally second half of first century A.D.); Fabbricotti, 1969, pl. IV, 30(mid first century A.D.); Menzel, 1969, Abb. 19, 9 (327) (Rome); Perlzweig, 1961, pl. 1, 14 and pl. 3, 68 (1st half of first century A.D.); Ponsich, 1961, pl. IV, 22 (Type IIA1—first century A.D.).

   For the decoration of the discus (leaves) cf. Ivanyi, 1935, pl. XLV, 16 (1151) (frag.); Lerat, 1954, pl. IV, 28 (A5) (Série 2A—first half of first century A.D.), pl. VII, 51 (D863–3–64) (Série 2B); Loeschcke, 1919, Taf. XI, 190, 191 (Type I—first century A.D.—laurel crown); Pompeii, 1973, 28; Waldhauer, 1914, pl. XV, 170, 171, (time of Claudius); Walters, 1914, pl. XXVI, 814 (first century A.D.).

Unillustrated fragments of lamps, in black glazed wares were:

   (i). Parts of nozzles, cf. no. 1 above, though smaller, in light brown paste with scanty remains of a black glaze (203, 524, 779f-h and 820).

   (ii). Parts of lamps cf. no. 5 above, with slight variations. In light brown paste with a dull black glaze except for 815 which has a chestnut glaze (603/1–2, 815 and 818).

   (iii). Indeterminate wall sherds from lamps, in buff and light brown paste, which have lost their glaze (779d-e).

   (iv). Ring handles in similar ware (136, 689 and 692).

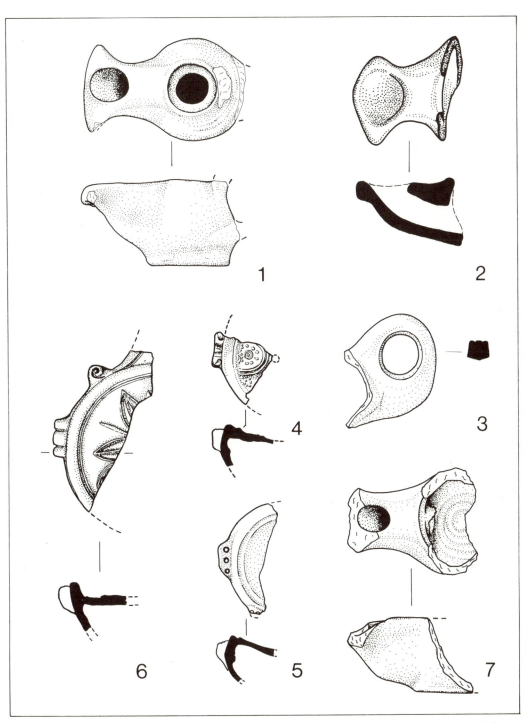

Fig. 14. Lamps in black glazed wares, *c.* 50 B.C.–A.D.1 or earlier (nos.1–6); in heavy red ware, first century B.C. (no.7). (Scale: 1/2)

(ii) *Unglazed lamp in heavy red ware. First century B.C.* (Fig. 14,7)

7. (813). Part of the body and the nozzle of a lamp in a heavy gritty coarse red paste, with a rough red surface. It has not been glazed. The base is flat, and the charred nozzle is angular. Probably first century B.C.

(iii) *Lamps in black glazed wares, with a decoration of raised dots. c. 50 B.C. to A.D. 1.* (Fig. 15, 8–10)

8. (193).[+] A lamp in buff paste with a thin glaze which shades from orange-brown to dull black. It is not glazed below the base. The handle, and part of the angular nozzle, are missing. The discus, with a central oil hole, has two raised circles. The top of the shoulder is decorated with four lines of raised dots, and there are six lines on the body. There is an eroded lug on one side. There is a small irregular perforation behind the wick hole. The base is stamped with five small impressed circles. c. 50 B.C. to A.D. 1.

Cf. Carettoni, 1957, fig. 34, f. (late Republican-early Augustan); Deneauve, 1969, pl. XXXIV, 265 (Type I—Republican); Dressel/Lamboglia, Type 2 (Republican); Ercolano, 1755–1792, 177, Tav. XXXVI; Fabbricotti, 1969, pl. III, 16,17 (second half of last century B.C.); Hanoune, 1970, pl. 3, 4 (up to first century A.D.); Loeschscke, 1911, pl. LXXVII, 1742 (Type V—second half of first century B.C.— Italian); Menzel, 1969, Abb. 21 (70) (second half of first century B.C.).

9. (100).[+] Part of the discus and nozzle of a lamp, in light brown paste with a dull orange glaze, charred around the nozzle. The discus is plain, with a central hole, and the top of the shoulder has a decoration of four rows of raised dots.

Cf. Fabbricotti, 1969, pl. III, 19 (second half of the first century B.C.); Loeschcke, 1911, pl. LXXVII, 1733 (Type III—first century B.C.—Italian); Pompeii, 1973, 36; Szentléleky, 1969, 47 (first century A.D.).

10. (22a).[+] Part of a lamp in a pinkish-buff paste, with a dull black glaze. The discus is bounded with a moulded circle, and the top of the shoulder has a decoration of four rows of raised dots interspersed with a dot-and-circle motif. c. 50 B.C. to A.D. 1.

Cf. Broneer, 1930, pl. VII, 373 (Type XX—chiefly Augustan—not later than first century A.D.); Ivanyi, 1935, pl. XVI, 5 (521) (Type II—Tiberius to end of first century A.D.—type found in Pannonia with coins of Nero and Vespasian). For discussions of lamps as 8–10 see Bailey, 1975, Q 711 (second half of the first century B.C.) and Pavolini, 1981, 161–5 (70–15 B.C.).

The following sherds of lamps of this type are not illustrated:

(774). The nozzle and part of the body of a lamp, cf. no. 8 above. The angular nozzle has a wick hole, and the body is decorated with rows of raised dots. The glazed base has five small dot-and-circle motifs.

(777). The nozzle and part of the body of a lamp, cf. no. 8 above and (774) above. It has part of a projecting lug on one side.

(778). Part of the discus and the lug, cf. no. 8 above. A raised circle bounds the central oil hole.

(167), (194a–d), (275) and (779i and k). Lamp sherds in light brown paste with remains of black glaze, decorated with raised dots.

(iv) *Lamps in orange-red glazed ware. c. 50 B.C. to A. D. 1.* (Fig. 15, 11–12)

11. (99).[+] The ring handle and part of the body of a lamp in buff paste with an orange-red

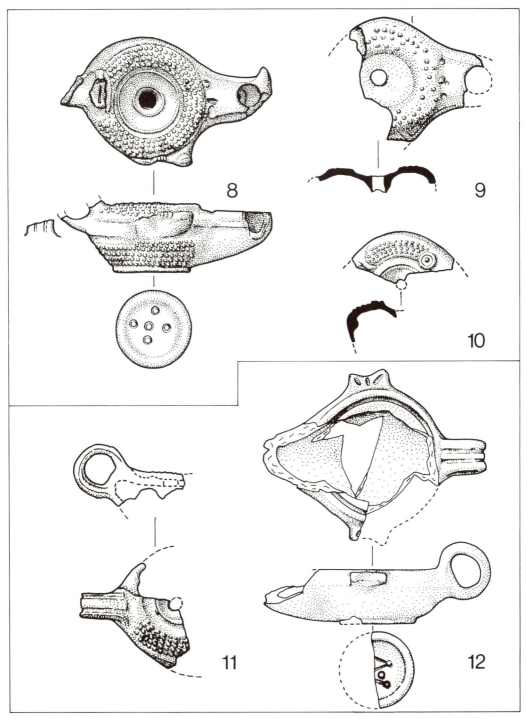

Fig. 15. Lamps in black glazed wares with raised dots (nos.8–10); in orange-red glazed ware (nos.11–12).
All *c.* 50 B.C.–A.D.1 (Scale: 1/2)

glaze. There is a raised circle round the central oil hole, and the top of the shoulder is decorated with five rows of raised dots. *c.* 50 B.C. to A.D.1.

Cf. Loeschcke, 1911, pl. LXXVII, 1733 (Type III—first century B.C.—Italian); Menzel, 1969, Abb. 19, 1 (71) (first century B.C.—this particular kind of 'Warzen-lampen', with side handles, grooved handle and hole in the centre of a small depressed discus disappears in the Augustan period.

12. (772). A lamp in soft buff paste with a good orange-red glaze. The ring handle is ribbed. There are bicornate lugs on each side. The missing discus had been demarcated by a deep groove. There is part of an impressed stamp on the base. *c.* 50 B.C. to A.D.1.

Cf. Benoit, 1958, 9, fig. 5 (first century B.C.); Brants, 1913, pl. V, 726 (Type XVII—begins in the time of Claudius and is most common in the two following centuries—from Carthage); Broneer, 1930, pl. X, 473 (Type XXIV—second half of the first century A.D.); Deneauve, 1969, pl. LXIV, 643 (Type VG—50—100 A.D.); Ercolano, 1755–1792, 153, Tav. XXX; Ivanyi, 1935, pl. XXVIII, 5 (752) (Type VII—first century A.D.); Lerat, 1954, pl. III, 21, 21b (A3) (Série 1), pl. XVII, 136 (A2) (Série 4—first-second centuries A.D.); Loeschcke, 1919, 242 Abb. 8, 3, (Type VIII with side handles—post Augustan to mid first century A.D.—less frequent in last third of the century—from Köln); Loeschcke, 1911, pl. LXXVII, 1715 and pl. LXXIX, 1738 (Type V—second half of first century B.C.—Italian); Menzel, 1969, Abb. 20, 1 (244) and Abb. 19, 4 (243) (lamp type of the second and third quarters of first century A.D.); Perlzweig, 1961, pl. 4, 80 (second quarter of first century A.D.—Italian), pl. 4, 84 (first half of first century A.D.—East Aegean), pl. 5, 119 (second half of first century A.D.), pl. 13, 403 (mid first century into second century A.D.—copied from imported lamps such as 84); Walters, 1914, pl. XLI, form 74, 516 (miscellaneous, mostly early varieties).

Unillustrated fragments of lamps of this category are:

(814). An angular nozzle with a good glaze.

(487). A similar nozzle, with part of the wall with a pattern of rows of raised dots, a base ring and an impressed circle on the base, cf. no. 12 above.

(268b). The base and part of the wall with a projecting lug.

(147). Part of a lamp very like no. 12 above.

(268d). Part of the discus with a small hole opposite the root of the nozzle, only part of which persists. At its attachment to the discus there is a decoration of three impressed circles.

(194e). A lamp fragment with a spiral motif impressed into the base of the nozzle.

(73), (165b), (166), (189), (266d), (268a and c), (604), (770), (771), (779k). Sherds from lamps of this type showing angular nozzles or decorations of rows of raised dots.

(v) *Lamps decorated with designs in moulded relief. c. A.D. 1. to 80.* (Fig. 16, 13–16)

13. (238).[+] Part of the discus of a lamp, in buff paste with an orange-brown colour coating. It is decorated with two grooves and a moulded rosette design *c.* A.D.1–80.

Cf. Bernhard, 1955, Tabl. LXXX,292 (first century A.D.—small leaf rosette); Ivanyi, 1935, pl. XVI, 3 (524) (Type II—Tiberius to end of first century A.D.—a type found in Pannonia with coins of Nero and Vespasian—12 leaves); Loeschcke, 1919, Taf. XVI, 688–90 (Type VIII—post Augustan—mid first century A.D.—less frequent in the last third of the century—rosette with 12 leaves), Taf. XVI, 566 (Type

IV—post Augustan but disappears north of the Alps in the first century—persists in Italy in later Imperial period—mussel with 13 ribs); Menzel, 1969, Abb. 11, 10 (162) (lamp type first century A.D. begins with Augustus and disappears at the beginning of the third century—10 leaf rosette—from Miletus); Ponsich, 1961, pl. V, 39 (Form IIB1—first century A.D.); Waldhauer, 1914, pl. XIV, 159 (time of Claudius).

14. (141).[+] Part of the discus of a lamp, in soft beige paste with an orange brown colour coating. It is decorated with two grooves, and a moulded relief motif of a winged victory. *c.* A.D. 1–80.

   This is probably the type of a Victory standing to the front on a globe and holding a wreath in her right hand and a palm branch in her left hand. The brownish glaze indicates a first century A.D. date (We are indebted to Miss Claireve Grandjouan for this suggestion).

   Cf. Bachofen, 1958, Taf. 17, 2; Bailey, 1965, pl. XI, 249 (second half of first century A.D.—made in Italy); Broneer, 1930, pl. X, 459 (Type XXIV—second half of first century A.D.), pl. XXV, 437 (Type XXII—chiefly Augustan—continued throughout the first half of the first century—not later than first century A.D.—fragment); Deneauve, 1969, pl. XXXVI, 299 (Type IVA—generally from the reign of Augustus to that of Claudius); Ercolano, 1755–92, 41, Tav. VI; Heres, 1972, Taf. 16, 120 (second half of first century A.D.); Libertini, 1930, Tav. CXXII, 1271; Loeschcke, 1919, Taf. VI, 389 (Type IV—post Augustan but disappears north of the Alps in the first century A.D.—persists in Italy to the later Imperial period), Taf. VI, 63 (Type I—first century A.D.); Menzel, 1969, Abb. 33, 21 (331) (fragment from Miletos); Osborne, 1924, pl. II, 26 (Augustan volutes); Ponsich, 1961, pl. V, 35 (Form IIB1—first century A.D.).

15. (158).[+] Part of a decorated lamp, in buff paste. It has lost its colour coating. There is a moulded lug, and a decorated design of impressed dot and circle motif. *c.* A.D. 30–80.

   Cf. Heres, 1972, pl. 35, 308 (second half of first century A.D. to first half of second century A.D.); Menzel, 1969, Abb. 19, 5 (268) (Form with round nozzle—second third of first century A.D.—main period mid first century A.D.—rare in last third of first century A.D.—from Miletos); Noll, 1937, Abb. 51, 7 (32) (mid first century A.D.).

16. (59).[+] A crescentic handle from a lamp, in buff paste, with the remains of an orange-brown colour coating. *c.* A.D. 30–80.

   Cf. Broneer, 1930, pl. VII, 396 (Type XXI—first century A.D.); Deneauve, 1969, pl. LVI, 544, 545, pl. LVII, 552, pl. LXIX, 570, 571 (Type VB—first half of first century A.D.); Dressel/Lamboglia Type 13 (Julio-Claudian); Ercolano, 1755–92, 5, Tav. II; 19, Tav. III; 43, Tav. VI; 63, Tav. X; 97, Tav. XVI; 141, Tav. XXVII; 149, Tav. XXIX; Hanoune, 1970, pl. 3, 17; Ivanyi, 1935, pl. XVII, 3 (530) (Type III—lamps of this type were found with Hadrianic medallions in *Aquincum*);Lerat, 1954, pl. IV, 31 (D863–3–52) (Série 2A—first half of first century A.D.); Loeschcke, 1919, Abb. 4, 1 and 2 (Type III—late Augustan—from Wollman collection); Menzel, 1969, Abb. 26, 1 (475), Abb. 26, 4 (89); Pompeii, 1973, 20, 22, 23; Ponsich, 1961, pl. VIII, 81 (Form IIB1—first century A.D.); Szentléleky, 1969, 86 (first century A.D.—of Italic origin); Waldhauer, 1914, pl. XXIII, 226, pl. XXIV, 229 (first century A.D.—from Italy); Walters, 1914, pl. XXVI, 837, 850 (first century A.D.).

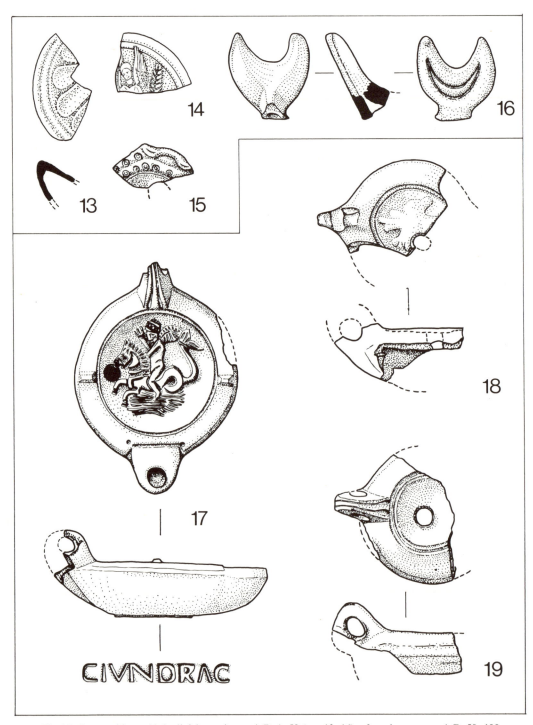

CIVNDRAC

Fig. 16. Lamps with moulded relief decoration, *c.* A.D. 1–50 (nos.13–16); of varying types, *c.* A.D. 50–100 (nos.17–19). (Scale: 1/2)

(vi) *Lamps of varying types. c. A.D. 90–180.* (Fig. 16, 17–9)

17. (50).[+] A lamp, in light brown paste with a brick-red colour coating. The ring handle is broken off, but it was ribbed. The nozzle is stubby and rounded, with one wick hole. The discus is demarcated by a deep groove, and the top of the shoulder has two opposed rectangular mouldings. The moulded relief design on the discus is of a winged *amorinus*, carrying a trident, riding a mythical fish-tailed sea-horse, over grooves representing the waves of the sea. The single hole for the oil is at one side. The base is stamped CIVNDRAC. *c.* A.D. 90–160.

For the shape of the lamp, cf. Deneauve, 1969, pl. LXXX, 879, 880 (Type VIIC), lamps with protuberances on rim and mark of Type VIIA (six of seven examples of CIVNDRAC in Deneauve are Type VIIA)—first half of second century A.D.); Loeschcke, 1919, 237, Type VIII, nozzle LI, (Claudian/Neronian main period); Menzel, 1969, Abb. 31, 20 (275), Abb. 44, 12 (290), Abb. 43 (273) (second third of first century A.D.—main period mid first century—rare in the last third of the first century); Bailey, 1980, Type P iii (*c.* A.D. 90–130+).

For the motif of a winged *genius* riding a hippocamp to the left, cf. Deneauve, 1969, pl. XLVIII, 449 and 451 (Type VA, lamps with rounded nozzle decorated with volutes—first half of first century A.D. to end of first century A.D.); Loeschcke, 1919, Taf. VI, 52–3 (Type I—first century A.D.—figure riding to the right); Menzel, 1969, Abb. 32, 25 (203) (Type Augustan—rare at the end of the first century A.D. and disappears in the second century A.D.—figure riding to the right); Ponsich, 1961, pl. VIII, 79, pl. IX, 86 (Form IIB1—first century A.D.—lamp with rounded nozzle decorated with volutes); Thouvenot, 1954, pl. XXIII, 4.

For the potter's mark, according to Leibundgut, 1963–64 (410–31 footnotes 96, with partial list of known examples, 97–99) the products of the workshop of C. IVNIVS DRACO (CIVNDRAC) are most strongly represented in North Africa, Campania, Sicily and Sardinia. They are rarely found north of the Alps and are lacking in the eastern provinces with one example found in the Danubian provinces. The workshop produced principally Loeschcke Type VIII with nozzle L and must have been active in the second half of the first century A.D. This statement must remain hypothetical because the *CIL* lists in many cases do not tell the type of lamp associated with the description. The workshop continued into the second century A.D. One of its lamps was found in a grave in Metauros with a coin of Antoninus Pius dated 140 A.D. Another (Dressel type 28) can be dated at the end of the second century to the beginning of the third century A.D. Some additional examples can be found in Ponsich, 1961, 70 and Illana, 1968, 23. Pavolini, 1976–7, Tav. II dates this workshop *c.* A.D. 160–200.

18. (2).[+] Part of a lamp in red paste, with orange-red colour coating. The ring handle is broken. The discus, bounded by a cordon, has a moulded relief pattern of a steering oar and a dolphin. *c.* A.D. 90–160.

Cf. Bernhard, 1955, pl. LXXII, 268; Brants, 1913, pl. V, 699 (Type XVII—begins in time of Claudius and is most common in the two following centuries); Deneauve, 1969, pl. LXXIII, 781 (Type VIIA—appears around the beginning of the second half of the first century A.D., found at Pompeii and Vindonissa, and continues into the first part of the second century A.D.); Heres, 1972, Taf. 33, 276 (second half of first century A.D. to first half of second century A.D.); Loeschcke, 1919 (for motif), Taf. VI, 601–2 (Type V, lamp with rounded nozzle and shoulder volute—post

Augustan—second and third quarters of first century A.D.); Loeschcke, 1911, pl. LXXXIII, 1897 (Type X—the type begins to be localised in the Claudian period—to be widespread in the following century in the Mediterranean region); Menzel, 1969, Abb. 32, 23 (248) (Type—second and third quarters of the first century A.D.); Osborne, 1924, pl. III, 34; Ponsich, 1961, pl. XXI, 286 (Form IIIB1—second century A.D.); Waldhauer, 1914, pl. XV, 162 (the time of Claudius—from Italy). Bailey, 1980, Type Pi.

19. (139).[+] Part of a lamp in buff paste with the remains of a dark brown coating. The ring handle is ribbed. The plain discus is bounded by grooves and carries an asymmetric oil hole. c. A.D. 90–180.

   Cf. Bernhard, 1955, Tabl. LXIV, 258 (Claudian—from Cherchell); Deneauve, 1969, pl. LXXXIII, 911 (Type VIIIA—50–100 A.D.); Heres, 1972, Taf. 35, 307 (second half of first century A.D. to first half of second century A.D.), Taf. 38, 333 (second half of first century A.D.), Taf. 51, 475 (first to third centuries A.D.); Leibundgut, 1963–64, Abb. 451, 38 (beginning in second third of the first century A.D.—flowering in mid to last third of the first century A.D.), Abb. 452, 45 (late antique—similar to 38 but differs in strikingly heavy weight, coarse thick walled clay, concentric furrows on base and lines in relief decorating end of spout. Similar to lamp dated in last third of second century to beginning of third century A.D.); Lerat, 1954, pl. X, 72 (A35) (Série 3B—not before the Flavians), pl. XI, 85 (Série 3D). Bailey, 1980, Type Pi.

Unillustrated lamp fragments of this type are:

   (11). A sherd from the discus and shoulder of a lamp in ware similar to that of no. 17 above. It has a rectangular raised moulding on the shoulder. c. A.D. 50–100.

   (105). The shoulder of a lamp, in red paste fired self colour, with a groove demarcating the discus which has part of a moulded relief decoration. The top of the shoulder has a rectangular raised moulding.

   (266a). The ring handle, ribbed on top, from a lamp in pink paste with a brown—red colour coating.

   (9), (118a), (215e), (220), (221b), (240), (372) and (473). Parts of lamps similar to no. 19 above.

(vii) *Lamps dated to c. A.D. 150–225.* (Fig. 17, 20–22)

20. (45).[+] A lamp, lacking the ring handle and nozzle, in hard red paste with a rough red surface. Its only features are two moulded raised rectangular 'stops' on the top of the shoulder. c. A.D. 150–225 or possibly later.

   Cf. Bernhard, 1955, Tabl. CXXXI, 454 (second century A.D.—Trajanic—Gallic workshop); Brants, 1913, pl. IV, 474 (Type XIII, Firmalampen—end of first century A.D. to beginning of second century A.D.); Loeschcke, 1919, Taf. I, Type Xk, 999 (Firmalampen short form—last quarter of first century A.D. to last third of third century A.D.); Perlzweig, 1961, pl. 9, 284 (first half of third century A.D.), pl. 24, 1181 (second half of third century A.D.—Attic); Pompeii, 1973, 35.

21. (110).[+] The ring handle and part of the shoulder of a lamp in soft yellow paste. The colour coating is lost. The top of the shoulder has a decoration of three rows of raised dots. c. A.D. 150–225 or possibly later.

   Cf. Bernhard, 1955, Tabl. XCII, 327 (third century A.D.—Italian); Deringer, 1965, Abb. 33, 341 and pl. XI, 342 (late antique); Fabbricotti, 1969, pl. VII, 53–9

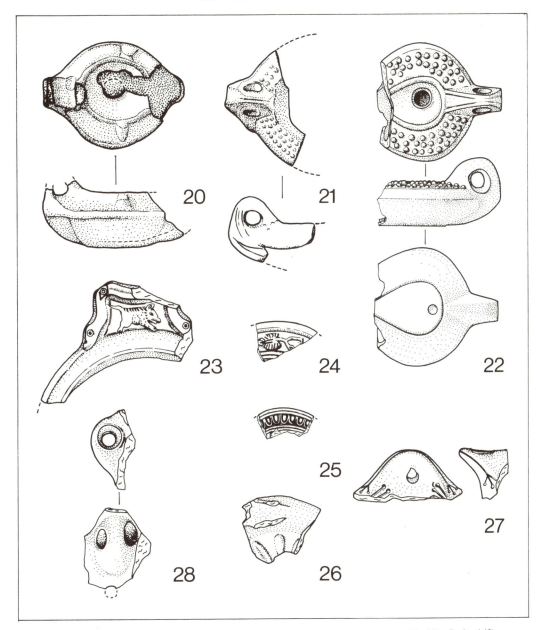

Fig. 17. Lamps dated *c*. A.D. 150–225 (nos.20–22); of miscellaneous dates, (nos.23–28). (Scale: 1/2)

(third—fourth centuries A.D.); Lerat, 1954, pl. XIII, 101 (A55–60) (Série 3E) (third—fourth centuries A.D.); Menzel, 1969, Abb. 72, 4 (559); Szentléleky, 1969, 180 (third century A.D.).

22. (471).[+] A lamp, in hard buff paste fired dull grey, with a rough surface. It has an angular ring handle, with an asymmetrical oil hole in a plain discus surrounded by a cordon. There are three irregular rows of raised dots on the top of the shoulder. The base is demarcated by a slight groove.*c*. A.D. 100–200.

Cf. Ercolano, 1775–92, 177, Tav. XXXVI; Fabbricotti, 1969, pl. VI, 42 (second century A.D.); Ivanyi, 1935, pl. XXV, 5 (710), 7 (711) (Type VI—no sure date, the second half of the first century A.D. to the beginning of the third assumed); Ponsich, 1961, pl. XIV, 152 (Form IIb 3—end of the first century A.D. to third century A.D.); Szentléleky, 1969, 183 (third century A.D.). For discussion of this type, see Fabbricotti, 1974, 23–30. Bailey, 1980, Q 1116 (*c.* A.D. 75–125).

Unillustrated lamps of similar form are:

(58a–b).[+] Part of a lamp, in ware and form similar to no. 21 above, but with four rows of raised dots. *c.* A.D. 150–225 or possibly later.

(106), (223), (391) and (539). Handles and tops of lamps like that of no. 22 above. Ten sherds from lamps in hard coarse red or grey paste, with a pattern of raised dots.

Seventeen lamp handles are probably from lamps of this category.

(viii) *Lamps and fragments of miscellaneous dates.* (Fig. 17, 23–8)

23. (609). The rim and decorated lug of a lamp in light brown paste fired yellow, with, inside the rim, the remains of orange-brown colour coating. The elaborate lug is flanked by two snakes, and it is decorated with a moulded relief of a small boar (?). Second century A.D.

    Cf. Broneer, 1930, pl. XXVIII, 677 (Type XXVII—practically limited to Greek sites—probably fully developed in the time of Hadrian and common in the Antonine period); Heres, 1972, Taf. 25, 201; Szentléleky, 1969, 88 (second century A.D.); Walters, 1914, fig. 156a, 841 (first century A.D.—from Knidos).

24. (817). A fragment of a lamp, in a hard buff paste, fired the same colour. It is decorated with a moulded relief pattern of a leaf. Probably second century A.D.

    Cf. Deneauve, 1969, pl. LXXXVIII, 967 and 972 (Type VIIIB, 100–150 A.D.); Ivanyi, 1935, pl. XXXV, 5 (873) (Type X); Walters, 1914, 166, fig. 230, 1105 (second century A.D.—from Cyprus).

25. (276). A fragment of a lamp in light brown paste with a brown colour coated surface. It is decorated with a moulded relief pattern of an ovolo, on top of the shoulder. For this piece, we are indebted to Miss Claireve Grandjouan for suggesting a date in the late second to early third centuries A.D.

    Cf. Pompeii, 1973, 28.

26. (215b). Part of the discus and shoulder of a lamp with the handle broken off. In hard light brown paste, fired the same colour. The discus shows part of a moulded decoration. Undated.

27. (204). A lamp handle, in a hard pink ware with a red colour coating. It was the only one found of this flattened form, and has an irregular circular piercing. There is a decorative motif of a line ending in three prongs, with impressed dots, on the edge.

    This is the back of a bird head lamp. Cf. Perlzweig, 1961, pl. 4, 86 (first half of first century A.D. and after A.D. 16—Italian). Bailey, 1980, Q 1158 (*c.* A.D. 175–225).

28. (569). A circular lamp handle, with a central round piercing, in pink paste fired the same colour. Possibly first century A.D.

    Cf. Bachofen, 1958, Taf. 43, 1; Baradez, 1961, pl. VIII, 1 (end of the first century A.D.); Deneauve, 1969, pl. XCVIII, 1070–74 (Type XC); Waldhauer, 1914, pl. XV, 168 (time of Claudius—from Italy).

Unillustrated pieces in this category are:

(200). A fragment, in ware similar to that of no. 23 above, has a deep groove demarcating the discus from the rim; and a three-ribbed lug.

(817). Part of the discus of a lamp, in hard buff ware, which is much worn and has lost its surface. It has an indistinguishable moulded relief pattern on the discus with a surrounding band.

(266b). An abraded fragment in pinkish paste which may have had an orange-red glaze. The discus is plain, but the top of the shoulder shows a moulded decoration, ? a leaf pattern.

(240a–c). Basal fragments of bases and walls of two lamps with flat bases and no decoration.

(48) and (215a). Two rounded nozzles from two lamps in buff paste with a red-brown colour coating.

(9). A fragment of the shoulder and a lug of a lamp in buff paste with a metallic brown colour coating. The lug has two concave indentations.

(ix) *Medieval lamps.* (Not illustrated)
Parts of two lamps, of medieval types, were found, but they were not sufficiently complete to type. (260) was a wavy-rimmed lamp in smooth buff paste, with an abraded dark green glaze. The rim was charred. (462), in very heavy coarse brown paste, with a pinkish-brown glaze outside, was possibly a lamp. The outside wall was charred. Both came from unstratified top soil.

The provenance of the lamps
(M. Aylwin Cotton).
(i) *Those dated c. 50 B.C. to A.D. 1.*
Periods I/IA. In the infill of the lower platform: No. (487); in the débris layer outside the W. wall of the Period I/IA villa: Nos. 6, 8, 9, 11, 12, (165b), (189), (268b), (774), (777), (778), (779a–k).
Period II. In the platform infill: Nos. 4, 5, (165b), (167), (603), (604), (771), (814), (815), (816); over the lower platform Nos. 7, (770); over the W. platform extension: (194e); in the makeup of the Period II floor of room 6: No. (166); in the lower fill over the W. cistern of the upper terrace: No. 3, and from its upper fill, No. 2/3.
Unstratified. Nos. 1, 10, (73), (136), (147), (194a–d), (203), (268a–d), (275), (524), (689), (692), (820).

The lamps of this date were, therefore, in use during the occupation of the Periods I/IA villa, and at the time that the Period II villa was built, indicating that all these three building phases could fall within the first century B.C. No. (487), in the infill of the lower platform, like no. 12, is dated as *c.* 50 B.C. to A.D. 1, which perhaps suggests that Period IA may have been later than *c.* 50 B.C.

(ii) *Those dated c. A.D. 1–80*
Destruction layer over the peristyle: Nos. 14 and 15.
Unstratified. To the S. of the Period II vats: No. 13; in the early slip from the upper terrace over the bath wing: No. 16.

These lamps would have been in use during the occupation of the Period II villa.

(iii) *Those dated A.D. 90–180*
All the lamps so dated were found in destruction layers, or in unstratified soil. They were presumably in use during the earlier part of the Period IIA occupation of the villa.

(iv) *Those dated c. A.D. 150–225 or possibly later*

None of the lamps of this group was found in a stratified layer. Some were in terrace spills and some in destruction layers or in sub- or top-soil. They represent some of the latest dated material in use. The fact that there is this amount of material datable to A.D. 150–225 or even later, and next to nothing of any later date, suggests that the villa was abandoned at some point in the third century and earlier rather than later. The evidence of the coin hoard (p. 130) shows that at some point before *c.* A.D. 160, part, at least, was in a state of disrepair. The combined evidence of the coins and the lamps suggests, however, that it was not abandoned until the late second or early third century A.D.

(v) *Lamps of miscellaneous dates*

These lamps, again, were all found in destruction layers or in disturbed or unstratified layers. No. 25 is noteworthy in that it is dated to the later second to early third century A.D., agreeing with the above suggestion about the date of the abandonment of the villa.

3. THE GLASS OBJECTS
(Figs. 18, 1–18; 19, 19–30 and 20, 31–37)
Dorothy Charlesworth, M.A.

(The late Miss Dorothy Charlesworth, then of the Department of the Environment, England, was kind enough to find time, during a visit to Italy, to examine this material, and to write this report. M.A.C.)

Flasks. (Fig. 18, 1–5)

1. (761). Small unguent flask in colourless blown glass with patches of brown weathering, rim knocked off, outsplayed and rounded in the flame, slight constriction at the base of the neck, thin globular body.
   Isings 1957, form 6. Mid-to late first century A.D.

2–4. (130), (185) and (432). Nos. 2–3 have infolded, flattened rims, and are in colourless blown glass with brown weathering. No. 4 is a flattened rim, rounded at the tip, in natural green blown glass.
   First to second century A.D. types. Cf. Cotton, 1979, 78–9 and fig. 16, 9.

5. (70). Flat circular base in natural green glass, probably from a bulbous-bodied flask rather than a cylindrical bottle, but it is impossible to be certain. The absence of any identical fragments of mould-blown square- or cylindrical-bodied handled bottles suggests the possibility that this is a free-blown flask.

Bowls. (Fig. 18, 6–9)

6–7. (441) and (485). Two very similar vessels represented by fragments of outsplayed, curved rims rounded at the tip, both in greenish blown glass, one thicker than the other, its surface heavily pitted with iridescent weathering. Two other examples (16) and (596).
   Isings, 1971. no. 57 is a similar type.

8. (546). Rim fragment of another bowl of similar type, but the tip of the rim is infolded.
   Cf. Isings, 1971, no. 60 from Opgrimby, Belgium.

9. (74). Rim fragment in colourless glass, rounded at the tip, upper surface probably

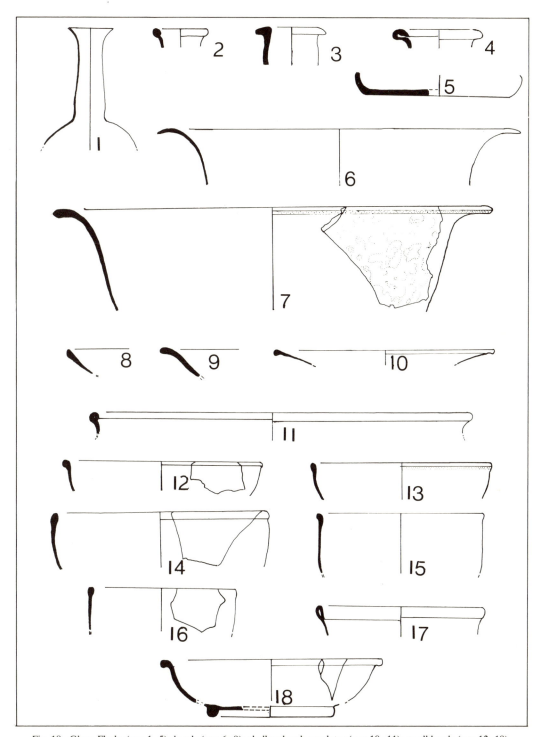

Fig. 18. Glass. Flasks (nos.1–5); bowls (nos.6–9); shallow bowls or plates (nos.10–11); small bowls (nos.12–18). (Scale: 1/2)

fire-polished, cloudy weathering. A similar example (509), but in thicker metal and with heavier brownish pitting of the surface. A rim and base, (32) and (137), possibly of the same vessel, were of this type.

Shallow bowls or plates. (Fig. 18, 10–11)
The rims are thinner, better quality, colourless metal and are probably from shallow bowls or plates, all apparently blown glass. Cf. Isings, 1971, no. 62 and nos. 136–9 in the Heerlen Museum.

10. (589). Flat outsplayed rim, rounded and thickened at the tip, striations in the metal indicate blown glass, spun to the required open shape. Iridescent weathering.
11. (72). Similar to no. 10, but slightly thicker glass. Another example (590) is also similar.

Small bowls. (Fig. 18, 12–18 and Fig. 19, 19–20)
12–16. (19), (762), (763), (594) and (448). All these bowls are in colourless glass with the rims rounded and slightly thickened in the flame and with a convex side. There are at least 7 examples besides those illustrated, all free-blown. See no. 17 below.

17. (542b). Small bowl with a hollow tubular rim formed by folding the edge inwards.
    This form is closely related to nos. 12–16 and both are common in the period *c.* A.D. 50–75. Isings 1957, form 44.
18. (185) and (184). A rim fragment in emerald green glass, formed in a mould and wheel-polished. Some iridescence. The base fragment could be from the same bowl, it had been in a fire and has deep strain cracking on the inner surface.
    Cf. Isings 1957, form 20. Early to mid first century A.D.
19–20. (542a) and (161). Two similar bowls, fire-blown, with a knocked-off ground rim, slight constriction below and a trail on the shoulder.
    This is not a familiar vessel in early contexts and is probably second rather than first century A.D. in date.

Beakers. (Fig. 19, 21–5)
21. (587). Rim rounded at the tip, tapered side of beaker in colourless glass with milky weathering.
    Cf. Isings, 1957, form 21?
22. (185)/(86). Similar to no. 21 above, but in thicker metal with a greenish tinge and brown weathering. Two rim fragments from the same vessel.
23. (13). Similar, but the rim is slightly outsplayed. White enamelled weathering.
24. (143). Beaker in colourless glass with faintly blue appearance where it is thicker in the base ring. Rim knocked off and ground, side tapering towards a punched-in base ring with neat domed centre.
25. (284). Base of a carinated beaker in colourless glass with brown weathering, faint wheelmarks on the side above the carination, flat thick base.
    Probably late first to early second century A.D.

Bases. (Fig. 19, 26–30)
26. (95). Base fragment in good colourless glass with facet-cut decoration underneath, under the base ring a circle of facets can just be traced, outside the base ring, and prob-

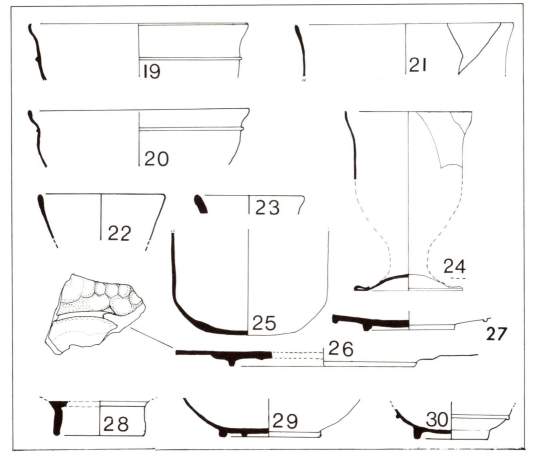

Fig. 19. Glass. Small bowls (nos.19–20); beakers (nos.21–25); bases (nos.26–30). (Scale 1/2)

ably continuing on the side of the vessel up to the rim, a closed diaper of hexagonal facets. The vessel was probably shaped in a mould.

Cf. Charlesworth, 1975, 404–6.

27. (15b). Base in greenish colourless glass with an applied ring and trailed decoration, slightly iridescent.

28. (522). Part of a high foot ring, probably made in the mould with vessel and ground. Iridescent.

29. (46). Base with two concentric trailed rings, greenish colourless with milky weathering.

These rings are associated with small bowls of second and third centuries date, cf. Charlesworth, 1971, 34–8.

30. (622). Base of a vessel with an applied ring and a trail on the body above the base. Greenish, colourless glass, some iridescence.

Miscellaneous. (Fig. 20, 31–7)

31. (440) and (760). Lid or shallow bowl, probably a bowl, in thick colourless metal. Fragments found in two different places have weathering in a different manner. The vessel appears to have been made in a mould and polished.

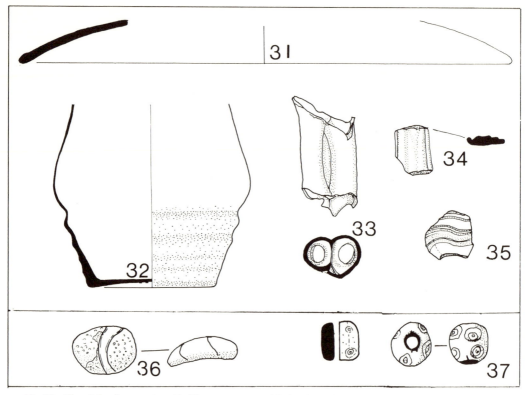

Fig. 20. Glass. Miscellaneous (nos.31–35); gemstone (no.36); bead (no.37). (Scale: 1/2, except nos.36–37, 1/1)

32. (431). Flask or beaker, mould-blown cylindrical body with horizontal ridges.
    It looks like the type of bottle made by 'Frontinus' and others, cf. Isings, 1957, form 89, but the inward curve of the upper part of the side does not fit in with this form.
33. (764). Double neck of flask in green glass. This appears to have been blown as a single tube and then drawn together down the centre with pincers.
34. (54). Part of a reeded handle, in green glass, with two grooves on the outer surface.
35. (97). Convex fragment of clear colourless glass with an opaque white marvered trail. Some iridescence and pitting of trails.
36. (712). Imitation gemstone, oval, in dark blue glass, for a ring or brooch. Iridescent and some pitting.
37. (96). Bead in green glass decorated with a marvered circle of yellow, blue and white. Iridescent and pitted surface.

Window glass. (Not illustrated)
All the fragments seem to be from the typical first to second century A.D. moulded sheets of glass and none of it is blown. Cf. Harden, 1961, 39–64.

Provenance and dating of the glass objects.
M.Aylwin Cotton

The provenance was:
Periods I/IA. No. 37 (gemstone).

Period II. No. 38 (bead).

Periods II/IIA. Nos. 2, 5, 6, 7, 33 and 34.

All the other pieces were from the destruction layers or top soil.

The glass vessels are dated to:

    Early to mid first century A.D. No. 18.

    A.D. 50–75. Nos. 12–17.

    Mid to late first century A.D. No. 1.

    Late first to early second century A.D. No. 25.

    First to second century A.D. Nos. 2–4.

    Second rather than first century A.D. Nos. 19–20.

    Second to third century A.D. No. 29.

This shows that, with the exception of the small bowl (no. 18), glass vessels seem to have come into use at San Rocco only from *c*. A.D. 50 onwards, the time at which the Period II villa was altered and acquired its bath wing. The small amount of material attributed to the second century A.D. agrees with the decline of the villa at the end of that century.

For window glass, 48 sherds were found, of which none was earlier than Period IIA, i.e. the same point at which the glass vessels came into use. There was no special concentration in any one place to suggest where windows may have existed.

4. BRONZES
(Figs. 21, 1–13; 22, 14–20 and 23, 21–31)

1.   (717). A bodkin or netting needle. The flattened head has two circular 'eyes', and the tapering shaft is of oval section with the angled edges in planes at right angles to the head flattening.

2 and 3. (281) and (309). Two dice, marked one to six.

4.   (310). A small fish hook with a barbed point.

5.   (523). A piece of binding.

6.   (607). A bronze wire fibula with a spiral spring of four turns, a hump-backed bow and the remains of a simple catchplate. The pin is missing.

7.   (670). A convex boss, or terminal decoration of an object of circular section. The central part of the attachment is broken off. The boss is decorated with two circular incised lines and there is another round the base.

8.   (403). A small buckle of semi-circular form, with expanded ends which carry a horizontal bar on which is threaded a small oval tongue.

9.   (382). A convex fitting, or clasp, pierced with three small holes. The short side has a rolled-over end for attachment.

10.   (606). A plain ring or a link from a chain.

11.   (666). An ornamental fitting, ? a handle. A highly arched bow bifurcated at one end to terminate in two stylised bird's heads with dot-and-circle eyes (one head is missing). Between them there is a tongue-like projection. There are three mouldings on top at the peak of the arch; the other end, also slightly upturned, bears three mouldings and is flattened underneath, but shows no evidence of a point of attachment. The point at which the bow bifurcated seems on its under surface to have been soldered.

12.   (553). A small flat strip pierced at one end with a small circular hole.

13.   (131). A small piece of thick circular wire, perhaps part of a bracelet.

14.   (149). A chain with two links of twisted bronze wire, attached to two small rings.

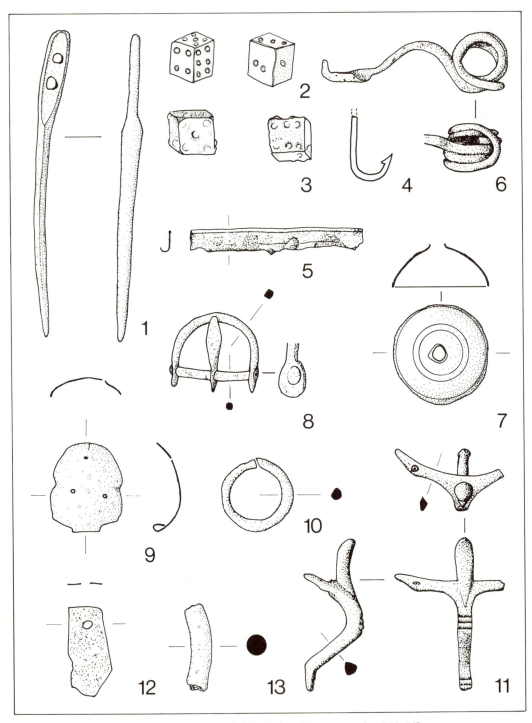

Fig. 21. Bronzes (nos. 1–13). (Scale: 1/1, except nos. 5 and 11, 1/2)

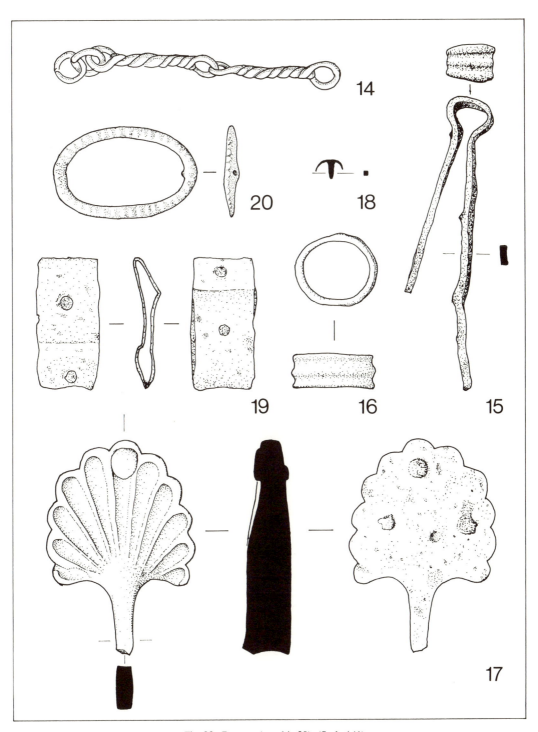

Fig. 22. Bronzes (nos.14–20). (Scale 1/1)

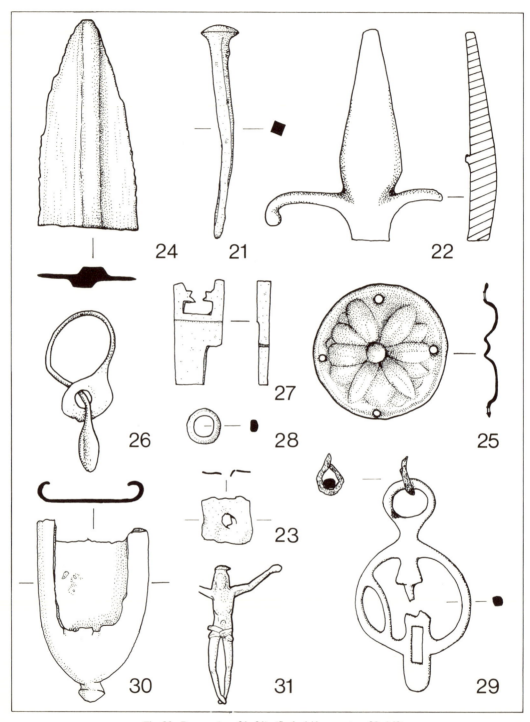

Fig. 23. Bronzes (nos.21–31). (Scale 1/1, except no.29, 1/2)

15. (722). A pair of tweezers with one leg missing.
16. (723a-b). Two similar rings with a raised central moulding externally, and a smooth internal surface. They were perhaps used to bind an object rather than to serve as finger rings, though they could fit on to the little finger. Only (723b) is illustrated.
17. (724). A heavy ornamental fitting in the form of a palmette. The back surface is flat for attachment to an object. The tip of the central division of the palmette, in front, has a large rivet; there seem to have been two additional rivets on the back surface.
18. (726). A very small tack with a convex head.
19. (727). A piece of flat strapping folded in two, ? round a leather strap. There are two iron rivets on each side, not opposite to each other.
20. (687). An oval ornament, possibly a buckle which has lost its tongue and central bar. It is decorated with notched lines.
21. (605). A nail with a circular head and a shaft of quadrangular section.
22. (172). An ornamental fitting in the form of a 'fleur-de-lis'.
23. (173). A small washer.
24. (84). The tip of a ribbed spearhead. Of uncertain date.
25. (20). A circular ornamental fitting of a disc decorated in repoussé with a rosette pattern. It has four piercings inside the edge for attachment.
26. (150). A ? pendant, consisting of a flattened wire and pierced with a circular hole. The looped wire ends in a thickened 'drop' which has been threaded through the hole.
27. (132). Part of a key. Possibly modern.
28. (23). A very small ring or link.
29. (381). Possibly a horse fitting and perhaps modern.
30. (182). A small chape, with a simple terminal knob.
31. (288). A small crucifix. Probably medieval.

Unillustrated bronze objects found in the top- or subsoil, which are probably modern, were:

(85). A piece of U-shaped binding.
(151) and (559). Two strap buckles.
(404). An oval-shaped fitting, pierced at one end with a small circular hole, and at the other with a larger oval hole.
(503). A simple bronze ring.
Ten unillustrated pieces of thin bronze sheet, or of bronze bar, with no decorative features, were found.

The provenance of the bronze finds
Periods I/IA. In a fill. No. 1.
Period II. From platform II infill: Nos. 2–3, 6, 12, 15–7; from the make-up of the pavement of room 6: No.11; from the fill in and over the Period I/IA vat of the lower working terrace: Nos. 4–5.
Unstratified. All other pieces.

5. IRON OBJECTS
(Fig. 24, 1–7 and Fig. 25, 8–11)

Many iron objects, and much iron scrap, were found, but mostly in unstratified layers. As the majority of the objects from these layers were modern, only those from stratified layers are described and illustrated.

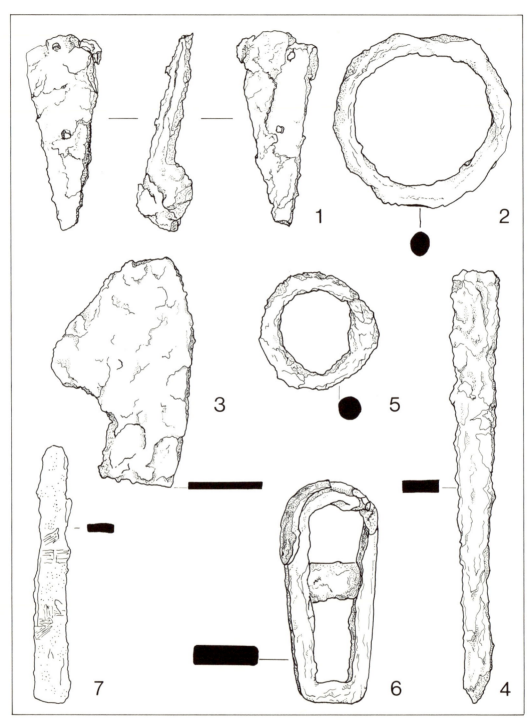

Fig. 24. Iron objects (nos.1–7). (Scale: 1/1, except no.7, 1/2)

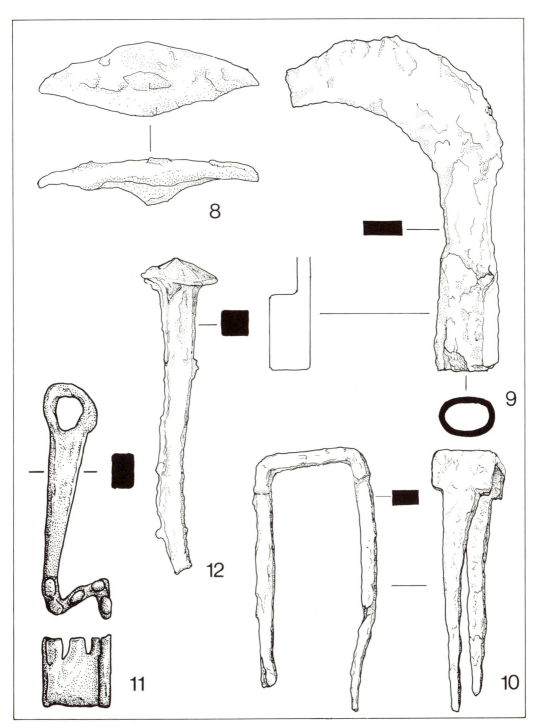

Fig. 25. Iron objects (nos.8–12). (Scale 1/1, except no.8, 1/2)

1.   (491). A hinge, associated with a nail and two pieces of scrap.
2.   (529). A large ring.
3.   (737). A broken piece of flat sheet.
4.   (319). A flat pointed bar.
5.   (254). A small ring.
6.   (664). A link.
7.   (416). A bar which possibly had a wooden haft, associated with a point and five pieces of scrap.
8.   (728). A small hammer head with two pointed ends.
9.   (469). A small bill-hook.
10. (562). A staple found embedded in the wall of the cisterns on the west side of the upper terrace.
11. (34). A key.

The provenance of the iron objects
Periods I/IA. No. 3, in the infill of the south terrace.
Period II. From the platform II infill: Nos. 4–9; in the wall of the W. cisterns: No.10.
Period II/IIA. Nos. 1–2 and 11.
Iron nails. (Fig. 25, 12)
  Nails were found in layers of all dates, together with 50 which came from unstratified layers.
12. (5). An example of a nail, from the mortar layer of the water tank over the W. cisterns of the upper terrace, to illustrate the rectangular section and conical head typical of the series.

6. BONE OBJECTS
(Fig. 26, 1–10)
1.   (637). A tooth-comb with coarse and fine teeth.
2.   (678). A small pin with a circular head and a bulbous shaft. The point is missing.
3.   (387). A pin with a long oval head, and a constriction above a bulbous shaft. The point is missing.
4.   (112). A large pin, with a circular tapering shaft and a carinated shoulder. The tip and head are missing.
5.   (267). A small spoon. Only the 'bowl' and part of the handle survive.
6.   (721). A worked point made from a tarsal or carpal bone of an ovine.
7.   (498). A large circular ring.
8.   (696). A stylus point.
9.   (798). A small circular ring.
10. (730). A plain rectangular plaque.
     Unillustrated objects were: (56). A pin similar to that of no. 2; (164), (496) and (646), shafts of three pins, lacking heads and points.

The provenance of the bone objects
From Periods I/IA layers. No. 5.
From Period II layers. From the platform II infill under room 23a: No. 10; over the south terrace working area: No. 9.
From Periods II/IIA layers. No. 2, over room 24; and (496) in the lower fill of the settling tank.

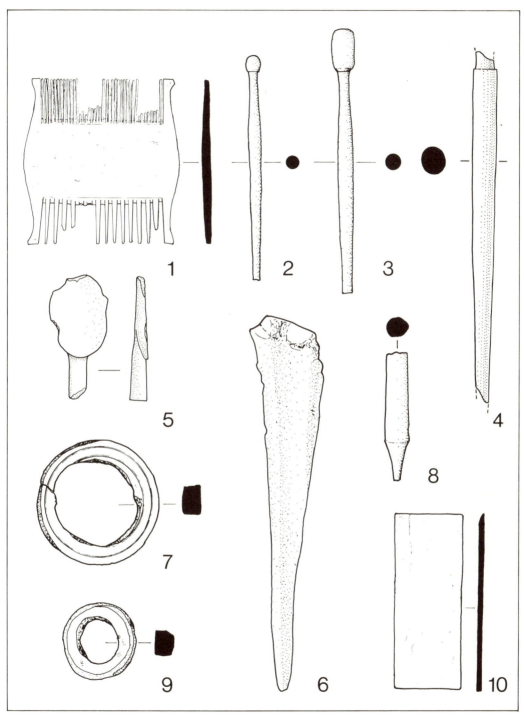

Fig. 26. Bone objects (nos.1–10). (Scale: 1/1, except no.10, 1/2)

Unstratified. Over the peristyle: Nos. 4 and (164); east of kiln 1: No. 7; in the drain outside the east entrance to the residential quarters: Nos. 1 and (646); in the S.W. corner of the Period II platform: Nos. 6, 8 and (56).

7. TERRACOTTAS
(Fig. 27, 1–5 and Pl. XXXVII)

1. (169). The head of a figurine, broken away from the eye level upwards. The base of the neck may have been inserted into a hollowed torso. The moulding is simple. There is some indication that the hair was long, ending in two curls, and that the head was probably that of a woman.

2. (356). A moulded object which copies the form of the ear of an ox. It is concavo-convex in section; the outside is smooth and the inside is roughly grooved to indicate the folds of the skin inside the ear. It has been broken away from the rest of the head.

3. (239). Part of a figurine of a woman wearing a draped garment. The head and the right side are missing.

4. (818). A small object of undetermined purpose. The top has a break as also does the projecting stalk at the back.

5. (249). Possibly this small object served as a plug or took the place of a cork.

Provenance: All these objects were in destruction and unstratified layers.

The Terracotta Mould. (Pl. XXXVII).

Two joining sherds from a terracotta mould, which was used to make antefixes or plaques, were found in the infill of kiln 2 in room 49. This object is the subject of an article by Professor Lionel Casson, 'Odysseus and Scylla on a Roman terracotta mould', *The International Journal of Nautical Archaeology and Underwater Exploration,* vii. 2, 1978, 99–104.

We are indeed grateful to Professor Casson for his interest and kind help over this mould. Hidden for some years in a large bag of amphorae sherds, it narrowly escaped being overlooked. Professor Casson showed it to Professor von Blanckenhagen and it was recognised that its interest, as an art historical piece, far surpassed that of the details of the ship's structure.

The find-spot of the plaque, though not truly stratified, suggests that it was not in use until after Period IIA, or *c.* A.D. 50, but that it could date from then up to A.D. 200+. Casson, on internal evidence, suggests a date from the second century A.D.

He describes the scene on the mould as that of a ship travelling under both oars and sail, with rowers and a helmsman. Odysseus stands amidships, and three of Scylla's multiple dogs-heads can be distinguished, one devouring a sailor. Scylla herself is missing, as only some two-thirds of the mould survives.

Pictures of Scylla, in various media, are known from the sixth century B.C. to the end of antiquity, but only a mere handful of examples show her with Odysseus and his ship. Hence the interest of the Francolise piece, which Casson sets against its art historical background, showing how it fills a chronological gap.

8. CLAY TOBACCO PIPES
(Fig. 28, 1–4 and Fig. 29, 5–6)

The bowls of 15 clay tobacco pipes were recovered from either the top soil, or the unstratified spill of the upper terrace over the main terrace. Though possibly not earlier than the

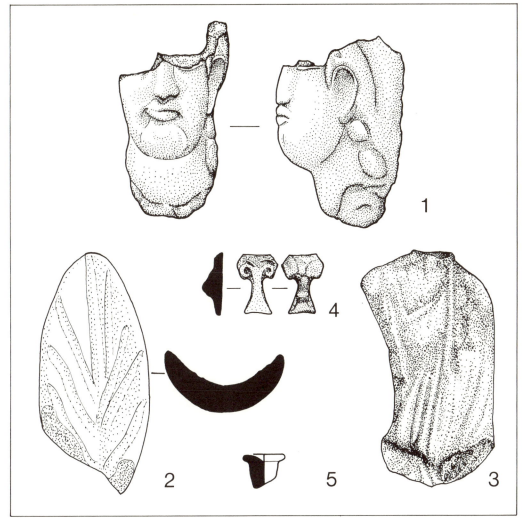

Fig. 27. Terracottas. (Scale: 1/1, except no.3, 1/2)

eighteenth century in date, the distinctive types have been illustrated here to serve as the start for a type series. While we excavated at San Rocco, residents of Sant' Andrea, the small town situated in the hot plain below, sometimes brought ailing children to the San Rocco plateau so that they might benefit from the cooler and more stimulating air. These tobacco pipes might form a reminder of the use of the plateau at an earlier date by local visitors relaxing there on Sundays or other *feste*.

1. (393). The bowl represents a moustached military man wearing a tall uniform hat with a badge in front. The mouth-piece is missing.
2. (796). The remaining part of the bowl represents a clean-shaven man's face.
3. (797). This simple design of a lower rounded moulded band, with an upper band with a verical leaf motif, seemed popular, for 7 other examples were found besides this one, all with the upper part of the bowl missing.
4. (711). Only part of the pattern decorating the lower part of the bowl remains. It is sharply defined.

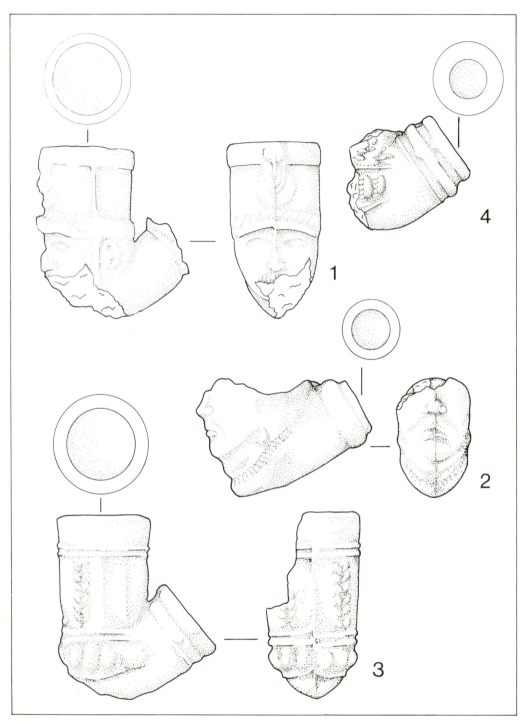

Fig. 28. Clay tobacco pipes (nos. 1–4). (Scale: 1/1)

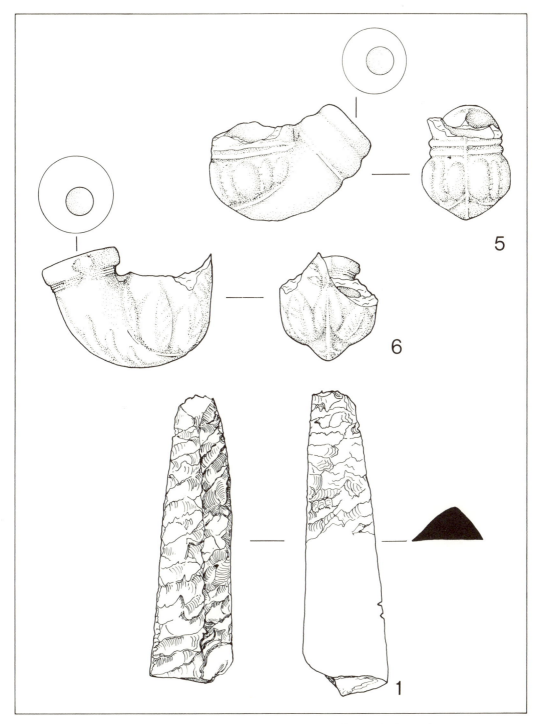

Fig. 29. Clay tobacco pipes (nos.5–6). Miscellaneous find (no.1) (Scale: 1/1)

5.   (11). This pipe has a simple bulbous moulding round the lower part of the bowl. Another, (720), is similar.

6.   (489). The curve of this pipe is decorated with a branched leaf or palmette motif and the lower part of the bowl is decorated with flat leaves. Another (392) is similar, but is from a worn mould.

9. LOOM WEIGHTS AND A SPINDLE WHORL
(Fig. 30, 1–4)

The finding of seven loom weights attests the practice of weaving at San Rocco. All but one were made of terracotta; the exception (no. 3) was made of tufa. Only one spindle whorl was found (and there were none at Posto). Spinning may not have been a widely practised local industry: the spun wool or thread may have been brought from elsewhere.

1.   (430). A large weight, heavier than the others.

2.   (279). This weight, with 4 others (316), (470), (80) and (640), has no distinctive markings. They vary little in size or weight.

3.   (512A). This loom weight, of tufa, is of interest in that its original top had been broken away along the line of piercing. It had been re-used by turning it upside down and by piercing the lower end.

4.   (188). A simple biconical spindle whorl with a circular piercing, made of terracotta.

Provenance: Period II. From platform II infill over the south terrace working area; Nos. 2, (316) and (470), No. 2 being in the fill of the round reservoir.

Periods II/IIA. From the upper fill of the settling tank: No. 1.

Unstratified. From the destruction layer: Nos. 3–4.

This scattered distribution gives no indication of where a loom, or looms, may have stood.

10. MISCELLANEOUS OBJECTS
(Fig. 29, 1)

1.   (613). A worked blade, triangular in section, of honey-coloured chert. On the ridged side, both faces are pressure-flaked the whole length of the blade; on the third flat face only the terminal half is flaked. The cutting edges and rounded tip are still quite sharp. Perhaps a Bronze Age rubbish survival found in the Period II platform infill under room 25.

A certain amount of lead was found. Most of it was scrap metal which came from Period II layers or was in unstratified soil. A lead rivet (317), still attached to two sherds, was a dolium mend, and is typical of a number of pieces found in the destruction layer over the south portico.

A very miscellaneous collection of modern objects, found scattered over the site in the top soil, illustrate the casual use to which this deserted site has been put. They include a collar stud; a nylon tooth-brush in an 'amber' plastic case, marked 'Made in U.S.A.'; a worn typewriter eraser; a small metal percussion hammer; a metal badge, perhaps from a car or motor cycle; half a pair of nail scissors; pieces of shrapnel; a cartridge case and a key for opening a sardine tin. Whilst the above sound like the remains of the occupation of an Army camp, a more recent deposit could be given a certain attribution. There must always have remained a hollow over the sunken floor

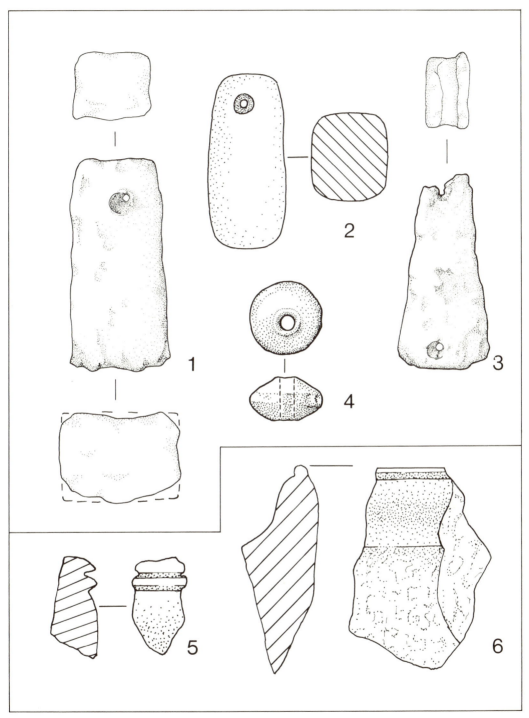

Fig. 30. Loom-weights (nos.1–3); spindle-whorl (no.4); carved tufa (nos.5–6). (Scale 1/2)

level of room A, for the first task of our excavators was to clear this area. It contained an incredible amount of discarded children's footwear derived from the nearby Orphanage.

11. BRICKS AND TILES
(Pl. XXXVI c; Fig. 31, 1–5 and Fig. 32, 6–11)

Brick stamps. (Pl. XXXVI c and Fig. 31, 1–5)

1–2. (641) and (132). The two pieces of stamped bricks illustrated are from a collection of 17 pieces found which bear part of a rectangular stamp of L. BILLIENVS. They are 2 · 3cm. thick and are baked red. Over two thirds of the pieces were found in or near the tile kilns, or near the bath wing—both Period IIA structures, and all were from destruction layers. The dimensions and shape of these particular bricks could not be determined, but it can be said that the triangular bricks used in the Period IIA build of the south wall of the bath wing's hot dry room did not have this stamp.

The name L. BILLIENVS MARATHVS, and that of his wife CORNELIA PREIMA are known from an inscription found in the villa of San Petri near Capua (*CIL* X.I, 4044). He may have been active c. A.D. 50. His name is not, however, included in Bloch, 1947–48, 56–7, nos. 1–128.

The association of these stamped bricks with the Period IIA kilns and bath wing suggests for them a date after A.D. 50. Whilst no brick so stamped was found built into a wall at San Rocco, it is just possible that at least some of the brick output of L. BILLIENVS was produced there, after the kilns had been installed. One cannot say whether or not he owned the villa.

In this connection one may quote Hartley, 1973, 39–40:-

'It is, however, interesting and useful to trace the origins of the mortaria imported to Britain in the first century. Types which were habitually stamped can be readily traced and Fig. 2 shows the distribution of stamps from Italian brickyards, dated primarily to A.D. 50–150. Many of these brickyards were in W. Italy; they made bricks, tiles, mortaria, dolia and even clay baths and sarcophagi, and the stamps of the potters are found on all these products. Often the yards were owned by senatorials, though, as was usual with commercial activity, they were directed by freedmen who often controlled larger staffs of slaves. Some of the tile-stamps record the names of the owner, the name of his manager and that of the maker of the tile, and at some periods a consular date is even given.' (See also Hartley, 1973[2], 49–60 for the distribution of tiles of Italian fabric.)

3. (694). Part of a brick, 3 · 4cm. thick, baked red, and stamped with very large letters perhaps in two lines. The letters of the lower line may be ? F L O. Unstratified over the eastern end of the underground cistern to the north of the garden.

4. (828). A large piece of dolium re-used as a brick and built into the east wall of the Period IIA kiln 1. It has a circular stamp with a rosette in relief, lettered between the points of the petals CN.$\sqrt{}$A VI.C?F. Unfortunately, no analogy for this stamp has been traced, for it would have helped with the date of the kiln. It is not a stamp which occurs in the vicinity of Rome.

5. (429). Part of a brick. 3 · 4 cm. thick, baked yellowish-grey. The remaining part of a rectangular stamp reads O [?D?V?T]. Unstratified, over the west end of the west portico.

Fig. 31. Brick stamps (nos. 1–5). (Scale: 1/1)

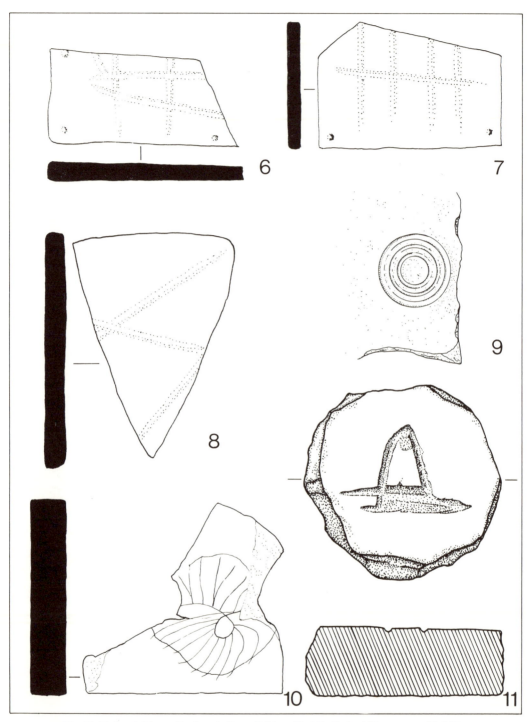

Fig. 32. Various bricks or tiles (nos.6–9); graffiti (nos.10–11). (Scale: 1/4, except no.11, 1/2)

The types of tiles recovered from kilns 1 and 2.

Most of the standard sizes and types of tiles were produced in these two kilns at San Rocco. The types listed below were collected from the collapsed infill of kiln 1, with the exception of the *tegula* and *imbrex* which came from kiln 2.

Bessalia. (20×20 cm. standard). The nearest example measured 23×? cm. and was 3 · 5 cm. thick.

Pedalis. (29×29 cm. standard). All examples collected were 3 · 5 cm. thick. One example was 29×? cm., and another was 27×? cm. A complete example, 29×29×3 · 5 cm. had incised guide lines for breaking the tile into segments of varying sizes.

Sesquipedalis. (42×42 cm. standard). A piece 2 cm. thick measured 41 cm. along one side.

Voussoir. An example measured 29×22 cm. tapering along the 29 cm. edge from 8 cm. to 6 cm. in thickness. On one face there was inscribed a St. Andrew's cross and it had three finger marks.

Tegula. An example measured 60×47 cm.

Imbrex. Its length was undetermined but it had an outside width of 13 cm.

Wasters. A number of badly distorted and ill-fired tiles were found in and around the kilns and scattered over the site.

Other bricks and tiles. (Fig. 32, 6–11)

Lozenge-shaped bricks. Three bricks of this type (128a–c) which measured 2 · 80×2 · 80 cm. were 1 · 70 cm. thick. They were baked yellowish-red, and came from the Period II fill A over the western cisterns of the upper terrace.

Holed roof tiles. (Fig. 32, 6–7). These measured 20×?20 cm. and were 0 · 6 to 0 · 8 cm. thick. Each corner had a pierced hole. They were fairly plentiful in the destruction layers over the peristyle and surrounding portico.

Quarter-round bricks. (Fig. 32, 8). These were used for building the cores of columns. They were plentiful on the site. The four bricks that formed the core had a diameter of 38 cm. and the bricks were from 1 · 7 to 2 · 0 cm. thick. They were scored on one side and smooth on the other. One had the imprint of the hoof of a goat or sheep. They were all found in destruction or surface layers and would have been derived from the Periods II/ IIA villa.

Stamped tile. (Fig. 32, 9). Part of a tile, from the collapsed fill of kiln 2, had a stamp of concentric circles.

Small rectangular bricks. Four of these (376a–b) and (775a–b) measured 8 · 0×5 · 5 cm. and were 3 · 0 cm. thick or 9 · 0×5 · 5 cm. by 2 · 75 cm. thick. They were baked red and were found in Period I and Periods I/IA layers.

Circular bricks. These were in use in the *suspensurae* of the Period IIA hypocaust under the warm dry room of the bath wing.

Box tiles. These tiles, 10cm. square, were built into the walls of the Period IIA hot dry and hot wet rooms of the bath wing.

Imbrices and tegulae. These were plentiful in all layers. Drain pipes were either circular, or formed of two imbrices in circular drains. When square built, small tegulae were used for roofing.

Graffiti on tiles. (Fig. 32, 10–11). Two were found. A squared tile (no. 10) had a central hole with a surrounding graffito of radiating lines. A broken circular tile or brick (no. 11), from the top soil in the western end of the upper terrace, had an indecipherable graffito.

12. CARVED TUFA.
(Fig. 33, 1–3)

1.   (115),(116). A slab of tufa carved with an egg-and-dart pattern with the remains of a white stucco finish. Perhaps from a cornice.
2.   (450). Part of a block of tufa carved with radiating lines. It may have served as a sun-dial.
3.   (6). Half a circular disc of carved tufa.
      Unillustrated pieces include 3 pieces of moulding with traces of white stucco coating (97),(149) and (310); a piece which seems to form the tip of an acanthus leaf (226); part of an ovolo (133); and a piece which may have come from a capital (222).

Provenance: All came from destruction levels, or top soil, with the exception of no. 3, which was associated with Period II build of the W. cistern in the upper terrace.

13. ARCHITECTURAL DETAILS
(Fig. 33, 4–5, Fig. 34, 1–4 and Fig. 35; Pls. XI and XV)

(a) *Stucco.* (Fig. 33, 4)
Much stucco was found and it was present in most layers. It included pieces of fluting which had clothed the columns made with cores of quarter-round bricks, and parts of cornices. Fig. 33, 4 illustrates the left hand volute of a stucco Ionic capital from a pilaster (261). It shows traces of yellow paint, and was found unstratified over the west end of the south portico.

(b) *Terracotta.* (Fig. 33, 5)
(428) Part of a circular brick, perhaps from a column base, baked yellow. In, or near, the centre, there is a rectangular stamp which reads AN[ ]. From a destruction layer.

(c). *The terracotta frieze and finish of the roof of the portico round the peristyle.* (Fig. 34, 1–2)
(i) *The tiles of the frieze.* (Fig. 34, 1)
Twenty eight pieces were found, all from destruction or unstratified layers. Seventy per cent of them came from the peristyle area. Whilst no complete tile was found, one large piece with its edge, and the conventional pattern, gave the size (34 · 5 cm. long×18 · 5 cm. high×2 · 5 cm. thick) as shown in the reconctructed drawing of one tile. These relief moulded tiles had a crenellated top edge, and were decorated with palmettes in which the medial fronds turned inwards or outwards alternately. Each tile had two palmettes flanked by half palmettes.
(ii). *The lion's head and forepaws antefixes.* (Fig. 34, 2)
A minimum of eight lions' heads and forepaws, one still attached to an imbrex, were found. All came from unstratified or destruction layers, suggesting that they were still in position until after the villa was deserted. Of these broken pieces, five were found over the peristyle area or its surrounding portico and a sixth was near room 4. The others were widely scattered in disturbed soil. That most were in the vicinity of the peristyle suggests that they had formed part of the finish of the roof of its surrounding portico.
      These terracotta antefixes consist of a vertical part with the mask of a lion with his mane and pointed ears. The back, or unseen surface is flat and smoothed. The sloping part con-

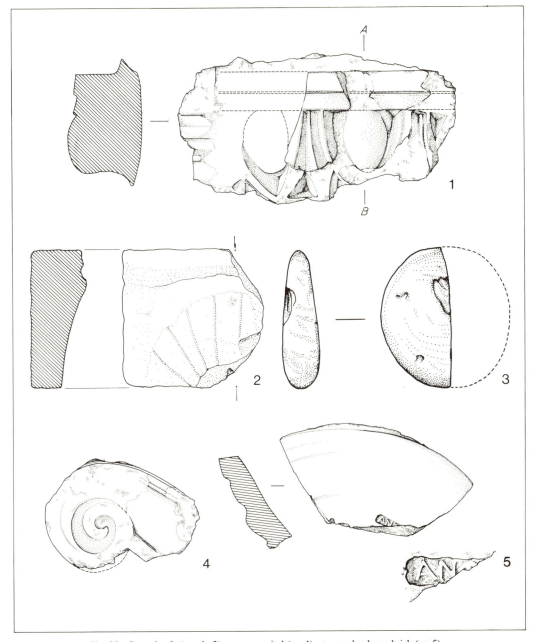

Fig. 33. Carved tufa (nos.1–3); stucco capital (no.4); stamped column brick (no.5).
(Scale: 1/3, except no.2, 1/6, brick stamp, 2/3)

sisted of the two front paws, which bounded a concave area, and which were moulded in one with the curved end of the imbrex tile they graced. They had all been broken at the weakest point, or the angle at which the upright head joined the tile.

(d). *Columns and column bases.* (Pls. XI*a* and *c*, XV*a–b* and Fig. 34, 3–4)
(i) *From the area of the peristyle.* Here there were found parts of four column bases in white marble (35), (209), (111) and (94); two bases in terracotta which had been joined by lead

Fig. 34. Frieze and antefix in terracotta (nos.1–2); profiles of column bases (nos.3–4). (Scale: 1/3)

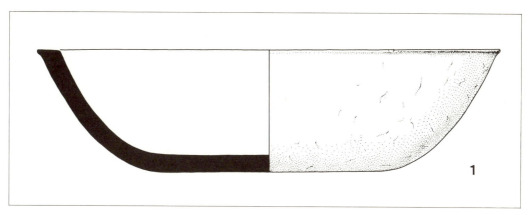

Fig. 35. Marble basin from the *viridarium*. (Scale 1/8)

rivets (65) and (196); and one in tufa which was incomplete and carried remains of stucco (127). Fig. 34, 3–4 shows the profile of these columns (29) and (30). A piece of stucco fluting from a fallen column (Pl. XI*c*) suggests that the diameter of the base had been *c*. 75 cm.

(ii) *From the west portico*. Three column bases of terracotta, joined with lead rivets, were found in the destruction layer (157a-c). In this area there was a fallen column of three brick courses which had lost its stucco finish (210) (Pl. XV*a-b*). It had probably fallen from one of the stone-built bases. Two other terracotta bases (89) and (113) were also in the destruction level.

(e). *Marble basin*. (Fig. 35, and Pl. XI*d*)
Two pieces of a large marble basin were found in destruction layers over the peristyle. It would probably have served there as a central ornamental feature.

(f). *Marble drain cover*. (Not illustrated). Part of a small drain cover (15 × 15 × 3 · 25 cm. thick), in white marble, of the usual form with a cup-shaped hollow pierced by one central and four radial holes (1 cm. in diameter), came from the destruction layer on the west side of the main terrace.

14. MARBLES
Rosemary Fleck and Demetrios Michaelides

(I am indebted to Dr. Rosemary Fleck and Dr. Demetrios Michaelides for their work in identifying and commenting on this material. M.A.C.)

Whilst no comprehensive study has been made of all the marbles and other coloured stones used in the various floors or in the construction of the villa, notes on the following pieces are of interest.

(i). *The floor of room A1*.
Two well-shaped pieces came from this floor, which was in use throughout the life of the villa, but was laid originally in Period I, with repairs in Periods IA and II: (a) A piece of *Africano*, which originated in Teos in Asia Minor; and (b) A piece of *Porta Santa*, which comes from the Greek island of Chios.

(ii). *The floor of the portico round the peristyle.*
Four pieces of thinner, irregularly shaped or rectangular pieces of stone were taken from
this floor: (a) A yellow stone of *Calcare Marmosa Giallo detto Paesina*; (b) A green stone
in *Calcare Marmosa Verde*; (c) A grey-black stone called *Olivine* (and not basalt); stones
(a)-(c) could be obtained locally.

It is of interest to note that for the important Period I floor of room A1 imported marbles
were used. For the extensive flooring of the Period II peristyle area, local coloured limestone sufficed, except perhaps for re-used chippings of marble imported earlier.

(iii). *The flooring of the Period IIA caldarium.*
Slabs of *cippolino* marble, found as a flooring in the Period IIA bath wing, were re-used,
and in an earlier period should have served as a screen or as a wall revetment.

15. PAINTED WALL PLASTER
Ann Laidlaw

(I am indebted to Professor P. von Blanckenhagen and Dr. Ann Laidlaw for their examination of the large amount of plaster found, and for their identification of the published
pieces. I wish also to thank Vivienne Hibbs for her recording of this material in the field.
M.A.C.)

(a). *A curved moulded cornice decorated with a figured frieze.*
The pieces that go to make up this frieze were found in the well in the lower terrace and
were not *in situ*. It was probably discarded in the Period II rebuild. Because of its fragmentary condition and poor preservation, it is not illustrated.

The decoration consisted of 35 curved and 13 straight pieces of a decorated frieze which
formed an arch which, on the arc of its lowest curve, had a radius of 123 cm. The rectangular moulding had three exposed sides coloured yellow, pink and blue. it measures 13 ×
7 · 5 cm. The yellow face has an indentation 1 · 50 cm. wide running along the centre. The
indentation is decorated with a guilloche design painted in indeterminate colours, but they
may have been black and white against the yellow background. It appears that the yellow
side was the horizontal surface of the moulding since the pink side has a painted frieze of
figures on it which would require that the pink surface should be vertical.

The pink side has a frieze of *putti*-like figures on it, in yellow paint. Only one block is preserved well enough to make out the painted figures, but on many of the other blocks there
are yellow splotches of paint, which may indicate that the frieze actually appeared on the
entire surface. A few details which were recorded at the time of discovery indicated a *putto*
facing left next to a yellow draped figure, a *putto* facing right which seemed to be floating in
space, with visible facial features, and touches of red paint on the wings, flanked by another
putto; and a small fragment with a figure with arms outstretched as though holding the
reins whilst driving something. The blue side is poorly preserved in all cases and shows only
that this side was so painted. Whether it was used for background or ornamental design is
impossible to determine.

The possible alternatives for the original disposition of the frieze are:
(i). The moulding for a hemicircular room with the moulding placed horizontally
between the ceiling and the wall. But no foundations for a hemicircle were found in the
excavation.

(ii). The moulding for a single-arched vault, but this idea was considered unlikely.

(iii). Part of the decoration of the vaulted end of a *cubiculum*. This would consist of a double arched moulding with one end larger than the other. Since the yellow curved moulding is slightly larger, it is possible that the two mouldings were used in this way, and that the straight yellow moulding would have been used horizontally on the straight wall. A *cubiculum* of this type existed at Boscoreale, and the double moulding is known from photographs. The cubiculum has been restored at the Metropolitan Museum of Art, New York, without the mouldings, since these are not included in their collection, but photographs of the originals are in the hands of the Greek and Roman Department of that Museum.

An analogy for a curved moulding is that of the *cubiculum* of room 16 of the Villa dei Misteri. For the ceilings, cf. the Casa del Cryptoportico in Pompeii and the tomb of Montefiore (*Archaeology*, Spring 1964, 2.). The earliest examples of *putti* come from the Samnite house at Herculaneum, from the top left side of the *fauces*, in Pompeian First style painting.

(b). *A rectangular frame moulding.*
Again from the well, there came 18 pieces and 3 corner pieces of a moulding from a rectangular frame. The frame had a painted design in black, white, blue and pink on its outer edge, the rest being yellow. The corner piece indicates that the fragments are part of a rectangular frame set into a wall, but the pieces cannot be matched closely enough to determine the original size of the frame.

(c). *A plain white moulding.*
This moulding is white except for a deep red border, and shows no figures. From room 24, in a Period II layer.

(d). One fragment of painted plaster (118), from the well, had a red painted background with, on it, the representation of an upright *console*.

16. MOLLUSCAE

The only shells noted from stratified layers were:

(a). From the Periods I/IA débris layer outside the west wall of the I/IA building, a snail shell, 3 mussel shells and a cockle shell.

(b). From the Period I fill over the Period I cisterns in the peristyle came part of a cockle shell.

Two oyster shells were unstratified.

Chapter IX. The Pottery: Fine Wares

I. *EARLY PAINTED WARE* (Not illustrated)

Only fragmentary pieces of this ware were found at San Rocco. It has a buff paste, smoothed on the outside, with horizontal bands in black to brown paint. The only form recognised was a jug or flagon, but no rims or bases were found. No sherds were found which could be related to the Spanish imported 'sombreros da copa', cf. Cotton, 1979, 88. The pieces found consisted of 2 jug handles, one with a cross between two horizontal bands: 2 handle roots; a carinated shoulder sherd, perhaps from an aryballos; the wall of a large jug or flagon and five wall sherds. Whilst all these fragments should belong to the earliest occupation of the site, only two could be attributed to the Periods I/IA occupation; four were from the Period II platform and the rest were unstratified.

II. *MEGARIAN BOWLS* (Fig. 36, 1–5)

Fabric. Two fabrics were found:— (a) A hard bright brown paste with a thin black slip on both sides (nos. 1–3). (b) A softer pink paste with a thin dull red slip on both sides. (nos. 4–5).

1. (P714). The rim and wall of a bowl. The rim is simple and pointed and has an angular junction with the wall. The external decoration on the wall consists of two bands of motifs between grooves. The upper band is of rosettes; the lower of larger rosettes inside two concentric circles demarcated with intervening small rosettes in a single circle. The spaces are filled with triangular groups of three dots. The curved wall has an imbricated leaf pattern. The base is missing.

2. (P704/705). A rim and wall of a form similar to that of no. 1 above. the wall decoration differs in having only one band of design bounded by two ridges below a groove. The band has a relief pattern of a wreath of small leaves above lozenges. The decoration of the rest of the wall is not known.

3. (P706/707). A reconstructed profile of the same form as the above with a narrow band of a blurred pattern above leaf imbrication on the curved wall. 2 examples.

4. (P2664). Some 10 sherds, probably from the same bowl. The simple pointed rim and body join without angularity. The single decorative band has a pattern of alternate lozenges and relief dots. The wall again has the imbricated leaf pattern and the base is flat and thinned.

5. (P2665). A wall sherd showing a different external wall decoration of rays of relief lines enclosing dots.

Provenance: Period II. No. 2.

        Periods II/IIA. Nos. 3 and cf. 5.

        Destruction. Nos. 1, 4 and 5.

Two unillustrated sherds were found in the topsoil.

For an article on first century B.C. relief types produced in Italy, see Adamsheck, 1972–3, 5–9. Whilst the San Rocco fragments do not belong to the groups described in this article (some examples of which are so like those found at Delos that Adamsheck speculated that, after the invasion of Sulla in 88 B.C., Delian potters emigrated to Italy and initiated this service, see Adamsheck, 1972–3, 5) the dating suggested for these relief

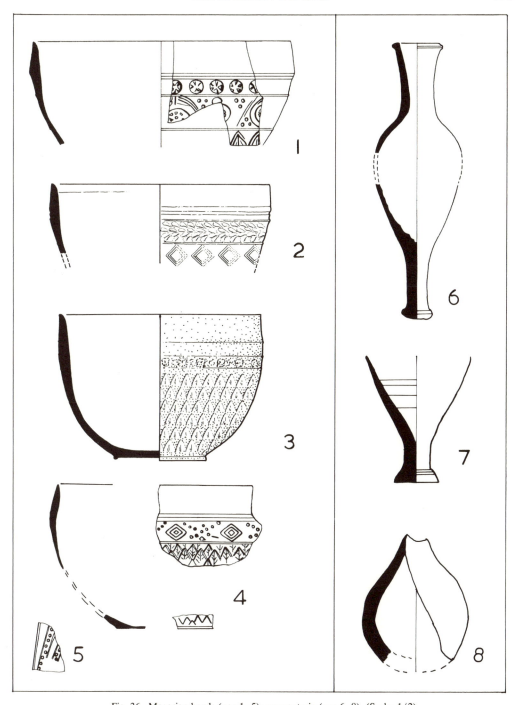

Fig. 36. Megarian bowls (nos.1–5); unguentaria (nos.6–8). (Scale: 1/2)

wares may well apply to the San Rocco pieces. Adamsheck states (8) that 'One would logically suppose that all this pottery was manufactured during the late first, second and third quarters of the first century B.C. with the Lapius–Popilius series beginning earliest and that production ended with the appearance of Arretine pottery'.

Though the San Rocco pieces are found out of context, they should belong to the Periods I/IA occupation of the villa, agreeing with an initial foundation date of 100−90 B.C.

III. *UNGUENTARIA* (Fig. 36, 6−8)

Fabric. Nos. 6−7 had a pink to buff paste, with a thin black wash on the inside and sometimes over the rim and neck, or outside, above the base. The globular example (no. 8) has a thicker wall in light brown paste with a thin black wash internally.

6. (P2663). A tall unguentarium with a slightly everted cylindrical neck with a flattened rim, an ovoid body and a long-stemmed base with a quoit-shaped finish. Six examples, five being less complete.

    Cf. Cotton, 1979, 135 for notes on dating. This type is equivalent to Haltern type 30 which is characteristic of the second and first centuries B.C.

7. (P420). A base of the type of no. 1 above but a better example of the quoit-shaped foot.

8. (P272). Part of the body of a globular unguentarium.

    Cf. Cotton, 1979, 135 and fig 38, 7, though the San Rocco example lacks the painted bands. A derivative of a Hellenistic type, it probably belongs to the first century B.C.

    A neck and 8 bases were also found.

Provenance: Periods I/IA. A base, cf. No. 8.

                  Period II. Nos. cf. 6 (2 exs.), cf. 8 (2 exs.).

                  Periods II/IIA. No. 6 (2 exs.).

                  Unstratified. No. 7 and eight other pieces.

These unguentaria were all probably in use during Periods I/IA, in the first century B.C. All were probably pre-Augustan in date.

IV. *BLACK GLAZED WARES* (Figs. 37−40)

The black glazed, or gloss, wares are described under the following headings:

1. Jugs and juglets. (Fig. 37, 1−5).
2. Kylikes. (Fig. 37, 6−7).
3. Skyphoi. (Fig. 37, 8).
4. Calenian relief ware. (Fig. 37, 9−10).
5. Small bowls. (Fig. 37, 11−15).
6. Salt-cellars. (Fig. 37, 16).
7. Pyxides. (not illustrated).
8. Flanged rim cups. (Fig. 37, 17−18).
9. Small plates or bowls. (Fig. 37, 19−20).
10. Cups (Fig. 37, 21−22).
11. Lids. (Fig. 37, 23−34).
12. Inturned rim bowls. (not illustrated).
13. Platters or dishes. (Fig. 38, 1−7)
14. Medium sized bowls (Fig. 38, 8−13).
15. Miscellaneous forms. (Fig. 39, 1−7).
16. Graffiti. (Fig. 39, 8−10)
17. Bases. (Fig. 40, 1−8).

For general notes on the fabric and forms of the black glazed wares, cf. Cotton, 1979, 88−117. These notes on the Posto series are also applicable to those from San Rocco. 'Local ware' indicates the predominant ware with a light brown to brown/red paste with a dull matt black glaze. Otherwise, only variations are noted. The forms found at Posto are not re-illustrated. In general, the San Rocco material has a rather later chronological *facies* than that of Posto.

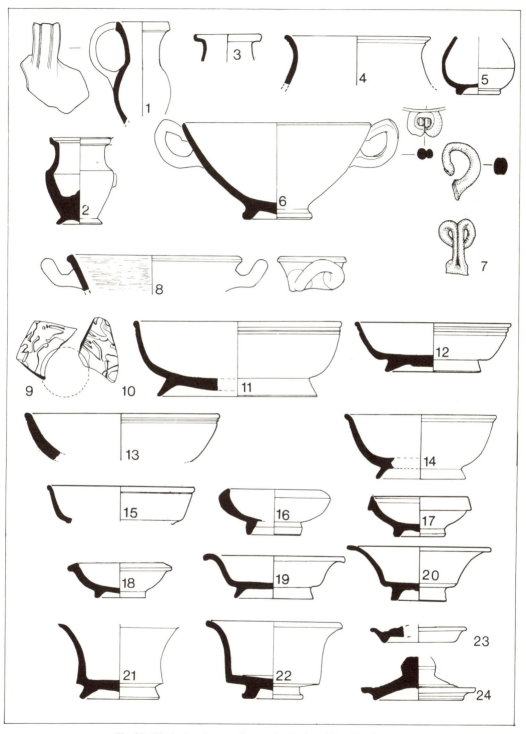

Fig. 37. Black glazed wares. Groups 1–11 of pp.176–180. (Scale: 1/3)

1. *Jugs and juglets.* (Fig. 37, 1–5).

Fabric. This group is in local ware though the paste tends more towards a buff colouring. Being closed vessels, they were not glazed internally, and only one base was glazed underneath.

1. (P2671). A narrow-mouthed jug with a collar rim, a vertical neck and a bulbous body. A wide ribbon handle, with two external grooves, springs from the rim and is attached on top of the shoulder. Two examples.
2. (P1102). A juglet with a cupped rim, a high concave neck above a well-defined shoulder, a pear-shaped body and a ring foot. The handle is missing, but its roots show that it sprang from the outside of the rim and was attached below the shoulder. One example and a rim sherd.
3. (P479). A rim sherd with a more marked cupping.
4. (P548). A rim sherd from a wide-mouthed jug, with a better black glaze than the rest of the group. The everted rim has two external grooves. Another example shows the root of a handle at the base of the neck. Four examples. Part of a ribbon handle, cf. Cotton, 1979, 91 and fig. 20, 10, was also found.
5. (P526). The wall and base of a juglet. Six examples.

Three other bases occurred with oblique pointed footrings, one misfired.

Provenance: Period I. No. cf. 5 (Two exs.).

        Periods I/IA. No. cf. 4.

        Period II. Nos. 1, 3, cf. 5 (2 exs.), and 2 bases.

        Periods II/IIA. No. 5.

        Destruction. Nos. cf. 1, 2, 4, cf. 4 (2 exs.), cf. 5 (2 exs.) and a base.

Nine of the 18 pieces in this group came from layers earlier than the Periods II/IIA occupation, or *c.* 30 B.C. No. 2 has some resemblance to the juglet of Lamboglia Form 11 in Campana B ware, cf. Lamboglia, 1952, 150, but the rim form differs.

2. *Kylikes.* (Fig. 37, 6–7)

Fabric. The few examples found were in local ware. The glaze extended underneath the base, even if only in part.

6. (P1124). A fairly complete example with a bifid handle. Three bases of this form were also found.
7. (P446). A bifid handle which has been attached vertically. Five examples.

Provenance: Of these nine pieces, all but two (from destruction layers) came from the build of the Period II platform, and were therefore derived from the Periods I/IA occupation.

For notes on this form, which is usually dated to the first half of the second century B.C., see Cotton, 1979, 92–3 and fig. 21, 1–6, where the relationship to Morel, 1963, 44–5, Form 82 a–b is discussed. That so few pieces of this early form were found at San Rocco supports the contention that the Period I villa does not go back beyond the beginning of the first century B.C.

3. *Skyphoi.* (Fig. 37, 8)

Fabric. Local ware, glazed all over.

8. (P2749). An example with a slightly everted rounded rim with an oblique wall and a curved upturned horizontal handle.

Provenance: From a destruction layer.

Cf. Lamboglia, 1952, 190–1 and Form 43A in Campana A ware, where an example from Minturnae is quoted. Although the form of the handle is closer to Form 43A, rather than the later Form 43C, it is also stated that the skyphos form is copied locally until the second century B.C. The San Rocco example is certainly in a local fabric, and, like the kylices, is a late survival.

4. *Calenian relief ware.* (Fig. 37, 9–10)
Fabric. Sherds of the local ware, glazed on both sides.
9–10. (P1098a–b). Two sherds, probably from the same vessel, with a relief pattern on the upper surface. The design is of horses galloping in opposite directions, being driven perhaps by winged figures or Victories.
Provenance: From a disturbed layer.
   The sherds bear some resemblance to, though they are not identical with, the sherd illustrated in Pagenstecher, 1909, 73–4, no. 113 and Taf. 15. Cf. Cotton 1979, 97 for a note on the imprecise dating. At San Rocco they should certainly be derived from the Periods I/IA occupation.

5. *Small bowls.* (Fig. 37, 11–15)
Fabric. All are in local ware.
11. (P710). An example of the larger size in this category. Five examples, of which two have maroon stacking rings and two were glazed underneath the base.
12. (P76). The smaller version of the above bowl. Four examples.
13. (P438). A rim sherd with a thicker wall. Two examples.
14. (P549). A variant version. Two examples.
15. (P74). A rim sherd with weak grooving. Eight examples.
In addition there were 25 bases of this form, seven of which were glazed underneath.
Provenance: Periods I/IA, Nos. cf.12 (4 exs.). 13 and 4 bases.
                   Period II. Nos. 11 (4 exs.), 12 (8 exs.), 14, 15 (3 exs.) and 2 bases.
                   Periods II/IIA. cf. No. 12 (3 exs.).
                   Destruction and topsoil. All others.
   Cf. the examples from Posto, Cotton, 1979, 101–2 and fig. 23, 15–21. Nos. 11–3 are of Lamboglia, 1952, 143–4, Form 1A in Campana B ware, and nos. 14–5 are Form 1B. Forms 1A–B are some of the commonest forms on all sites in the first century B.C. Cf. also Taylor, 1957, 159–60. At San Rocco this form predominates up to *c.* 30 B.C.

6. *Salt-cellars.* (Fig. 37, 16)
16. (P2672). A section, in buff paste with a very poor and thin grey/black glaze which does not extend underneath the base. One example and one rim sherd, both unstratified.
       Cf. Lamboglia, 1952, 174–5, Form 21/25B in Campana A ware; and Cotton, 1979, 99 and fig. 23, 3–4, both of which lacked the base. Unfortunately, neither the Posto nor the San Rocco examples were attested in the first phases of the villas.

7. *Pyxides.* (Not illustrated)
   For this form cf. Lamboglia, 1952, 145 for the form in Campana A ware and 158 for the form in Campana C ware, both Form 3; and also Cotton, 1979, 99 and fig. 23, 5–8.
   At San Rocco, three rim sherds, three wall sherds and 17 bases could be assigned to this form, but no section was available. The ware was the usual local one. Of these pieces, one

rim and two bases came from the Periods I/IA occupation; two wall sherds and two bases were in Period II layers, but these were probably rubbish survivals.

8. *Flanged rim cups.* (Fig. 37, 17–8)
17. (P72). A small example, in the local ware, with most of the glaze missing.
18. (P1104). The rim of this example has a flange of variant form. In brown paste with a matt black glaze all over including underneath the base. Two examples.
Provenance:Periods I/IA. No. cf. 18.
                    Periods II/IIA. Nos. 17 and 18.
    Cf. Lamboglia, 1952, 196, Form 52 in Campana A ware; and Cotton, 1979, 101 and fig. 23, 9–14. No. 18 has some resemblance to the Lamboglia illustration taken from Minturnae. The form is not rare in S. Italy.

9. *Small plates or bowls.* (Fig. 37, 19–20)
Fabric. In light brown paste with a matt grey/black glaze except for half of the underside of the base.
19. (P622). A small shallow bowl or plate, with a flared and rounded rim, a slightly incurved wall and an oblique foot. There is a V *graffito* on the outside of the wall which may be an owner's mark. Nearly complete.
20. (P70). A deeper bowl with a wider foot. Four examples.
*Provenance:*Two examples of no. 20 came from Period II layers and the rest were unstrati-
                fied.
    Cf. Lamboglia, 1952, 160, Form 17 in Campana C ware. In one example the wall is less curved and, though the base is horizontal, the oblique foot differs in profile. The form has its optimum circulation in the first century B.C. It was not differentiated at Posto.

10. *Cups.* (Fig.37, 21–2)
Fabric. Light brown paste, with a black glaze all over, including the underside of the base.
21. (P2748). A small cup. Eight rims and seven bases.
22. (P2672). Though essentially the same, the basal form differs. Three examples.
Provenance:Periods I/IA. No. 21 (4 exs.), 22 (2exs.).
                Periods II/IIA. No. 21. (1 ex.).
                Destruction. The remainder.
    Cf. Cotton, 1979, 99 and fig. 23, 1–2. These cups are of Form 2, cf. Lamboglia, 1952, 144–5 in Campana B ware. The San Rocco examples were probably all derived from the Periods I/IA occupation.

11. *Lids.* (Fig. 37, 23–4)
Fabric. No. 23 is in local ware; no. 24 has a much lighter buff paste with a thin dark brown glaze on top and over the rim and flange and it is not glazed underneath.
23. (P2675). Part of a lid with the rim upturned above the flange and with a flat cordon on top.
24. (P2674). A nearly complete lid with a horizontal bevelled rim above the flange and three grooves inside on top of the rim. The knobbed handle is symmetrical and well moulded.
*Provenance:*No. 23 was from a Periods II/IIA layer; no. 24 was unstratified.
    The lid of Lamboglia, 1952, 151, in Campana B ware, Form 14, has a rim and flange similar to that of no. 24, but its knob handle is more sophisticated.

12. *Inturned rim bowls.* (Not illustrated)
For this form, see Cotton, 1979, 93 and fig. 21, 7–11. At San Rocco, only rim sherds were found and no profile was obtained. With one exception, the glaze was thin and patchy or worn away. One small fragment was in pink paste, the rest were in the usual light brown colour.

This early form (cf. Lamboglia, 1952, 176–7, Forms 26 and 27) really only exists at San Rocco in late local copies which should belong to the earliest occupation. Of the 25 rim sherds found, only two could be attributed to Periods I/IA layers, the rest being displaced or unstratified.

13. *Platters or dishes.* (Fig. 38, 1–7)
Fabric. Unless noted otherwise, these were in local ware.
(i). *Platters and dishes of Lamboglia Form 6.* (Not illustrated)
For this form cf. Cotton, 1979, 108–10 and fig. 27, 1–2. At San Rocco some eight rims were found. The Lamboglia form was in Campana C ware, but it was a copy of an A ware form. The San Rocco examples were probably late copies of the A ware form in the local ware, and were almost certainly derived from the Periods I/IA layers.

(ii) *Platters or dishes of Lamboglia Form 16.* (Not illustrated)
A series is illustrated in Cotton, 1979, 106–8 and fig. 26, 1–5. The form is less common at San Rocco and no profiles were obtained. 12 examples.

(iii) *Platters or dishes of Lamboglia Form 36a-b.* (Not illustrated)
These forms are illustrated in Cotton, 1979, 108–10 and fig. 27, 8–12. Five rim sherds, in the local fabric, were found at San Rocco, comparable to those of fig. 27, 8 and 11 of the Posto series. Again, these are late copies of the Lamboglia form in Campana A ware.

(iv) *Platters or dishes of Lamboglia Form 5.* (Fig. 38, 1–3)
Fabric. All were in the usual local ware.
1. (P1123). A small sized example of this form. Nearly complete.
2. (P2751). A larger sized example, with rouletting on top of the base.
    For this form, cf. Lamboglia, 1952, 146–7, Form 5 in Campana B ware, and Cotton, 1979, 106–8 and fig. 26, 7 and 11. At San Rocco this form was the most abundant of all the black glazed ware forms found. A minimum of 76 pieces represented an indefinite number of platters. Perhaps they were the remains of the dinner service of the Periods I/IA villa.
3. (P2666). An example of this form with a decoration on top of the platter of five rouletted circles between two lots of grooves.
    Lamboglia, 1952, 147, states that the later examples of Form 5 have this decorative addition. The number of circles varies from 2–5 and there are variations in the grooves. 11 examples were found.

(v) *Platters or dishes of Lamboglia Form 7.* (Fig. 38, 4)
Fabric. All were in the local ware.
4. (P13). An example of this form.
    Cf. Lamboglia, 1952, 148, Form 7 in Campana B ware. At San Rocco 21 rim pieces were found.

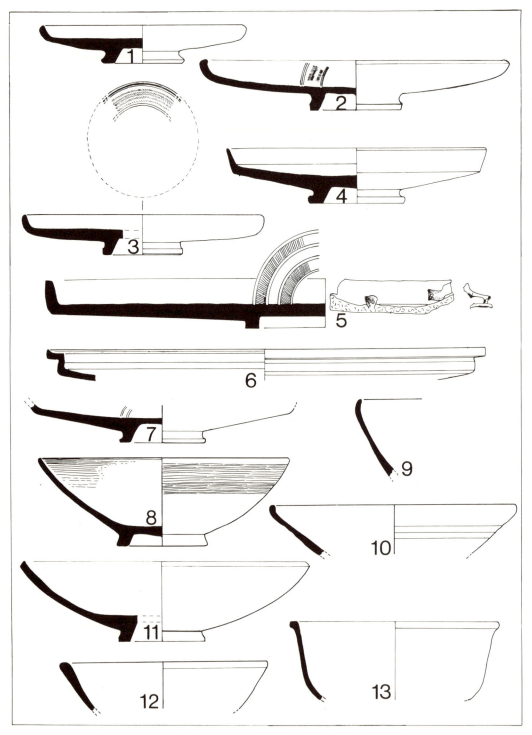

Fig. 38. Black glazed wares. Platters and dishes (nos.1–7); medium sized bowls (nos.8–13). (Scale: 1/3)

(vi) *Platters or dishes of Lamboglia Form 7 in Campana C ware.* (Fig. 38, 5)
Fabric. This example differs from the other platters in having a heavy gritty grey paste with a dull peeling black glaze, which does seem to resemble the Campana C ware.

5. (P89). A very large platter or dish. The centre of its top is decorated with circles of paired grooves and two bands of rouletting. The dish has been repaired in antiquity. Where the rim was rivetted, one lead rivet persists.

    Cf. Lamboglia, 1952, 159, Form 7 in Campana C ware. The San Rocco example should be an import.

(vii) *Other platters or dishes.* (Fig. 38, 6)

6. (P2676). A large platter, in the local ware, with a flanged upturned rim and a carinated wall. Two pieces (probably of the same platter) were found.

(viii) *Bases of platters or dishes.* (Fig. 38, 7)

7. (P279). In addition to the rouletted bases listed under no. 3 above, there are bases without rouletting, which could belong to either Lamboglia Form 5 or Form 7. These have a decoration of two grooved circles, sometimes with a smaller more central one, or are plain. 22 examples.

Provenance: Periods I/IA. Form 5 (20+ exs), Form 7 (6 exs.) No. 6 and No. 7 (2 exs.).
        Period II. Form 16 (2 exs.), Form 6 (4 exs.), Form 36a-b (2 exs.), Form 5 (many exs.), Form 7 (4 exs.).
        Periods II/IIA. Form 16 (3 exs.), Form 6 (2 exs.), Form 5 (many exs.), Form 7 (3 exs).

The remainder were unstratified.

As the Period II examples would have been in use *c.* 30 B.C., since they were derived from the Periods I/IA occupation, all these platter forms found at San Rocco were ascribable to *c.* 100/90–30 B.C., though Forms 5–7 and 16 may have continued in use after that date.

14. *Medium sized bowls.* (Fig. 38, 8–13)
Fabric. Unless otherwise noted, they are in the local ware, though some have a poor brown wash which only covers the inside and the upper part of the outside wall.

8. (P86). A medium sized bowl with a simple rim and a stumpy foot ring. 44 rims. Some 20 bases were probably of this form.

9. (P452). As no. 8 above, but the rim is pointed and inturned. 15 rims.

10. (P429). As no. 8 above, but the rim is rounded and inturned. The form of the base was not determined. Some examples have three slight ridges on the outside of the wall. 36 rims.

11. (P2752). As no. 10 above, but the inturned rim is bevelled. 16 examples. These range from those with a dull matt black glaze on both sides to those with only a thin brown wash inside and over the top of the outside wall.

    The medium sized bowls of nos. 8–11 are variations of a local type assignable to the first century B.C. Those from Cotton, 1979, 103 and fig. 24, 5–6, are comparable, where some resemblance to those of Lamboglia, 1952, 182, Form 33b in Campana A ware is noted. It is a form much copied by post-Campana and provincial potteries, and one which was found at Albintimilium in the first century B.C. layers.

12. (P478). A medium sized bowl with a thickened rounded rim. 21 rims.

13. (P2753). An example with an everted rounded rim. 29 rims.

      For the form cf. Lamboglia, 1952, 177–8, Form 28 in Campana A ware, a form which was copied for a considerable time.

Not illustrated. 8 bases, with oblique pointed foot rings, possibly belonged to this category. For the shape, cf. Cotton, 1979, 103 and fig. 24, 4.

Provenance: Periods I/IA. Nos. 8 (6 rims and 5 bases), 10 (6 exs.), 11 (4 exs.), 12 (1 ex.), 13 (7 exs.).

          Period II. Nos. 8 (2 rims and 3 bases), 9(4 exs.), 10 (4 exs.), 12 (1 ex.), 13 (6 exs.) 4 bases.

          Periods II/IIA. Nos. 8 (8 rims), 10 (7 exs.), 11 (4 exs.), 13 (3 exs.).

          The rest were displaced.

The note on the provenance of the platters or dishes, for their use and dating, also applies to these medium sized bowls.

15. *Miscellaneous forms.* (Fig. 39, 1–7)

Fabric. These were all in the usual local ware.

1. (P447). The rim of a vase which probably had a stemmed base. 2 examples.

2. (P2750). The stem and base of a vase like that of no. 1 above. 5 examples.

      For these 'stemmed vases' see Lamboglia, 1952, 145–6, form 4 in Campana B ware, and 167, Form 4 in Campana A ware. The base of our no. 2 is between the A and B ware forms.

3. (P464). A well-moulded base with a short stem. Two examples.

      Cf. Lamboglia, 1952, 167 (illustration at the bottom right) from Minturnae, for one example, and the top left illustration, also from Minturnae, for our other example.

4. (P320). Part of the rim of an inkpot, in buff paste with all of the glaze worn away.

      Cf. Lamboglia, 1952, 150, Form 13 in Campana B ware, where an example is quoted from the Republican levels in the Forum, Rome, cf. Morel, 1965, Form 102, 220.

5. (P2755). A small beaker.

      Cf. Lamboglia, 1952, 199, Form 60 in Campana A ware, described as an *urnetta* with or without handles. The form occurred at Minturnae.

6. (P2756). A rim from a jug or jar.

7. (P2757). A jar with an everted thickened rim with external grooving. Two examples.

Not illustrated. Fragments of four flanged rim bowls, for which cf. Cotton, 1979, 110 and fig. 27, 20–21.

Not illustrated. Part of the neck of a jug with 4 perforations through the base of the neck to serve as a strainer.

Provenance: Period I/IA. Nos. 2 (2 exs.), 3 (1 ex.).

          Period II. Nos. 1 (1 ex.), 4, 5.

          Periods II/IIA. Nos. 1 (1 ex.), the jug with a strainer.

          The rest were unstratified.

These miscellaneous pieces were all probably current in Periods I/IA.

16. *Graffiti.* (Fig. 39, 8–10)

8. (P12). A sherd from the base of a platter with the graffito SIL incised underneath. The top of the sherd has a wide band of rouletting as in Fig. 38, 3 above. In local ware, it came from a destruction layer.

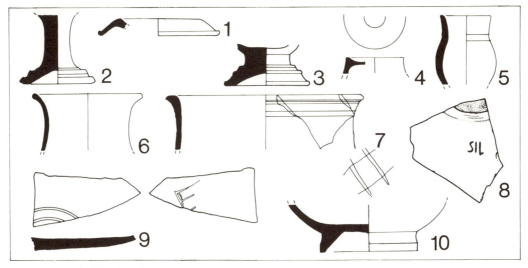

Fig. 39. Black glazed wares. Miscellaneous forms (nos.1–7); graffiti (nos.8–10). (Scale: 1/3)

9.   (P281). A similar sherd, in a similar ware, with the graffito ?E underneath and two grooved circles on top. From a Periods I/IA layer.

10.   (P2758). A base, in light brown paste, glazed dull black on top only. The graffito, perhaps an owner's mark, is part of a rough checkerboard. From a Period II building layer.

17. *Bases.* (Fig. 40, 1–8)

Fabric. Unless otherwise stated, these are in the usual local ware.

(i) *Bases with palmette stamps.* (Fig. 40, 1–3)

1.   (P2667). A base with a rouletted circle inside which are four very rudimentary palmette stamps.

2.   (P2754). A base with one remaining rudimentary palmette stamp inside two grooved circles.

3.   (P611). Part of a base with three remaining palmette stamps. Worn.

      Another basal fragment had part of a palmette stamp of a better form. Four fragmentary bases, which had rouletted circles, may also have had rudimentary stamps.

      By the time that San Rocco was founded, black glazed ware forms with palmette stamped bases should have nearly reached the end of their period of use. Indeed, of the above pieces, only one (no. 3) was stratified, in a Period II level, and they should all go back to the earlier part of the occupation. At San Rocco, there were even fewer examples than at Posto; and only the small degenerate type of palmette is found. For the Posto examples, see Cotton, 1979, 111–13 and fig. 28, 1–9 and fig. 29, 10–13. No. 2 above is similar to that of Cotton, 1979, fig. 29, 12. Rosette and lozenge-shaped stamps were not found at San Rocco.

(ii) *Bases with moulded mask feet.* (Not illustrated)

Part of the base of a bowl (P1088), which originally had three feet consisting of moulded comic masks, was found. Only one and a half feet persist and these were worn and are poorly moulded. Unstratified.

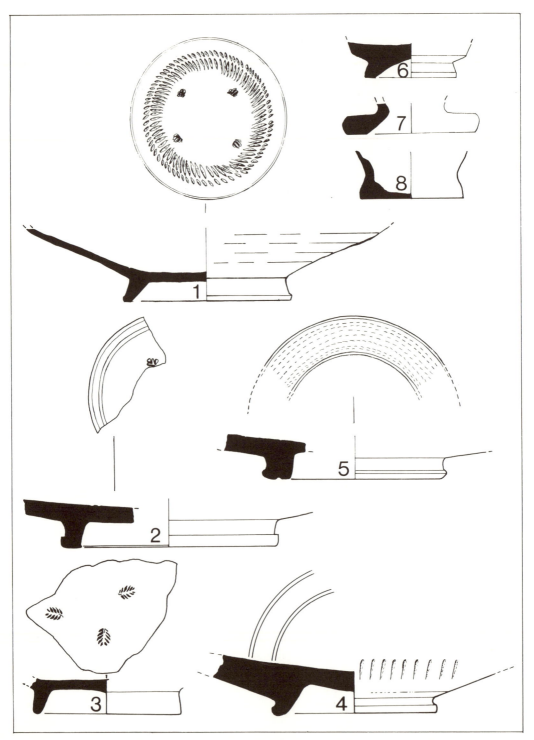

Fig. 40. Black glazed wares. Palmette-stamped bases (nos.1–3); miscellaneous bases (nos.4–8). (Scale: 1/2)

For a similar bowl, see Cotton, 1979, 98 and fig. 22, 8, though it has better shaped feet. This example does, however, add to the list of those quoted by Morel which are given in the Posto report, cf. Cotton, 1979, 98.

(iii) *Bases with an external decoration on the wall.* (Fig. 40, 4)
4. (P309). A base with two circular grooves on top and with a band of oblique impressed lines on the outside of the wall. From a Period II layer.

(iv) *Bases with grooved footrings.* (Fig. 40, 5)
5. (P2668). A base showing this feature. There is also a band of fine rouletting between twin grooves on its upper surface, 4 examples, 1 from a Period II layer and the rest unstratified.

The grooved foot is characteristic of Campana A pottery and is an early feature. The scarcity of bases of this form at San Rocco is consistent with the dating for its foundation. However, the San Rocco examples are in the usual local ware and are not glazed underneath the base, so they should belong to the very end of the series.

(v) *Miscellaneous bases.* (Fig. 40, 6–8)
6. (P574). A pedestal base with a footring below a carinated wall. Three examples, in the local ware. From the Period IIA occupation on the floor of the kitchen area, a Period II infill and unstratified.
7. (P2759). A quoit-shaped base. Its paste has a pinkish tinge, but it is not the typical Ischitana pink of the Campana A ware. Above and below, it has worn matt black glaze, but the rounded edge is reserved. This piece may be a late and degenerate example of Campana A ware. It is formed of two joining pieces from the Period II infill over the lower S. terrace.
8. (P445). A flat base with an incurved wall. This is in a light grey paste with scant traces of a peeling dull glaze outside and below the base, but the roughly finished inside has never been glazed. Probably from a closed vessel, or a misfired piece, it is also reminiscent of Campana C ware, though the paste is a paler grey than is usual. From the Period II infill under room 15.

Many bases, with oblique footrings and of the smaller size, or perhaps from medium sized bowls, were found and occurred in most layers.

V. *THE TERRA SIGILLATA WARES*
These ware are grouped as follows:
A. Arretine.
B. Local terra sigillata.
C. Late Italian terra sigillata.
D. African Red Slip ware.

A. ARRETINE. By Joanna Bird. (Fig. 41, 1–9)
(I wish to offer my grateful thanks to Mrs Joanna Bird (née Morris) for identifying and dating the Arretine and local terra sigillata material. M.A.C.)

Fabric. See Cotton, 1979, 118–20, for the classification used for Arretine and Late Italian terra sigillata fabrics.

(i) *Decorated.* (Fig. 41, 1)
1.   (P263). Fragment of a crater (Dr. 11). The decoration is bordered at the top by a stylized olive wreath. The partial mould-stamp [ ] H, *in tabella ansata,* is probably of Xanthus, a mould-maker of the Arretine Ateius family. Fabric Al. First half of first century A.D.

(ii) *Stamped.* (Fig. 41, 2)
2.   (P329). Part of a large platter with a rouletted circle on the interior. The radial square stamp, [ ] VI, is not certainly identifiable: the preceding letter is probably L or E. Fabric Al. Late first century B.C. to early first century A.D.

(iii) *Plain forms.* (Fig. 41, 3–9)
3.   (P266). Foot from a crater. Fabric Al. Augustan.
4.   (P2639). Base, large platter with rouletted circle on base. Fabric Al, partially unslipped under base; very lustrous slip. Slightly burnt in one place. First half of first century A.D.
5.   (P260). Base and wall of a small bowl. The fabric and footring suggest a date in the first half of the first century A.D.
6.   (P262). Bowl rim; both surfaces show turning marks. The form and ware suggest a mid-first century A.D. date.
7.   (P333). Small bowl or cup with rouletting on the underside of the rim. Cf. Goudineau, 1968, 307, type 41 (B) b. Tiberian-Claudian probably.
8.   (P2638). Cup, decorated with an applied garland on the upper wall. Tiberian-Claudian probably.
9.   (P567). Rim of a small platter, cf. Dr. form 17. Tiberian-Claudian probably.
Not illustrated. (P118). A platter rim as no. 9. Dr. 17 or perhaps Dr. 15/17. First half of first century A.D.
   In addition, 1 worn rim, 3 basal fragments and 9 wall sherds were found.
Provenance: Periods II/IIA. Nos. 1, 5, 6, a basal fragment and 2 sherds.
The rest were in destruction layers or top soil.
Summary of dating. Late first century B.C. to early first century A.D. No. 2.
                           Augustan. No. 3.
                           c. A.D. 1–50. Nos. 1, 4, 5 and (P118).
                           c. A.D. 50. No. 6.
                           Tiberian-Claudian. Nos. 7, 8 and 9.
   Unlike Posto, San Rocco produced only a small amount of Arretine ware. There was no evidence to show that it was in use at the time that the Period II villa was built, for all the stratified pieces came from the Periods II/IIA occupation layers. But one piece could be of Augustan date, which suggests that it came into use there soon after the occupation of the Period II villa started.

B. LOCAL TERRA SIGILLATA. By Joanna Bird. (Fig. 41, 10–12)
Fabric. The paste is fairly micaceous and rather uneven.
10. (P2657). Rim from large platter; the ware is probably a local terra sigillata fabric, slightly burnt. Probably first century A.D. and likely to be within the first half.
Not illustrated. (P510). Rim, deep dish, in a similar ware to that of no. 10, slightly burnt. First half of first century A.D.

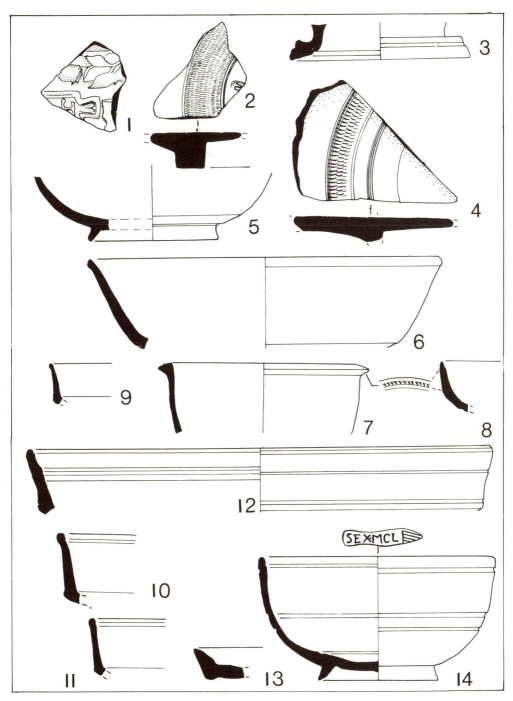

Fig. 41. Arretine ware (nos.1–9); local terra sigillata (nos.10–12); Late Italian terra sigillata (nos.13–14). (Scale: 1/2, except potter's stamp, 1/1)

11. (P30). Platter, smaller than that of no. 10, but a similar form and in the same ware; and presumably a similar date.

12. (P2512). Rim, large platter. The ware is better fired than nos. 10–11, but it is likely to come from the same source, and is of the same date.

Provenance: These four pieces all came from the destruction layers or top soil, but should have been derived from the phase of the Periods II/IIA occupation succeeding the first use of the Arretine pottery, as they are all datable to the first half of the first century A.D.

C. LATE ITALIAN TERRA SIGILLATA. (Fig. 41, 13–14)

This ware is dated to approximately the mid-first century to the mid-second century A.D. Whilst it was well represented at Posto (see Cotton, 1979, 124 and fig. 34, 1–3, 7–11 and 13 and fig. 35, 4–6 and 12) it was scarce at San Rocco, and only two pieces merit illustration.

13. (P2659). The rim of a platter in pale red paste, with a dull red slip inside and a dull brown/red slip outside. The fabric is probably Late Italian 1, see Cotton, 1979, 120.

14. (P1106). A bowl, in soft pink paste with a thin dark red slip. The simple rim has internal and external grooves below it, the wall has two external grooves below its maximum girth and two internal ones in its lower part. The ring foot is oblique and pointed. On the top of the inside there is a potter's stamp SEX. MCL in an elongated *planta pedis*.

Klumbach, 1956, 119, records stamps in this ware, of Sex. (Murrius?) Fest (us), and Sex. Mu. Pi and C.P.P., with references. This may be a related stamp. (I am indebted to Philip Kenrick for this reference).

The other pieces found were a fragmentary foot, 5 ring and 1 flat bases and 11 sherds.

Provenance: Unfortunately, none of these pieces came from a stratified layer, but they must have been derived from the Period IIA occupation. The use of this ware attests occupation during the last half of the first century until the early second century A.D.

D. AFRICAN RED SLIP WARE. (Fig. 42, 1–14 and Fig. 43, 15–22)

(Most of this material was examined by Dr. John Hayes, to whom I wish to express my thanks for his help and advice. M.A.C.)

The form references used below are those of Hayes, 1972.

Fabric. The fabric of the San Rocco material was of a very uniform character. Cf. Hayes, 1972, 13–14 for a description.

The forms found were as follows:

1. (P409). A rim sherd from a dish with a broad convex rim decorated with a leaf in barbotine.
    Cf. Hayes Form 3B, 21–25 and fig 2, 28. *c.* A.D. 75–150.
2. (P26). In this sherd, the rim is more convex. Two examples.
    Cf. Hayes Form 3B, 21–25, and fig. 2, 79. *c.* A.D. 75–150.
3. (P345). A rim fragment from a large sized dish with a plain wide convex rim. 5 examples.
    Cf. Hayes Form 3B, 21–25, and fig. 2, 79. *c.* A.D. 75–150.
4. (P48). A dish with a broad flat rim and a shallow body, slightly carinated. There is a

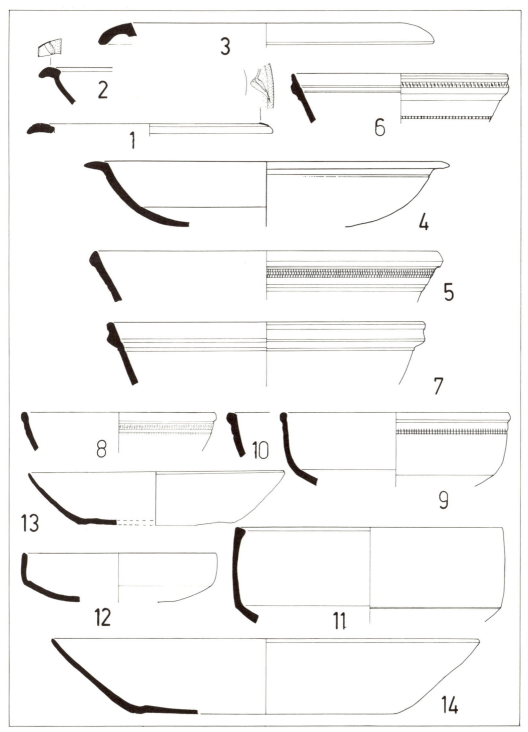

Fig. 42. African Red Slip ware (nos.1–14). (Scale: 1/3)

groove inside matching the carination. As the tip of the lip is broken away, it is not known whether or not it had a groove, but two other fragmentary rims showed this feature. The base is missing. Two examples.

Cf. Hayes Form 6A–B, 29–31 and fig. 3, 16 or 17. Dated from the end of the first to the end of the second century A.D.

5. (P2649). A bowl with a steep wall, a thickened or rolled rim and, on the outside, one remaining row of rouletting below a deep groove.

Cf. Hayes Form 7B, 31–33 and fig. 3, 6. Dated to the early to mid-second century A.D.

6. (P417). The rim of a carinated bowl with a large convex moulding below the lip with a small ridge below, matched by two corresponding grooves on the inside. There are two lines of rouletting on the moulding below the rim and a single row, forming a groove above the (missing) carination. Nine examples.

Cf. Hayes Form 8A, 33–35 and fig. 4, 3 c. A.D. 80/90–160 +.

7. (P25). A rim like that of no. 6, but plain and with a more flaring wall. 5 examples.

Cf. Hayes Form 8B, 33–35 and fig. 4, 32. Second half of second century A.D.

8. (P24). The rim from a bowl with a curved body with a plain rounded lip below which there is a band of rouletting between two grooves and a single band below the lower groove. Fourteen examples.

Cf. Hayes Form 9A, 35–37 and fig. 4, 12. c. A.D. 100–160+.

9. (P2648). A larger version of the above, with simpler rouletting.

Cf. Hayes Form 9A, 35–37 and fig. 4, 3. c. A.D. 100–160+.

10. (P2646). A rim sherd from a plain version of no. 9. Six examples.

Cf. Hayes Form 9B, 35–37 and fig. 4, 16. Second half of second century A.D.

11. (P2653). A carinated bowl with a vertical wall. Ten rims, 4 bases and 7 sherds were found.

Cf. Hayes Form 14B, 39–41 and fig. 6. c. A.D. 160–200+.

12. (P2650). A shallow open bowl with a low inward-sloping rim and a sloping floor.

Cf. Hayes Form 14C, 39–41 and fig. 6, 11. Late second century A.D. but may last into the third century.

13. (P2654). A bowl with a simple rim, a curved wall and a small ridge separating it from a flat base.

Cf. Hayes Form 17B, 42–43 and fig. 6, 11, dated perhaps to the second half of the second century A.D.

14. (P2656). A large example of no. 13 above, nearly half of which was found.

15. (P23/31/34). Three joining sherds from a flanged rim lid of shallow conical form which has a broad flat rim with a small vertical flange below. There is a raised fillet on the body above the rim, with a small ridge at its junction, and bands of simple rouletting on the fillet and rim. The knob is missing. The slip is on top only and extends down to the edge of the rim. Two examples.

Cf. Hayes, Form 20, 44–5 and fig. 7, 1. Of late first to early second century A.D. date. Form 19, which goes with this lid, was not identified.

16. (P2655). Part of a casserole, with an inward sloping wall and rounded bottom separated by a more or less pronounced flange. There is a pronounced internal rim roll. This form was fairly plentiful at San Rocco, 16 rims and 10 sherds being noted.

Cf. Hayes Form 23B, 45–8 and fig. 7, 24. Mid second to early third century A.D.

17. (P346). The rim of a dish with a flaring wall curving upwards to a more or less vertical

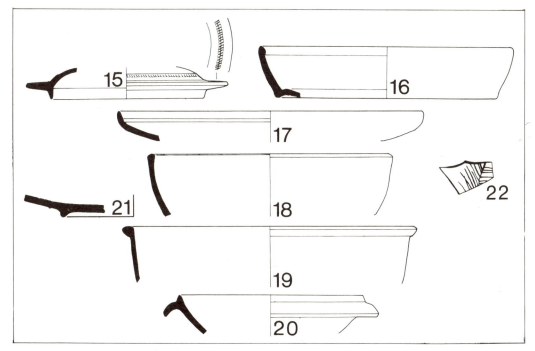

Fig. 43. African Red Slip ware (nos.15–22). (Scale: 1/3)

rim. There is a groove on the inside below the rim. The slip is thin and dull. Two rims and two basal fragments.

Cf. Hayes Form 27, 49–51 and fig. 8, 2. The suggested date is *c.* A.D. 160–220. The main period of production seems to be within the second century.

18. (P406/407). This rim is possibly a variant form of that of no. 17. The rim is thickened and it lacks the internal groove. The slip is dull. 18 examples.

Cf. Hayes Form 27, 49–51 and fig. 8, 9. *c.* 160–220 or mainly in the second century A.D.

19. (P347). The rim from a bowl with a steep wall and a narrow flattened rim. Two examples.

Cf. Hayes Form 28, 51–2 and fig.. 8, 1, though the San Rocco examples lack the groove near the inner edge of the rim. Hayes writes that 'The general form and thick bright slip...indicates an early third century date.'

20. (P2652). A small bowl with a flanged rim and a curved wall. The flange is pointed and curves downwards. The good red slip covers the inside and rim top only.

21. (P50). An example of the base of a dish with a low foot and a band of rouletting on the top of the base. There is not enough of the wall to show the form of the vessel. Two examples. In addition, 21 basal fragments, probably from bowls, were found.

22. (P410). A sherd from a vessel with a scratched graffito on the outside.

54 sherds of this ware were also found.

Provenance: Of the 124 rims, 21 bases and 54 sherds found, 12 rims, 1 base and 3 sherds came from the Periods II/IIA occupation level. 11 of the rims came from the peristyle area and the rest were scattered. The remainder were unstratified.

The dating evidence. At San Rocco, the earliest forms of African Red Slip ware, or those which first appear during the last quarter of the first century A.D., are represented, but only in small quantity (nos. 1–6 above which account for 21 pieces). The bulk of the material is of later date. At the time that Dr. John Hayes saw the material, he considered that there was nothing later than the second century A.D. and pieces found later are consistent with this view. Whilst some of them, nos. 16–19, could be as late as the early third century, they are all forms which were already in use at the end of the second century. On this ware, therefore, the occupation of the San Rocco villa is certainly attested throughout the second century, but, at its end, or early in the third century at latest, it seems to have been deserted.

A comparison with African Red Slip ware found at the Posto villa is of interest. There, there were only 10 pieces and 16 sherds of the earlier series, in contrast to all the San Rocco material here described, perhaps indicating the difference in wealth between the two villas. At Posto, on this slighter evidence, the occupation was attested until at least A.D. 160, or later, but there was nothing of third century date. The desertion of the two sites may have occurred at roughly the same period. Again, in contrast, the later re-occupation of Posto, which produced a fair quantity of this ware of fifth to sixth century date, has no parallel at San Rocco, where not a single sherd has been attributed to this later phase.

VI. *THIN WALLED WARES*

For a type series of these wares from Cosa see Moevs, 1973. The Moevs references quoted below refer to the type series depicted on the pull-out plate at the end of her volume.

The forms found at San Rocco were:
1. Bowls (1a, decorated; 1b, plain).
2. Situlae.
3. Jugs.
4. Jars.
5. Beakers (5a, decorated; 5b, plain).
6. Bases.

1a. *Decorated Bowls.* (Fig. 44, 1–5)
Fabric. This is described individually.
1. (P614). A bowl with a moulded rim with a close-set rouletted decoration on the outside of the wall. In buff paste with a good red/brown colour coating on both sides, similar to that of the decorated beakers nos. 2–4 below. Two examples.
2. (P2735). A handled bowl, or cup, in buff paste fired the same colour. It has a moulded rim and a simple rouletted decoration of vertical strokes. Two examples.

   Nos. 1 and 2 are thin-walled versions of the plentiful type found in colour-coated wares, see below pp. 203–206 and Figs 47–8, 1–17.
3. (P2736). An inturned rim bowl with two external grooves below the lip and an oblique stroke rouletted decoration. In brown paste fired the same colour. Two examples (the second coarser and with a variant rouletting).

   Again, this type is a finer version of the forms in coarse colour-coated ware as were nos. 1–2 above.
4. (P2722). A sherd from a handled bowl, or beaker, with a decoration of incised grooves.
5. (P2723). A sherd with a band of high relief barbotine decoration. In gritty paste fired red inside and dark grey outside.

Provenance: Period II. Nos. 4 and 5.
The 6 remaining examples came from destruction layers (2) and top soil (4).
   These types were not found at Posto.

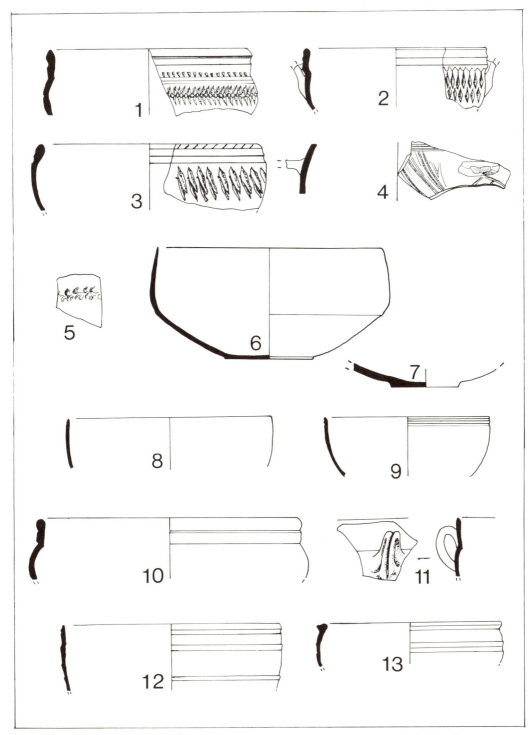

Fig. 44. Thin-walled wares. Small bowls, decorated (nos. 1–5), plain (nos. 6–13). (Scale: 1/2)

1b. *Plain Bowls.* (Fig. 44, 6–13)

(i) *Bowls in metallic glazed ware.* (Fig. 44, 6–7)

Fabric. In the Augustan period, Moevs, 1973, 99, writes 'Two new classes of thin-walled ware, the metallic and the proto-orange glaze, which now appear on the market, testify to the new effort toward the realisation of a coloured surface in competition with the incipient activity of the Arretine factories.' And (127) 'Two new decorative devices are adopted by the metallic glaze: floral decoration in barbotine, and sand decoration... the second, derived from the La Tène tradition, makes sporadic appearances from the end of the third quarter of the first century B.C. throughout the Augustan period, and becomes popular, in turn, during the time of Tiberius'.

6.   (P2599). A hemispherical bowl with a thinned pointed lip, a curved body and a small flat base with a slightly marked ring. In a red/brown paste, both sides are colour-coated in a purple/brown colour with a metallic sheen, except for the outside of the wall between the lip and the point of maximum girth. Below this there is a faintly marked groove.

For this form, in this ware, cf. Moevs, 1973, Form XXXVI. For the Augustan examples, see Moevs 132–3; for the Claudian-Neronian period, see Moevs 254. The one San Rocco example cannot be dated exactly, as it came from a destruction layer, but it may perhaps belong to the Claudian-Neronian group. Two examples from Posto (Cotton, 1979, 138 and fig. 40, 4–5) were also unstratified, but were compared with examples from the Sutri kiln dated to *c.* A.D. 60–70, i.e. of Neronian date.

7.   (P528). A flat base with a ring foot of the same form as that of no. 6, but in a metallic glazed ware with a sanded surface. One example from the destruction layer over the peristyle and 1 sherd.

For the sand decoration on Form XXXVI hemispherical bowls, see Moevs, 1973, 133 ff., for Augustan examples; and 176–9 for Tiberian-Early Claudian examples. The San Rocco piece may perhaps belong to the later group. The unstratified bowl of Cotton, 1979, 138 and fig. 40, 3, had a sanded surface and is similar to that of Moevs, 1973, pl. 35, 316, a form which was popular during the Tiberian period.

(ii). *Bowls in non-metallic wares.* (Fig. 44, 8–13)

8.   (P460). A small bowl with a simple thinned rim. In pink paste with the remains of a red/orange colour coating on both sides. Three examples.

9.   (P2681). A small bowl with a simple thinned rim with two external grooves. In pink paste, fired pink/red.

10. (P606). A fragment from a bowl with a moulded rim. In brown paste fired dark brown. Two examples.

This is probably a finer undecorated version of the series of rouletted bowls in Early colour-coated ware, of Figs. 47–8, 1–17.

11. (P2683). A handled bowl, in worn gritty orange ware. The vertical rim has a simple lip above a well-rounded body. The two-ribbed handle springs from the junction of the rim and body and is attached on the shoulder.

12. (P573). A rim fragment, in orange ware with traces of colour-coating. The simple rim has a pointed lip, and the wall has two grooves and a cordon outside.

13. (P2744). A bowl with a rim of triangular section. In dark brown paste fired the same colour.

Provenance: Periods I/IA. Cf. no. 8.

          Periods II/IIA. No. 8.

The remaining seven pieces came from the destruction layers (5) and the top soil (2).

  There are no exact parallels for this group in the Posto series.

2. *Situlae.* (Fig. 45, 1–6)

1. (P2679). A small situla with an everted moulded lip, an elongated body with thin walls and a flat base. In pale grey paste fired grey inside and dull red outside and inside the rim. Some 44 fragmentary rims, similar to the internally concave moulded one of the type illustration, probably came from situlae of this form or perhaps from beakers with a similar rim form.

    For information on this form, see Moevs, 1973, Form I, 49–50 and 57–8. The form is dated from the second half of the second century B.C. to the end of the third quarter of the first century B.C.

2–3. (P2713) and (P443). One sherd and one base were found of the variety of the above situla with a barbotine decoration on the outside of the wall. In hard pink paste, fired orange/pink and in grey paste fired brown, with thin walls.

    Cf. Moevs, 1973, Form I, 50–3, and Small, 1977, 170–1 with fig. 33, 261, for references to situlae so decorated. Though the type starts as early as c. 175/150 B.C., it is in the majority amongst thin walled wares in the first century B.C., and all examples are pre-Augustan in date, at latest.

4. (P1097). A small situla with a thin simple rim, a tapered body and a flat base with a rudimentary foot. In red paste fired dull to light red. It is difficult to attribute fragmentary rims to this type, so only one example is quoted.

5–6. (P433) and (P2732). Examples of small and large sized flat bases, mostly from situlae of the above types, though some may have belonged to beakers. Thirty-five examples, of which 14 were in red paste with a dull smoothed red finish and 21 were in grey paste with a smoothed grey/brown finish.

Provenance: Periods I/IA. Cf. no. 1 (15 exs.), 5, cf. 5 (7 exs.).

          Period II. Nos. 1, cf. 1 (7 exs.), 3, cf. 5 (10 exs.).

          Periods II/IIA. Cf. no. 1 (1 ex.) 2, cf. 5 (1 ex.).

In addition to these 45 stratified examples, the remainder, 37 examples in all, came from destruction layers or top soil. The examples from the Period II layers would have been derived from the Periods I/IA occupation, which means that only three of the stratified pieces were not of this phase. The whole group can, therefore, be assigned to the Periods I/IA phase, or to pre-Augustan times, which is in conformity with the dating given to the Cosa material.

3. *Jugs.* (Fig. 45, 7–12)

7. (P2718). A globular, one-handled jug with an everted rim. Only two rims of this type showed evidence of a handle and it is assumed that only one handle was present. In buff paste with an orange/brown colour coating outside and over the rim.

    For an analogy, see Moevs, 1973, Form L, 153–154 and pl. 26, 246. It is stated that the form, which may start in Augustan times, enjoyed a moderate popularity in Tiberian times and survived into the reign of Claudius.

8. (P2682). A jug fragment with a flanged rim cupped internally. In brown paste fired dark grey.

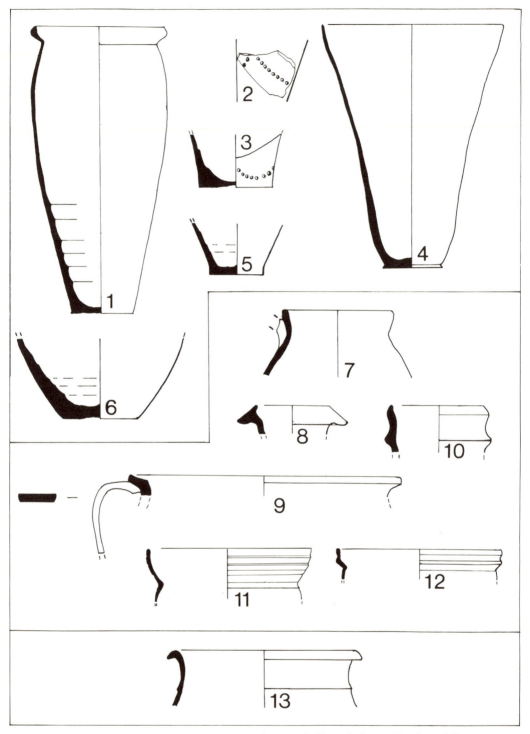

Fig. 45. Thin-walled wares. Situlae (nos.1–6); jugs (nos.7–12); and a jar (no.13). (Scale: 1/2)

9. (P2740). A handled jug in cream ware. The rim is concave and the ribbon handle springs from its outer side. Two examples.

10. (P2741). A jug fragment with a collar rim, in buff paste with a dark brown colour-coating outside.

11. (P2742). A rim fragment, in orange/pink paste fired self colour. The cup-shaped rim has a pointed lip and it has shallow grooves externally.

    Possibly similar to Moevs, 1973, Form LVIII, a globular ampulla with a flaring mouth, cf. Moevs, 1973, 168–9, nos. 301–3 and pl. 33, 75. The form first appears there in the later Augustan period and continues until Tiberian times.

12. (P323). A small fragment of a moulded rim, in red/brown paste with very thin walls fired the same colour. Perhaps from a jug. Two examples.

Provenance: Period II. Cf. no. 7(1 ex.), cf. 9(1 ex.) and 10.

     Periods II/IIA. Cf. no. 7(2 exs.)

Twenty pieces, including nos. 8, 9 and 11, came from destruction layers and 6 pieces came from top soil. The 5 pieces from stratified layers tend to show that the jug types found did not exist before Period II and were probably not earlier than the Augustan period.

4. *Jars.* (Fig. 45, 13)

13. (P2712). The rim of a jar with a down-turned lip and an oblique neck which has a ridged junction with the body. In hard grey/brown paste with a light to dark brown surface. Four examples.

Provenance: One piece each came from Periods I/IA and Periods II/IIA and the rest were unstratified.

5a. *Decorated Beakers.* (Fig. 46, 1–7)

1. (P421). A beaker with an oblique everted rim and a bulbous body on which, below a shallow groove, there is a reticulate pattern. In pale brown paste fired the same colour.

2. (P267). A rim fragment, in buff paste with a good brown/red colour coating on both sides. The lip is rounded above a cordon. Below a groove, the wall is decorated with a closely-set rouletted pattern.

3. (P264). This rim fragment differs from no. 2 above in being of larger size and in having larger simpler rouletting. Two examples.

Not illustrated. A rim fragment (P411) had simple oblique stroke rouletting and was in the same ware as nos. 2–3. Two examples.

4. (P412). A rim fragment with a turned-back rim and a bulbous body. There is oblique stroke rouletting above and below a horizontal line. In pink paste with an orange/red colour coating on both sides.

5. (P2734). A coarser example with a buff paste and the remains of red/brown colour coating outside. The rim is everted and the outside of the bulbous body has a simple decoration of an oblique stroke rouletting.

6. (P2720). The neck and wall of a beaker decorated with barbotine ribbing. In red paste fired a dull red.

7. (P2721). A sherd from a beaker with a barbotine decoration of elongated pine scales. In brown paste fired brown. Two examples.

    Cf. Moevs, 1973, 54–5, for comments on this decoration which first appears there from the first century B.C.

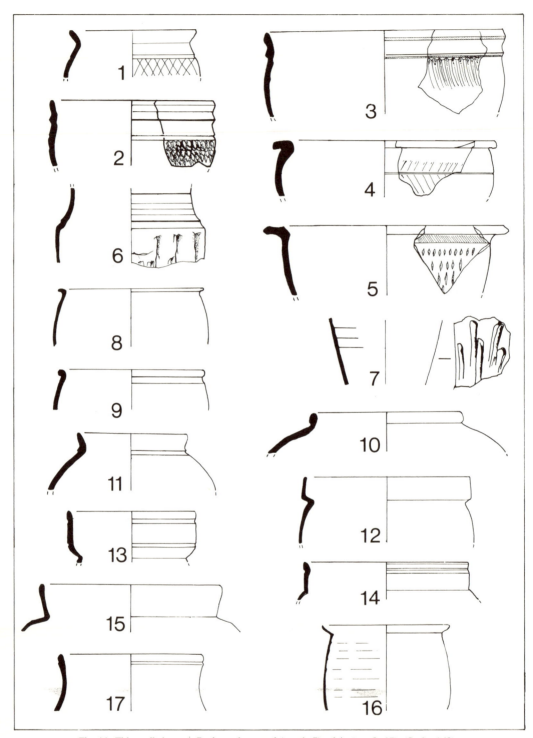

Fig. 46. Thin-walled wares. Beakers, decorated (nos.1–7); plain (nos.8–17). (Scale: 1/2)

Provenance:Periods I/IA. Cf. no. 7.

          Period II. Cf. no. 7.

          Periods II/IIA. Nos. 3, cf. 3 (2 exs.), 4 and 7.

Nos. 1 and 2 came from the destruction layer; nos. 5 and 6 were in top soil.

At Posto, there were no decorated beakers of these types. At San Rocco only no. 7 is attested before Augustan times.

5b. *Plain Beakers.* (Fig. 46, 8–17; Fig. 46a, 18–20)

8.   (P2506). Part of a beaker with a small turned-over rim. In pink paste fired dull pink/red. Three examples.

     Cf. Moevs, 1973, Form VIII, 69 and pl. 80, 806, there described as an elipsoidal beaker with an everted lip. Dated to the third quarter of the first century B.C.

9.   (P481). A small rolled rim. In the same ware as no. 8 above. Two examples.

10. (P393). An almond-shaped rim. In grey paste fired orange outside and grey inside. The paste can also be buff and orange. Three examples.

11. (P2733). A beaker with an everted rim and a small cordon at the junction of the rim and body. The lip is thinned. In pink paste fired a dull pale red. Eight examples.

     Cf. Moevs, 1973, Form LXVIII, 237 and pl. 46, 432; described as a one-handled jug, and dated as Claudian-Neronian.

12. (P2737). A beaker with an internally concave rim, a simple lip and a necked demarcation externally between the rim and the body. In brittle yellow or brown ware. Four examples.

     Cf. Moevs, 1973, Form IV, 59 and pl. 4, 37; with a cup-shaped rim. The range of this form is dated from the middle of the second century B.C. to the early Augustan period.

13. (P436). A beaker, the outside of which is decorated with two grooves. In the same ware as no. 12. 5 examples.

14. (P480). In this type, the rim is vertical. Pink paste with a red/brown colour coating.

15. (P2738). This concave rim is everted above a sharp shoulder.

16. (P2739). A very thin-walled beaker, in pink paste fired self colour. The everted rim is concave internally and is similar to those of the situlae of Fig. 45, 1.

17. (P583). A rim fragment from a necked beaker with a simple rim. In pink or red paste with a red/brown or brown colour coating. Five examples.

18. (P2680). A handled beaker or jug, in dull pink paste, fired pink/red, with a rough external surface. It may have had two handles, which spring outside the rim and are attached to the shoulder. The rim is almond-shaped and the neck is curved. Five examples.

19. (P599). A small beaker, with an everted rim and the root of a grooved handle. In pale buff paste fired the same colour.

20. (P349). A small two-handled beaker with an everted rim and arched handles which spring from the neck and are attached below the shoulder. In pink paste fired pink.

Not illustrated. (P465). A beaker with a cupped rim and a thinned lip. In orange pasted fired the same colour. Two examples.

     Cf. Moevs, 1973, form IV, cf. no. 12 above; cf. Cotton, 1979, 137 and fig. 39, 7.

Not illustrated. (P312) and (P313). A bulbous beaker, in local ware. Three examples.

     Cf. Cotton, 1979, 137 and fig. 39, 20 for a description of the form and ware. These examples in local ware are usually of early date.

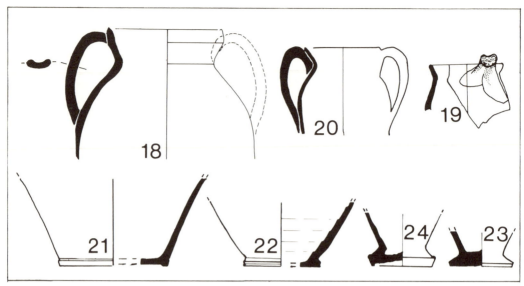

Fig. 46a. Thin-walled wares. Beakers, plain (nos. 18–20); bases (nos. 21–24). (Scale: 1/2)

Provenance: Periods I/IA. Cf. no. 8, cf. no. 11(2 exs.), cf. no. 12, 13, cf. no. 16 (3 exs.).
　　　　　　Period II. Cf. no. 11, cf. 12, (P312) and (P313) (1 ex.).
　　　　　　Period II/IIA. Nos. 11, cf. 12, cf. 13, cf. 16.
Seventeen examples, including nos, 8, 9, 10, 14–8 and 20 came from destruction layers
and 10 examples came from top soil.

Of these types, unfortunately only five were found in stratification, nos, 8, 11, 12, 13
and 16. All these, however, were attested in the Periods I/IA occupation layers, and
should go back to the first century B.C. and be pre-Augustan in date. These types were in
plain ware, only type nos. 14 and 17 above are in colour-coated ware.

6. *Bases* (Fig. 46a, 21–4)
21. (P592). An incipient ring base, in red paste with a patchy red colour coating on both
　　sides.
22. (P2745). An example of a pad base, in grey paste fired brown with a smoothed sur-
　　face. Two examples.
23. (P2746). A small pedestal base, flat underneath, in gritty grey paste fired light red.
　　Three examples, two in brown ware.
24. (P2747). A base similar to that of no. 23, but hollowed underneath. In grey paste fired
　　buff to brown.
Provenance: All, except one example of no. 22, which was in top soil, came from the des-
　　　　　truction layers.

Chapter X. The Pottery: Coarse Wares

VII. *EARLY COLOUR-COATED WARES*

Fabric. This ware has a pink to light red or a buff paste which fires to a buff or pinkish-buff colour. The colour coating varies from dark brown, through light brown to varying shades of brown/red or light red, with occasionally a purplish tinge. Some forms are coated all over the inside and the outside: for others, whilst the inside is coated, only the lower half of the wall and the base are coated outside. Some have a patchy colour coating.

Provenance: At San Rocco, these wares are not attested before the last phase of the occupation, for the majority of the pieces found were displaced in the destruction and unstratified layers. It could be that they were only in use from around the mid-first century A.D. onwards. If so, it is tempting to think of them as the domestic table ware in use during the gap between the decline of Arretine and the introduction, *c.* A.D. 75/80, of the Early African Red Slip ware.

The forms found were:
1. Bowls (1a, decorated; 1b, plain).
2. Dishes (2a, with decorated and 2b, with plain rims).
3. Jugs.
4. Jars.
5. Cups.
6. Bowl/Lids.
7. Miscellaneous.
8. Bases.

1a. *Decorated Bowls.* (Fig. 47, 1–9 and Fig. 48, 10–22)

(i) *Rouletted flanged rim bowls.* (Fig. 47, 1)
1.   (P1110). A bowl with a sloping rim with a pointed lip above a flat horizontal flange, a rounded wall and a ring base. In a pink paste, it is colour coated dark red inside, below the base and on the lower half of the wall outside. The rim, flange and upper part of the wall are fired cream to pink. There are six rows of simple rouletting on the outside of the wall below the flange. Four examples, in two of which the colour was purplish.
      Cf. Cotton, 1979, 140 and fig. 57, 4, with fine rouletting.

(ii) *Rouletted carinated bowls.* (Fig. 47, 2–3)
2.   (P2655). A carinated bowl with an upright wall with an inturned and rounded lip, an oblique wall below the carination and a ring base. There are two grooves outside, below the lip, and the upright wall is decorated with three rows of simple rouletting. In pink paste, it is colour coated brown/red all over. Four examples, three of which are not completely coated and 1 was fired buff.
3.   (P49). Similar to no. 2 above, but with only one groove outside below the lip, and with the rouletting differently spaced. Four examples.
      Cf. Cotton, 1979, 140 and fig. 57, 7, which lacks most of the decoration.

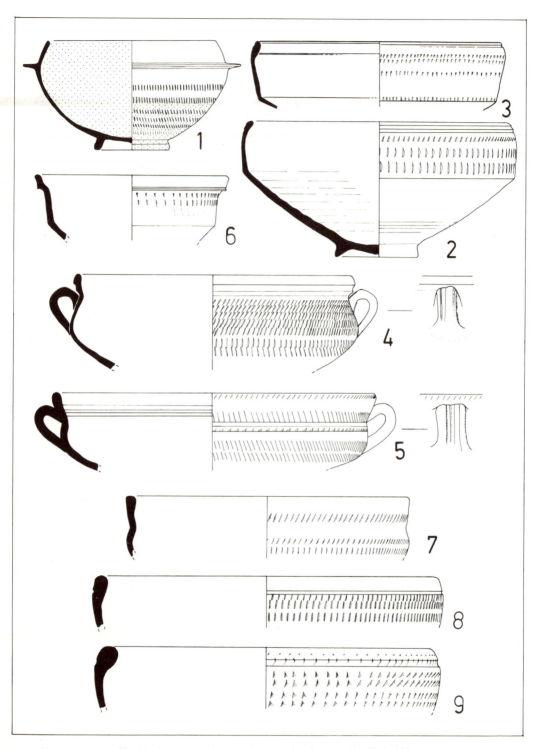

Fig. 47. Colour-coated wares. Rouletted bowls (nos.1–9). (Scale 1/3)

(iii) *Rouletted handled bowls with rounded walls and moulded rims* (Fig. 47, 4–7)

4. (P2688). A bowl with a moulded vertical rim and a well curved body. The base is missing. Two ribbon handles, externally grooved, spring from the body below the rim. The upper part of the body is decorated with 7 rows of rouletting consisting of simple oblique strokes. In red paste, colour coated red/brown all over. This form was very plentiful, 55 examples being found, with colouring varying from dark brown to light red, or fired buff with little remaining colour coating.

5. (P2689). An example with a simple rim form, and with the handle springing from the rim. There are two rows of rouletting on the outside of the rim, a row of triangular punchings below the rim and two lines of oblique line rouletting on the curved wall at the level of and below the point of attachment of the handle. In buff ware with traces of colour coating inside. Four examples.

6. (P2686). A variant rim form. Pink paste, fired self colour, with traces of dark brown colour coating. Evidence for handles was missing.

7. (P2690). A bowl with a simple vertical rim with a thickened rounded lip. There is a row of rouletting at the base of the rim and two rows, at least, on the curved wall. In pink paste, fired red, with the remains of dark brown colour coating. Evidence for handles was missing.

For bowls of this type, see Cotton, 1979, fig. 57, nos. 5 and 12.

(iv) *Rouletted bowls with rounded walls and a thickened inturned rim.* (Fig. 47, 8–9 and Fig. 48, 10–16)

Handles that might have belonged to this form were not found. The form, which was very plentiful, shows much variation in the rouletted decoration, and can be sub-divided, on rim form, into:

Group a. Those with a single groove below the rim which can be wide and well below the lip (nos. 8–9), shallow and often nearer the lip (nos. 10–11) and just outside the lip (nos. 12–13a).

Group b. Those with two grooves below the lip (nos. 14–15).

Group c. Those with a slight line, or with no grooves, below the lip (no. 16).

All variants of the fabric and colour coating occur.

Group a. (Fig. 47, 8–9 and Fig. 48, 10–13a)

8. (P2692). An example with a deep groove well below the lip. This bowl is decorated with simple vertical rouletted strokes. One of the commonest types, 52 rims being found.

9. (P2691). A larger bowl with a deep wide groove well below the lip with a rouletted decoration of triangular punches as well as a row of dots above the groove. In buff paste coated dark brown. Two examples.

At Posto, there were no exact analogies for the above two types.

10. (P2693). The groove is shallow and closer to the lip. This example is decorated with simple strokes. Fourteen examples.

11. (P2694). An example with a minimum of five rows of rouletting or triangular punches. Two examples.

Nos, 10 and 11 are both in pink paste with pink/red colour coating. No examples were found at Posto.

12. (P2695). A rim with the single groove close to the lip and with triangular punch rouletting. The majority of the other examples have stroke rouletting. In buff paste, fired buff, with a pink colour coating inside. Seventeen examples.

13. (P570). An unusual example, in dark red/brown paste with a similar colour coating on both sides, and with a more complex rouletted decoration.
13a. (P354). A small bowl with a pointed inturned rim with one external groove, and a single band of simple triangular punched rouletting. In buff paste with a brown wash. Two examples.

Group b. (Fig. 48, 14–15)
14. (P2696). A large bowl with two wide grooves below the thickened inturned lip, and a curved wall. The wall is decorated outside with six rows of vertical stroke rouletting. In buff paste, fired buff, it has a dark brown colour coating inside but a thinner patchy coating outside. Fifty-three examples.
15. (P605). An example with a variant pattern of rouletting. Four examples.
    For examples of this group, see Cotton, 1979, 140 and fig. 57, 2, 3 and 8.

Group c. (Fig. 48, 16)
16. (P249). A rim with a thickened inturned lip but with no external grooves. There is a minimum of six rows of triangular punched rouletting, but vertical and oblique strokes are also found in this type. In pale red paste, fired self, with a dark red colour coating. Twenty-one examples.
    For examples of this group, see Cotton, 1979, 140 and fig. 57, 1.

(v) *Rouletted bowls with 'pie-dish' rims.* (Fig. 48, 17)
17. (P2697). A bowl with an oblique wall and a 'pie-dish' or small beaded flanged rim. In pink paste, fired pink, it has a worn red colour coating inside and over the rim. The outside of the bowl is decorated with six rows of rouletting of oblique strokes.
    This type did not occur at Posto.

(vi) *Bases from rouletted bowls.* (Fig. 48, 18–21)
18. (P2698). A ring base from a large bowl, in pink paste with a light red colour coating on both sides. The remaining wall is decorated with three bands of rouletting of oblique strokes.
19. (P2699). A similar bowl which shows the disc centre underneath the base and which has six bands of fine rouletting of oblique strokes.
20. (P2700). Part of a ring base, in buff paste with a deep red colour coating on the outside. The rouletting is of deeper oblique strokes.
21. (P2701). A flat base, in pink paste fired buff. It has a row of oblique strokes outside the lower part of the wall.

(vii) *Bowls with barbotine decoration.* (Fig. 48, 22)
22. (P1091a). Part of the wall of a hemispherical bowl decorated with pine scales in barbotine. In rather coarse red paste, fired dull red, and with a red to brown colour coating outside. Two examples.
    Cf. Moevs, 1973, Form XXXVI, 239, no. 488 and pls. 4–6 and 86, an example from the group of unglazed pottery of the Claudian-Neronian period. The analogies quoted, which are dated to this period, are all glazed examples. These two unglazed examples may not be of the same date.

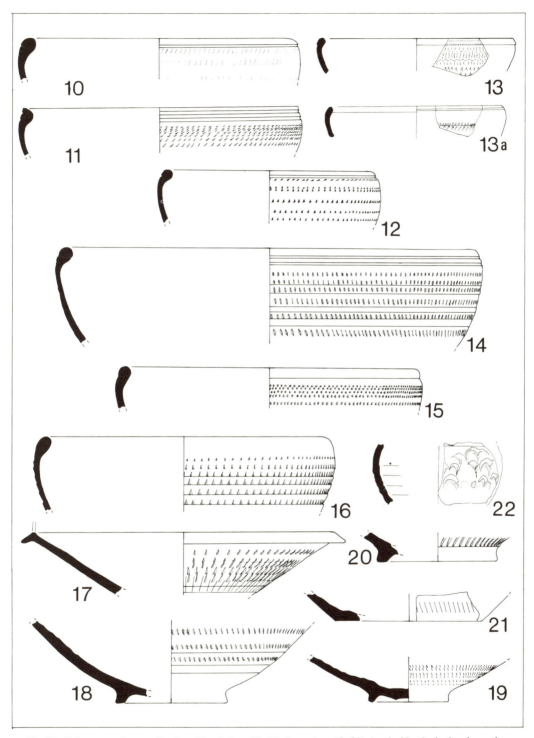

Fig. 48. Colour-coated wares. Rouletted bowls (nos.10–17); bases (nos.18–21); bowl with a barbotine decoration (no.22). (Scale: 1/3)

226 examples of these decorated colour-coated bowls were found at San Rocco (compared with 21 at Posto, cf. Cotton, 1979, 140 and fig. 57, 1–12). All came from destruction layers or top soil, and should have been derived from the Period IIA occupation. For a series of bowls decorated with rouletting or barbotine, cf. Duncan, 1964, Form 7, 56 and fig. 8, 32–4 and 37–42, from the Sutri kiln dated to c. A.D. 60–70. The barbotine decorated bowl, though in an unglazed fabric, might still be of Claudian-Neronian date (or A.D. 40–70). So that, at San Rocco, these decorated bowls in this ware, almost certainly from Period IIA layers, provide evidence that the structural alterations of that period were most probably not earlier than c. A.D. 50.

1b. *Plain Bowls.* (Fig. 49, 1–19)
The types found were:
Group a. With inturned rim and curved walls. (Fig. 49, 1–5)
Group b. With angled rim and carinated walls. (Fig. 49, 6–7)
Group c. With inturned rim and external grooving. (Fig. 49, 8–13)
Group d. With flat-topped rim. (Fig. 49, 14)
Group e. With turned-over rim. (Fig. 49, 15–6)
Group f. With a bead rim. (Fig. 49, 17)
Group g. Miscellaneous. (Fig. 49, 18–9)

Group a. With inturned rim and curved walls. (Fig. 49, 1–5)
1.   (P2551). A typical example. In light brown paste, fired cream, it has a brown colour coating inside and on the lower part of the wall outside. Six examples some of which are coated all over on both sides.
2.   (P2625). An example with a more marked shoulder. In orange paste, fired cream, with a red/brown colour coating as in no. 1 but it extends over the top of the rim outside.
3.   (P522). An example in thinner ware. The paste is pink or buff and the colour coating varies from red to a dull brown, usually only the inside and lower part of the outside wall being coated. 48 examples.
4.   (P373). This type has a thickened rim with a suggestion of a beading. In buff paste with a brown colour coating all over, though patchy outside below the rim.
5.   (P2564). A bead-rim bowl in buff paste with a brown/red colour coating on both sides. It has an inside groove below the thickened rim. A second example (not illustrated), in a pink paste with a brick-red colour coating, has the same thickened rim, but has two external groovings below the lip.

   These bowls were plentiful, 58 examples being found. All came from destruction or disturbed layers and were probably not in use before the Period IIA occupation. Cf. Duncan, 1964, Form 12, 57 and fig. 9. which were also colour-coated, but they were rare there. The form recalls that of Lamboglia's Form 21 in black glazed wares.

Group b. With an angled rim and carinated walls. (Fig. 49, 6–7)
6.   (P2702). A bowl with an angular inturned rim and a vertical wall above a carination. In buff paste, fired the same colour, with a dark brown colour coating inside and also outside below the carination. Thirty-seven examples, some with pink or grey paste.
7.   (P470). This type, though carinated, has a thickened rim which lacks the sharp angle of no. 6 above. In buff paste with a brown colour coating on both sides. Three examples.

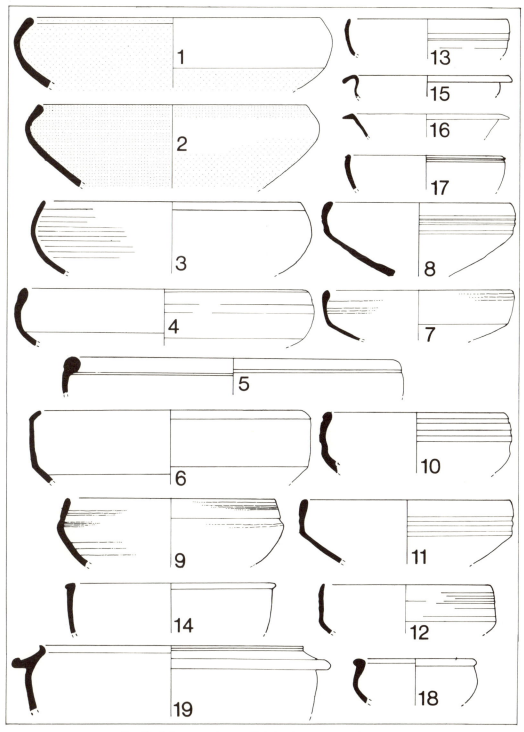

Fig. 49. Colour-coated wares. Plain bowls (nos. 1–19). (Scale 1/3)

The 40 examples of this group were all found in destruction or disturbed layers. They again probably all belong to the Period IIA occupation. Analogies for the type have not been traced.

Group c. With inturned rim and external grooving. (Fig. 49, 8–13)

8. (P2703). A plain bowl with a thickened inturned rim and a curved wall. There are three grooves outside below the lip and above a carinated shoulder. In buff paste with a purple/brown colour coating inside and outside below the grooving. Some examples are colour coated all over. Seven examples.

9. (P367). In this type the ill-defined external grooving is spaced above and below a ridge and the carination is more pronounced. In pink paste with a red to brown colour coating on both sides. Six examples.

10–11. (P2704) and (P593). Two examples, in pink paste with brick-red colour coating on both sides, which have variant external grooves. Another example, as no. 11, was in thinner brown ware.

12. (P268). An example in a hard thinner red/brown ware with three external grooves. Four examples.

13. (P334). An example typifying the simple variety with two external grooves. Six examples.

    None of this group was found in a stratified layer and they should be related to the Period IIA occupation. No analogies have been noted.

Group d. With flat-topped rims. (Fig. 49, 14)

14. (P519). A carinated bowl, with a stubby flattened rim and a slightly curved wall. In pink paste, coated red to pink inside and a dull dark brown outside and under the base which bears scratches. A similar form (P533) had a shorter rim. Four examples.

    All were unstratified and should be from Period IIA layers. Cf. Duncan, 1964, Forms 20/21, 59 and fig. 10, from the Sutri kiln dated *c.* A.D. 60–70.

Group e. With turned-over rim. (Fig. 49, 15–6)

15. (P458). The rim of a small bowl with a well-curved body and a turned-over rim with a rounded lip. In pink paste with a worn-away dark red colour coating. Four examples.

16 (P532). The rim of a small bowl with an oblique wall and a flattish turned-over rim with a thinned lip. In the same ware as no. 16. Two examples.

    All six bowls were unstratified.

Group f. With a bead-rim. (Fig. 49, 17)

17. (P2713). A small bowl with a bead-rim, in the same ware as nos. 11-2. Two examples, both unstratified.

Group g. Miscellaneous. (Fig. 49, 18–9)

18. (P2525). A small squat bowl with a thickened rolled rim. The outside of the wall is faintly rilled. In pink paste fired the same colour, with traces of a light brown colour coating.

19. (P1110). A large flanged rim bowl in brick-red paste fired red inside and dull yellow outside. The inside has a red colour coating and so has the lower part of the body outside.

This bowl is of the same form as the coarse ware examples of p. 222 and Fig. 55, 1–2.

Both nos. 18 and 19 were derived from Period IIA layers.

These plain bowls of groups *a-g*, 138 in number, were very plentiful at San Rocco. They are not certainly attested before Period IIA.

2. *Dishes.* (Fig. 50, 1–3)

Whilst the majority are plain, a few have rouletted decoration on the top of their flat rims.

2a. *With rouletted rims.* (Fig. 50, 1–3)

1. (P278). A large dish with a flaring rim and a curved wall. The top of the rim has a groove inside the lip, and a rouletted decoration of irregular herring-bone form. In brown/red paste with a similar colour coating on both sides. Two examples.
2. (P303). A dish with a flat rim and a lightly curved wall. The top of the rim is grooved, as in no. 1 above, and it is decorated with irregularly spaced punch holes. In pink paste with a pinkish/red colour coating on both sides. Three examples.
3. (P2705). Of the same form and ware as no. 2 above, this dish has the same groove on the top of the rim, but the rouletted decoration consists of two bands of simple oblique strokes.

2b. *With plain rims.* (Fig. 50. 4–10)

The types found are those with (a) turned-over rims; (b) flanged rims; (c) inturned rounded rims; and (d) thickened bevelled rims.

(a) *With turned over rims.* (Fig. 50. 4–5)

4. (P615). The rim is thinned and pointed and the wall is oblique. In hard red paste with a good deep red colour coating on both sides. Some examples are in brown paste with an orange/brown colour coating. Nine examples.
5. (P534). As no. 4 above, and in the same ware, but there is a groove on top of the rim inside the lip which is not thinned. Two examples.

Not illustrated. A rim fragment, in the same ware, has a second groove at its inner edge.

(b) *With flanged rims.* (Fig. 50, 6–8)

6. (P2608). The rim of a flanged dish, in buff paste with a red colour coating under and over the rim. Three examples, the second with a brown coating.
7. (P248). A shallow dish with a small flanged rim and small bead. In pink paste with a pink/red colour coating on both sides. Four examples.
8. (P610). A small dish with a flanged and beaded rim. In red paste with a dark red/brown colour coating on both sides. Four examples.

(c) *With inturned rounded rims.* (Fig. 50, 9)

9. (P517). A shallow dish of this type in a red paste with brick/red colour coating outside and brown inside. Six examples.

(d) *With bevelled rims.* (Fig. 50, 10)

10. (P2707). The rim of a dish of this type, in buff paste fired the same colour with a light brown colour coating inside and over the bevelled part of the rim.

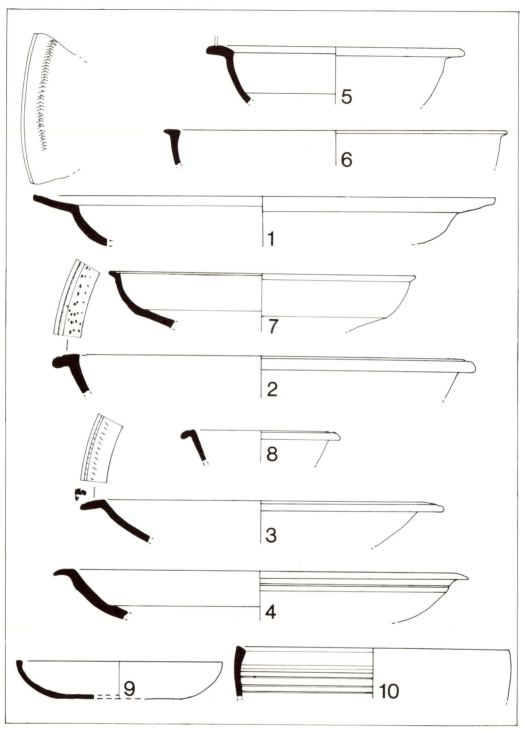

Fig. 50. Colour-coated wares. Dishes (nos.1–10). (Scale 1/3)

Provenance: At San Rocco, 36 examples of dishes were found in this ware, 6 decorated and 30 plain. Most came from destruction or unstratified layers, or from unsealed fills in the large kiln or the settling tank, but 2 were in layers that were probably not earlier than Period IIA.

Analogies for dishes, in this ware, have not been traced.

3. *Jugs.* (Fig. 51, 1–10)
(i) *Wide-mouthed jugs.* (Fig. 51, 1–8)

(a) *With everted rims and a simple lip.* (Fig. 51, 1–2)
1. (P525). A jug, in a hard thin ware of buff paste, fired buff, with a dark brown colour coating over the top of the outside and handle and inside the rim. The body is bulbous and slightly corrugated, the ribbon handle has two external grooves, arises below the lip and is attached above the point of maximum girth. Four examples.
2. (P520). The wall and base of a type like that of no. 1 above, but with more marked corrugations. In pink paste with red/brown colour coating on the outside and splashes on the inside.

(b) *With everted rims with a thickened rounded lip.* (Fig. 51, 3–4)
3. (P2560). The rim tends to be concave internally. In pink or buff paste with red or brown colour coating. Ten examples.
4. (P2534). A rim fragment with a ribbon handle, concave on the outside.

(c) *Everted rims with a groove inside the lip.* (Fig. 51, 5)
5. (P459). The simple everted rim has a groove inside. In buff paste with a red/brown colour coating outside and over the rim.

(d) *Trefoil mouthed.* (Fig. 51, 6)
6. (P2555). Part of the rim and handle of a trefoil-mouthed jug in brown paste with a dark brown colour coating on both sides. Two examples.

(e) *With collar rims.* (Fig. 51, 7)
7. (P2708). A collar rim with a thickened lip. In buff paste with a dark brown colour coating on both sides.

(f) *With flared rims with an external groove below the lip.* (Fig. 51, 8)
8. (P2601). Part of a rim of this type with part of a ribbon handle with a wide central external groove.

(ii) *Narrow-mouthed jugs.* (Fig. 51, 9–10)
9. (P2709). A rim with an everted simple lip and a small cordon at its base. In buff paste, with a red/brown colour coating outside and over the rim.
10. (P2710). A flat-topped everted rim fragment, in buff paste with a dark brown colour coating outside and over the rim.

Provenance: There were 20 examples of wide-mouthed jugs in this ware, none of which was attested earlier than Period IIA. The two examples of narrow-mouthed jugs were unstratified.

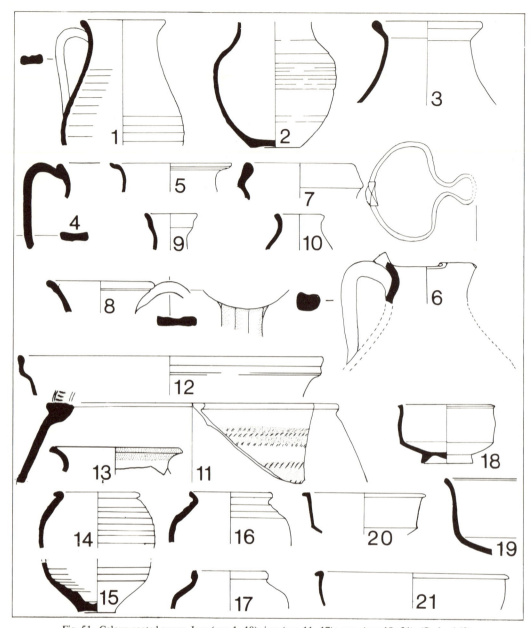

Fig. 51. Colour-coated wares. Jugs (nos. 1–10); jars (nos. 11–17); cups (nos. 18–21). (Scale: 1/3)

Nos. 1, 3–5 and 8 have rims and profiles not unlike those of Duncan, 1964, Form 30, though the Sutri examples were not in a colour-coated ware.

4. *Jars.* (Fig. 51, 11–17)

(i) *A rouletted jar.* (Fig. 51, 11)

11. (P2684). Only one decorated jar was found. In red/brown paste with a grey core at the rim, it was fired buff. Of barrel-shaped form, it had a flat rim, with two grooves on top, enclosing a row of rouletting. The outside is decorated with two bands of rouletting of oblique strokes. Over these, and on top of the rim, are bands of dark brown colour coating.

(ii) *Plain jars.* (Fig. 51, 12–17)

12. (P457). A jar with a moulded collar rim, in pink paste with a red/brown colour coating on both sides. Four examples.

13. (P81). A bevelled rim from a jar of S-shaped form. In soft buff ware, fired brown, with a brown colour coating inside and outside the rim.

14. (P391). A small jar with a folded back rim and a globular body corrugated externally. Fifteen examples, in all colour washes from pink and grey to yellow.

15. (P2714). A base from a jar of the same type as no. 14 above. Ten examples, in varying shades of colour-coated ware.

16. (P2716). A small jar, with an everted rim with a cordon at its base. It has a globular body which was probably corrugated. In buff paste with a brown/red colour coating outside and part way down the inside. Eight examples.

17. (P2717). An example with an almond-shaped rim and a high shoulder above a corrugated body. In gritty red paste with a red colour coating on both sides. Three further examples were in buff paste with a red/brown colour coating.

Provenance: At San Rocco there were 43 examples of jars in this ware, of which 8 may have been in Period IIA layers whilst the rest were unstratified.

5. *Cups.* (Fig. 51, 18–21)

18. (P1108). A fairly complete cup, with an oblique rim, a curved vertical body above a sharp carination and a pointed ring base. In pink paste, the inside and all the vessel outside below the carination has a red colour coating.

19. (P2621). A cup with a simple everted rim and a curved wall with a rounded shoulder. In pink paste with a red colour coating inside and orange outside. Two examples, the second having a sharper shoulder.

20. (P370). Small cups with a flat-topped rim and an oblique wall above a sharply carinated shoulder. Two examples.

21. (P461). A larger cup, or bowl, with a turned-over rim and a curved wall. In pink paste with a deep red colour coating on the inside and a poor thin red/brown outside. Two examples.

Provenance: Of these seven examples, two were from layers probably of Period IIA date. For the cup, or bowl, of no. 21, cf. Duncan, 1964, Form 15, 54 and fig. 9, 56–57, c. A.D. 60–70, though the Sutri example is larger and is certainly a bowl. It too was in colour-coated ware.

6. *Bowl/Lids.* (Fig. 52, 1–6)

(i) *With simple rims.* (Fig. 52, 1–5)

1. (P523). A large example with a simple rim and an oblique wall. In pink paste with a brown/red colour coating on both sides. Six examples, five being of smaller size.

2. (P2712). This is a smaller shallower version of no. 1 above which shows the ring base or knob top. In brick-red paste with a similar colour coating on both sides.

3. (P448). In this type the wall is curved. In buff paste with a red/brown colour coating on both sides. Two examples.

4. (P604). An example with a very vertical wall. In buff paste with a golden to dark brown colour coating on both sides. Three examples, the other two in red paste but with a similar colour coating.

5. (P375). An example in red paste with a dark red colour coating on both sides but brown on the outside below the lip. The rim is almond-shaped. Two examples.

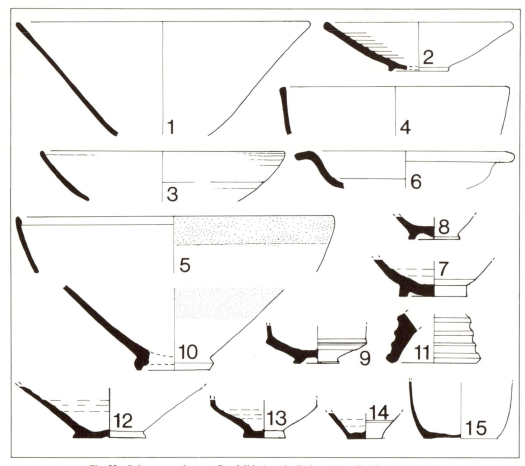

Fig. 52. Colour-coated wares. Bowl/lids (nos.1–6); bases (nos.7–15). (Scale: 1/3)

(ii) *With turned-down rims.* (Fig. 52, 6)

6.   (P2616). A domed example, in buff paste, fired pink and cream, with remains of dark brown colour coating.

Provenance: Of these 15 examples, five were probably from Period IIA layers and the rest were derived.

7. *Miscellaneous forms.* (Not illustrated)

Pieces not included in the above type series were:— (a) a nozzle from a feeding vessel, in buff paste with red/brown colour coating outside, and (b) some of the many broken off ring, ribbon or ribbed handles found which probably belonged to this series.

8. *Bases.* (Fig. 52, 7–15)

(i) *Ring bases.* (Fig. 52, 7–10)

7.   (P2724). A ring base with a narrow hollowing underneath. Five examples.

8.   (P2725). A type with a wide hollowing underneath and the centre an inverted dome. Eight examples.

9.   (P2726). The hollowing below the base is almost flat. Two examples.

10. (P277). The base of a large bowl with a moulded ring foot. In buff paste, fired pink/ buff, and colour coated red inside and on the outside of the wall except for the lower part and under the base.

(ii) *Pedestal base.* (Fig. 52, 11)
11. (P483). A tall pedestal base with four external cordons. In pink paste with a dull red colour coating all over, except at the top of the underneath of the base.

(iii) *Pad bases.* (Fig. 52, 12–13)
12. (P2728). An example of a pad base with an oblique wall. The paste and colour coating vary. 25 examples.
13. (P2729). An example of a cup with a pad base. Most of these are in buff paste with an orange/red colour coating on one or both sides. 13 examples.

(iv) *Flat bases.* (Fig. 52, 14–15)
14. (P2731). An example of small size with an oblique wall. In red paste with a red/brown colour coating on both sides. 12 examples.
15. (P2730). An example of large size with a curved wall. The paste and colour coating vary. 12 examples.
Provenance: Of these 77 bases, 19 were found in layers that could be of Period IIA date and the rest were in destruction layers or were unstratified. The number of bases found emphasises the use of this ware, at San Rocco, probably from *c.* A.D. 50 onwards.

VIII. *DARK AND LIGHT SURFACED WARES*

As in the Posto report, these two wares are considered together, so that similar forms are not duplicated. For notes on the forms and fabrics see Cotton, 1979, 148–72.

The Posto categories described as 'Late Roman hard red ware' and 'Late Roman colour-coated ware' are not given in this report, as the period in which these occurred, at Posto, was later than the end of the occupation at San Rocco.

The categories described below are:
1. Casseroles.
2. Dishes, including baking dishes and plates.
3. Bowls.
4. Jugs or flagons.
5. Jars.
6. Lids.

1. *Casseroles.* (Not illustrated)
At San Rocco, only two examples were found in fabric A (i.e. dark-surfaced or cooking-pot ware, cf. Cotton 1979, 148). They are of the types shown in Cotton, 1979, 149 and fig. 44, 1–5. One (P581) consisted of part of a rim with its handle, cf. Cotton, 1979, 149 and fig. 44, 1; and the other (P325), again with part of the rim and a handle, was like Cotton, 1979, 149 and fig. 44, 2.
Provenance: Both were unstratified, in the tank on the upper terrace and in a destruction layer outside the east retaining wall.

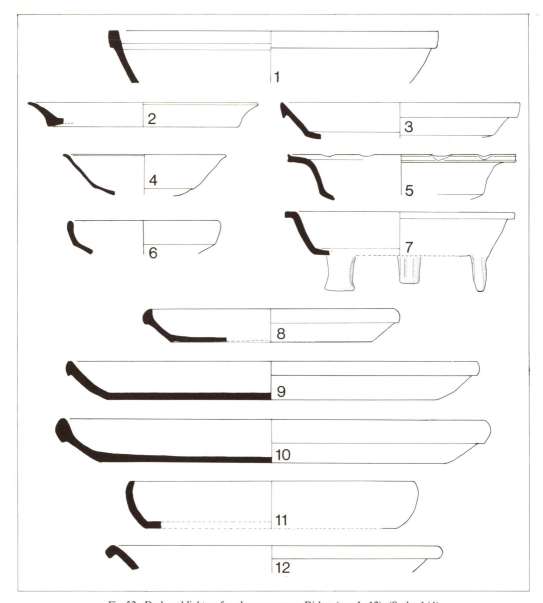

Fig. 53. Dark and light surfaced coarse wares. Dishes (nos.1–12). (Scale: 1/4)

With reference to the Posto casserole types of Cotton, 1979, 149 and fig. 44, 6–7, San Rocco produced many examples, but they were no longer in the same dark-surfaced ware, but were in a thinnish red ware, though some are charred from use. These have been described here in the bowl series (see pp. 222–223 and Fig. 55, 1–2) rather than as casseroles.

2. *Dishes.* (Figs. 53, 1–10 and 54, 1–8)
Dishes are described under the following headings:
(i) Dishes in fabric A, or dark-surfaced ware. (Fig. 53, 1)
(ii) Dishes in fabric D, or light surfaced wares. (Fig. 53, 2–7)
(iii) Dishes in fabric B, or Pompeian Red ware. (Fig. 53, 8–10)

(iv) Large baking dishes or cooking stands in a heavy coarse ware. (Fig. 54, 1–7)
(v) Baking plates or serving dishes. (Fig. 54, 8).

(i) *Dishes in fabric A*. (Fig. 53, 1)
1.   (P499). A dish, in heavy coarse ware, with a squared collar rim. Other types were:
     (P2529), cf. Cotton, 1979, 151 and fig. 45, 15; (P2593), cf. Cotton, 1979, 151 and
     fig. 45, 10; and another as Cotton, 1979, 151 and fig. 45, 11; (P147/103a-b), cf.
     Cotton, 1979, 151 and fig. 45, 6–7.
Provenance: (P147/103a-b) came from a Period I layer, (P2529) was derived in a Period
          II layer and the rest were unstratified.
   As with the casseroles above, dishes in this ware are scarce at San Rocco.

(ii) *Dishes in fabric D*. (Fig.53, 2–7)
2.   (P2629). A shallow dish, in bright red ware, with a simple rim and a curved wall above
     a flat raised base.
3.   (P536). A type with a collar rim and an oblique wall above a carination. In red ware.
     Two examples.
4.   (P2609). A small dish with a thinned rim and a thin oblique wall above a sharp carina-
     tion. Thin red ware, misfired to a grey colour.
5.   (P2776). A carinated dish or bowl with a flared rim, misfired as no. 4 above.
6.   (P2548). A shallow type with a simple vertical rim and a curved wall above a carina-
     tion.
7.   (P2636). Part of a footed dish or cooking stand, with a flat topped rim with a squared
     lip, an oblique wall above a flat base which stands on three rectangular feet, hollowed
     internally.
        Cf. Dyson, 1976, 77, Class 4 and 92, Class 6, where this form is described as a
     'legged skillet' with a curved floor, or as a flat-floored version of the form. These came
     from Deposit 4 (V–D), or from an area deserted shortly before 70 B.C. The later
     form, with the flat bottom, came from Deposit 5 (PD), dated from the first quarter of
     the first century B.C. to early in the last quarter of that century. The San Rocco
     example (and that of the baking dish of Fig. 54, 7) are of the later or flat-bottomed
     variety, but no exact parallels for their rim forms can be quoted. At San Rocco they
     could well go back to the Periods I/IA occupation, though not attested there before
     Period II.
Not illustrated. Dishes with simple rims and oblique or curved walls were also found. For
(P608), cf. Cotton, 1979, 151 and fig. 45, 15; and one as Cotton, 1979, 151 and fig. 45, 13.
Provenance: Nos. 3 and 7 came from Period II layers; the rest were unstratified.

(iii) *Dishes in fabric B, or Pompeian Red ware*. (Fig. 53, 8–12)
For a note on the ware, forms and dating of these dishes, see Cotton, 1979, 148–9.
8–10. (P2539), (P2761), (P2760). Three dishes, of type 1, of varying sizes and rim form.
1 example of no. 8, 4 examples of no. 9 and 7 examples of no. 10.
        Cf. Cotton, 1979, 149–51 and fig. 45, 1–4. This is the earlier form of the first century
B.C. onwards.
11. (P616). A dish of the type 2 form, with a slacker shape and a simpler rim, slightly
     inturned. Five examples.
        Cf. Cotton 1979, 151 and fig. 45, 5.

12. (P432b). A variant form with a rounded turned-over rim. Burnished inside and over the top of the rim. Three examples.

Provenance: At San Rocco, the type 1 form is, as at Posto, attested as being in use from the first century B.C., but there is no evidence available for the initiation of the type 2 form. 1 example of no. 12 came from a Period I/IA layer and another from a Period II layer.

(iv) *Large baking dishes or cooking stands.* (Fig. 54, 1–7)

This is a form which scarcely existed at Posto. It is in heavy, gritty coarse paste, grey or red in colour, and it is fired to grey, red or buff. These vessels probably served as baking dishes, or as serving platters for hot food.

1. (P390). An example of the lighter type with a curved wall ending in a rounded rim and with a flat base. Two examples.
2. (P515). A shallow thick-walled dish with a bevelled rim.
3. (P302). A type similar to no. 2, but with a pointed rim.
4–5. (P3080) and (P301). Two very similar dishes. No. 4 has a thinned pointed rim (lacking in no. 5) and both have a constriction between the wall and the base. No. 5 shows a break where a foot could have been attached, and a circular hole in its wall to lighten the weight or to let steam escape. Two examples of no. 4 and one of no. 5.
6. (P286). Similar in form to no. 4, this dish is distinguished by a decoration of finger-tip impressions on the top of its rim. It also has a hole pierced in the wall. A third (P2583) had the top of the rim hollowed.
7. (P292). A more complete example which shows the form of the triangular feet and, again, has at least one hole in its wall.

Eight feet, from stands of the type of no. 7, also of triangular form, were found. One very large rectangular foot (12 cm. high and 4 cm. thick at the tip) must have come from a very large stand.

Provenance: The 11 examples (and 8 feet) were all in destruction layers or top soil, except for no. 5 and the very large foot. These came from Periods II/IIA layers.

These very heavy examples do not seem to be shown in the Cosa series, but they may be later versions of the lighter form quoted in Dyson, 1976, 69 and fig. 18, 7.

(v) *Baking plates or serving dishes.* (Fig. 54, 8)

8. (P78). A plate with a very oblique wall and a hollowed rim top decorated with a pie-crust edge and with a pattern of indented circles on the rim top. In thick gritty brick-red paste fired the same colour. A second example (P295), in the same ware, lacked the circle pattern. A third example (P305) was similar to and in the same ware as the last.

Provenance: Of the three examples found, two came from Period II layers, and could have been derived from the Periods I/IA occupations, and the third was in a destruction layer.

3. *Bowls.* (Figs. 55, 1–18; 56, 19–32; and 57, 33–42)

Fabric. These vessels were found in fabrics A, C, D and E.

Bowls are described under the following headings:

(i) Flanged rim bowls in fabrics A and E. (Fig. 55, 1–2)

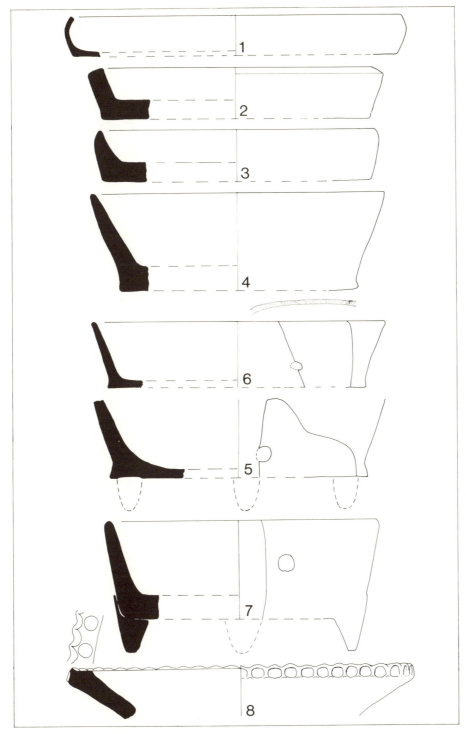

Fig. 54. Dark and light surfaced coarse wares. Large baking dishes, cooking stands and baking plates (nos. 1–8). (Scale 1/4)

(ii) Rilled ware bowls in fabric E. (Fig. 55, 3)
(iii) Other bowls in fabric A. (Fig. 55, 4–15)
(iv) Bowls in fabric C. (Fig. 55, 16–18)
(v) Bowls in fabrics C and D. (Fig. 57, 19–32 and 57, 33–40)
(vi) Bowls with internal ledges in fabrics C and D. (Fig. 57, 41–42)

(i) *Flanged rim bowls in fabrics A and E.* (Fig. 55, 1–2)
Some, but not all of them, in fabric A, are charred and were used as casseroles (cf. p. 217).
Others, in fabric E, show no sign of charring.
1.   (P365). An example in fabric A. The flanged rim, which served well as a lid seating,
      has a rounded lip and beading. Eight examples.
2.   (P518). An example in fabric E. Both the lip and beading are hooked. Twenty-one
      examples.
Provenance: Five examples of no. 1 and 10 examples of no. 2 came from the Periods
          II/IIA occupation layers.
    Cf. Cotton, 1979, 149 and fig. 44, 6–7. There, this type was not found in a stratified con-
text. At San Rocco, it is attested from Period II onwards, but it is more plentiful, in fabric E,
in the latest occupation level. This type was not found in the Sutri kiln (Duncan, 1964),
which suggests that it was later in date than A.D. 60–70 to which that kiln is dated. Nor are
they figured at Sutri II (Duncan, 1965) or Gabii (Vegas, 1968). The differing numbers
found between the earlier and later levels show the change of fabric from A to E.

(ii) *Rilled ware bowls in fabric E.* (Fig. 55, 3)
For this type, see Cotton, 1979, 158 and fig. 47, 1–4. At San Rocco they were found in
fabric E, but they sometimes showed evidence of charring below the carination. In a typical
example the rim is almond-shaped, with a more or less pronounced groove on its lip. The
wall is vertical above a carination, with marked internal grooving. The wall below the carination has marked external 'rilling', and the base sags. At San Rocco there were 22
examples.
3.   (P2614). An atypical example, with an oblique wall. The internal groovings are
      faintly marked, and there is no 'rilling' externally.
Provenance: About 50 per cent of the examples of typical form came from Period II/IIA
          occupation layers, but 1 example came from a Period II layer. The atypical
          example of no. 3 was unstratified.
    For an account of this type cf. Dyson, 1976, 141, Class 13 and fig. 54, LS6–7. The type
is Hayes, 1972, Form 197, known from N. Africa, Spain and Italy. It was concluded that
this was a ceramic type which was not local but was widely distributed over the Mediterranean, within the chonological period of the 'Late Shops' group at Cosa, i.e. late first to
early third century A.D. This dating coincides with that of Period IIA at San Rocco.

(iii) *Other bowls in fabric A.* (Fig. 55, 4–15)
4–6. (P364), (P524) and (P540). Three bowls, in fabric A, of differing profiles, with
      turned-back rims. Sherds show that these bowls can have a carinated shoulder.
      Twenty-five examples of no. 4; five of no. 5 and one of no. 6.
7–9. (P2603), (P366) and (P2522). Three similar bowls, but the rims are horizontal and
      are hollowed for a lid seating. Two examples of no. 7; eight of no. 8 and one of no. 9.
          For nos. 4–9, there was no evidence for handles, so they are described here as bowls

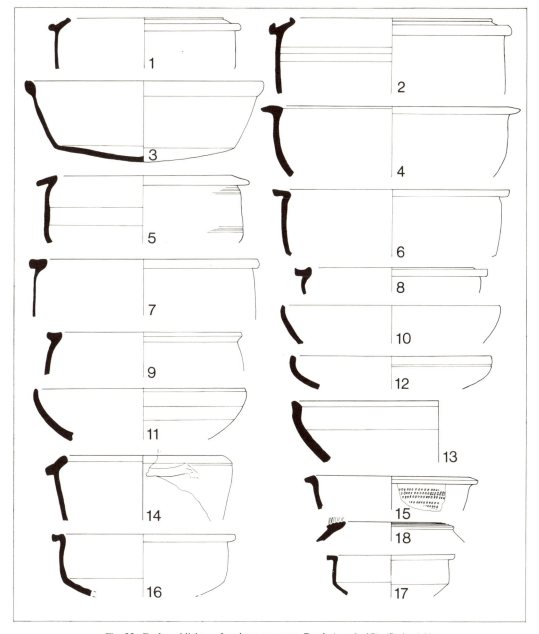

Fig. 55. Dark and light surfaced coarse wares. Bowls (nos.1–18). (Scale: 1/4)

rather than as casseroles, although most of them have been charred by fire, probably did have handles and could also be called casseroles.

Cf. Cotton, 1979, 156 and fig. 44, 8–9, which have wider rims. At Posto, the type goes back to period IA. For no. 4, see also Dyson, 1976, 102, Class 13, and fig. 37, 109. This example, described as a wide-mouthed bowl, is in the equivalent of our fabric D, but is related to the 'round-bottomed pans' in kitchen ware of an earlier period. The analogy is from the coarse ware of the pottery dump deposit, dated to the earlier three-quarters of the first century B.C.

For no. 5 cf. Dyson, 1976, 142–143, Class 22 and fig. 56, LS23. These are described as saucepans in kitchen ware, and the deposit is dated as late first to early third century B.C.. But close in form are those of Sutri, Duncan, 1964, Form 20, 59 and fig. 10, 67, dated c. 60–70 A.D.

For no. 6, with an upturned rim, cf. Sutri, Duncan, 1964, Form 20, 59 and fig. 10, 70, which is in a finer ware, but is of the same date as above.

Whilst the San Rocco examples of bowls (or saucepans) in this ware are not attested before Period II, they did probably originate in Periods I/IA, but would seem to have continued in use well into the first century A.D.

10. (P502). A bowl with a curved wall and an inturned rim which is grooved on top. Three examples, whilst a fourth has a bead rim with a groove on top.
11. (P501). A type like that of no. 10, but it lacks the groove on top. There are faint grooves on the outer wall. Fifteen examples.
12. (P539). A shallow bowl with a simple rim which has a groove below it.
13. (P2771). An example in a very heavy coarse paste with white grits. It has a curved wall and an internally thickened rim.

Nos. 12–13 are bowl/dishes of simple form which were probably in use from Periods I/IA times onwards. No. 10 is the equivalent, in fabric A, of the bowl/dish of Fig. 56, 31, in fabric E.

14. (P2520). A bowl with an inturned rim which forms an angle with the wall externally. Below the angle, there are horizontal lug handles, of which only one persisted. Two examples.
15. (P2772). A bowl with a stubby flanged rim. The outside wall has five or more rows of rouletting of impressed squares.

Provenance: Period II. Nos. 6, 12, 14 (1 ex.).
　　　　　　　Periods II/IIA. Nos. 4 (1 ex.), 5 (3 exs.), 8 (3 exs.), 9, 10 (1 ex.), 11 (10 exs.), 14 (1 ex.).
The rest were in unstratified layers.

In general, the bowls of the above forms, in fabric A, whether they were used as bowls, casseroles or saucepans, belong chiefly to the Periods II/IIA occupation, but the three examples from the Period II layers could have been derived from the Period I occupation. The A fabric tends to be replaced in Periods II/IIA by the D and E fabrics.

(iv) *Bowls in fabric C.* (Fig. 55, 16–18)

16–17. (P2642) and (P368). Two carinated bowls in this ware, of differing sizes. The rim of no. 16 is hollowed for a lid; that of no. 17 is flat. One example of no, 16 and two of no. 17.
18. (P2619). A rim fragment, from a bowl or jar, with an oblique rim with four grooves on its upper surface.

Provenance: No. 18 was from a Periods II/IIA layer; the others were unstratified.
No close analogies have been traced.

(v) *Bowls in fabrics D and E.* (Figs, 56, 19–33 and 57, 33–42)
This group is sub–divided, on rim form, into those with:
(a) Decorated rims in fabric D. (Fig. 56, 19–22)
(b) Flanged rims in fabrics D and E. (Fig. 56, 23–30)
(c) Inturned rims in fabrics D and E. (Figs. 56, 31–32 and 57, 33–35)

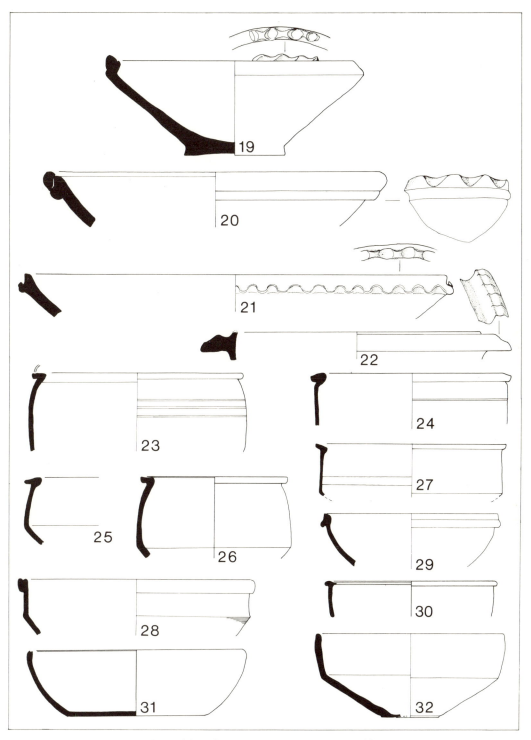

Fig. 56. Dark and light surfaced coarse wares. Bowls (nos.19–32). (Scale 1/4)

(d) Grey rim bowl/lids in fabric E. (Not illustrated)
(e) Oblique flat–topped rims in fabric D. (Fig. 57, 36–39)
(f) Rounded rims in fabric E. (Fig. 57, 40)

(a) *Decorated rims in fabric D.* (Fig. 56, 19–22)

19. (P2559). A bowl, in coarse heavy dull red paste fired the same colour inside and with a smoothed pink/cream surface outside. It has a flat rim, an oblique wall and a pad base. On top of the rim, one strip persists of a band with finger–tip impressions, which would have served as a handhold.

20. (P572). A sherd from a large bowl, in pink paste with a cream smoothed surface on both sides. The flanged rim is covered with a thick band decorated with finger–tip impressions. Whether this is just a handhold, or is continuous, could not be determined. Three examples.

21. (P2582). A flanged rim bowl in which the top of the flange has been decorated in 'pie-–crust' fashion. This bowl has been misfired to a black to grey colour.

22. (P594). A large flanged rim bowl, with oblique grooves on the top of the flange.

Provenance: Nos. 19, 21 and 22 came from Periods II/IIA occupation layers; no. 20 was unstratified.

For no. 21 cf. Dyson, 1976, 89 and fig. 28, 8, where they are described as flanged pans of Class 4 type. They occurred in the pottery dump deposit dated *c.* 75–20 B.C. A related example, from the 'late shops' deposit of late first to early third century A.D. (145 and fig. 57, LS37) was thought to be a stray, but its dating fits also with the San Rocco example.

(b) *Flanged rims in fabrics D and E.* (Fig. 56, 23–30)

23. (P276). An example with a short horizontal flange with a groove on the top of its lip, and with three grooves on the outside of the wall. Nine examples, three of which lack the grooves on the lip, and two of which have two outside grooves.

24. (P2543). The stubby flange is turned down and is not grooved. There is only one groove on the outside of the wall.

25. (P2588). The plain turned–down flange has a pointed lip, there are no grooves on the outside wall and the bowl is carinated. Four examples.

26. (P2773). The flange is nearly horizontal and the bowl is carinated. Four examples.

27. (P488). A carinated bowl with an upturned flange with a thinned lip.

28. (P379). A stubby flange with a beaded rim from a carinated bowl. Ten examples.

29. (P2630). A type with a drooping flange.

30. (P442). A small flange above a slightly curved wall. Six examples.

Nos. 26–30 were in fabric D; some of no. 28, and the rest, were in fabric E.

Provenance: Periods I/IA. No. 30 (1 ex.)

Periods II/IIA. Nos. 24, 25 (2 exs.), 26 (1 ex.), 28 (1 ex.), 29 (1 ex.), 30 (2 exs.).

The rest were unstratified.

For a series of carinated bowls with flanged rims, or with projecting rims, with or without grooves on them as nos. 23–27 above, cf. Sutri, Duncan, 1964, Forms 18 and 20–4, 59 and fig. 10, from the kiln dated *c.* A.D. 60–70. Cf. also Dyson, 1976, 116, Class 6, 1–5 and fig. 42, 22II–1 to–5, from the deposit dated as Caligulan to Early Claudian. At San Rocco, these bowls were probably in use during the Period IIA occupation.

(c) *Inturned rims in fabrics D and E.* (Figs. 56, 31−2 and 57, 33−5)

31. (P2590). A fairly complete bowl with an inturned rim, grooved on top, a curved wall and a flat base.

32. (P2643). This type, which is fired orange, has a simple almost vertical rim, with a faint groove outside and a slightly curved wall above a carinated shoulder with a small flat base.

33. (P441). A hemispherical bowl with a simple rim, almost vertical but slightly inturned. Five examples.

34. (P2775). A small bowl with a simple inturned rim. Four examples.

35. (P2565). The inturned rim of this large bowl is almond-shaped and there is an external groove below the rim.

Nos. 32−3 were in fabric D; nos. 31 and 34−5 were in fabric E.

Provenance: No. 33 came from a Periods I/IA layer; nos. 31 and 2 exs. of no. 33 were from Periods II/IIA layers. The rest were unstratified.

For no. 31, cf. Dyson, 1976, 119 and fig. 45, 22II−24, Class 1 of flat-bottomed pans in kitchen ware. The suggested range of dates, at Cosa, is *c.* 100 B.C. to A.D. 50. The type is also found in a first century A.D. deposit at Ostia.

For nos. 33−4, cf. Dyson, 1976, 100−1, and fig. 36, PD99, Class 1 coarse ware bowls, a type which has a long history at Cosa.

(d) *Grey rim bowl/lids.* (Not illustrated)

For this type see Cotton, 1979, 158 and fig. 47, 5. These reversible vessels served as lids for rilled ware bowls. San Rocco produced 11 examples.

Provenance: Two examples came from Periods II/IIA layers, but the rest were unstratified.

Cf. Dyson, 1976, 126 and fig. 48, 22II−74 and fig. 49, 22II−75−77, where they are described as lid/plates. They are common in this group dated to Caligulan to Early Claudian times, and continue into the second century A.D. At San Rocco they belong to the Period IIA occupation: the Posto examples were unstratified.

(e) *Oblique flat-topped rims in fabric D.* (Fig. 57, 36−9)

36. (P2568). A small bowl with a well-rounded shoulder and a wavy line groove below the rim. Two examples.

37. (P603). A large heavy bowl with an oblique rim which has a faint groove on its inner side, and with a well-rounded body.

38. (P402). This type differs from that of no. 37 in having a less rounded body and it lacks the groove on the rim. Three examples.

39. (P2524). In this type the rim is thickened internally. Two examples.

Provenance: Period II. No. 38 (1 ex.).

       Periods II/IIA. Nos. 36 (1 ex.), 38 (1 ex.) and 39 (2 exs.).

For nos. 37−8, cf. Duncan, 1964, Form 17, 58 and fig. 9, 61, and Form 51, 67 and fig. 16, 186, from the kiln dated as *c.* A.D. 60−70.

(f) *Rounded rims in fabric E.* (Fig. 57, 40)

40. (P2524). A bowl with a well-rounded rim and body. From the Periods II/IIA occupation layers.

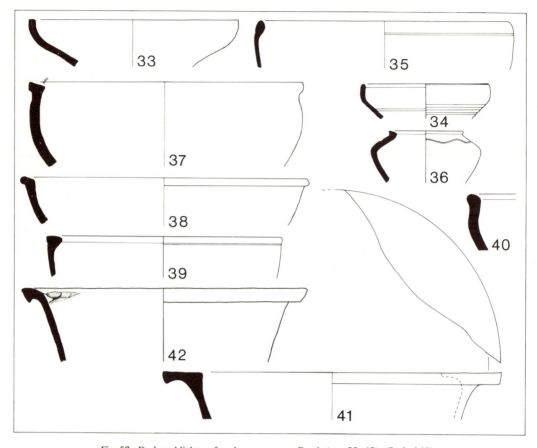

Fig. 57.   Dark and light surfaced coarse wares. Bowls (nos.33–42). (Scale 1/4)

(vi) *Bowls with internal ledges in fabrics C and D.* (Fig 57, 41–2)

These bowls are large and heavy and they have internal ledges at rim level for ease in lifting them.

41. (P289). The rim is wide and flaring and the lifting ledge is semi-circular. They are fairly common at San Rocco, 12 examples being in the red paste of fabric D.

42. (P15). In this type the flared rim is shorter. The internal ledge was broken away on the example illustrated, but others show that, though again semi-circular, it projected a short way into the interior of the bowl. Six examples in fabric C.

*Provenance:*Only 1 example of no. 42 was stratified in a Periods II/IIA layer. The form belongs, most probably, to the Period IIA occupation

4. *Jugs or Flagons.* (Fig. 58, 1–21)

For a note on the definition of jugs or flagons, see Cotton, 1979, 153. As at Posto, these two forms are grouped together, but some of the San Rocco examples do have a spout. *Fabric.* They were found in fabrics C and D.

   The forms are sub-divided into:

(i) Narrow-mouthed (Fig. 58, 1–10)

(ii) Cup-mouthed with narrow necks (Fig. 58, 11–15)

(iii) Trefoil-mouthed. (Fig. 58, 16)

(iv) Wide-mouthed. (Fig. 58, 17–21)

(i) *Narrow-mouthed.* (Fig. 58, 1–10)

1. (P2634). The upper part of a jug in fabric D. The rim is everted above a narrow sloping neck and the upper part of the body is globular. The plain handle springs from the neck and is attached to the shoulder above the point of maximum girth. Five examples.

2. (P2765). A type which, though of the same form as no. 1 above, has a wider mouth and the handle is hollowed externally. Three examples in fabric C and 11 in fabric D.

3. (P2581). The rim, neck and part of the handle, in fabric D. The rim is thickened and flat-topped above a narrow vertical neck. The two-ribbed ribbon handle springs from the neck nearly horizontally. It is decorated at the sides of its neck with two 'confetti' roundels. Two examples.

4. (P2762). The rim and neck of a vessel in fabric D. The ware is thicker than that of the others in this group and the sherd is very worn. The rim is turned over above a vertical neck. The scar of a handle root is immediately under the rim.

5. (P2596). A rim in fabric D. It has a small flange. The handle springs from the neck.

6. (P2763). An example, in fabric D, with a hollowed rim with a pointed lip. The two-ribbed handle springs from the neck below the rim and arches above rim level.

7. (P618). This example, in fabric C, has an outward sloping neck, which ends in a simple rounded rim above two ill-defined grooves. There is a small cordon at the junction of the neck and body. The handle was missing.

8. (P546). A rim in fabric D. The vertical neck swells at the top and ends in an inturned thinned pointed lip. The handle was missing. Three examples, one showing part of a spout.

9. (P564). A wider mouth, with an oblique neck and bevelled rim. In fabric D. Two examples.

10. (P2597). Part of a rim, in fabric C, which is of collar form.

Provenance: Of the 31 examples of these types, three examples of no. 2 and two of no. 8 came from Period II layers; one example of no. 1, two of no. 2 and one of no. 7 came from Periods II/IIA layers. The rest were unstratified. Therefore, only nos. 2 and 8 are attested before *c.* 30 B.C.

For no. 1, cf. Cotton 1979, 155 and fig. 46, 24–5, which were unstratified.

For nos. 5–6, cf. Vegas, 1968, 32 and fig. 11, 106–7, which are compared with the Augustan type of Haltern 46 (Vegas, 1968, 53).

For no. 8, cf. Dyson, 1976, 111, and fig. 41, 169 from deposit 5, dated from the first quarter of the first century B.C. until early in the last quarter of that century. On these analogies, nos. 2, 5, 6 and 8, at least, of San Rocco should certainly go back to the Periods I/IA occupation.

(ii) *Cup-mouthed with narrow necks.* (Fig. 58, 11–15)

11. (P2612). The upper part of a jug or flagon in fabric D. The cup-shaped rim, with a rounded lip, has two external grooves. A narrow curved neck slopes out to a bulbous body. The ribbon handle, with an external groove, springs from the neck below the rim and is attached on the top of the shoulder.

12. (P617). An example, in fabric C, which resembles no. 11 above, but the wider ribbon handle has three well-defined grooves outside.

13. (P506). A larger version of the type which has a pointed lip to an oblique rim which lacks the external grooving. The short neck is vertical and the handle springs from it below the rim.

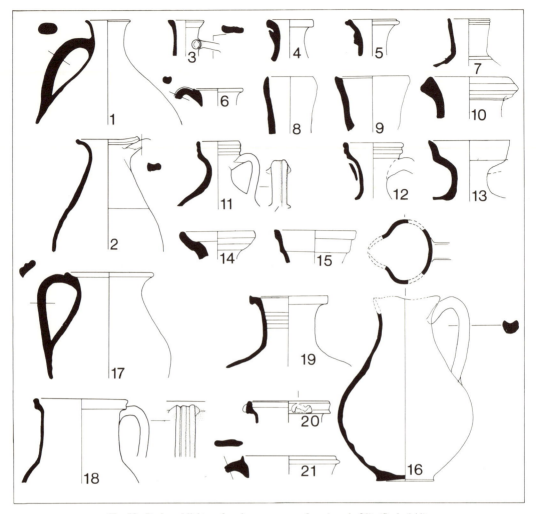

Fig. 58. Dark and light surfaced coarse wares. Jugs (nos. 1–21). (Scale 1/4)

14. (P2764). Part of a rim (the handle is missing) in fabric D. The rim, above the neck, curves to a rounded lip.

15. (P545). Part of a rim in fabric D with a deep cream slip. The handle is missing and the slightly cupped collar rim has a projecting lip and an angular junction with the neck. Two examples.

Provenance: Of the six examples of this form, only one example of no. 15 came from a Period II layer, but three examples of nos. 11, 12 and 14 came from Periods II/IIA occupation layers, and the other two were unstratified.

   For no. 11, cf. Cotton, 1979, 155 and fig. 46, 18, which was unstratified. Cf. also Duncan, 1964, Form 35, 64 and fig. 14, 141, from the kiln of *c.* A.D. 60–70, though there the mouth is wider.

(iii) *Trefoil-mouthed.* (Fig. 58, 16)

16. (P2640). A fairly complete jug in fabric C. The trefoil-shaped mouth has a pointed lip with a spout above a short oblique neck. The body is piriform and the pad base is

slightly convex. The ribbon handle, deeply hollowed outside, springs from the upper part of the neck and is attached above the point of maximum girth.

Not illustrated. (P252). The rim and neck of another example which was in thicker ware of fabric D. The lip is flattened and the short neck was more vertical. Four examples. A third variety (P2766) had part of a rim of this type, but the vessel was neckless. The fabric had a coarse and rather heavy paste of light brown colour, fired the same colour inside, but with a patchy buff surface outside.

Provenance: Three examples of (P252) came from Periods II/IIA layers. All other examples were unstratified.

(iv) *Wide-mouthed.* (Figs. 58, 17–21)

17. (P1109). A type with an everted hollowed rim with a rounded lip, a very short neck which slopes into a bulbous body and a handle with two external grooves. It springs from below the rim and is attached at the point of maximum girth. Four examples in fabric C. Cf. Cotton 1979, 153 and fig. 46, 3.

18. (P2613). The upper part of a jug or flagon in fabric D. The collar rim has a well-rounded lip. The neck is vertical above a swelling body, and the handle, which springs from below the rim, has two deep external grooves. Two examples.

19. (P563). As no. 17, but the rim is a variant form and the handle is missing. In fabric C. In a second variant (P398), the collar rim lacks the hollowing. Four examples, three in fabric D and one in C.

20–21. (P2626) and (P2606). Two examples of collar rims which are concave internally. They had had handles, that of no. 20 apparently a two-ribbed one which sprang from the external concavity of the collar rim; that of no. 21 was a wide ribbon handle with two grooves which sprang from below the collar rim. No. 20 was in fabric D; no. 21 was in fabric C.

Provenance: No. 21 came from a Periods I/IA layer: nos. 17 (four examples), 18 (two examples) and 19 (two examples) came from Periods II/IIA layers and the rest were unstratified.

For no. 17, cf. Dyson, 1976, 130 and fig. 50, 96, from deposit 6, dated as Caligulan to Early Claudian. The San Rocco examples probably belong to the Period IIA occupation.

For no. 18, cf. Cotton, 1979, 153 and fig. 46, 7, where two examples were found in period III layers of *c.* A.D. 50 or later. Cf. also Duncan, 1964, Form 30, 62 and fig. 13, 112, from the kiln of *c.* A.D. 60–70, and Dyson, 1976, 111 and fig. 41, 160 from deposit 5, of the first quarter of the first century B.C. to early in the last quarter of that century. At San Rocco, this type also belongs, in all probability, to the Period IIA occupation.

For no. 19, cf. Duncan, 1964, Form 30, 62 and fig. 13, 114, from the kiln of *c.* A.D. 60–70.

For no. 20, cf. Dyson, 1976, 83 and fig. 27, VD104, from deposit 4, from an area deserted shortly before A.D. 70. The San Rocco piece was unstratified, but it seems to be an earlier type.

For no. 21, cf. Cotton, 1979, 155 and fig. 46, 22–23, the former being stratified in a period I layer. This again should be an early type as, at San Rocco, it came from a Period I/IA layer.

Additional material found in this category was (i) part of a 'rope' handle (P409), in fabric D, cf. Cotton, 1979, 155 and fig. 46, 29; (ii) half of the body and the base, probably from a narrow-mouthed jug, in fabric D; and (iii) the upper part of the body with the lower part of one handle with a single external groove, in fabric D. This was distinguished by having vertical lines of red paint on the upper part of the body below the neck. It, too, seemed to be of the narrow-mouthed type.

Provenance: (ii) came from the Period II platform infill; the other two pieces were unstratified.

5. *Jars.* (Figs. 59, 1–20 and 60, 21–38)
Fabric. Jars were found in fabrics A, C and D.
Jars in fabric A. (Fig. 59, 1–12)
(i) *With S-shaped profile.* (Fig. 59, 1)
1.   (P2768). A large wide-mouthed jar, without handles, but with a rounded rim and a flat base. Eight examples.
Provenance: One example from a Period I layer; four from Periods II/IIA and three from destruction layers.

For rim sherds of this type, cf. Cotton, 1979, 163 and fig. 51, 2. The scarcity of this type at San Rocco, where there were so few examples compared with the 42 found at Posto, suggests that its life-span had neared its end by the time that the San Rocco villa was founded. Cf. Dyson, 1976, Class 1 kitchen-ware pots, found in the deposits CF (23f.), PG(42), and 16IV(55), all dated earlier than *c.* 70 B.C.

(ii) *With bevelled rims.* (Fig. 59, 2–3)
2.   (P2632). A jar of this type with a typical rim, a piriform body, and a flat base. Three examples.
3.   (P2615). A large wide-mouthed jar with a bevelled rim and a bulbous body. Two examples.
Provenance: One example of no. 3 was from a Period I layer; two examples of no. 2 were from Period II layers and the rest were unstratified.

For this type, cf. Cotton, 1979, 163 and fig. 51, 8–15, where there were 141 examples in this fabric. Again, the type was almost superseded when San Rocco was founded. This type is that of Dyson, 1976, 55, Class 2 kitchen pots, where the series is given a range from 275–25 B.C. But the San Rocco examples are nearer to those of the earlier deposits, before 70 B.C., cf. Dyson, 1976, fig. 13, 16IV28.

(iii) *With everted rims.* (Fig. 59, 4)
4.   (P516). An everted rim with a sharp division between it and the wall. Three examples.
Provenance: One example from a Period I layer and two from destruction layers.
Cf. Dyson, 1976, 94 and fig. 33, PD51, from the deposit dated *c.* 75–25/20 B.C.

(iv) *With almond-shaped rims.* (Fig. 59, 5–6)
5.   (P2509). A short rim of this type, above two ridges, three examples.
6.   (P2618). A deeper rim.
Provenance: No. 6 was from a Period I layer; the rest were unstratified.
Cf. Duncan, 1965, 165 and Form 38B on fig. 12, A89–A95 for a series of jars with half-almond rims, which could continue into the first century B.C. Posto (Cotton, 1979, 166 and fig. 52, 24–25) produced eight examples.

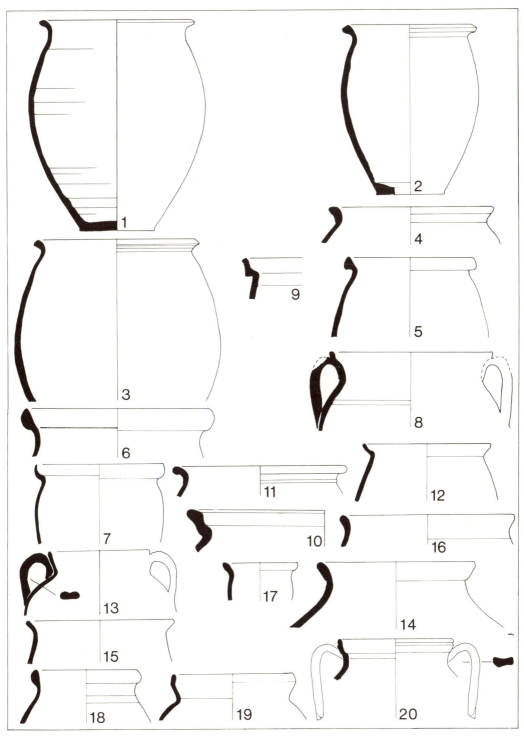

Fig. 59. Dark and light surfaced coarse wares. Jars (nos.1–20). (Scale 1/4)

(v) *With internally concave rims.* (Fig. 59, 7–10)

7. (P467). A typical example of this type, as found in the thin-walled pottery of situla form (cf. p. 197) and Fig. 45, 1–6), but larger and thicker-walled, and in the coarse fabric A. Six examples.
8. (P247). A handled jar with a rim of this type. Only one handle persists which springs from the neck, is attached on the shoulder of the jar and is slightly hollowed externally. One example with a second of smaller size.
9. (P2605). A rim sherd, with a collar rim hollowed internally. Four examples.
10. (P2569). A rim from a large jar, in thick ware, which is concave internally.

Provenance: From Period I, one ex. of no. 7; from Period II, two exs. of no. 9; from Periods II/IIA, no. 7 and 2 exs. of no. 9. The rest were unstratified.

For no. 7, cf. Dyson, 1976, 45 and fig. 21, V–D40, where it states that the form becomes much more popular at the beginning of the first century B.C. with numerous examples appearing in the deposit deserted shortly before 70 B.C. and also that of *c.* 75–25/20 B.C.

For no. 8, cf. Duncan, 1964, Form 34. Posto also produced six examples (Cotton, 1979, 166–8 and fig. 52, 28).

(vi) *Necked jars.* (Fig. 59, 11)

11. (P2541). A rim fragment from a necked jar with a well-rounded lip and a cordon at the base of the neck.

Provenance: From the Period II infill of the south terrace.

(vii) *Lidded jars.* (Fig. 59, 12)

12. (P521). A type with the rim hollowed to take a lid. Seven examples.

Provenance: Three examples were from Period II layers.

For the 12 types in fabric A described above, nos. 1–7 were attested in Period I/IA layers; nos. 9 and 11–12 were not found earlier than Period II and nos. 8 and 10 were only found unstratified. In general, the kitchen cooking pots, in this ware, were probably outdated, at San Rocco, by Period II.

Jars in fabric D. (Figs. 59, 13–20 and 60, 21–32)

(i) *With bevelled rims.* (Not illustrated)

Only two examples, in orange fabric, were found of this type. Both came from Period II layers, but they could have been derived from Periods I/IA layers.

Cf. Cotton, 1979, 163–6 and fig. 51, 16. As with fabric A, jars of this type, in this fabric, were nearly obsolete by the time of the foundation of the San Rocco villa.

(ii) *With everted rims* (Fig. 59, 13–17)

13. (P585). An example with an everted rim with a simple rounded lip and with handles with a central external groove which spring from the outside of the rim. Sixteen examples, fired red or brown.
14–17. (P2536), (P493), (P486) and (P547). Four jars, of different sizes, with rims of this type, but which lacked evidence for handles. No. 17 is a very small example. One example each of nos. 14, 15 and 17 and three examples of no. 16.

Provenance: One example of no. 16 and no. 17 came from Period II layers. The rest were unstratified.

For no. 13, cf. Dyson, 1976, 80 and fig. 25, V–D84, of Class 12 jars in coarse ware. From deposit 4 from the area deserted before 70 B.C.

(iii) *With almond-shaped rims.* (Fig. 59, 18)

18. (P497). A narrow-mouthed jar with a rim of this type. Five examples. For this unstratified jar, cf. Duncan 1965, 165 and Form 38B on fig. 12, A89–A95 for the form.

(iv) *With internally concave rims.* (Fig. 59, 19–20)

19–20. (P387) and (P2641). Two variants of this rim type. Sixteen examples of no. 19 and two of no. 20.

Provenance: There were three examples of no. 19 in Period II layers and the rest were unstratified.

(v) *Necked jars.* (Fig. 60, 21–23)

21. (P2645). A large jar with a rounded rim above a high vertical neck, a ridged shoulder and a bulbous body. Six examples.
22. (P2533). This type lacks the ridge or distinction between the neck and shoulder. Four examples.
23. (P84). An almost complete example of a smaller jar with a rounded rim above a short oblique neck, a bulbous body and a small flat base. The example illustrated lacked handles, but a smaller jar had two handles. Six examples.

Provenance: Periods II/IIA produce one example of no. 22 and two of no. 23. The rest were unstratified.

(vi) *Lidded jars.* (Fig. 60, 24–26)

24. (P250). A handled jar with a rim hollowed deeply to take a lid. Only the root of one handle persists.
25. (P2607). The lid seating is shallow and takes a lid of different form.
26. (P2585). A flat-topped rim with a deep concavity to take a lid with a rounded rim. Two examples.

Provenance: Nos. 24 and 25 came from Periods II/IIA layers.

Cf. Dyson 1976, 104 and fig. 38, PD122, a coarse ware jar from the deposit of *c.* 75–25/20 B.C.

(vii) *With vertical rims.* (Fig. 60, 27–28)

27. (P386). A handled jar with a thickened vertical rim. Only part of one ribbon handle persisted, which rose to an angular bend above the rim. Four examples.
28. (P474). The rim of this type is not thickened but is slightly bevelled. The root of only one handle persisted, of indeterminate form, but it may not have arched above the rim.

Provenance: All five examples were unstratified.

(viii) *Shouldered jars with thick rims.* (Fig. 60, 29–31)

29–31. (P317), (P565) and (P2628). Three examples of this type, nos. 29 and 30 having walls in very coarse thick ware, whilst no. 31 is in the usual fabric D. Two examples each of no. 29 and 31; one of no. 30.

Provenance: Two examples of no. 31 came from Period II layers; and one of no. 29 from Periods II/IIA layers. Nos. 29 and 30 were unstratified.

Cf. Duncan, 1964, 66 and fig. 15, 173–4. This is Duncan's Form 46, which he describes as pipes, with inset neck for joining the next pipe in a row. However, he considered that they were made in the kiln dated to *c.* A.D. 60–70.

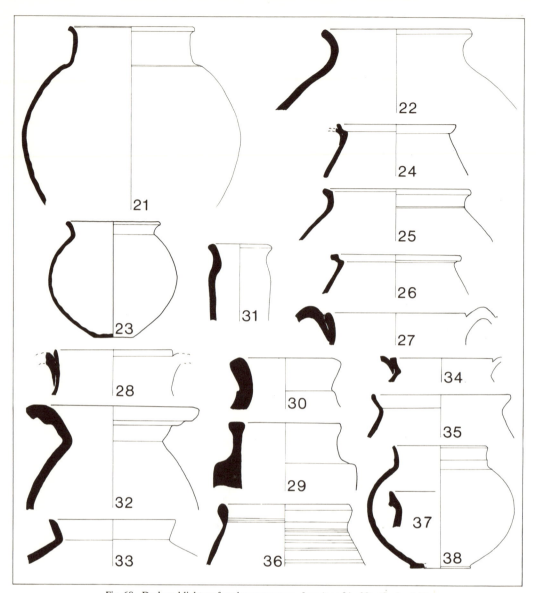

Fig. 60. Dark and light surfaced coarse wares. Jars (nos.21–38). (Scale: 1/4)

(ix) *With flared rims.* (Fig. 60, 32)

32. (P2545). An example with a widely flared rim with a hooked lip above a thickened cordon. The neck is oblique and is demarcated from a piriform body. This jar has the red paste of fabric D, but it has a cream surface over the outside and over the top of the lip. From a destruction layer.

At San Rocco, jars in fabric D are only attested from Period II onwards. Group (i), with bevelled rims, may be an exception as they may be derived, but, as noted, the form was practically obsolete by then. It would seem that, for the cooking jars, fabric D superseded fabric A from Period II onwards.

Jars in fabric C. (Fig. 60, 33–38)
(i)   *With everted rims.* (Fig. 60, 33)

33. (P2584). A sherd with a sharply everted and pointed rim.
Provenance: From a Periods I/IA layer in the south terrace fill.

(ii) *With internally concave rims.* (Fig. 60, 34–35)
34. (P440). A two-handled jar with a flat-topped rim, concave internally. The handles are too broken to ascertain their form.
35. (P454). An example with a slight concavity and a simple rounded rim. Two examples.
Provenance: No. 34 came from a Periods I/IA layer; and one example of no. 35 came from a Period II layer.
For no. 35, cf. Duncan, 1964, 61 and fig. 12, 108, Form 28, from the kiln of *c.* A.D. 60–70.

(iii) *With almond-shaped rims.* (Fig. 60, 36)
36. (P576). A rim of this type. Two examples.
Provenance: Both were unstratified.

(iv) *With a collar rim.* (Fig. 60, 37)
37. (P2561). A rim fragment only, from a Periods I/IA layer in the south terrace fill.

(v) *Necked jars.* (Fig. 60, 38)
38. (P2644). An almost complete example with a simple rim. From a destruction layer. Jars in fabric C, perhaps a domestic ware which was not used for cooking, appear at San Rocco, though sparsely, in Periods I/IA (nos. 33, 34 and 37). They are not well represented in Period II, as jugs or flagons became more plentiful and these jars were perhaps less used.

6. *Lids.* (Fig. 61, 1–15)
Fabric. Lids were found in fabrics A, C and D.
Lids in fabric A. (Fig. 61, 1–4)
1. (P2587). Part of a large lid with a flanged and beaded rim. The handle is missing, but the wall is decorated on top with four bands of wedge-shaped impressions. Probably it was used with a casserole.
2. (P2767). A plain casserole lid, with a thickened rounded rim and an asymmetric knobbed handle.
3. (2589). A jar lid with a simple rounded rim and an asymmetric knob handle. Six examples.
4. (P271). A lid sherd with a flanged rim. Five examples.
Provenance: One example of no. 3 and two examples of no. 4 came from Periods I/IA layers. The rest were unstratified.
These are the types, in fabric A, found at San Rocco, but they are not to be taken as a quantative estimate, for numerous small rim fragments were not counted.
For no. 3, cf. Cotton, 1979, fig. 54, 1. San Rocco also produced a more symmetrical knob handle like that of Cotton, 1979, fig. 54, 10, though without the groove on the wall. Again, almost exclusively, the types in fabric A belong to Periods I/IA.
For a series of lid forms, dated as *c.* 75–25/20 B.C., see Dyson, 1976, 99–100 and fig. 35, PD80–PD95.

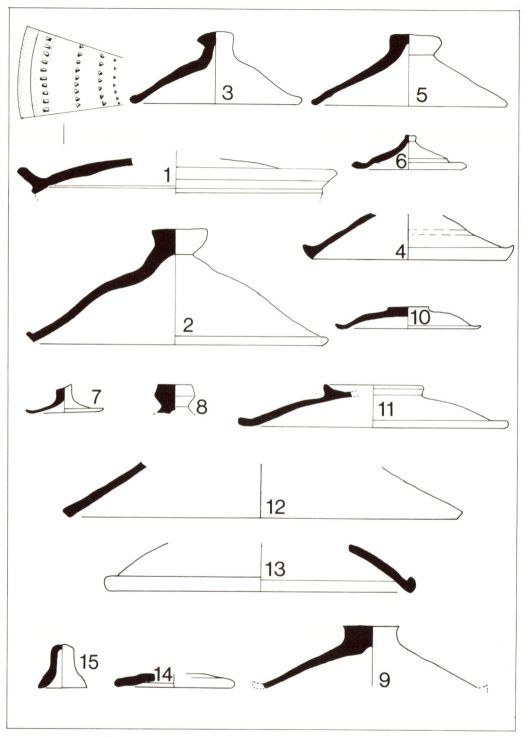

Fig. 61. Dark and light surfaced coarse wares. Lids (nos. 1–15). (Scale: 1/3)

Lids in fabrics C and D. (Fig. 61, 5–15)

Fabric. With the exception of one example of no. 6 and of no. 15, which were in fabric C, these lids are in fabric D.

5. (P2610). A jar lid, with a simple rounded rim, sometimes slightly upturned below a hollowed wall and with a small asymmetric knob handle. Many examples.
6. (P1107). A smaller lid, with an upturned rounded rim below a hollowed wall and a small asymmetric handle. Two examples.
7. (P265). A small lid, two examples.
8. (P2505). A small knob handle, of symmetric form. This example was one of the very few found of this type.
9. (P596). A larger version of the symmetric form. Three examples.
10. (P258). A small example of the bowl/lid form, with a flat top (or pad base) and an upturned rim. Two examples.
11. (P2627). A larger example of the lid/bowl form, with a hollowed top (or ring base) and an upturned rim. Two examples.
12. (P423). A rim sherd with a squared lip. Many examples.
13. (P361). A rim sherd, with the lip folded back. Fairly common.
14. (P2507). A small flat lid.
15. (P360). A thick crude lidlet.

Provenance: Types nos. 5, 9, 12 and 13 came from Periods I/IA layers; nos. 6 and 14 from Periods II/IIA layers; the rest were unstratified.

At San Rocco, the earlier types (nos. 5, 9 and 12–13), which were plentiful, were in fabric D, unlike the jars in this fabric, which were predominantly in layers of Period II onwards.

For a series of lid forms of Republican date, which may be of second, or even first century B.C., see Duncan, 1965, 167 and fig. 14, A119–A127, Form 51. This group has both asymmetrical and symmetrical knob handles, and rim forms which are parallels to those of the San Rocco group.

For a series of lid forms dated *c.* A.D. 60–70, see Duncan, 1964, and fig. 15, 175–85, Forms 49–51, which again offer a few parallels.

IX. *AMPHORAE.* (Figs. 62, 1–11 and 63, 12–21)

(I wish to thank Professor Zevi for advice on these pieces, but any misinterpretations or errors are my responsibility. M.A.C.)

Fabric. This is described individually.

1. *Amphorae of Dressel Form 1.* (Fig. 62, 1–2)

1. (P556). A large rim, with a deep collar well inclined from the vertical. Two examples. The one figured has a cream/buff paste with a dull cream slip, the other has a red paste with a cream surface.
2. (P2567). A large amphora with a more vertical collar rim. In a light brown paste fired a lighter brown.

Not illustrated. (P482). Cf. Cotton, 1979, 141 and fig. 41, 2, for profile, although it lacks the rough finish at the lower edge of the collar rim. In red paste fired lighter red and with a smoothed surface. For four more examples, see Cotton, 1979, 141 and fig. 41, 3, which have collar rims and are in a ware like that of (P482).

Provenance: No. 1 came from a Periods I/IA layer; cf. no. 1 and one of the group of four came from Periods II/IIA layers; the rest were from destruction levels.

A newly discovered kiln, at Mondragone on the coast very near to Francolise, produced amphorae of Dressel Forms 1A and 1B (see Peacock, 1977, 262–5 and 267–8). This could be a likely source for these Francolise examples. Peacock describes the ware (264–5) as, "hard, reddish-brown in colour . . . Traces of a pale slip can be seen on the outer surface . . .' and he gives details of the microscopic appearance. The San Rocco pieces, except for no. 1, seem to fit with this ware.

On the chronology of the Mondragone kiln, Peacock (265) suggests that it may have been operative from the late second century to the second half of the first century B.C., as 'Dressel 1A is generally held to have been current from the latter part of the second century until about the middle of the first century, while Dressel 1B belongs to the second part of the first century B.C.'. The Ager Falernus is known to have been one of the main production areas (267).

The three stratified pieces from San Rocco fit into this period. The sparsity of its occurrence (eight pieces at San Rocco and 11 at Posto) does not suggest that the two villas were themselves producing wine.

2. *Amphorae of Dressel Forms 2–4.* (Fig. 62, 3–4)
3. (P381). A wide-mouthed amphora with a rounded rim, an oblique neck and the stump of a double-roll handle. In buff paste with a smoothed cream surface. Five examples, three of which have a red paste.
4. (P1115). Part of a narrow-mouthed amphora with a rounded rim and a vertical neck. The handle is of double-roll form. In a buff paste with a smoothed cream surface.
Not illustrated. (P282) and (P619). Cf. Cotton, 1979, 142 and fig. 41, 6. Eleven examples. They are in red paste with quartz particles and are fired red. Two have a cream surface. In addition, eight handles were found which have the double-roll form.
Provenance: No. 4, cf. (P282) and (P619) (two exs.) came from Periods II/IIA layers and the rest were unstratified.

Koan style vessels of Dressel Forms 2–4 were found in association with Dressel 1B forms at another kiln site at Albinia, near Orbetello, north of Rome (Peacock, 1977, 266–8). The ware is very similar in appearance to that of Mondragone, but its microscopic texture makes it readily distinguishable. This form indicates activity which continues into the last two decades of the first century B.C., or perhaps even into the first century A.D. (Peacock, 267).

For this form, the fabrics of the San Rocco examples do not seem to be those of the Albinia kiln, which is far away from Francolise. But this form was produced over a wide area of Italy, Spain and France. Whilst the origin of the form goes back to at least the first century B.C., its *floruit* was in Augustan–Tiberian times and examples are attested throughout the first century A.D. They served, in Italy, for the transport of wines, especially those of Campania and Lazio. For a recent article on the wine industry of Campania, see Zevi, 1972, 35–67. It includes macrophotographs of the paste, in colour, and from varying provenances, some with potters' stamps. For the contrast between the potters' stamps found in Campania and Etruria, see Manacorda, 1978, 128–9.

At San Rocco, this form is not attested until after *c.* 30 B.C. The 17 rims and eight handles show an increase in quantity over that of the Dressel Form 1 of earlier date, which is perhaps in keeping with the grandeur of the Period II villa. But it may not be sufficient to suggest a local production and sale of wine. This is supported by the absence of a wine press.

3. *Amphora of Dressel Forms 38–9 or Ostia Form LXIII.* (Fig. 62, 5)
5. (P383). An amphora with an everted hooked collar rim and a wide oblique neck. In a cream/buff paste fired the same colour.
Provenance: From a destruction level.

The rim fragment is rather small for identification, but it might perhaps be an example of this form, see *Ostia* III, 512–15 and 626, fig. 11. If so, it belongs to the series that was used to transport *garum* or conserved fish products from Spain, and would be of Augustan-Claudian date.

4. *Amphorae of Ostia Form L.* (Fig. 62, 6–7)
6. (P2620). A wide-mouthed flat-topped rim with an expansion where it joins the neck. The scar of one root handle persists below this expansion. In a dull red paste fired the same colour.
7. (P2661). This rim is more everted and has a rounded lip above the expansion. The neck is more oblique. In a pink/red paste fired pale buff on both sides. The scar of the handle root is placed higher.
Provenance: Both rims were unstratified.

Cf. *Ostia* II, 109, Form L and Tav. XXXIV, 551 for no. 6 and Tav. XXXIII, 550 for the A and B variant forms of Form L. For a discussion of the form, see *Ostia* III, 551–5, where it states that it is well attested in strata of the second half of the first century and the beginning of the second century A.D. The character of its contents is not known.

5. *Amphora of small dimensions of Schöne-Mau Form XXXV.* (Fig. 62, 8)
8. (P2511). An almost complete example of a smaller type amphora, with an everted almond-shaped rim, a fairly vertical neck, angular shoulders above a long narrow body which ends in a hollow spiked base. The double-rolled handles spring from the upper part of the neck and are attached on top of the shoulders. In well levigated paste, pale red in colour, but not showing quartz particles. It is fired to a rose tone and the surface is smoothed.
Provenance: From a Period II layer.

For a discussion of this type see *Ostia* III, 478–9 and 632, fig. 42 (an example of Form XXXV of the Pompeian typology of Schöne-Mau in *CIL* IV, Suppl. II, Tav. III, no. XXXV). They are dated to the first to second centuries A.D., but their contents are not known securely. It is possible that they were used for the transport of wine.

6. *Amphorae of Tripolitanian II Form.* (Fig. 62, 9–10)
9. (P382). A rim in a pink paste fired red.
10. (P2598). A variant rim form, in a pink/red paste with cream inclusions, and a cream slip on both sides.
Provenance: Both examples were unstratified.

These rims seem to be of the Tripolitanian I–III series, see *Ostia* IV, 153–4 and 256, fig. 7, with references to *Ostia* I–III. They are not sufficiently complete to determine where their handles were situated, a point which differs in the three types, and especially shows how type II differs from I and III. Our rims seemed nearer to those of type II.

At Ostia the form occurred from Flavian times and, in reduced numbers, up to A.D. 250. It seems probable that the form was used in the transport of oil.

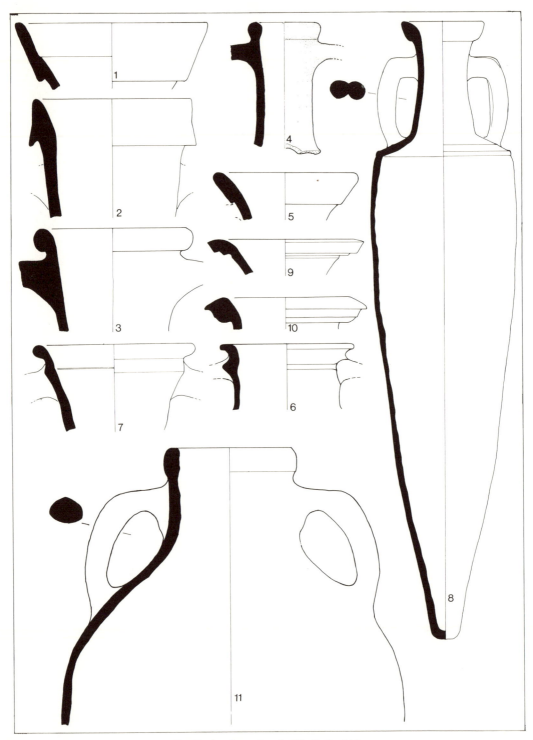

Fig. 62. Amphorae (nos.1–11). (Scale: 1/4)

Its occurrence at San Rocco might be earlier rather than later in this long span, at a time before the villa's own production of olive oil got under way, unless it was a different type of oil that was being imported.

7. *Amphorae of African Type IIB.* (Fig. 62, 11)
11. (P2660). The neck, handles and shoulder (with some body sherds) of a large amphora. The rim is almond-shaped, the neck is troncoconical, the shoulders are well-rounded, and the ribbon handle is applied to the neck below the rim and on the slope of the shoulder. Seven examples.
Provenance: Only one piece was stratified in a Periods II/IIA level.

Cf. *Ostia* III, 585–6 and 630, fig. 69; and *Ostia* IV, 162–3, and 257, fig. 14. These are similar to the form of Zevi, 1969, 173–9 and fig. 4, and are African Form IIB, of Tunisian origin, in the Ostia classification. They are dated from the first ten years of the third century A.D. onwards. The contents of these amphorae are uncertain, but their origin in an oil-producing area suggests that they were used for the transport of the oil.

At San Rocco, they should belong only to the very last years of the occupation, perhaps after local production had ceased. No internal residue was noted.

8. *Amphorae of ? Form Beltran IIB or Ostia LVIII.* (Fig. 63, 12)
12. (P588). A wide-mouthed vessel with a projecting rim and a curved neck. Handle stumps rise from the neck but the form of the handles is not clear. In red paste, fired pink/red inside and with a cream slip outside.
Provenance: Unstratified.

Perhaps, but not securely, of this form. Cf. *Ostia* III, 510–11 and 616, fig. 10. These amphorae were usually used for the transport of fish paste. They were initiated in Tiberian-Claudian times and continued in use throughout the first and second centuries A.D.

Other rims. (Fig. 63, 13–8)
13. (P2573). A rim with the scar of the base of one handle. In rose-red sandy paste, fired lighter outside and the same colour inside. The collar rim, with a thickened rounded lip, is everted and the neck is oblique. The handle springs from the base of the rim.
14. (P275). A flat-topped and thickened rim. In dull red paste with a smoothed cream surface outside.
15. (P384). A wide-mouthed vessel with an almond-shaped rim. In red paste fired red to orange.
16. (P251). An everted almond-shaped rim. In orange/brown gritty paste with a yellow to cream external surface. Two examples.
17. (P601). A stubby rim above a vertical neck. In gritty brown paste with a smoothed yellow surface outside.
18. (P2550). A turned-over rim, thickened underneath. In dull red paste with a few inclusions, with a yellowish smoothed surface outside.
Provenance: None was stratified.

9. *Amphora handle.* (Fig. 63, 19)
19. (P11). A stamped handle, in plain buff ware, smoothed externally. It was found in unstratified top soil.

I am grateful to Miss Virginia R. Grace, of The American School of Classical

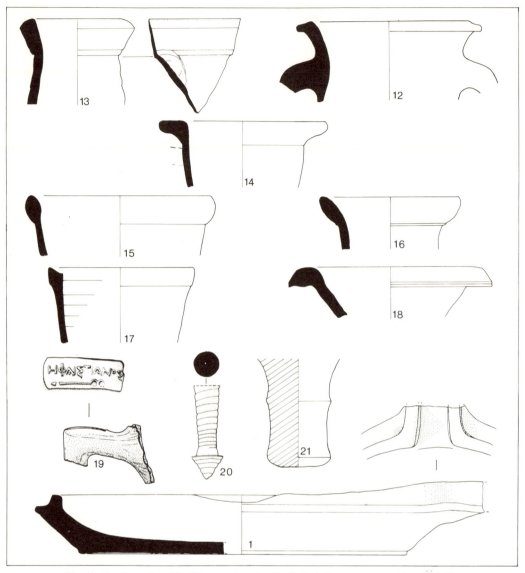

Fig. 63. Amphorae (nos.12–21); mortarium (no.1). (Scale 1/4, except stamp of no.19, 1/2)

Studies in Athens, for her help, and for her references for this find. Also, may I thank Miss Joyce Reynolds, of Newnham College, Cambridge, who identified the inscription originally and supplied me with helpful information.

The handle is stamped with the name of the fabricant, HΦAIΣTIANOΣ, above a *caduceus*. This is a Rhodian amphora stamp. There is an example in the British Museum (*IG* XII.1.1310) and a number have been found in various parts of the Mediterranean world, cf. Nilsson, 1909, 427–8, no. 226, and Grace, 1952, 516 ff. (which records eight examples found in Delos). Miss Grace quotes the names of Rhodian eponymous priests, which show that Hephaistion worked in the second quarter of the second century B.C., and possibly into the third quarter. (For her revisions of Early Hellenistic chronology, see Grace, 1974, 193–200. For lists of Rhodian eponyms, cf. Bleckman, 1912, 249 f.; Hiller von Gaertringen, 1931; and Grace and Savvatianou-Pétropoulakou, 1970, 277–382).

There is a whole jar by Hephaistion in the Nicosia Museum, Cyprus, dated in the term of Pausansias the Third (cf. Grace and Savvatianou-Pétropoulakou, 1970, 304–5 and pl. 53, no. E12; published in the *Classical Journal,* xlii, 1947, 450, fig. 8) linking the two names. This eponym is dated to the first half of the second century B.C. Another jar of Hephaistion, also from Cyprus, is in the Metropolitan Museum in New York, dated in the term of Pythogenes. Nilsson (1909, 117) corrected the reading of the eponym's name. His suggestion that this stamp could be read as that of Pythogenes was hesitant, but Miss Grace (who has seen the jar, which he had not) finds that his guess was right. Both Pausanias the Third and Pythogenes are datable to the second quarter of the second century B.C.

The San Rocco handle was found in unstratified top soil. On the above dating, *c.* 175–150 B.C. or somewhat later, at its original source in Rhodes, it seems to fall into the same class as the small group of Greek coins (see p.129) which are prior to the establishment on the site of the first villa.

10. *Amphorae bases.* (Fig. 63, 20–1)
20. (P2574). A pointed amphora base in a dull pale red paste. The stem has a grooved spiral decoration and the triangular tip has a decoration of four grooved circles.
21. (P587). A solid pointed amphora base, in a red paste with a smoothed pink to yellow surface.

   This is an example of a type which was not shown in the Posto series, cf. Cotton 1979, 146 and fig. 43, 30–6. Other San Rocco types were similar to those found at Posto.

*Provenance:*Both bases were unstratified.

The amphorae in the economy of the villa
The occupation of Periods I/IA. *c.* 100/90–30 B.C.

The amphorae found, which could have been used in this period, are perhaps the Rhodian one with a stamped handle, eight pieces of Dressel Form 1 and 17 rims and eight handles of Dressel Forms 2–4. All these vessels probably contained wine. The Rhodian one, an import, may have been a rare luxury, but for the other supplies it was not perhaps necessary to go far afield, for the containers for this wine were being manufactured at Mondragone and elsewhere in the Ager Falernus. But the number suggests but a very modest use of wine, which was bought locally, and was not produced on the estate.

The occupation of Periods II/IIA. *c.* 30 B.C.—A.D. 200+.

During this long phase, amphorae of six different forms have been postulated, but, with the exception of the latest of Form African IIB, there were only one to two examples of each. The evidence for the use of wine could not be more slender. Only two rims of Ostia Form L, of uncertain provenance, and one of Schöne-Mau Form XXXV, of Pompeian type, might have contained wine. It could be that local supplies were plentiful, and easily accessible, so that jugs or small table amphorae were filled, and the large transport amphorae were not needed. The villa's inhabitants needed to go no farther afield than Cales, as can be understood from Horace *Od.* i, xx,; 'An Invitation to Maecenas' (Loeb, ed. 1927, translation by C. E. Bennett):

   Caecubum et prelo domitam Caleno
   tum bibes uvam; mea nec Falernae
   temperant vites neque Formiani
      pocula colles.

('Then thou [Maecenas] shalt drink Caecuban and the juice of grapes crushed by Cales' presses; my cups [of cheap Sabine wine] are flavoured neither with the product of Falernum's vines nor of the Formian hills').

Two rims, of Ostia Form LXIII and Ostia Form LVIII, of Augustan-Claudian and Tiberian-Claudian to second century date respectively, testify to rare purchases of *garum* or preserved fish products derived originally from Spain. Shellfish were not found to be a staple diet of the inhabitants of the villa so these were indeed an unusual luxury.

On the other hand, olive oil, from perhaps mid-first century onwards, was an important product. It is of interest to note that the two rims of Form Tripolitanian II, datable from Flavian times onwards, and used for the transport of oil from N. Africa, may have been early purchases before the villa's own production got under way; whilst the seven rims of African IIB, from Tunisia, and dated as *c.* A.D. 210 onwards, could only have been purchased at the very end of the occupation of the villa, perhaps at a time when its own *oletum* had ceased to function.

Addenda and corrigenda

SAN ROCCO

Between the time that this report was written, and that of going to press, available information about Campanian amphorae has increased greatly. Much of this is due to recent survey work, and excavation of newly found kilns in Campania (some of them near to the San Rocco site) by Paul Arthur. Cf. his article. 'Roman amphorae and the Ager Falernus under the Empire', *PBSR* 1, 1982, 22–33. This study not only shows the extent of local production of amphorae, both in coastal and later in inland areas, but it also indicates something of the local density of villa sites, and it gives important conclusions about the Falnernian wine trade. It is now essential reading for any consideration of the amphorae of the San Rocco area.

POSTO. (Cf. Cotton, 1979, 140–6)

Amphora handle stamped ΙΑΣΟΝΟΣ

Cf. 146 and fig. 43, 27. I am indebted to Dr. David Whitehouse for the information that an amphora handle stamped with this name has been found as far away as the Persion Gulf. It was excavated, in 1973, at Mleiha, in the United Arab Emirates (T. Madhloom, 'Excavations of The Iraqi Mission at Mleiha, Sharjah, UAE', *Sumer,* xxx, 1974, 149–58). The stamp is published by J-F. Salles, 'Notes on the archaeology of the Hellenistic and Roman periods in the United Arab Emirates', *Archéologie aux Emirats Arabes Unis,* ii-iii, 1978–9, 79–87, especially 79, colour photo 80, drawing 89. Salles cites M. P. Nilsson, *Timbres amphoriques de Lindos,* Copenhagen, 1909, 247, 3 and says it is Rhodian.

Other amphorae

I am indebted to Mr. Paul Arthur for the following information, published in his review of Posto in *The Bulletin of The Institute of Archaeology* (University of London), no. 18, 1981, 274–76.

Cf. 141. (a). Falernian wine is not mentioned on stamps, though it does occasionally appear in *tituli picti.*

(b) For 1. (P634), 'the deep almost vertical lip' of Dressel 1B, is not 'characteristic of the mid-first century B.C.', for the form continued, at least, into Augustan times.

(c). For 3. (P131). This is not a developed Dressel 1 form. Rather it is a Dressel 1A, probably of late second to mid-first century B.C. date.

Cf. 142. 'The amphora form Dressel 2–4 was certainly produced in Campania and Latium, but also in Etruria, Apulia/Calabria, southern France, noth-west Spain, southern Spain and other areas (including Britain!). The characteristic bifid handle is also found on the original form from Cos (and on the Tripolitanian form Schöne-Mau XXXV) which, the reviewer believes, can be identified by its distinctive fabric and nuances of typology. Therefore, without careful examination, one cannot be sure that all the Dressel 2–4/5s from Posto are of Italian origin; indeed, fig. 41, 6, looks and sounds distinctly Tarraconesian.'

Cf. 144. 16–17 (P857, P892). These appear to be north African 'Punic' types.

Arthur comments that:— 'A notable absence amongst the amphorae series is the Baetican Dressel 20 oil amphora. There are a few known from Pompeii, but they do not really appear in quantity in Campania. Perhaps this is due to the strength of local oil production.'

X. *MORTARIA.* (Fig. 63, 1)

At San Rocco, pieces of mortaria that could be recognised were even more scarce than at Posto. Only two types were noted. Possibly some of the larger bowls, which lacked bases, may belong here.

1. (P1113). An example in pink/white coarse paste with white grits. About one-third of the vessel, including the spout, persisted.

For the form, cf. Cotton, 1979, 172 and fig. 55, 1. The San Rocco example shows the flatness of the base and the fact that the inner surface was gritted. Evidence for hand holds was missing. This is an early form.

Not illustrated. (P2582). Part of a pie-crust rim, in dark grey gritty paste fired dark grey. Probably misfired.

For the form, cf. Cotton, 1979, 172 and fig. 55, 2.

Provenance: Both pieces came from Period II building levels, so that they could well be derived from the Periods I/IA occupation. No. 1 was under room 39; no. 2 was in the fill of the vat of room 25.

XI. *LARGE STORAGE JARS, DOLIA AND THEIR COVERS.* (Figs. 64, 1–7 and 65, 1–8)

Large storage jars. (Fig. 64, 1–7)

Fabric. No. 1 was in fabric A; nos. 6–7 were in fabric D and the others were in fabric C. There was one example of each type, with the exception of no. 8, which had two examples.

1. (P2768). A necked jar with a thickened everted rim.
2. (P2633). A two-handled jar with an everted rim.
3. (P2572). In this type the rim is thicker and bevelled and the ribbon handle is wider.
4. (P2566). A type with a thickened everted rim and an even wider ribbon handle with three flat grooves externally.
5. (P2631). This jar has a flat-topped everted rim which is hollowed internally to take a lid. The ribbon handle has two external grooves.
6. (P2563). A jar with an almond-shaped rim, decorated on the shoulder with an incised wavy line between two grooves.
7. (P2594). A jar with a well-rounded inturned rim.

Provenance: No. 2 was from a Period II layer; no. 1 was from a Periods II/IIA layer and the rest were unstratified.

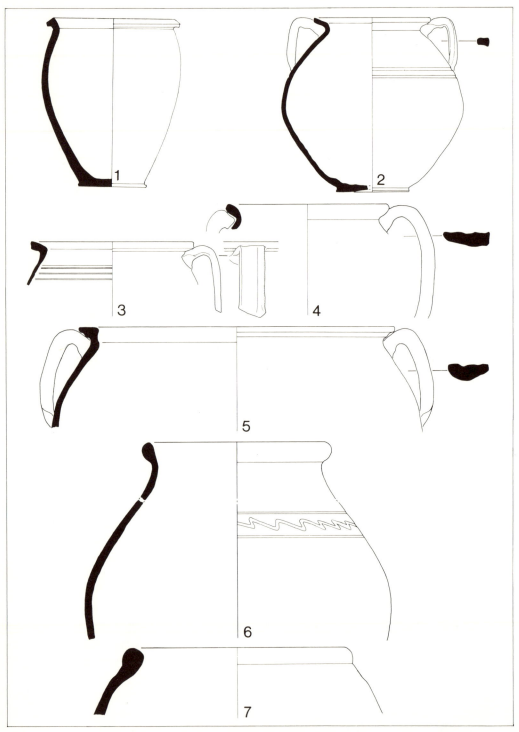

Fig. 64. Large storage jars (nos. 1–7). (Scale: 1/4)

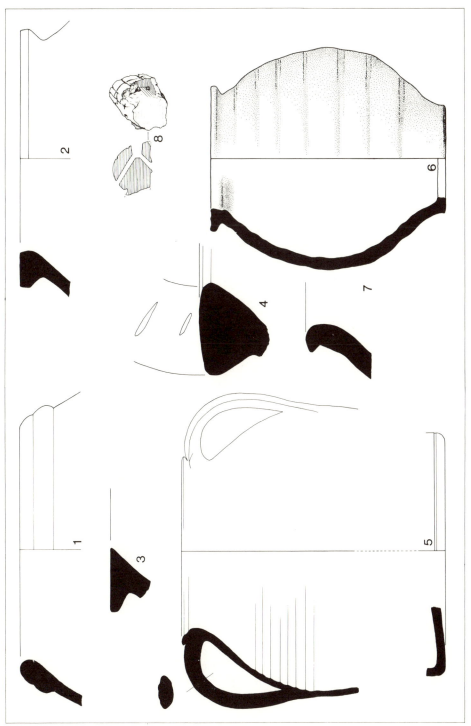

Fig. 65. Dolia (nos.1–8). (Scale: 1/5)

Dolia. (Fig. 65, 1–8)

Fabric. There was no uniformity, so the fabric is described individually.

1. (P307). A rim in a dull red gritty paste fired the same colour and slightly charred. Two examples.

2. (P274). A rim, in coarse red paste fired orange, with a flat top and a squared lip. Four examples, of which one was a waster with dark grey to black gritted paste fired light brown.

3. (P371). A rim as no. 2 above, but the top is less flattened and the angle with the body is sharper. Four examples, in red paste fired red to brown.

4. (P2592). A rim from a very large and heavy dolium, in paste with a dark grey core with the outer side fired red. The rim is of triangular section.

5. (P2769). A dolium with an everted rim, hollowed internally to take a lid.

6. (P199). A dolium in grey paste fired brown/red and with a smoothed surface, burnt in places. The flat rim has two hollowings on top, the globular body is corrugated and the base is flat.

7. (P2617). In this type the everted rim has a pointed lip. In grey paste fired dark brown.

8. (P668). A shattered dolium rim which has been doubly pierced to take lead rivets when it was repaired. A second rim, with wall sherds, still had the rivets *in situ*.

Not illustrated. A shoulder sherd from a very large dolium, in pink paste fired the same colour, seems to have had a collar rim whose lower edge was decorated with rough finger-tip impressions.

Eight further, untyped, dolia rims were found.

Provenance: None was stratified.

Six out of the 24 examples listed came from the industrial area near the oil presses and kilns. Some may perhaps have served as storage jars for the olive oil.

Jar or dolia covers. (Not illustrated)

At San Rocco, these were fairly plentiful and were of the same two types as those found at Posto.

Of the type with a plain rounded edge, rough underneath and with a central handle from which six grooves radiate (cf. Cotton, 1979, 174 and fig. 64, 3), there was at San Rocco one example (P1100), complete with handle, and seven pieces.

Of the type with a single raised cordon on top, inside the rounded edge (cf. Cotton, 1979, 174 and fig. 64, 2), San Rocco produced six pieces.

Provenance: Two pieces of the first type came from Periods II/IIA layers; the rest were unstratified.

Well or pit cover. (Not illustrated)

One rim sherd had part of one of the four handles like those of Cotton, 1979, 175 and pl. XVIII*d.* It was found in a destruction layer.

Piatti. San Rocco did not produce any piatti like those of Cotton, 1979, 174 and fig. 64,4.

XII. *MINIATURE VESSELS.* (Fig. 66, 1–3)

1. (P1111). A small cup, in fabric C, with a pointed everted rim, a vertical wall and a thick base with a small pad. One side has a circular hole, which should have been for the insertion of a handle.

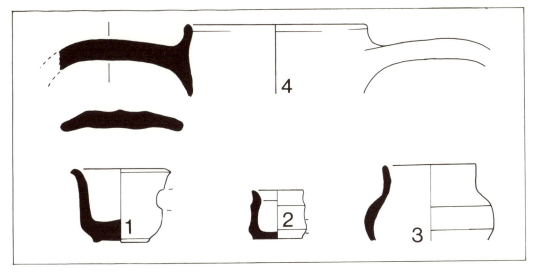

Fig. 66. Miniature vessels (nos.1–3); 1 medieval jar (no.4). (Scale 1/2)

2. (P2508). A miniature jar, which has lost its single handle. In fabric D, with orange paste.
3. (P537). A small jar, in orange fabric D, with a rounded rim above a vertical neck and a bulbous body. There was no evidence for handles.

Not illustrated. Two wall sherds, with small pad bases, one with the lower end of a handle on the wall, probably came from very small cups or juglets. In orange fabric D.

Provenance: No. 1 came from a Periods I/IA layer; no. 3 from a Periods II/IIA layer and the rest were unstratified.

XIII. *MISCELLANEOUS POTTERY.* (Not illustrated)

Only a few pieces were not classified. They consist of: a long nozzle in fabric D (P2557); a sherd with a short, but broken off, nozzle from a feeding vessel (P1089), in fabric C; and a sherd with a lug handle, in fabric A, which has finger-tip decoration at its extremities.

Provenance: Only (P1089) was stratified, in a Period II layer.

XIV. *MEDIEVAL POTTERY.* (Fig. 66, 4)

Some nine pieces of glazed ware were found in the top soil. I am indebted to Dr. David Whitehouse for examining them. He considered them to be either modern or of fairly recent date. The only piece identified as certainly of medieval origin was the coarse ware jug described below.

(P2770). The rim and part of the handles of a large amphora or jug in buff paste fired cream. The short vertical neck has a thinned lip and the wide strap handle has five shallow grooves on top. One example, unstratified, over the kiln area.

Cf. Cotton and Cherry, 1971, 165 and fig. 11, 1–2. The occupation at Monte d'Irsi ended no later than *c.* 1350, but these jugs are prevalent in the thirteenth and fourteenth centuries.

CHAPTER XI. The Assemblies of Material and their Dating

The several hundred layers excavated at San Rocco have been phased and dated, using the structural evidence and its associated material. The sequences are illustrated in the composite section ABCD of Fig. 4; and the section EF of Fig. 6. The details of the assemblies are given here.

SUMMARY OF THE DATING

Period I. c. 100/90 B.C.
The building of the southern terrace and rooms G–I; and the building of the northern terrace and rooms A–F. Levels (6) and (5) of Fig. 4.
Period IA. Before 30 B.C.
The alterations to the Period I building. Level (4) of Fig. 4.
Periods I/IA. c. 100/90–30 B.C.
Occupation layers associated with the use of the villa during Periods I and IA. Levels (5) and (6) of Fig. 4 and (4) of Fig. 6.
Period II. c. 30 B.C.
The building period of the Period II villa. Level (3) of Fig. 4.
Period IIA. c. A.D. 50 or a little later.
The alteration and additions to the Period II villa.
Periods II/IIA. c. 30 B.C.–A.D. 200+.
The occupation layers associated with the use of the villa.
Unstratified. From the late second to early third centuries A.D. onwards.
   The desertion and decay of the villa. Levels (2) (destruction) and (1) (Top and sub-soil) of all sections.

ANTERIOR TO THE PERIOD I VILLA. Before *c.* 100/90 B.C.

Whilst no real occupation of the site was found before the Period I villa was built, a few stray coins were found in the old turf-line, in such places as were excavated down to bed rock. These were three Greek coins, nos. 1–3 of p. 129, *c.* 250–100 B.C., or a little later. They indicated that it was unlikely that the villa was built until a time early in the first century B.C. The stamped amphora handle of Rhodian origin (p. 243) belongs with these coins.

THE PERIOD I BUILDING LEVEL. *c.* 100/90 B.C.

The layers which constitute this phase were excavated as:
1.   The Period I building phase of the southern terrace and rooms G–I. (Fig. 4, section ABCD, level 6).
2.   The Period I building phase of the northern terrace and rooms A–F. (Fig. 4, section ABCD, level 5).

1.   *The Period I building phase of the southern terrace and rooms G–I.* (Fig. 4, level 6)
The layers of the southern terrace which belong to this period were excavated as: *164,*

(10B) (13B) (18B) (19B); *166*, (12B); *167*, (10); *168*, (9); *169*, (15C) (16C) (17C) (18C) (19C) (21C); *172*, (19) (20); *173*, (10B1) (11B1) (12B1).

These layers produced no material, as would be expected when moving soil and building on a virgin site.

The rooms G–I were excavated as:

Room G. 173, (10B1) (11B1) (12B1); *173 S. Ext.*, (10A) (12B); *181*, (3).

Room H. 164, (10B) (13B) (18A) (19A); *166*, (12B); *167*, (10); *163*, (15C) (16C) (17C) (18C) (19C) (21C).

Room I. 47, (9) (10); *163*, (15C) (16C) (17C) (18C) (19C) (21C).

Again, no material was obtained from these layers.

2. *The Period I building phase of the northern terrace and rooms A–F.* (Fig. 4, level 5)

The layers of the north terrace were excavated as:

1B/1C, (6B) (7B); *2B Area A*, (5AB) (6A1) (6A2) (6A4); *2B/3B*, (5B) (5E) (6A) (6C) (6D); *2C*, (6C) (8B); *3B*, (6A) (6B) (6C); *3C*, (6); *47*, (9) (10); *Tr. 1* (7); *Tr. 2* (6); *Tr. 3* (7); *Tr. 4* (6); *106N*, (6A) (7).

The Period I fills associated with the walls of the villa, again as was to be expected, were essentially of newly dug, clean earth, which contained little or no occupation material. The only layers in this group which produced anything were those of *2B Area A*, (6A1) and *47*, (9) and (10). This material consisted of an iron nail; the rim of a juglet in black glazed ware (see Fig. 37, 5) with three basal fragments and five sherds of the same ware; a number of sherds of thin-walled ware; a basal piece from a Pompeian red ware dish of the first century B.C.; and the rim of a dish in coarse ware of fabric A (see p. 219, (P14/103a–b), not illustrated).

The layers in rooms A–F were excavated as:

Room A. None.

Room B. 2B Area A, (6A1) (6A2) (5AB) (6A4); *2B/3B*, (6A) (5B) (6Z) (6D) (5E); *2C*, (8B) (4C); *3B*, (6A) (6B) (6C); *30*, (6); *Tr. 1*, (7); *Tr. 2*; (6); *Tr. 3*, (7); *Tr. 4*, (6).

Room C. None.

Room D. 2C, (6B) (8B); *room 9/D*, (13).

Room E. 2B Area A, (5AB) (6A1) (6A2) (6A4); *2B/3B*, (5E) (6A) (6C) (6D); *2C*, (6C) (8B); *3B*, (6A) (6B) (6C); *3C*, (6).

Room F. 174, (8B) (10B) (11B) (13B).

These layers produced no material.

The problem of the dating of the Period I villa

Insofar as the contemporary pottery or finds are concerned, there is nothing in the above handful of sherds (and one iron nail) that could be used as firm datable evidence. One can only consider the black glazed ware juglet which is but a fragment; and the base of a Pompeian Red ware dish, which is of a type usually attributable to the first century B.C. The Periods I/IA occupation material (listed below) does, however, contain painted wall plaster which was derived from the Period I/IA villa, and this plaster is considered as being of Pompeian Style I, *c.*150–80 B.C. The late Republican black glazed wares from this occupation are at home in the first century B.C., but some of them could perhaps be of earlier date.

The important evidence is, therefore, the dates that can be assigned to the *opus incertum* structure and to the mosaic pavement of room A (*op. mus.* 1). The geographically closest analogy for the *opus incertum* is in the Loreto sanctuary in Teanum Sidicinum (see Chapter III, n. 2) but see the difficulties of dating *opus incertum* outside Rome in F. Rakob in Coarelli, 1976, 32–3 and Rakob, 1976, 370–72. For the *scutulatum pavimentum* (*op. mus.* 1), the very striking similarity between it and the pavement in a house between the *Scalae Caci* and the foundations of the temple of the Palatine Apollo in Rome, Morricone, 1980, 44, 71–3, no. 38, pl. IV, 38, gives a date in the first decade of the first century B.C. to the pavement, a date consistent with *opus incertum* structures outside Rome and with the material evidence, such as it is, as detailed above. The Period I villa, therefore, appears to have been built sometime between 100 and 90 B.C., perhaps a little after period I at the nearby *villa rustica* at Posto where *opus quadratum* was still in use at the initial construction (see Cotton, 1979, 16-7).

THE PERIOD IA ALTERATIONS TO THE VILLA. Before 30 B.C.
The following layers were associated with the Period IA floors and structures. They appear as level 4 on the section ABCD of Fig. 4 and were excavated as:
Room A1. Pit 1, (3) (4).
Room B1. 2A Area B, (5B) (6B); *2A/2B,* (5A) (6B); *2B Area A,* (5A1) (5A2) (5A4) (7A1); *2B/3B,* (5A) (5C) (5D); *3A N, Ext,* (5A) (7A); *3A/3B,* (5) (6); *3B,* (5A) (5B).
Room D1. 2C, (7B) (5C); *3C,* (5); *room 9/D,* (6B) (7B) (8B) (11) (12).
Material was found in layers *3C, Pit 1,* (3) and *room 9/D,* (6B). It consisted of:
Black glazed wares. 1 rim of a small bowl of Lamboglia Form 1A, (see Fig. 38, 12), a form common on all sites of the first century B.C.; 2 indeterminate rims (1 very worn); and 3 sherds.
Thin-walled wares. 1 handle and 2 tiny sherds.
Coarse wares. A bowl rim in fabric A, cf. Fig. 55, 11; a ring base, and a number of sherds.
   This trifling amount of contemporary material offers no help in dating this phase between those of Periods I and II.

THE PERIODS I/IA OCCUPATION LEVEL. *c.* 100/90–30 B.C.
Owing to re-use or destruction of the Periods I/IA villa when the Period II villa was built, no sealed occupation layers were left inside the building. The chief source of material was the accumulation of débris outside the west retaining wall of the Periods I/IA villa, which was sealed by the Period II west extension of the terrace.
   The Periods I/IA débris level is shown as layers (5) and (4) on the section EF of Fig. 6. They were excavated as:
173 S.Ext., (10A) (12B) (13B) (14B); *179* (7) (9); *180* (6); *181* (9); *182* (5); *187* (7).
   Fortunately, some of these layers were rich in material, which would have continued to accumulate throughout the use of the villa during Periods I and IA, and cannot be subdivided. The material consisted of:

FINDS (room 7)

Lamps. Fig. 14, 6, Fig. 15, 8–9, 11–12, dated *c.* 50 B.C. to A.D. 1.

Glass. Fig. 20, 36. A gemstone.

Bronzes. Fig. 21, 1. A bodkin or netting needle.

Iron objects. Fig. 24, 3. Flat sheet.

Bone objects. Fig. 26, 5. A small spoon.

Pottery. Fine Wares

Early Painted ware. Two pieces, p.174.

Unguentaria. One base, see p.176. First century B.C. and pre-Augustan.

Black glazed wares.

1. *Jugs and juglets.* Cf. Fig. 37, 4.

5. *Small bowls.* Fig. 38, cf. 12, 13 and four bases. First century B.C. and probably pre-30 B.C.

7. *Pyxides.* See p. 179, one rim and two bases.

8. *Flanged rim cups.* Fig. 37, cf. 18.

10. *Cups.* Fig. 37, 21 (four exs.), 22 (two exs.).

12. *Inturned rim bowls.* Two rims. See p. 181. An early form.

13. *Platters or dishes.* See p. 181, Form 5 (20 exs.); Form 7 (six exs.); Fig. 38, 6 and 7 (two exs.).

14. *Medium-sized bowls.* Fig. 38, 8 (six rims and five bases), 10 (six exs.), 11 (four exs.), 12, 13 (seven exs.). First century B.C.

15. *Miscellaneous forms.* Fig. 39, 2 and 3.

16. *Graffiti.* Fig. 39, 9.

Thin-walled wares.

1b. *Plain bowls.* Cf. Fig. 44, 8.

2. *Situlae.* Fig. 45, cf. 1 and 3. 23 exs., dated as pre-Augustan.

4. *Jars.* Fig. 45, 13.

5a. *Decorated beakers.* Fig. 46, cf. 7.

5b. *Plain beakers.* Fig. 46, cf. 8, cf. 11, cf. 12, 13, cf.16. Pre-Augustan.

Pottery. Coarse Wares

Dark and light surfaced wares.

2. *Dishes.* Fig. 53, 12 *in fabric B.*

3. *Bowls.* (v) *Bowls in fabrics D and E,* (a) *with flanged rims.* Fig. 56, 30.
      (b) *With inturned rims.* Fig. 57, 33. From *c.* 100 B.C. onwards.
      (iv) *Wide-mouthed.* Fig. 56, 21. First century B.C.
      5. *Jars. In fabric A,* (i) *with S-shaped profile.* Fig. 59, 1. First century B.C. (ii) *with bevelled rims.* Fig. 59, 3. Early first century B.C. (iii) *with everted rims.* Fig. 59, 4. *c.* 75–25/20 B.C. (iv) *with almond-shaped rims.* Fig. 59, 6. Early first century B.C. (v) *with internally concave rims.* Fig. 59, 7. Early first century B.C. to *c.* 25/20 B.C. *In fabric C,* (i) *with everted rims.* Fig. 60, 33. (ii) *with internally concave rims.* Fig. 60, 34. (iv) *with a collar rim.* Fig. 60, 37. Fabric C, a domestic ware, is sparse in this phase.
      6. *Lids. In fabric A.* Fig. 61, 3–4. Second and third quarters of the first century B.C. *In fabric D.* Fig. 61, 5, 9, 12 and 13. First century B.C.

Amphorae. Dressel Form 1. Fig. 62, 1. First century B.C.

Miniature vessels. Fig. 66, 1.

Whilst there is nothing in this assembly which can be dated very precisely, the overall dating of the group favours the period covered by the first half and into the third quarter of the first century B.C. For the lower end of the bracket there is nothing which has to be as late as Augustan. But, most important, is the fact that there is no Arretine pottery which indicates that the end of this occupation phase preceded *c.* 30 B.C.

Painted plaster (see below p. 257), in the infill of the Period II terrace, which must have come from the Periods I/IA villa, was believed to be of Pompeian Style I, *c.* 150–80 B.C. The black glazed wares found in the Period II infills must also belong to this phase and they are Late Republican types of the first century B.C. The derived thin-walled wares (see below p. 258) are also predominantly pre-Augustan.

A date of *c.* 100/90–30 B.C. is, therefore, suggested as that most appropriate for Periods I/IA.

THE PERIOD II BUILDING LEVEL. *c.* 30 B.C.

The levels associated with the Period II villa are grouped as:

1. The western terrace (*domus*) rooms, trenches and layers (Fig. 4, section ABCD, level 3).
2. The eastern terrace (*villa rustica*) rooms, trenches and layers.

1. *The western terrace (domus) rooms, trenches and layers.* (Fig. 4, section ABCD, level 3)

Room 1. 20, (3); *27*, (7) (8).

Room 2. None.

Room 3. 24, (5) (6) (7) (8).

Peristyle. 111, (4); *180*, (4) (5).

Room 4. Tablinum. 2A, (3B) (4B) (8B); *2A/2B*, (3B) (4B) (8B); *2B*, (3A1) (3A2) (3A3) (3A4) (4A1) (4A2) (4A3) (4A4); *2B/3B*, (3A) (3B) (3C) (3D) (3E) (4A) (4B) (4C) (4D); *3A N. Ext.*, (3A) (4A) (6A); *3A/3B*, (3) (4); *3B*, (3A) (3B) (3C) (4A) (4B) (4C) (5C).

Room 5. Triclinium. Tr. 1, (2); *Tr. 2*, (2); *Tr. 3*, (2); *Tr. 4*, (2).

Room 6. 2C, (3C) (4B) (4C) (5B) (6B); *3C*, (4); *3C Pit 1*, (1) (2) (3).

Rooms 7–13. None.

Room 14. 20, (3).

Rooms 15–26 None.

Room 17. 23, (5); *24*, (5) (6) (7) (8); *26*, (7) (8) (9) (9A).

Room 18. 26, (7) (8) (9) (9A); *33*, (4) (5).

Room 19. 33, (4) (5).

Rooms 20a and b. None.

Room 21. 4D, (2) (3) (4) (5); *4D S. Ext.*, (2) to (7); *27*, (3) to (6).

Room 22. 4D, (3) (4) (5).

Room 23a. 27, (4) (5) (6).

Room 23b. None.

Room 24. 169, (4B) (5B) (7C) to (14C).

Room 25. 164, (2) (6) (7) (9) (11) (14A) (16A); *166*, (3) (6) (8) (11B) (14); *167*, (4) (5) (6) (8); *168*, (5) (6) (10); *174*, (4) (5) (7A) (8A) (12A).

Room 26. None.

Western terrace. *106N,* (1A) (2A) (3) (3A) (4) (4A) (5A) (6); *170,* (3A) (4B); *182,* (2)(3) (3A) (4); *186,* (2) to (6).

Southern terrace. *4F,* (2)(3)(4)(5); *33,* (4); *172,* (4) to (6) and (8) to (18); *178,* (10) (11); *181,* (2) to (8).

Rooms 27–28. None.

Room 29. 185, (2).

Room 30–30a. None.

Rooms 31a and b. 188, (2).

Room 32. 2C, (4C) (5C).

Rooms 33–34. None.

Room 35. Room 9/D, (2) (4) (5B) (9C) (10) (10D).

Room 36. None.

Room 37. 173, (3A) (7A) (7B) (8A) (9B1); *173 S. Ext.* (4) (5) (6B) (7B); *177,* (4) (5) (6) (7); *179,* (4) (5) (6) (8).

Room 38. None.

Room 39. 183, (5A) (6B); *184,* (2) (3A).

Entrance road, main and back entrances. None.

Upper terrace, west. None.

The assembly of material from this area of the Period II villa was:

FINDS

Coins. Five Republican coins, nos. 9, 12–13 and 15–17 of p. 129, dating from after 211 to 109/108 B.C.

Lamps. Fig. 14, 2–5 and 7. Dated *c.* 50 B.C.–A.D. 1.

Glass. Fig. 20, 37. A bead.

Bronzes. Fig. 21, 11–12 and Fig. 22, 15–17.

Iron Objects. Fig. 24, 4, and Fig. 25, 10, a hammer and a bill-hook.

Bone Objects. Fig. 26, 9–10. A ring and a plaque.

Loom weights and spindle whorls. Fig. 30, 2.

A worked chert blade. Fig. 29, 1. Perhaps a Bronze Age survival.

A tufa disc. Fig. 33, 3.

Painted plaster. Possibly of Pompeian First Style, *c.* 150–80 B.C.

Pottery.

Fine wares.

Early Painted ware. Four pieces, see p. 174.

Megarian bowls. Fig. 36, 2, *c.* 75 B.C.–A.D. 1.

Unguentaria. Fig. 36, cf. 6 and cf. 8. First century B.C., and pre-Augustan.

Black glazed wares.

1. *Jugs and juglets.* Fig. 37, 1, 3, cf. 5 and two bases.

2. *Kylikes.* Fig. 37, 6–7 (seven pieces). First half of second century B.C.

5. *Small bowls.* Fig. 37, 11, 12, 14–15 and two bases. First century B.C. and probably pre-30 B.C.

7. *Pyxides.* See p. 179. Two sherds and two bases.

9. *Small plates or bowls.* Fig. 37, 20 (two exs.). First century B.C.

13. *Platters or dishes.* See p. 180, Form 16 (two exs.), Form 6 (four exs.), Form 36a–b (two exs.), Form 5 (many exs.), Form 7 (four exs.).
14. *Medium sized bowls.* Fig. 38, 8 (two rims and three bases), 9 (four exs.), 10 (four exs.), 12 (one example), 13 (six exs.), four bases. First century B.C.
15. *Miscellaneous forms.* Fig. 39, 1, 4, 5.
16. *Graffiti.* Fig. 39, 10.
17. *Bases.* Fig. 40, 3 (palmette stamped), 4–8.

Thin-walled wares.
1a. *Decorated bowls.* Fig. 44, 4 and 5.
2. *Situlae.* Fig. 45, 1, 3 and 5, 19 examples. Dated as pre-Augustan.
5a. *Decorated beakers.* Fig. 46, cf.7.
5b. *Plain beakers.* Fig. 46, 11, cf. 12, (P312), (P313).

Coarse wares
Dark and light surfaced wares
2. *Dishes.* p. 219, (P2529) *in fabric A*; Fig. 53, 3, 7 *in fabric D*; Fig. 53, 12 *in fabric B*.
2. *Baking plates.* Fig. 54, 8.
3. *Bowls.* (iii) *Other bowls in fabric A*. Fig. 55, 6, 12 and 14.
4. *Jugs.* (i) *Narrow-mouthed.* Fig. 58, 2 and 8. *c.* 100–25/20 B.C.
5. *Jars. In fabric A.* (ii) *With bevelled rims,* Fig. 59, 2. Early first century B.C. (v) *With internally concave rims.* Fig. 59, 9. First century B.C. (vi) *Necked jar.* Fig. 59, 11. (vii) *Lidded jars.* Fig. 59, 12. Jars in fabric A were probably out-dated by Period II. *In fabric D.* (i) *With bevelled rims.* p. 234 and cf. Cotton, 1979, fig. 52, 12. (ii) *With everted rims.* Fig. 59, 16–17. Early first century B.C. (iv) *With internally concave rims.* Fig. 59, 19. (vii) *Shouldered jars with thick rims.* Fig. 60, 31.
Amphorae. Schöne-Mau Form XXXV, Fig. 62, 8. Starts in the first century B.C.
Mortaria. Fig. 63, 1 and (P2582). Probably first century B.C.
Large storage jars. Fig. 64, 2.
Miscellaneous pottery. p. 251, (P1089).

    Whilst much of this material, in the Period II infills, is derived from the previous Periods I/IA occupation phases, this assembly does show that there was nothing which, at the time of the rebuild, has to be as late as the Augustan period. It is consistent with a suggested date of *c.* 30 B.C., at latest, as that of the new Period II villa, because of the absence of Arretine ware.

2.   *The eastern terrace (villa rustica), rooms, trenches and layers.*
In the *villa rustica* there were found courtyard 1 (on the west), courtyard 2 (on the east) and rooms 40–60 (44 being a portico and 47 a stable). In this area the terrace had been levelled, as opposed to its being raised for the *domus*, to take the new structures for the Period II eastern extension. As a result, there were no terrace infills. Whilst the structures could be shown to be of Period II date, with later alterations of usage in Period IIA, cultivation and other disturbances had left no securely sealed layers. The material from this area has, therefore, been treated as unstratified. The trenches of the area were excavated as 9–15, 37, 39, 50–61, 102, 104, 112, 116 and 200–234.

THE PERIOD IIA ALTERATIONS AND ADDITIONS. *c.* A.D. 50 or a little later. No stratified layers could be associated with these structural alterations. The dating for this period, therefore, insofar as the material is concerned, depends on deductions made from that found in the occupation layers, listed below.

THE PERIODS II/IIA OCCUPATION LEVEL. Before 30 B.C.–A.D. 200+
Owing to ploughing, and disturbances caused by the start of the hospital building, in many places these occupation layers were no longer intact. Material found in layers on intact floor surfaces, where sealed by slip from the upper terrace, or by a destruction layer which sealed an earlier undisturbed one, has been grouped here. These layers were excavated as: *0*, (3); *1B/1C*, (3B) (4B) (5E); *1E*, (3A); *1Z*, (7B) (8B); *1Z/2Z*, (4); *27*, (4) (5); *2Z*, (7A) (7B) (7Bb) (8A) (8C) (8D) (8E); *3Z*, (7A) (7B) (8) (9C) (9D) (10D); *3Z/47*, (5); *4D*, (1) (2); *4D S. Ext.* (2); *4F*, (3W); *4G*, (4); *4W(E)*, (8); *4X*, (2A) (3) (5A) (5Aa); *4Y*, (2A) (3) (4); *4Z*, (5A) (5B) (5C) (6D) (6E) (6W); *5E*, (2); *8B Ext.*, (4) (6); *14*, (3); *15*, (3); *20*, (3); *23*, (3) (4) (5); *24*, (4); *26*, (5) (6); *27*, (2); *32*, (5); *33*, (3); *35*, (3) (4); *36*, (5) (6); *38*, (4A); *40*, (7) (8); *44*, (4); *45*, (4); *45/47*, (4); *48*, (4) (5); *100*, (3) (3b) (4); *123*, (6A); *124*, (3); *125*, (4); *166*, (4) (5); *167*, (3); *168*, (4); *171*, (4); *172*, (7); *174*, (9A) (9B); *180*, (2) (3); *181 S. Ext.*, (5); *183*, (4A); *room 9/D*, (10B) (10C) (10D).

The material retrieved was:
FINDS
Lamp. Fig. 14, 4. *c.* 50–0 B.C.
Glass. Fig. 18, 2, 5–7; Fig. 19, 33–34, mid-first to early second century A.D.
Iron objects. Fig. 24, 1–2 and Fig. 25, 11. A hinge, a ring and a key.
Bone objects. Fig. 26, 3. A pin.
Loom weights and spindle whorls. Fig. 30, 1.

Pottery.
Fine wares.
Megarian bowls. Fig. 36, 3 and cf. 5, p. 174. *c.* 75 B.C.–A.D. 1.
Unguentaria. Fig. 36, 6. First century B.C. and pre-Augustan.
Black glazed wares.
1.   *Jugs and juglets.* Fig. 37, 5.
5.   *Small bowls.* Fig. 37, cf. 12. First century B.C. and probably pre-30 B.C.
8.   *Flanged rim cups.* Fig. 37, 17–18.
10.   *Cups.* Fig. 37, 21.
11.   *Lids.* Fig. 37, 23.
13.   *Platters or dishes*, See p. 181. Form 16 (three exs.), Form 6 (two exs.), Form 5 (many exs.), Form 7 (three exs.).
14.   *Medium sized bowls.* Fig. 38, 8 (eight exs.), 10 (seven exs.), 11 (four exs.), 13 (three exs.).
15.   *Miscellaneous forms.* Fig. 39, 1.
17.   *Bases.* Fig. 40, 6.
Arretine ware. Fig. 41, 1, 5, 6, a basal fragment and two sherds, four of the pieces found were of Augustan (2) and late first century B.C. to early first century A.D. date (2), which shows that this ware only came into use at San Rocco after the occupation of the Period II villa had started, thereby placing its building date as *c.* 30 B.C. at the latest, if that date is accepted for the early circulation of Arretine ware.

Local terra sigillata ware. None, but the four pieces of this ware found unstratified should have been derived from this occupation. *c.* A.D. 50–100.

Late Italian terra sigillata. Fig. 41, 13–14. *c.* A.D. 50–100.

African Red Slip ware. See pp. 190–194. Twelve rims, one base and three sherds. From A.D. 75/80 to the end of the second century. See below, p. 262, where four pieces might possibly be as late as the early third century.

Thin-walled wares.

1b. *Plain bowls.* Fig. 44, 8.

2.   *Situlae.* Fig. 45, cf. 1, 2, cf. 5. These three examples are dated as pre-Augustan.

3.   *Jugs.* Fig. 45, cf. 7, cf. 9, 10. Probably Augustan onwards.

4.   *Jars.* Fig. 45, 13.

5a.   *Decorated beakers.* Fig. 46, 3, 4, 7.

5b.   *Plain beakers.* Fig. 46, 11, cf. 12, cf. 13, cf. 16.

Coarse wares

Dark and light surfaced wares.

2.   *Cooking stands.* Fig. 54, 5.

3.   *Bowls.* (i) *Flanged rim.* Fig. 55, 1, 2. In fabric A and E and possibly posterior to *c.* A.D. 60/70; (ii) *Rilled ware in fabric E.* p. 222 and cf. Cotton, 1979, fig. 47, 1–4. Late first to early third century A.D.; (iii) *Other bowls in fabric A.* Fig. 55, 4–5, 8–11 and 14. First century B.C. (iv) *Bowls in fabric C.* Fig. 55, 18; *Bowls in fabrics D and E.* (a) *with decorated rims.* Fig. 56, 19, 21–22. Late first century A.D. to early third; (b) *with flanged rims.* Fig. 56, 24–26 and 28–30. First century A.D.; (c) *with inturned rims.* Fig. 56, 31 and Fig. 57, 33. First century A.D.; (d) *Grey rim bowl/lids.* p. 227 and cf. Cotton, 1979, fig. 47, 5. *c.* A.D. 50 to early second century; (e) *oblique flat-topped rims.* Fig. 57, 36 and 38–39. Mid-first century A.D.; (f) *rounded rims.* Fig. 57, 40. (vi) *Bowls with internal ledges in fabrics C and D.* Fig. 57, 42.

4.   *Jugs.* (i) *Narrow-mouthed.* Fig. 58, 1, 2 and 7. First century B.C.; (iii) *Trefoil-mouthed.* p. 231, (P252); (iv) *Wide-mouthed.* Fig. 58, 17–19. Mid-first century A.D. onwards.

5.   *Jars. In fabric A.* (i) *with S-shaped profile.* Fig. 59, 1. First century B.C.; (v) *with internally concave rims.* Fig. 59, 7 and 9. First century B.C.; in *fabric C*; (ii) *with internally concave rims.* Fig. 59, ?3, 5. Mid-first century A.D.; *in fabric D* (v) *necked jars.* Fig. 60, 22–23; (vi) *lidded jars.* Fig. 60, 24–25. Second and third quarters of the first century B.C.; (viii) *shouldered jars with thick rims.* Fig. 60, 29.

6.   *Lids. In fabrics C and D.* Fig. 61, 6 and 14. Mid-first century A.D.

Amphorae.

Dressel Form 1. Fig. 62, cf. 1 and (P330).

Dressel Forms 2–4. Fig. 62, 4 and cf. (P282) and (P619). Plentiful in Augustan-Tiberian times and persist throughout the first century A.D.

Form African IIB. Fig. 63, 11. *c.* A.D. 210 onwards.

Large storage jars. Fig. 64, 1.

Jar or dolia covers. p. 250.

Miniature vessels. Fig. 66, 3.

The material from this grouping of layers is spread over a wide date, but belongs, in fact, to three separate phases, though it was not possible to separate them stratigraphically, because of the amount of surface destruction. These phases are:

1. The residual material from the Periods I/IA occupation.
2. The occupation material associated with the Period II villa.
3. The occupation material associated with the Period IIA villa.

1. *Periods I/IA residual material. c.* 100/90–30 B.C., at latest.
Some of the fine wares belong here, as some of the Megarian bowls; the unguentaria; part of the black glazed wares, as the small bowls and perhaps some of the platters and dishes; the thin-walled situlae, so plentiful in the I/IA periods, of which only three examples were here found; and probably some of the beakers. Amongst the coarse wares, forms in fabric A are now scarce, and some would be survivals. The Dressel Form 1 amphorae also are more at home here than later.

2. *Period II occupation material. c.* 30 B.C.—A.D. 50 or a little later
The few finds offer little help for this phase, and it is the occurrence of new fine wares that indicates the date at which it started. Black glazed wares are still current to begin with. But the Augustan, and later, Arrentine wares give the initial date. Much of the coarse ware is datable to the first century B.C. or to the first half of the first century A.D., and the Dressel Forms 2–5 amphorae, of Augustan-Tiberian date through the first century A.D., now appear.

3. *Period IIA occupation material. c.* A.D. 50–200+.
This third phase is marked by the appearance of Late Italian and local terra sigillata of *c.* A.D. 50–100, followed by the African Red Slip ware (mostly Early), from 75/80 until the end of the second century A.D. or even just into the third century. Later lamps also bracket this phase, and, for the first time, glass of mid-first century date and onwards comes into use. In the coarse wares the early colour coated category seems to bridge the gap, for table wares, between the decline of Arretine and the diffusion of Early African Red Slip ware. Much of this material is datable from *c.* A.D. 50 onwards.

The problem remains, insofar as material is concerned, to relate it to the time at which the Period IIA alterations and additions were made. On structural grounds, a date of *c.* A.D. 50 or a little later seems feasible.

MATERIAL FROM DESTRUCTION AND UNSTRATIFIED LEVELS. After A.D. 200.
Much of the occupation material left on the site, of all periods, was retrieved from the destruction levels, or from the ploughed subsoil and top soil. Understandably, the architectural fragments, which resulted from the decay of the villa, would only occur here. The levels concerned are shown in Fig. 4, section ABCD, levels 2 and 1; Fig. 6, section EF, levels 2 and 1.

Only significant material, or types which were not found in earlier levels, are listed here.
FINDS
Coins. One undistinguishable Greek coin of Magna Grecia, no. 4 of p. 129. Eight Republican coins, nos. 5–8, 10–11, 14 and 16 of p. 129, dating from 215/212–135 B.C.
12 Imperial coins, nos. 18–20 and 28–36 of p. 130, dating from after A.D. 22–320/324. The seven-coin hoard of silver *denarii,* nos. 21–7 of p. 130, which was not deposited before the last third of the second century A.D., in the then ruined west terrace retaining wall.

Two medieval and five modern coins.

Lamps. Fig. 14, 1 and Fig. 15, 10, dated *c.* 50 B.C.—A.D.1.

Fig. 15, 14–6, dated *c.* A.D. 1–50.

Fig. 16, 17–9, dated *c.* 50–100.

Fig. 17, 20–2, dated *c.* 150–225+.

Fig. 17, 23–8, dated late second to early third centuries A.D.

Parts of two medieval lamps, see p. 143.

Glass. Most of the series, including that of Fig. 19, 29, dated to the second to third century A.D., was, with the exception of one small glass bowl, attributable to *c.* A.D. 50 onwards.

Bronzes. Fig. 21, 2, 7–10, 13 and Fig. 22, 14 and 18, and Fig. 23, 31. These include a small crucifix, probably medieval.

Terracotta objects. Fig. 27, 1–5, including two figurines and an ox-ear copy.

The terracotta antefix mould of Ulysses and Scylla. p. 158.

Late medieval clay tobacco pipes. Fig. 28, 1–4, and Fig. 29, 5–6.

Lead and lead piping.

Brick stamps. Of Billienus, Fig. 31, 1–2; others, Fig. 31, 3–4.

Tiles from kilns. p. 164–7.

Architectural details. Fig. 33, 4, stucco Ionic capital; Fig. 34, 1–2, the terracotta frieze from the portico of the peristyle; Pl. XI *d* and Fig. 34, 3–4, columns and bases. Marble basin, Fig. 35; marble drain cover, p. 171.

Pottery

Fine wares

Black glazed wares. A skyphos, Fig, Fig. 37, 18; Calenian relief ware, Fig. 37, 9–10; salt-cellar, Fig. 37, 16; base with moulded mask feet, p. 185.

Arretine wares. Fig. 41, 2–4, 7-9. From late first century B.C. to Tiberian-Claudian date.

African Red Slip ware. 112 rims, 20 bases and 51 sherds. From A.D. 70/80 to the end of the second century A.D. See p. 194 for four pieces of Fig. 43, 16–9, which might be as late as the early third century A.D.

Thin-walled wares. Decorated bowls, Fig. 44, 1–3; and plain bowls, Fig. 44, 6–7 and 9–13. Nos. 6 and 7 are dated as possibly Claudian-Neronian.

Coarse wares

Early colour-coated wares. All forms, in this ware, were unstratified. Analogies quoted were not earlier than *c.* A.D. 50.

Dark and light-surfaced wares.

5. *Jars. In fabric D* (iii) *with almond-shaped rims.* Fig, 59, 18; (vii) *with vertical rims.* Fig. 60, 27–8; (viii) *with flared rims.* Fig. 60, 32.

In fabric C (iii) *with almond-shaped rims* Fig. 59, 16; (v) *necked jars* Fig.60,38.

Amphorae. Form Tripolitanian II. Fig. 62, 9–10. A.D. 75–250.

Form Ostia L. Fig. 62, 6–7. *c.* A.D. 50. Early second century.

Other types. Fig. 62, 8 and Fig. 63, 12. First and second centuries A.D.

Untyped rims. Fig. 63, 13–18.

Stamped handle. Fig. 63, 19, *c.* 175–150 B.C.

Dolia. Fig. 65, 1–8.

Well or pit cover. p. 250.

It is the Roman material from these layers which determines the date at which the villa was deserted. The latest dated lamps are those of Fig. 17, 20–22 and 25, all *c.* A.D. 150–225 or later. For the glass, only one piece, that of Fig. 19, 29, is dated as late as the second or third centuries A.D. Unfortunately, the brick stamps have not been helpful. The African Red Slip ware, with the exception of three pieces, Fig. 43, 16–19, which could persist into the third century, was otherwise not later than the second century. But the African (Tunisian) amphorae, of the last group, purchased perhaps when the villa was declining, do indicate an early third century date, for their manufacture is not believed to start before *c.* A.D. 210.

The evidence from the coins shows a more gradual decline, which may have started earlier. The deposition of the seven-coin hoard of silver *denarii*, possibly *c.* A.D. 175–200, in the west terrace retaining wall, already in a state of decay, shows that the *domus* at least was no longer maintained at the end of the century. Only the coin of Constantinus, as Caesar, of A.D. 320–324, is later than this.

BIBLIOGRAPHY

Abbreviations used:

AE	*L'Année Épigraphique.* Revue des publications épigraphiques relatives à l'antiquité romaine. Paris: P.U.F.
AJA	*American Journal of Archaeology.* New York: Archaeologiccal Institute of America
AntJ	*The Antiquaries Journal.* London: The Society of Antiquaries of London
Archaeology	*Archeology.* Quarterly Journal of The Archaeological Institute of America. New York
ArchClass	*Archaeologia Classica.* Rome: Ist. di Archeologia e Storia dell' Arte Greca e Romana e di Etruscologia e Antichità Italiche dell'Università di Roma
Athenaeum	*Athenaeum.* Studi periodici di letteratura e storia dell'antichinà. Pavia: Univ. di Pavia
Ath.Mitt.	*Mitteilungen des Deutschen Archäologischen Instituts (Athenische Abteilung).* Berlin: Mann
AttiCeSDIR	*Atti del Centro di Studi e Documentazione sull' Italia Romana.* Milan: Ist. ed. Cisalpino La Goliardica
BCH	*Bulletin de Correspondance Hellénique.* Paris: École française d'Athènes
Bd'A	*Bolletino d'Arte.* Rome: Libr. dello Stato
BMC Italy	*A catalogue of the Greek coins in the British Museum, Italy.* London: Trustees of the British Museum, 1873
BMC Sicily	*A catalogue of the Greek coins in the British Museum, Sicily.* London: Trustees of the British Museum, 1876
BonnJahr	*Bonner Jahrbücher des Rheinischen Landesmuseums in Bonn und des Vereins von Altertumsfreunden im Rheinlande.* Cologne and Vienna: Böhlau
BullCom	*Bulletino della Commissione Archaeologica Comunale di Roma.* Rome: L'Erma di Bretschneider
CIGr	*Corpus Inscriptionum Graecarum* ed. Boeckh. Berlin: Vogt, 1828–1877
CIL	*Corpus Inscriptionum Latinarum* ed. Mommsen et al. Berlin, 1863–
CVAr	*Corpus Vasorum Arretinorum.* Compiled by A. Oxé and edited by H. Comfort. Bonn: Habelt, 1968
Dr	Dragendorff
Dressel	Dressel, H. in *CIL* XV,2, tav.2
EAA	*Enciclopedia dell' arte antica classica e orientale.* Rome: Ist. della Enciclopedia Italiana, 1958–1970
FI	*Forma Italiae.* Rome: Ist. di topografia antica dell'Università di Roma. Regio I, I *Latium e Campania.* Regio I, II *Surrentum.* Regio I, III *Tibur (Pars altera).* Regio I, IV *Tellenae.* Regio I, V *Cora.* Regio I, VI *Agnania.* Regio I, VII *Tibur (Pars prima).* Regio I, IX *Apiolae.* Regio I, X *Collatia*
Gallia	*Gallia.* Fouilles et monuments archéologiques en France métropolitaine. Paris: C.N.R.S.
Hellenismus in Mittelitalien	see Zanker, 1976
Hesperia	*Hesperia.* Journal of the American School of Classical Studies at Athens. Baltimore
Inscr.It.	*Inscriptions Italiae.* Rome: Libr. dello Stato, 1931–

JHS	*Journnal of Hellenic Studies.* London: The Society for the Promotion of Hellenci Studies
JRS	*Journal of Roman Studies.* London: The Society for the Promotion of Roman Studies
Klio	*Klio.* Beiträge zur alten Geschichte. Berlin: Akademie Verlag
Latomus	*Latomus.* Brussels: Societé des Études Latines de Bruxelles
Libyca	*Libyca.* Service des Antiquités de l'Algérie
MAAR	*Memoirs of the American Academy in Rome.* Rome: American Academy in Rome
M. and S.	Mattingley, H. and Sydenham, E.A. et al., *The Roman Imperial coinage.* London: Spink & Son, 1923–
MEFR	*Mélanges d'archaéologie et d'histoire de l'École française de Rome.* Paris: de Boccard
MonAnt	*Monumenti Antichi.* Rome: Accademia Nazionale dei Lincei
NSc	*Notizie degli scavi di antichità.* Rome: Accademia Nazionale dei Lincei
NZ	*Numismatische Zeitschrift.* Vienna: Num. Gesellschaft
Ostia I–IV	see *Studi Miscellanei* xiii, 1968; xvi, 1970; xxi, 1973; xxiii, 1975–6
Palladio	*Palladio.* Rivista di storia dell'architettura. Rome: Libr. dello Stato
PBSR	*Papers of the British School at Rome.* London: The British School at Rome
PIR²	*Prosopographia Imperii Romani. Saec. I–II–III.* 2nd ed. by E. Groag et al. Berlin: de Gruyter, 1933–
PLRE	*Prosopography of the later Roman Empire* I by A.H.M. Jones, J.R. Martindale and J. Morris, 1971; II by J.R. Martindale, 1980. Cambridge: C.U.P.
RCRF	*Rei Cretariae Romanae Fautorum.* Tongres: Michiels
RE	*Paulys Realencyclopädie der classischen Altertumswissenschaft.* hrsq. von G. Wissowa. Stuttgart, 1893–
Recherches	see Baldacci, 1972
Rend.Napoli	*Rendiconti dell'Accademia di Archaeologia, Lettere e Belle Arti di Napoli.* Naples: Società reale
RGKomm	*Bericht der Römisch- Germanischen Kommission des Deutschen Archäolischen Instituts.* Berlin: de Gruyter
Röm.Mitt.	*Mitteilungen des Deutschen Archeologischen Instituts (Römische Abteilung).* Mainz: von Zabern
RSL	*Rivista di Studi Liguri.* Bordighera: Ist. Internazionale di Studi Liouri
Sibrium	*Sibrium.* (Centro di Studi Preistorici e Archaeologici). Varese: Musei Civici di Villa Mirabello
Studi Miscellanei.	*Studi Miscellanei.* Seminario di Archeologia e Storia dell' Arte Greca e Romana dell''Università di Roma. Rome: L'Erma di Bretschneider

Adamsheck, Beverly, 1972–73. 'Hellenistic relief wares from Italy', *RCRF* Acta xiv–xv, 5–9

Alexander, Margaret A., and Ennaifer, Mongi, 1973. *Corpus des mosaïques antiques de Tunisie,* i, fasc.1. Tunis: Inst. Nat. d'Archéol. et d'Art

Alföldi, A., 1965. *Early Rome and the Latins.* Ann Arbor: Michigan U.P.

André, J.M., 1966. *L'otium dans la vie morale et intellectuelle romaine.* Paris: P.U.F.

Bachofen, Johann Jakob, 1958. 'Die Unsterblichkeitslehre der Orphischen Theologie. Römische Grablampen'. *Gesammelte Werke* vii. Basel/Stuttgart: Schwabe

Bailey, D.M., 1965. 'Lamps in the Victoria and Albert Museum'. *Opuscula Atheniensia* vi, 1–83. Lund: Gleerup

— —, 1975. *A catalogue of the lamps in the British Museum* i, London: The British Museum

— —, 1980. *A catalogue of the lamps in the British Museum* ii, London: The British Museum

Baldacci, P. et al., 1972. *Recherches sur les amphores romaines. Coll. de l'École française de Rome* x. Paris: de Boccard

Baradez, J., 1961. 'Nouvelles fouilles à Tipasa'. *Libyca* ix, 7–199

Becatti, Giovanni, 1961. *Scavi di Ostia* IV. *Mosaici e pavimenti marmorei.* Rome: Ist. poligrafico dello Stato

Beloch, Karl, 1890. *Campanien,* 2nd ed. Breslau: Morgenstern

— —, 1926. *Römische Geschichte bis zum Beginn der Punischen Kriege.* Berlin: de Gruyter

Benoit, Fernand, 1958. 'Nouvelles épaves de Provence'. *Gallia* xvi, 5–39

— —, 1961. 'Fouilles sous-marines. L'épave du Grand Congloué à Marseilles'. *Gallia* Suppl. xiv

Bergonzoni, Federigo, 1965. 'Bologna, Via Cà Selvatica. Edificio romano'. *NSc* xix Suppl., 59–68 and fig.5

Bernhard, M.L., 1955. *Lampki starozytne.* Warsaw: Museum Narodowe w Warszawie

Blake, Marion Elizabeth, 1930. 'The pavements of the Roman buildings of the Republic and Early Empire'. *MAAR* viii, 9–159

— —, 1947. *Ancient Roman construction in Italy from the prehistoric period to Augustus.* Washington: Carnegie Institution

— —, 1959. *Roman construction in Italy from Tiberius through the Flavians.* Washington. Carnegie Institution

Blanckenhagen, Peter von, see under Cotton, 1965 and 1965[2]

Bleckmann, F., 1912. 'Zu den rhodischen eponymen Heliospriestern'. *Klio* xii, 249–58

Bloch, Herbert, 1947–8. 'The Roman brick-stamps not published in Vol.xv.1 of the *CIL*'. *Harvard Studies in Classical Philology* lvi–lvii, 1947, 1–128 and 'Indices to Roman brick-stamps', ibid. lviii–lix, 1948, 1–104

Boëthius, Axel and Ward-Perkins, J.B., 1970. *Etruscan and Roman architecture* (The Pelican History of Art). Harmondsworth: Penguin

Brandizzi Vitucci, Paola, 1968. *FI* I, V, no.37, 116–17 and no.200, 181–2

Brants, Johanna, 1913. *Antieke terra-cotta lampen uit het Rijksmuseum van oudheden te Leiden.* Leiden: Ministerie van Binnenlandsche Zaken

Broneer, Oscar, 1930. *Terracotta lamps. Corinth* iv,2. Cambridge, Mass.: American School of Classical Studies at Athens

Brouette, E., 1948. 'Vinum Falernum. Contribution à l'étude de la sémantique latine au haut moyen âge'. *Classica et Medievalia* x, 267–73. Copenhagen: Gyldendal

Brown, Frank E., 1970–71. 'Contributo dell'archeologia alla storia sociale. Discussione'. *Dialoghi di Archeologia* iv–v, 362–3. Rome: Via Arenula 21

Brunt, P.A., 1971. *Italian manpower, 225 B.C.–A.D.14.* Oxford: Clarendon Press

Camps-Fabrer, Henriette, 1953. *L'olivier et l'huile dans l'Afrique romaine.* (Gouvern. Génér. de l'Algérie, Service des Antiquités.) Algiers: Impr. Officielle

Caprino, C., 1944–45. 'Guidonia. Villa rustica con "torcularium"'. *NSc* v–vi, 39–51

Carandini, A. and Settis, S., 1979. *Schiavi e padroni nell'Etruria romana.* Bari: De Donato

Carandini, A. and Tatton-Brown, T., 1980. 'Excavations at the Roman villa of "Sette Finestre" in Etruria, 1975–9. First interim report', in Painter, 1980,7–44

Carettoni, Gianfilippo, 1957. 'Roma, Paltino. Saggi nell'intorno della Casa di Livia'. *NSc* xi, 72–119

Carrington, R.C., 1931. 'Studies in the Campanian "villae rusticae"'. *JRS* xxi, 110–30

Castagnoli, Ferdinando, 1955. 'I più antichi esempi conservati di divisioni agrarie romane'. *Bulletino del Museo della Civiltà Romana* xviii, 1953–55, 3–9

— —, 1956. 'La centuriazione di Cosa'. *MAAR* xxiv, 147–65

Cerulli Irelli, G., 1965. 'San Sebastiano al Vesuvio. Villa rustica romana'. *NSc* xix, 161–78

Charlesworth, Dorothy, 1971. 'A group of vessels from the Commandant's House, Homesteads'. *Journal of Glass Studies,* Corning, xxxiv, 34–8

— —, 1975. 'A Roman cut glass plate from Wroxeter'. *AntJ* lv, 404–6

Cherry, John, see under Cotton, 1971

Chianese, G., 1938. 'Ruderi di villa romana a Napoli, in contrada S. Rocco di Capodimonte'. *Campania romana* i, 79–87. Naples: Rispoli

Coarelli, Filippo, 1976. 'Architettura e arti figurative in Roma: 150–50 a.C.', in Zanker, 1976, i 21–51

— —, 1977. 'Public building in Rome between the Second Punic War and Sulla'. *PBSR* xlv, 1–23

Cohen, Henry, 1880–92. *Description historique des monnaies frappées sous l'empire romaine . . .* 2nd ed. Paris: Rollin & Feuardent

Corradi, G., 1949. *Le vie romane da Sinuessa a Capua a Literno, Cumae, Pozzuoli, Atella, Napoli, Aversa*

Cotton, M. Aylwin, Blanckenhagen, P.von, and Ward-Perkins, J.B., 1965. 'Francolise (Caserta). Rapporto provvisorio del 1962–4 sugli scavi di due ville romane della Repubblica e del Primo Impero'. *NSc* xix, 237–52

— —, Blanckenhagen, P.von, and Ward-Perkins, J.B., 1965[2]. 'Two Roman villas at Francolise, Prov. Caserta. Interim report on excavations, 1962–4'. *PBSR* xxxiii, 55–69

— —, 1965[3]. 'Excavations at Francolise, Southern Italy'. *History Today* xv no.11, 799–800

— —, 1970–1. 'Contributo dell'archeologia alla storia sociale. Discussione'. *Dialoghi di Archaeologia* iv–v, 473–6

— — and Cherry, John, 1971. 'A trial excavation at Monte d'Irsi, Basilicata'. *PBSR* xxxix, 138–70

— —, 1979. *The late Republican villa at Posto, Francolise. PBSR* Suppl. Vol. London: The British School at Rome

Cozza, Lucos, 1952. 'Roma. (Via Anagnina, vocabolo Centroni Grotte). Natatio nell'antica villa detta dei Centroni'. *NSc* vi, 257–83

Crawford, Michael H., 1974. *Roman Republican coinage* I and II. Cambridge: C.U.P.

Crova, Bice, 1942. *Edilizia e tecnica rurale inRoma antica.* Milan: Bocca

Cuomo, Lucio, 1974. 'La colonia di Urbana'. *RendNapoli* xlix, 29–36

Cuomo di Caprio, Ninina, 1971–2. 'Proposta di classificazione delle fornaci per ceramica e laterizi nell'area italiana, dalla preistoria a tutta l'epoca romana'. *Sibrium* xi, 371–464

D'Arms, J.H., 1970. *Romans on the Bay of Naples* (Loeb Classical Monograph 846). Cambridge, Mass.: Harvard U.P.

— —, and Kopff, E.C. (eds.), 1980. *The seaborne commerce of ancient Rome: studies in archaeology and history. MAAR* xxxvi

Day, John, 1932. 'Agriculture in the life of Pompeii'. *Yale Classical Studies* iii, 165–208. New Haven: Yale U.P.

De Franciscis, Alfonso, 1966. 'Teanum'. *EAA* vii, 638–40

Degrassi, A., 1938. 'Problemi cronologici delle colonie di Luceria, Aquileia, Teanum Sidicinum'. *Rivista di Filologia* lxvi, 129–43, Torino: Loescher

Delano Smith, Catherine, 1979. *Western Mediterranean Europe. A historical geography of Italy, Spain and southern France since the Neolithic.* London: Academic Press

Della Corte, Matteo, 1921. 'Pompeii. Scavi eseguiti da privati nel territorio Pompeiano'. *NSc,* 415–67

— —, 1922. Ibid (secondo rapporto). *NSc,* 459–85

— —, 1923. Ibid (terzo rapporto). *NSc,* 271–87

— —, 1929. 'Teano. Avanzi di una vila suburbana e di una via publica'. *NSc,* 173–7

— —, 1929[2]. 'Boscoreale. Parziale scavo della villa rustica "M. Livi Marcelli"'. *NSc,* 178–89

— —, 1929[2]. 'Valle di Pompeii. Parziale esplorazione di una villa rustica nella cava di lapillo di Angelantonio De Martino'. *NSc,* 190–9

Della Valle, Guido, 1938. 'La Villa Sillana ed Augustea PAUSILYPON (Contributo alla storia dell'epicureismo campano)'. *Campania romana* i, 205–67. Naples: Ist. di Studi Romani

Deneauve, Jean, 1969. *Lampes de Carthage.* Centre de Recherches sur L'Afrique Mediterr. Paris: C.N.R.S.

Deringer, Hans, 1965. *Römische Lampen aus Lauriacum* (Forschungen in Lauriacum ix). Linz: Inst. für Landeskunde von Oberösterreich

De Rossi, Giovanni Maria, 1967. *FI* I, IV no.97, 133

— —, 1970. *FI* I, IX no.122, 71–4

De Vos, Mariette, 1975. 'Pitture e mosaico a Solunto'. *Bulletin Antieke Beschaving* l, no.2, 195–224. Leiden: Rapenburg 26

Di Cicco, V., 1903. 'Tricarico. Scoperta di avanzi di una villa romana'. *NSc*, 350

Drachmann, A.G., 1932. *Ancient oil mills and presses.* Copenhagen: Levin and Munksgaard

Drerup, H., 1959. 'Die römische villa'. *Marburger-Winckelmann Programm*

Dressel, H., in *CIL* XV.2 (part iii), 491 ff; 657 ff. and tav.II for amphorae forms

Dressel/Lamboglia, see under Lamboglia 1955, which gives Lamboglia's revision of Dressel's classification of lamp forms

Duncan, G.C., 1964. 'A Roman pottery near Sutri'. *PBSR* xxxii, 38–88

— —, 1965. 'Roman Republican pottery from the vicinity of Sutri'. *PBcSR* xxxiii, 134–76

Dyson, Stephen L., 1976. 'Cosa: the utilitarian pottery'. *MAAR* xxxiii

Ercolano, 1755–92. *Le antichità di Ertcolano esposte* viii. *Le lucerne ed i candelabri d'Ercolano.* Naples: Reale Accademia Ercolense

Fabbricotti, E., 1969. 'Le lucerne antiche dell'Antiquarium della Badia di Grottaferrata'. *Bolletino della Badia Greca di Grottaferrata*, n.s. xxiii, Jan.–Jun. 9–13. Rome: Semestrale

— —, 1974. 'Osservazioni sulle lucerne a Perline'. *Cenacolo* iv, 23–30

— —, 1976. 'I bagni nelle prime ville romane'. *Chronache pompeiane* ii, 29–111. Naples: Ass. Internaz. Amici di Pompei

Facenna, Domenico, 1957. 'Tivoli (Località Granaraccio). Resti della parte rustica di una villa'. *NSc* xi, 148–53

Fasolo, F., and Gullini, G., 1953. *Il santuario della Fortuna Primigenia a Palestrina.* Rome: Ist. di Archeol.

Felletti Maj, Bianca Maria, 1955. 'Roma (Via Tiberina). Villa rustica'. *NSc* ix, 206–16

Fraenkel, Ed., 1957. *Horace.* Oxford: Clarendon Press

Frederiksen, Martin, 1959. 'Republican Capua: a social and economic study'. *PBSR* xxvii, 80–130

— —, 1970–1. 'The contributionof archaeology to the agrarian problem in the Gracchan period'. *Dialoghi di Archeologia* iv–v, 330–67

Gentile, A., 1955. *La romanità dell'agro campano alla luce dei suoi nomi locali* i. *Tracce della centuriazione romana.* (Ist. di glottologia, Quaderni linguistici l) Naples: Univ. degli studi di Napoli

Giuliani, Cairoli F., 1970. *FI* I, VII, no.209, 315–35

Goudineau, C., 1968. *La céramique arétine lisse. MEFR,* Suppl. vi

Grace, Virginia R., 1952. 'Timbres amphoriques trouvés à Delos'. *BCH* lxxvi, 514–40

— —, 1953. 'The eponyms named on Rhodian amphora stamps'. *Hesperia* xxii, 116–28

— —, 1974. 'Revisions in early Hellenistic chronology'. *Ath.Mitt.* lxxxix, 193–203

— —, and Savvatianou-Pétropoulakou, Maria, 1970. 'Les timbres amphoriques grecs'. *Exploration archéologique de Délos* xxvii, chap.XIV, 277–382. Paris: de Boccard

Graziani Abbiani, M., 1969. *Lucerne fittili paleocristiane nell'Italia settentrionale. studi di antichità crist.* (with Dressel's classification revised by Lamboglia). Bologna: Pàtron

Greenidge, A.H.J., and Clay, A.M., 1960. *Sources for Roman history 133–70 B.C.,* 2nd ed., rev. by E.W. Gray. Oxford: D.U.P.

Gros, Pierre, 1978. *Architecture et société à Rome et en Italie centroméridionale aux deux derniers siècles de la République.* Coll. Latomus clvi. Brussels: Soc. des Études Latines de Bruxelles

Gullini, Giorgio, 1953, see under Fasolo, F.

— —, 1973. 'La datazione e l'inquadramento stilistico del santuario della Fortuna Primigenia a Palestrina', in *Aufstieg und Niedergang der Römischen Welt* i,4, 746–99. Berlin: de Gruyter

Hanoune, Roger, 1970. 'Lampes de Graviscae'. *MEFR* lxxxii, 237–62

Harden, Donald B., 1961. 'Domestic window glass, Roman, Saxon and Medieval', in *Studies in building history, presented to B.H. St. J. O.'Neill,* ed. E.M. Jope, 39–63. London: Odhams

Hartley, Katherine F., 1973. *The marketing and distribution of mortaria,* C.B.A. Research Report x, 39–51. London: The Council for British Archaeology

— —, 973[1]. 'La diffusion des mortiers tuiles et autres produits en provenance des fabriques italiennes'. *Cahiers d'archéologie subaquatique* ii, 49–60. Gap: Louis-Jean

Hayes, J.W., 1972. *,ate Roman pottery.* London: The British School at Rome

Heres, Gerald, 1972. *Die römischen Bildlampen der Berliner Antikensammlung.* Berlin: Akademie Verlag

Heurgon, Jacques, 1942. *Recherches sur l'histoire, la religion et la civilisation de Capoue préromaine des origines à la deuxième guerre punique.* Bib. des Écoles françaises d'Athènes et de Rome cliv. Paris: de Boccard

— —, 1976. 'Viaggi dei Romani nella Magna Grecia', *Atti del xv convegno di studi sulla Magna Grecia, Taranto 1975.* 9–29. Naples: Arte tipogr.

Hiller von Gaertringen, F., 1931. 'Rhodos'. *RE* Suppl. v, 731–840

Hülsen, C., 1899. 'Cales', *RE* iii, 1351–2

1971–2

— —, 1909. 'Falernus Ager', *RE* vi, 2, 1971–2

Illana, Alberto Balil, 1968. *Lucernae singulares.* Coll. Latomus xciii. Brussels: Soc. des Études Latines de Bruxelles

Isings, C., 1957. 'Roman glass from dated finds'. *Archaeologica Traiectina* ii. Groningen: Wolters

— —, 1971. 'Roman glass in Limburg'. *Archaeologica Traiectina* ix. Groningen: Wolters

Ivanyi, Dora, 1935. *Die Pannonischen Lampen.* (Diss. Pannonicae ser. 2.2). Budapest: Ist. Numismatico

Jacopi, Giulio, 1936. 'Sabaudia. Scavi nella villa di Domiziano in località Palazzo sul lago di Paola'. *NSc,* 21–50

Jashemski, Wilhelmina F., 1973. 'A large vineyard discovered in ancient Pompeii'. *Science* clxxx, 821–30

— —, 1974. 'The discovery of a market garden orchard at Pompeii: The garden of the House of the ship Europa'. *AJA* lxxvii, 391–404

Johannowsky, Werner, 1961. 'Relazione preliminare sugli scavi di Cales'. *Bd'A* xlvi, 258–67

— —, 1963. 'Relazione preliminare sugli scavi di Teano'. *Bd'A* xlviii, 131–65

— —, 1965. 'L'occupazione etrusca di Campania', in Alföldi, 1965

— —, 1970–1. 'Contributo dell'archeologia alla storia sociale. La Campania'. *Dialoghi di Archeologia* iv–v, 460–71

— —, 1974. 'L'attività archeologica nel Casertano'. *Atti del xiii convegno di studi sulla Magna Grecia, Taranto 1973.* 353–6. Naples: Arte tipogr.

— —, 1975. 'Problemi archeologici campani'. *Rend. Napoli* l, 3–38

— —, 1976. 'La situazione in Campania', in Zanker, 1976, i 267–99

— —, 1977. 'L'atività archeologica nel Casertano'. *Atti del xvi convegno di studi sulla Magna Grecia, Taranto 1976.* 771–3. Naples: Arte tipogr.

Jones, G.D.B., 1962. 'Capena and the Ager Capenas, I'. *PBSR* xxx, 116–207

— —, 1963. 'Capena and the AGer Capenas, II'. *PBSR* xxxi, 100–58

Juengst, E., and Thielscher, P., 1954 and 1957. 'Catos Keltern und Kollergänge. Ein Beitrag zur Geschichte von Oel und Wein'. *BonnJahr* cliv, 32–93 and clvii, 53–126

Kahane, A., Murray-Threipland, L. and Ward-Perkins, J.B., 1968. 'The Ager Veientanus, north and east of Veii'. *PBSR* xxxvi, 1–218

Klumbach, Hans, 1956. 'Das Verbreitungsgebiet der spätitalischen Terra Sigillata'. *Jahrbuch des Röm.-Germ. Zentralmuseums Mainz* iii, 117–33

Koethe, Harald von, 1940. 'Die Bäder römischer Villen im Trierer Bezirk'. *RGKomm* xxx, 43–131

Lacchini, Magda, 1972–3. 'Il territorio di Altinum. Confini, configurazioni geografiche e centuriazione'. *AttiCesDIR* iv, 191–226

Laidlaw, Ann, 1964. 'The tomb of Montefiore. A new Roman tomb painted in the Second Style'. *Archaeology* xvii, 33–42

— —, 1975. 'A reconstruction of the First Style decoration in the Alexander exedra of the House of Faun'. *Neue Forschungen in Pompeji,* ed. B. Andreae and H. Kyrieleis, 39–52. Recklinghausen: Bongers

Lamboglia, Nino, 1950. *Gli scavi di Albintimilium e la cronologia della ceramica romana.* Coll. di Monog. Preist. & Archeol. ii. Bordighera: Ist. Int. di Studi Liguri

— —, 1952. 'Per una classificazione preliminare della ceramica campana'. *Atti del i congresso int. di studi Liguri, 1950.* Bordighera: Ist. Int. di Studi Liguri

— —, 1955. 'Sulle cronologia delle anfore romane di età repubblicana'. *RSL* xxi, 241–70

Lehmann-Hartleben, Karl, see under Noack, 1936

Leibundgut, Annalis, 1963–4. 'Antike Lampen im Bernischen Historischen Museum'. *Jahrbuch des Bernischen Historischen Museums in Bern* xliii–xliv, 408–60

Lerat, Lucien, 1954. *Les lampes antiques* (Catalogue des collections archeólogiques de Besançon, 2e série, i, fasc.1). Paris: Les Belles Lettres

Levi, M.A., 1921–2. 'I confini dell'agro campano'. *Atti della Accademia delle Scienze di Torino* lvii, 604–16

Libertini, Guido, 1930. *Il Museo Biscari*. Milan/Rome: Casa Editrice d'Arte Bestetti e Tumminelli

— —, 1947. 'Lipari. Villagio neolitico e necropoli classiche.' *NSc*, 214–20

Lissi Caronna, E., 1971. 'Fondi (Latina). Resti di parte di un impianto termale in piazza della Unità'. *NSc*, 330–63

Loeschcke, S., 1911. *Beschreibung römischer Altertümer gesammelt von Carl Anton Niessen*, 3rd ed., Bd 1, text, Bd 2, illustrations. Cologne: von Greven & Bechtold

— —, 1919. *Lampen aus Vindonissa*. Zurich: Baer

Lugli, Giuseppe, 1921. 'Albano Laziale. Avanzi di antiche ville sui colli Albani'. *NSc*, 263–73

— —, 1927. 'Villa Adriano. Una villa di età repubblicana'. *BullCom* lv, 139–204

— —, 1930. 'Via Nomentana. Scavo di una villa di età repubblicana in località San Basilio'. *NSc*, 529–35

— —, 1946. 'Albano Laziale. Scavo dell'Albanum Pompeii'. *NSc*, 60–83

— —, 1952. 'Osservazioni sulle stazioni della Via Appia antica da Roma ad Otranto', in *Beiträge zur älteren europäischen Kulturgeschichte. Festschrift für Rudolf Egger*, 276–93. Klagenfurt: Geschichtsver. fur Kärnten

— —, 1957. *La tecnica edilizia romana*. Rome: G.Bardi

— —, 1965. *Studi minori di topografia antica*, 384–97. Rome: De Luca

McDonald, Alexander H., 1966. *Republican Rome*. London: Thames and Hudson

Maciariello, N., 1964. *Un fiume che fa rumoroso e pigro—il savone.* (Tavolette per la storia di Francolise 1). Santa Maria di Capua Vetere

McKay, A.G., 1975. *Houses, villas and palaces in the Roman world.* London: Thames and Hudson

MacMullen, Ramsay, 1970. 'Market days in the Roman Empire'. *Phoenix* xxiv, 333–41. Toronto: Classical Assoc. of Canada

Maetzke, Guglielmo, 1958. 'Orbetello. Trovamenti archeologici vari'. *NSc*, 34–41

Maiuri, Amedeo, 1938. 'La villa augustea di Palazzo a Mare a Capri'. *Campania romana* i, 115–41. Naples: Ist. di Studi Romani

— —, 1947. *La villa dei Misteri*, 2nd ed. Rome: Libr. dello Stato

— —, 1957. *Passegiate campane*, 3rd ed. Florence: Sansoni

— —, and Pane, Roberto, 1947. *La case di Loreio Tiburtino e la villa di Diomede in Pompei.* Rome: Libr. dello Stato

Manacorda, Daniele, 1977. 'Anfore spagnole a Pompei', in *L'instrumentum domesticum di Ercolano e Pompei nella prima età imperiale:* Quad. di cultura materiale i. Rome: L'Erma di Bretschneider

— —, 1978. 'The Ager Cosanus and the production of the amphorae of Sestius: new evidence and a reassessment'. *JRS* lxviii, 122–31

Mansuelli, Guido Achille, 1958. *Le ville del mondo romano*. Quad. di storia dell'arte viii. Milan: Pleion

Mau, Auguste, see under Overbeck, 1884

Meiggs, R., 1973. *Roman Ostia*, 2nd ed. Oxford: Clarendon Press

Menzel, Heinz, 1969. *Antike Lampen im Römisch-Germanischen Zentralmuseum zu Mainz*, Kat.15. Mainz: Philip von Zabern

Mercando, Liliana, 1962. *Lucerne greche e romane dell'Antiquarium Comunale*. Rome: Musei Monumenti Scavi. Grafio Tiberino

Mingazzini, P., and Pfister, F., 1946. 'La villa sullo Scoglio dell'Isca (o Galluzzo)'. *FI* I, II, 153–7

Moevs, Maria Teresa Marabini, 1973. 'The Roman thin-walled pottery from Cosa (1948–54)'. *MAAR* xxii

Moore, Richard E., 1968. 'A newly observed stratum in Roman floor mosaics'. *AJA* lxxii, 57–68 and figs.1–11

Morel, Jean-Paul, 1963. 'Notes sur la céramique etrusco-campanienne. Vases à vernis noir de Sardaigne et d'Arrezzo'. *MEFR* lxxv, 1–58

— —, 1965. *Céramique à vernis noir du Forum et du Palatin. MEFR* Suppl.iii

— —, 1976. 'Aspects de l'artisanat dans la Grand-Grèce romaine'. *Atti del xv convegno di studi sulla Magna Grecia, Taranto 1975*, 263–324. Naples: Arte tipogr.

Moritz, L.A., 1958. *Grain-mills and flour in Classical Antiquity.* Oxford: Clarendon Press

Morricone Matini, Maria Luisa, 1965. 'Mosaici romani a cassettoni del I secolo a.C.'. *ArchClass* xvii, 79–91 and pls. xxiii–xxix

— —, 1967. *Mosaici antichi in Italia. Regione prima, Roma. Reg.X, Palatium.* Rome: Ist. poligr. dello Stato

— —, 1971. *Mosaici antichi in Italia. Studi monografici I, Pavimenti di signino repubblicani di Roma e dintorni.* Rome: Ist. poligr. dello Stato

— —, and Scrinari, V.S.M., 1975. *Mosaici antichi in Italia. Regione prima, Antium.* Rome: Ist. poligr. dello Stato

— —, 1980. *Scutulata pavimenta.* Rome: L'Erma di Bretschneider

Munro, J.A.R., 1890. 'Excavations in Cyprus, 1889. Second season's work. Polis tes Chrysochou—Limniti. III. Contents of the tombs'. *JHS* xi, 31–60

Murray-Threipland, Leslie, see under Kahane, 1968

Mustilli, Domenico, 1956. 'La villa pseudo-urbana ercolanese'. *Rend. Napoli* xxxi, 77–97

Muzzioli, Maria Pia, 1970. *FI* I,VIII, no.15, 43–8 and fig.37

Nilsson, Martin P., 1909. *Timbres amphoriques de Lindos. Exploration archéologique de Rhodes* v. Copenhagen: Luno

Nissen, Heinrich, 1902. *Italische Landeskunde* ii. Berlin: Weidmann

Noack, Ferdinand and Lehmann-Hartleben, Karl, 1936. *Baugeschichtliche Untersuchungen am Stadtrand von Pompeji.* Berlin: de Gruyter

Noll, Rudolf, 1937. 'Eine neue oberitalische Lampentöpferei'. *Jahresheft des Österreichischen Archäologischen Instituts in Wien* xxx, Beiblatt, 108–19. Vienna: Rudolf M. Rohrer

Oates, David, 1953. 'The Tripolitanian Gebel: settlement of the Roman period around Gasr-ed-Daun'. *PBSR* xxi, 81–117

Osborne, Alfred, 1924. *Lychnos et Lucerna. Catalogue raisonné d'une collection de lampes en terrecuite trouvées en Egypte.* Alexandria: Soc. Arch. Alex.

Ostia I: *Studi miscellanei* xiii, 1968

Ostia II: *Studi miscellanei* xvi, 1970

Ostia III, i and ii: *Studi miscellanei* xxi, 1973

Ostia IV: *Studi miscellanei* xxiii, 1975–6

Overbeck, Johannes, and Mau, Auguste, 1884. *Pompeji in seinen Gebäuden, Alterthümern und Kunstwerken dargestellt.* 4th ed. Leipzig: Engelmann

Pagano, Mario, and Ferrone, C., 1977. *Sinuessa, ricerche storiche e topograpfiche (Archeol.e Storia della campania ant.* ii) Naples: Athena Mediterranea

Pagano, M., 1978. 'Note su una località della Via Appia fra Sinuessa e Capua: il "pons Campanus"'. *RendNapoli* liii, 227–34

Pagenstecher, Rudolf, 1909. *Die Calenische Reliefkeramik. Jahrbuch des Deutschen Archäologischen Instituts,* Ergänzungsheft viii. Berlin: de Gruyter

Painter, Kenneth (ed), 1980. *Roman villas in Italy: recent excavations and research.* British Museum Occasional Paper xxiv. London: British Museum

Pallottino, Massimo, 1937. 'Capena. Resti di construzioni romani e medioevali in località Montecanino'. *NSc,* 7–28

Panella, Clementina, 1977. 'Anfore tripolitane a Pompei', in *L'instrumentum domesticum di Ercolano e Pompei nella prima età imperiale,* 135–49. Rome: L'Erma di Bretschneider

— —, 1980. 'Retroterra, porti e mercati: l'esempio dell'ager Falernus', in d'Arms and Kopff, 1980, 251–60

Paribeni, R., 1903. 'Boscoreale. Villa rustica rinvenuta nella Contrada Centopiedi, al Tirone'. *NSc,* 64–7

— —, 1924. 'Roma. Via Latina'. *NSc,* 423–4

Parlasca, Klaus, 1959. *Die römischen Mosaiken in Deutschland.* Berlin: de Gruyter

Pasqui, A., 1897. 'La villa pompeiana della Pisanella. Presso Boscoreale'. *MonAnt* vii, 398-554

Pavolini, C., 1976–7. 'Una produzione italica di lucerne: le *Vogelkopflampen* ad ansa trasversale'. *Bulletino della Commissione Archeologica Comunale di Roma* lxxxv, 45–134. Rome: Comune di Roma

— —, 1981. 'Le lucerne nell'Italia romana', in A.Giardina and A.Schiavone, *Merci, mercati e scambi nel Mediterraneo* (*Societa romana e produzione schiavistica* ii), 139–184. Bari: Laterza

Peacock, David, 1977. 'Recent discoveries of Roman amphora kilns in Italy'. *AntJ* lvii, 262–9

Pellegrino, Angelo, 1978. 'Iscrizione di Mondragone', *Miscellanea greca e romana,* Studi pubblicati dall'Ist. Ital. per la Storia Antica, vi, 383–94. Rome

Percival, John, 1976. *The Roman villa. An historical introduction.* London: Batsford

Perlzweig, Judith, 1961. *Lamps of the Roman period. The Athenian Agora,* vii. Princeton, N.J.: The American School of Classical Studies at Athens

Pernice, Erich, 1938. *Die hellenistische Kunst in Pompeji,* Band vi, *Pavimente und figürliche Mosaiken.* Berlin: de Gruyter

Pfister, Fredericus, see under Mingazzini, 1946

Pompeii, 1973. *Catalogue of Exhibition, Pompeii* (Jan.–March 1973), Petit Palais, Paris

Ponsich, Michel, 1961. *Les lampes romaines en terre cuite de la Maurétanie tingitane. Publications du Service des Antiquités du Maroc* xv. Rabat

Potter, T.W., 1980. 'Villas in south Etruria: some comments and contexts', in Painter, 1980, 73–81

Poulsen, V.H., 1960. A.Boëthius et al. *San Giovenale. Etruskerna landet och folket.* Malmö: Allhems

Quilici, Lorenzo, [1974]. *FI* I,X. *Collatia*

— —, 1976. 'Castel Giubileo (Roma). Saggi di scavo attorno a Fidenae'. *NSc,* 263–326

Quilici, L., and Quilici Gigli, S., 1978. 'Ville dell'Agro Cosano con fronte a torrette'. *Riv. dell'Ist. Naz. di Archeologia e Storia dell'Arte* iii, I, 11–64. Rome: L'Erma di Bretschneider

Radke, Gerhard, 1973. 'Viae publicae Romanae'. *RE* Suppl.xiii

Rakob, Friedrich, 1976. 'Hellenismus in Mittelitalien. Bautypen und Bautechnik', in Zanker, 1976, ii, 366–86

Rawson, Elizabeth, 1976. 'The Ciceronian aristocracy and its properties', in *Studies in Roman property,* ed. M.I.Finley. Cambridge: C.U.P.

Richardson, Lawrence, 1976. 'The evolution of the Porticus Octaviae'. *AJA* lxxx, 57–64

Robotti, Carlo, 1973. 'Una sinopia musiva pavimentale a Stabia'. *Bd'A* lviii, 42–4 and figs. 1–5

Rocco, Anna, 1954. 'S. Rocco di Marano (Napoli). Ricognizione archeologica nella frazione di S. Rocco'. *NSc,* 33–8

Rolland, Henri, 1951. *Fouilles de Saint-Blaise (Bouches-du-Rhône). Gallia* iii, Suppl.

Rose, H.J., 1936. *A handbook of Latin literature.* London: Methuen

Rostovtzeff, M., 1911. *Hellenistisch-römische Architekturlandschaft. Röm. Mitt.* xxvi

— —, 1957. *The social and economic history of the Roman Empire,* 2nd ed. revised by P.M. Fraser. Oxford: Clarendon Press

Ruoff-Väänänen, E., 1978. *Studies on the Italian fora. Historia* Einzelschrift xxxii. Wiesbaden: Steiner

Salmon, E.T., 1967. *Samnium and the Samnites.* Cambridge: C.U.P.

Schiavo, Armando, 1939. 'La villa romana di Minori'. *Palladio* iii, 129–33

Schmiedt, G. (ed), 1972. *Il livello antico del mar Tirreno. Testimonianze dei resti archeologici.* Florence: Olschki

Schöne-Mau=Schöne, R., and Mau, A., in *CIL* IV, Suppl.2, Tav.III

Schumm, Stanley A., 1977. *The fluvial system.* New York: Wiley

Scullard, H.H., 1959. *From the Gracchi to Nero.* London: Methuen

Shatzman, Israel, 1975. *Senatorial wealth and Roman politics.* Coll. Latomus cxlii. Brussels: Soc. des Études Latines

Sirago, Vito Antonio, 1958. *L'Italia agraria sotto Traiano.* Louvain: Pub. Universitaires

Skydsgaard, J.E., 1961. *Den Romerske villa rustica* (*Studier fra sprog-og oldtidsforskening* ccxlvi). Copenhagen

— —, 1969. 'Nuove ricerche sulla villa rustica Romana fino all'epoca di Traiano'. *Analecta Romana Instituti Danici* v, 25–40

— —, 1970. *Pompeii en Romersk Provinsby.* Copenhagen

Small, Alastair, (ed.) 1977. *Monte Irsi, Southern Italy.* British Archaeological Reports. Suppl. series xx. Oxford

— —, 1980. 'San Giovanni di Ruoti: some problems in the interpretation of the structures', in Painter, 1980, 91–109

Spano, G., 1927. 'Formia. a) Ruderi di una villa romana in contrada Vendicio'. *NSc,* 434–43

Spinazzola, Vittorio, 1953. *Pompei alla luce degli scavi nuovi di Via dell'Abbondanza.* 2 vols. Rome: Libr. dello Stato

Staccioli, Romolo Augusto, 1958. 'Sugli edifici termali minori'. *ArchClass* x, 273–8

Stefani, Enrico, 1944–5. 'Grottarossa (vocabolo Monte delle Grotte). Ruderi di una villa di età repubblicana'. *NSc,* 52–72

Swoboda, K.M., 1924. *Römische und romanische Paläste,* 2nd ed. Vienna: Schroll

Szentléleky, Tihamér, 1969. *Ancient lamps.* Amsterdam: Hakkert

Tamaro, B., 1928. 'Isola. Costruzione romana'. *NSc,* 412–4

Taylor, Doris Mae, 1957. 'Cosa: Black-glaze pottery'. *MAAR* xxv, 65–193

Tchernia, André, see under Zevi, 1969 and 1972

— —, 1980. 'Quelques remarques sur le commerce du vin et les amphores', in d'Arms and Kopff, 1980, 305–23

Thielscher, Paul, 1963. *Des Marcus Cato Belehrung über die Landwirtschaft.* Berlin: Duncker and Humblot

— —, see under Juengst, 1954 and 1957

Thomsen, R., 1947. *The Italic regions from Augustus to the Lombard invastion.* Copenhagen: Gyldendal

Thouvenot,R., 1954. 'Lampes en terre cuite'. *Publications du Service des Antiquités du Maroc* xi, 113–25. Rabat

Tibiletti, Gianfranco, 1950. 'Ricerche di storia agraria romana I'. *Athenaeum* n.s. xxviii, 183–266

Uenze, Otto, 1958. *Frührömische Amphoren als Zeitmarken in Spät-La-Tène.* Marburg: Elvert

Vallat, J-P., 1979. 'Le vocabulaire des attributions de terres en Campanie: analyse spatiale et temporelle'. *MEFR* xci, 977–1017

— —, 1980. 'Cadastrations et contrôle de la terre en Campanie septentrionale (IVe siècle av.J.C.– Ier siècle ap. J.C.)'. *MEFR* xcii, 387–444

— —, 1981. 'Les dossiers—Les villas gallo-romaines: L'agriculture en Campanie du nord'. *Histoire et Archéologie* lviii, 12–19

Valletrisco, Anna, 1977. 'Note sulla topografia di Suessa Aurunca'. *RendNapoli* lii, 59–73

Vegas, Mercedes, 1968. 'Römische Keramik von Gabii (Latium)'. *BonnJahr* clxviii, 13–55

Vita-Finzi, Claudio, 1969. *The Mediterranean valleys. Geological change in historical times.* Cambridge: C.U.P.

von Gaertringen, see Hiller von Gaertringen

Waldhauer, Oskar, 1914. *Die antike Tonlampen.* St Petersburg: Hermitage Museum

Walker, D.S., 1967. *A geography of Italy.* 2nd ed. London: Methuen

Walters, H.B., 1914. *Catalogue of the Greek and Roman lamps in the British Museum.* London: British Museum

Ward-Perkins, J.B., see under Cotton, 1965 and 1965[2]

— —, see under Kahane, 1968

— —, see under Boëthius, 1970

— —, 1970[2]. 'Francolise'. *EAA* Suppl., 338

White, K.D., 1970. *Roman farming.* London: Thames and Hudson

— —, 1975. *Farm equipment of the Roman world.* London: C.U.P.

Widrig, Walter M., 1980. 'Two sites on the ancient Via Gabina', in Painter, 1980, 119–40

Wiseman, T.P., 1970. 'Roman republican road building'. *PBSR* xxxviii, 122–52

— —, 1971. *New men in the Roman Senate, 139 B.C.–A.D. 14.* Oxford: O.U.P.

Yeo, Cedric, 1948. 'The overgrazing of ranch-lands in ancient Italy'. *transactions and Proceedings of the American Philological Association* lxxix, 275–307. Cleveland, Ohio: Case Western Reserve University

Zanker, Paul (ed.), 1976. *Hellenismus in Mittelitalien. Kolloquium in Göttingen vom 5. bis 9. Juni 1974*. Göttingen: Vandenhoeck and Ruprecht

Zevi, Fausto, 1966. 'Appunti sulle anfore romane'. *ArchClass* xviii, 208–47

— —, and Tchernia, A., 1969. 'Amphores de Byzacène au Bas-Empire'. *Antiquités Africaines* iii, 173–95. Paris: C.N.R.S.

— —, and Pohl, Ingrid, 1970. 'Ostia, Saggi di scavo'. *NSc* Supp.1, 18–22 and figs.12–13

— —, and Tchernia, A., 1972. 'Amphores vinaires de Campanie et de Tarraconaise à Ostie', in Baldacci et al., 1972, 35–67

INDEX

PLATE I

Photo: J. B. W. P.

View of the Ager Falernus and Monte Massico, from the platform of the San Rocco villa.

PLATE II

Photo: J. B. W. P.

a. The platform of the villa and the chapel of San Rocco.

Photo: R. Borwick

b. The village of Francolise and its Castle.

PLATE III

a. Water buffaloes in the Ager Falernus.

Photo: R. Borwick

Photo: G. Sansbury

b. View of the upper and lower terraces showing the Period I retaining wall of the upper terrace and the peristyle and *viridarium*.

PLATE IV

a. Room A and its Period I floor (*op. mus.* 1).

Photo: *J. B. W. P.*

Photo: *G. Sansbury*

b. The round reservoir in room A.

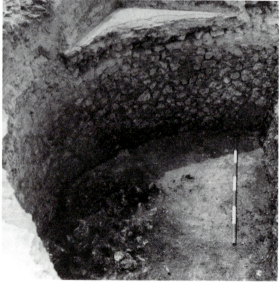

Photo: *G. Sansbury*

c. The interior view of the reservoir.

PLATE V

a. Room D. The Period I main hall, showing two of the buttresses.

b. Room H. Parts of the Period I threshing floors under Period II walls and the *op. sig.* 2 floor.

PLATE VI

Photo: P. Wallace-Zeuner

a. The cut-down southern retaining wall of the Period I villa under the Period II
terrace fill.

Photo: J. B. W. P.

b. The *dolium* under a Period II wall.

PLATE VII

Photo: P. Wallace-Zeuner

a. Room D1, a *cubiculum.* The Period 1A pavement (*op. mus.* 3) and an island of Period II
fill under a Period II mosaic (*op. mus.* 29 of room 35).

Photo: J. B. W. P.

b. Room D4. A Period 1A *cubiculum.* Floors of *op. mus.* 4 and 30 (swastika mosaic) with
op. sig. 11 beyond it.

PLATE VIII

b. The lime-coated interior of one of these cisterns.

a. Broken eastern end of the Period II water cisterns in the west upper terrace

PLATE IX

Photo: J. B. W. P.

a. The exposed outer face of the Period II west terrace retaining wall, in *opus incertum.*

Photo: P. Wallace-Zeuner

b. The Period II doorway blocking in the north terrace retaining wall.

Photo: J. B. W. P.

c. The inside face of the Period II west terrace retaining wall, and the I/IA debris layer and II fill.

Photo: P. Wallace-Zeuner

d. The inner face of the Period II east terrace retaining wall.

PLATE X

The Period II *exedra*, *tablinum* and *triclinium*, looking N.

PLATE XI

Photo: P. Wallace-Zeuner

b. Displaced columns found in the *villa rustica.*

Photo: M. A. Cotton

d. The broken marble basin, in the *viridium.*

The peristyle and *viridarium.*

Photo: M. A. Cotton

a. The seating for a column in the peristyle.

Photo: M. A. Cotton

c. Stucco coating from a fallen column.

PLATE XII

Photo: E. Nash

Room 8. The Period II mosaic floor (*op. mus.* 18), truncated by a Period IIA wall when the room was converted into a *frigidarium* and *sudatorium*.

PLATE XIII

Photo: E. Nash

Room 10, the *culina*, with its floor (*op. spic.* 1). The seating for the *testudo*, and the Period IIA bath wing, are in the background. Looking W towards the castle of Francolise.

PLATE XIV

Photo: J. B. W. P.

a. Room 10. The ramp from the corridor down to the *culina*, with its *op. spic.* 1 floor.

Photo: J. B. W. P.

b. Room 12. The mosaic floor (*op. mus.* 20) destroyed by the hospital walls.

PLATE XV

Photo: J. B. W. P.

a. Room 39. The west portico, with a fallen column.

Photo: J. B. W. P.

b. Detail of the structure of the column.

Photo: M. A. Cotton

c. A pier in the west portico.

Photo: M. A. Cotton

d. The *lavabo* and drain.

PLATE XVI

Photo: E. Nash

a. View, looking east, towards the *villa rustica,* south terrace and the *hortus. Cubicula* D1 and D4 are in the foreground, with their floors (*op. mus.* 3 and 4).

Photo: J. B. W. P.

b. Room 52. The Period II latrine and its floor (*op. spic.* 3).

Photo: G. Sansbury

c. The drain from the latrine in courtyard 2.

PLATE XVII

a. The Period II threshing floor in courtyard 2, and the limestone base set in a niche. *Photo: J. B. W. P.*

b. Structural detail of the threshing floor. *Photo: J. B. W. P.*

PLATE XVIII

Photo: G. Sansbury

a. The Period IIA bath suite. The *frigidarium* and doorway to the *sudatorium*.

Photo: G. Sansbury

b. The cold bath to the N of room A1.

Photo: E. Nash

c. The *sudatorium*, with the room with the *praefurnium* in the background.

PLATE XIX

Photo: J. B. W. P.

a. The Period IIA bath suite. The *caldarium* with its marble floor.

Photo: J. B. W. P.

b. The hot bath in the *caldarium*.

PLATE XX

Photo: J. B. W. P.

a. Kiln 1 in room 49.

Photo: J. B. W. P.

b. The interior of kiln 1.

Photo: G. Sansbury

c. Kiln 2 in room 49.

Photo: G. Sansbury

d. The drying oven.

The Period IIA *figlina*

PLATE XXI

Photo: J. B. W. P.

a. The Period IIA *oletum*. General view of rooms 53 and 54, with *op. spic.* 6 and *op. sig.* 14 floors. Room 52, the destroyed latrine, is in the background.

Photo: J. B. W. P.

b. Room 53, showing the *ara, trapetum,* one of the grooved stones, and the *op. spic.* 6 floor.

Photo: J. B. W. P.

c. Room 54, with the round platform and open basin, and *op. sig.* 14 floor.

PLATE XXII

Photo: G. Sansbury

a. The *trapetum, ara* and *arbores* in room 54; and the sedimentation tank, round basin and *capulator's* tank in room 53.

Photo: J. B. W. P.

b. Details of the *trapetum.*

Photo: J. B. W. P.

c. The oil channel, in the floor, between the *ara* and the sedimentation tank.

PLATE XXIII

a. The oil separating vats in rooms 57 and 58.

Photo: E. Nash

Photo: P. Wallace-Zeuner

b. The 'standing platform' and pit for water settlement in the larger vat.

Photo: P. Wallace-Zeuner

c. The grooves or slots in the sides of the raised compartment of the smaller vat.

PLATE XXIV

Photo: E. Nash

a. Room A/A1. *Op. mus.* 1, on the right, showing basketweave in its background tesserae; *op. mus.* 2, on the left, showing square background tesserae.

Photo: E. Nash

b. Rooms A/A1/29. *Op. mus.* 1, on the lower right; *op. mus.* 2, on the upper left, *op. mus.* 27 along the N wall and *op. mus.* 19 in the passage between the rooms. Looking NE.

PLATE XXV

Photo: J. B. W. P.

a. Room D1, in the background, with its floor of *op. mus.* 3; an island of Period II fill under *op. mus.* 29 of room 35. Room D4/36, in the foreground, with *op. mus.* 4 and *op. mus.* 30 (swastika mosaic) and *op. sig.* 11 to its left. Looking NE.

Photo: J. B. W. P.

b. Room D4 (background) and 36 (foreground). *Op. mus.* 4 in background, *op. mus.* 30 (the swastika band) and *op. sig.* in the foreground. Looking E.

Photo: J. B. W. P.

c. Room 4D. Detail of *op. mus.* 30.

PLATE XXVI

Photo: E. Nash

a. Room 1. *Op. mus.* 5. *Cancellum* on right, threshold on lower left. In background, *op. mus.* 6. Looking NE.

Photo: E. Nash

b. Room 2. *Op. mus.* 6. The diagonal wall is a modern intrusion. Looking NE.

PLATE XXVII

Photo: J. B. W. P.

a. Room 1. *Op. mus.* 6 threshold in foreground; *op. mus.* 8 of the peristyle in the background. Looking N.

Photo: E. Nash

b. Peristyle. *Op. mus.* 8. A section of *scutulatum pavimentum* in front of the *tablinum*. Looking E towards the borders and *viridarium*.

PLATE XXVIII

Photo: M. A. Cotton

a. *Op mus.* 9, on the E side.

Photo: M. A. Cotton

b. *Op. mus.* 10, on the S side.

Photo: P. Wallace-Zeuner

c. *Op. mus.* 11, on the S side.

Peristyle 'mats' between the columns

Photo: P. Wallace-Zeuner

d. *Op. mus.* 12, on the W side.

The top of the plate is to the N.

PLATE XXIX

Photo: M. A. Cotton

Photo: M. A. Cotton

a. Bed with *nuclei* of prefabricated hexagons and *nucleus* of hexagonal borders with laying-out lines and guidelines for pattern of tesserae.

b. Marble border; *nucleus* with laying-out lines and guidelines; preserved parts of hexagonal borders.

Photo: M. A. Cotton

Photo: J. B. W. P.

c. The extension, to the S. of *b* above, showing the *opus sectile* insets.

d. Detail of the N end. Prefabricated hexagon and half hexagon laid *in situ; nucleus* with laying-out lines and guidelines.

Room 4. *Tablinum,* threshold mosaic *op. mus.* 13. The top of the plate is to the N.

PLATE XXX

Photo: Joanna Bird

a. In situ.

Photo: E. Nash

b. After lifting and repair.

The threshold between room 4, the *tablinum*, and room 31a. *Op. mus.* 15, the 'city gate' mosaic.

PLATE XXXI

Photo: M. A. Cotton

Photo: M. A. Cotton

a. Room 4. The *tablinum. Op. mus.* 14 showing the preserved part of the crosslets and the chevrons border of the central *emblema.*

b. Room 3. The *triclinium* threshold. *Op. mus.* 16, the NW corner.

Photo: M. A. Cotton

Photo: M. A. Cotton

c. Room 5. The *triclinium. Op. mus.* 17. Part of the *cancellum* in the carpet.

d. Room 5. The *triclinium. Op. mus.* 17. Part of the runner.

The top of the plate is to the N.

PLATE XXXII

Photo: M. A. Cotton

a. Room 5. The *triclinium. Op. mus.* 17, with *scutulatum pavimentum* on the left, the 'runner' at the centre and the carpet with the *cancellum* on the right. Looking S.

Photo: J. B. W. P.

b. Details of the *scutulatim.* Looking W.

Photo: M. A. Cotton

c. Room 8. *Op. mus.* 18. S part of the room.

Photo: M. A. Cotton

d. Room 8. N. part of the room showing *op. mus.* 18 truncated in Period IIA. Looking W.

PLATE XXXIII

Photo: J. B. W. P.

a. Room 12. *Op. mus.* 20. N part of the room with preserved coffers of border. Diagonal
walls are modern.

Photo: M. A. Cotton

b. The preserved NW corner of the frame for the *emblema* of *op. mus.* 20.

The N is at the top of the plate.

PLATE XXXIV

Photo: M. A. Cotton

b. N side showing coffers 5–7.

Photo: M. A. Cotton

a. NW corner showing coffers 3–5.

Photo: M. A. Cotton

d. N side showing coffers 6–8.

Photo: M. A. Cotton

c. W side showing coffers 1–3.

Room 12. Details of *op. mus.* 20. The N is to the top of the plate.

PLATE XXXV

Photo: M. A. Cotton

b. Rooms 31a and b. *Op. mus.* 28. NE corner of room. Looking N.

Photo: M. A. Cotton

d. Room 6. *Op. sig.* 3. The truncation of the floor by the W wall is modern.

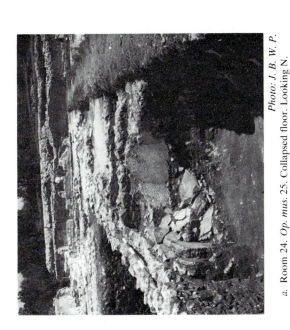

Photo: J. B. W. P.

a. Room 24. *Op. mus.* 25. Collapsed floor. Looking N.

Photo: M. A. Cotton

c. Room 35. *Op. mus.* 29. Central motif near the centre of the room. Looking W.

PLATE XXXVI

Photo: M. A. Cotton

a. Lifting the mosaics.

Photo: M. A. Cotton

b. Transporting a floor for repair.

Photo: P. Wallace-Zeuner

c. Bricks stamped BILLIE [NVS].

PLATE XXXVII

Photo: D. Whitehouse

a. Positive of the terracotta mould for producing antefixes, showing Ulysses in his ship, and some of Scylla's monsters devouring sailors.

Photo: D. Whitehouse

b. The mould itself.